IMMIGRATION POLICY AND
THE WELFARE SYSTEM

In association with
The William Davidson Institute
at the University of Michigan Business School

Immigration Policy and the Welfare System

A Report for the
Fondazione Rodolfo Debenedetti

Edited by

TITO BOERI
GORDON HANSON
BARRY McCORMICK

with

Herbert Brücker, Gil S. Epstein, Gilles Saint-Paul,
Kenneth Scheve, Matthew Slaughter,
Antonio Spilimbergo, Alessandra Venturini,
and Klaus Zimmermann

OXFORD
UNIVERSITY PRESS

*This book has been printed digitally and produced in a standard specification
in order to ensure its continuing availability*

OXFORD
UNIVERSITY PRESS

Great Clarendon Street, Oxford OX2 6DP
Oxford University Press is a department of the University of Oxford.
It furthers the University's objective of excellence in research, scholarship,
and education by publishing worldwide in
Oxford New York
Auckland Cape Town Dar es Salaam Hong Kong Karachi
Kuala Lumpur Madrid Melbourne Mexico City Nairobi
New Delhi Shanghai Taipei Toronto
With offices in
Argentina Austria Brazil Chile Czech Republic France Greece
Guatemala Hungary Italy Japan South Korea Poland Portugal
Singapore Switzerland Thailand Turkey Ukraine Vietnam

Oxford is a registered trade mark of Oxford University Press
in the UK and in certain other countries
Published in the United States
by Oxford University Press Inc., New York

© Fondazione Rodolfo Debenedetti 2002

The moral rights of the author have been asserted

Database right Oxford University Press (maker)

Reprinted 2008

ISBN 978-0-19-925631-0

Preface

BREAKING A EUROPEAN VICIOUS CIRCLE

Migration is one of those issues which is inevitably bound to divide public opinion and put social cohesion at stake. In every country of the world, there are, on the one hand, those who are keen to host more migrants, who need them desperately to fill vacant positions or to find someone who can pay for their pensions, and, on the other hand, those who fear that migrants will ultimately steal their jobs, increase the crime rate and abuse the state transfers paid out of their pockets. The same individual may, at the same time, both support and oppose migration, do so vigorously. One may frequently hear employers stating that they wish to have migrants from 7 a.m. to 5 p.m., rigorously just during working hours, and then, when it is time to shift to their private life, prefer not to see them around any longer.

Two-sided problems are food for economists. Economics is, after all, the science of trade-offs. When there are non-trivial choices to be made, costs and benefits need to be carefully weighed against each other, appropriate positions, policies, to be found along these trade-offs, then economists typically have something to say.

Economists are also notoriously pragmatic and pragmatism is something seriously lacking when talking about migration. Many positions around are just too extreme to have any chance of being feasible. Consequently, they just feed a debate which is both sharp and inconclusive at the same time.

This book aims at offering a balanced and pragmatic view of the problems associated with international migration. As in previous volumes for the Fondazione Rodolfo Debenedetti, it assembles contributions from two teams of leading scholars of the field. In both groups economists are over-represented. Part I presents the contribution of the first team—co-ordinated by Barry McCormick and involved Herbert Brücker, Gil Epstein, Gilles Saint-Paul, Alessandra Venturini, and Klaus Zimmermann—and is focused on Europe. Part II is devoted to the contribution of the second team—led by Gordon Hanson, with Kenneth Scheve, Matthew Slaughter and Antonio Spilimbergo—and draws entirely on the US experience.

The two parts of the volume are self-contained and complementary in that they take a different theoretical and empirical perspective. For instance, Part I goes into more depth in evaluating the consequences of allowing migrants to have free access to the generous welfare state of European countries, whilst Part II has more to say on policies repressing illegal migration as there is much more evidence on this in the US than in Europe.

Much can be learned by comparing the findings of the two parts and trying to interpret the asymmetries between Europe and the US in migration policies, and perceptions of public opinion on this phenomenon. The comments following the two parts by Giuseppe Bertola, George Borjas, Michael Burda, and Riccardo Faini as well as the final remarks by Olivier Blanchard, Dani Rodrik, and Giovanni Sartori offer useful insights in this direction. This introductory chapter is also adopts this comparative approach. It aims at highlighting the key asymmetries between Europe and the US and querying their potential determinants.

Self-fulfilling perceptions?

In Europe the conflict over migration policy is sharper and less informed than in the US. Radical positions—such as those advocating multi-ethnic societies and full liberalization of migration flows or conversely those, based on xenophobic and racist arguments, strongly opposing any type of migration—are generally more represented in Europe than in the US. Such radical positions develop almost exclusively on ideological grounds. Rarely do movements supporting or opposing migration in Europe bother to find evidence and statistics to supporting their claims. In the US the debate is more informed. It suffices to navigate over the Internet to find many websites of US-based organizations taking a stance on migration, and offering data backing their arguments. This style of discussion has promoted a better knowledge of the issue among politicians and militants as well as among public opinion at large.

A majority of Europeans, according to the Eurobarometer survey, is against increasing the *stock* of migrants, that is to say, they are in favour of a zero migration scenario. Polls carried out in the US point to a different attitude: here citizens wish to maintain migration *flows* at their current levels; they accept the idea of an increasing share of migrants in the total population, but would prefer annual inflows not to continually increase. The perception in Europe is one of 'the boat is full' type whilst in the US is just one of gradualism, it looks like a 'go slowly in letting them in as we have a limited absorption capacity'.

These differences in the preferences of voters across the two sides of the Atlantic dictate different migration policies. In Europe migration is strongly restricted and Governments generally take a very negative and often hypocritical stance on the issue. To give an example, in Germany only 'temporary migration' has been legally tolerated for a long time, while thousands of migrants were coming in and finding a permanent residence in the Teutonic lands. More broadly, there are tight restrictions on migration which are poorly enforced. Poor enforcement of migration restrictions is common to the US. But there are important differences in degree: restrictions are looser and more strongly enforced. Europe has more porous borders than the US.

It is difficult to find reliable data on illegal migration as most statistics come from administrative sources which, by definition, cannot capture illegal migration. Illegal migration is generally underestimated, but this seems to be more the case in Europe than in the US, where scholars can draw from better statistics on border controls. With the above caveats in mind, the estimates reproduced in the two parts of this volume suggest that illegal flows as a proportion of the population can be about one fourth larger in Europe than in the US. At the same time, legal flows are in broadly the same proportions (+ 25 per cent) larger in the US than in Europe.

There is an obvious issue that comes to mind by looking at these figures. Is illegal migration larger in Europe than in the US simply because restrictions to legal migration are too tight in the Old Continent? Part II of this volume repeatedly hints at substitution between legal and illegal migration. In particular, it suggests that restrictions to temporary migration in the US have been associated with a pickup of illegal migration flows.

The substitutability between legal and illegal migration stems also from the fact that illegal migration is fostered by the illegal employment of foreign workers: the latter face the high costs of migration and take the risk of apprehension because they have a realistic expectation of getting a job and an income in the country of destination. At the same time, illegal employment of foreign workers tends to increase in the presence of restrictions to the number of work permits allowed. Indeed, the policy prescriptions in Part II draw on the claim that border controls tend to be less effective than internal controls in repressing illegal migration. Internal controls, however, face strong opposition by employers and, consequently, are poorly enforced. Tight migration restrictions, either encouraging them to enter illegally or keeping their status as 'temporary', also heighten uncertainty among migrants, which reduces their incentives to assimilate, both economically and culturally.

Overall, a vicious circle seems to be at work in Europe. Negative perceptions of migration induce Governments to adopt restrictive policies *vis-à-vis* legal migration, and hence generate more illegal migration. Perceptions are self-fulfilling in that more illegal migration, in turn, strengthens the negative perceptions of migration to start with.

A better understanding of the differences in opinions over migration across the two sides of the Atlantic can give us better tools to break this vicious circle. What can economists say about preferences of Europeans and Americans over migration? To what extent do such differences reflect economic factors, for example, related to institutional asymmetries between the two Continents? Is it possible to make the Europeans more open-minded with respect to migration and support more realistic migration restrictions?

There is much material enabling one to address these issues in this book. One should just read the two parts in a loop and draw comparisons between the two experiences.

Migration as a tax on immobile labour

Europe is a Continent whose workers are less keen to change residence in response to changes in the allocation of employment opportunities. Less than half-a-percentage point of the European labour force changes region of residence within a year (compared with 2.5 per cent moving across states in the US). These are small numbers. Acute skill shortages and high labour slack tend to become chronic conditions of specific regions; they coexist within the same country even a few kilometers apart. This makes migrants more needed and at the same time more a reason for concern: they are desired and hated at the same time.

A number of institutions are responsible for the low mobility of the European workforce. Some of these institutions play a role within each country: mobility is hindered by the combination of wage compression induced by centralized wage agreements, employment protection regulations making it harder for workers in poor regions to find jobs elsewhere and subsidies to inactivity which also prevent wage underbidding, by marginal workers, to occur. Housing markets often operate inefficiently and owner-occupied dwellings are often subsidized, which makes it more costly to change jobs in response to geographical differences in the allocation of employment opportunities.

Other institutions discourage mobility across EU countries. Linguistic differences are certainly a major obstacle to cross-country labour flows. There are currently eleven different languages within the EU and, after the Eastern Enlargement, they will become 21! But there are also important barriers to mobility arising from a lack of co-ordination of institutions across EU countries, which de facto put a tax on labour flows. For instance, different national regulations of pension funds and no harmonization of taxation rules concerning retirement savings can significantly reduce the pension wealth of workers moving from one EU country to another.

Whatever the reasons for the low mobility of European workers—and the list of potential determinants spans far beyond the usual shopping list of economists, including a number of cultural (the 'culture of immobility' discussed in Michael Burda's comments to Part I) as well as historical factors—there is little doubt that labour in Europe is an immobile factor.

The growing share of non-EU citizens resident in the EU is instead more mobile than the rest of the workforce: according to the European Community Household Survey (ECHP), a pan-European survey tracking individuals even when they change dwelling, about seven out of every hundred non-EU citizens in the working age group change residence every year compared with less than one (0.6) among EU natives. Having more migrants will help Europe become a Continent with a more mobile labour force. Migration can 'grease the wheels' of the EU labour market. This fact is often ignored in many debates over migration.

Are immobile workers less keen to accept migrants?

As Europeans are, for a number of reasons, less mobile than Americans, they do not arbitrage away the large spatial differences in labour market conditions across nations and regions which are present in Europe. It is mainly left to the European population of non-EU citizens who accomplish this task. Migrants locate in the areas which offer the best employment opportunities. They may initially settle at a location close to the border-crossing, but if local labour market conditions appear to be less favourable than elsewhere, it is highly unlikely that they will remain there. Chart 1 offers a visual characterization

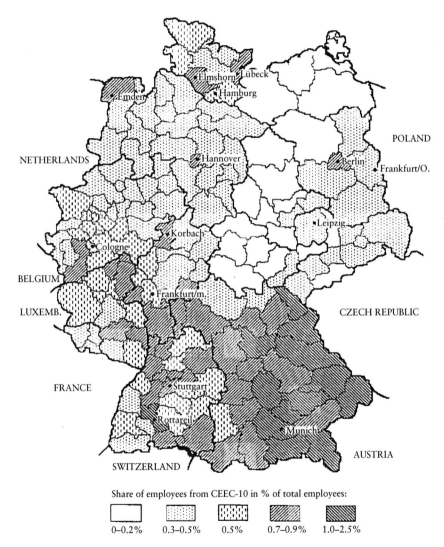

Share of employees from CEEC-10 in % of total employees:

| 0–0.2% | 0.3–0.5% | 0.5% | 0.7–0.9% | 1.0–2.5% |

Chart 1. *The reciprocal distribution of employees from Central and Eastern European countries working in Germany*

Source: Federal employment services, authors' calculations.

of the spatial arbitrage accomplished by foreign migrants in Germany, the EU country with the largest foreign population after Austria. It shows that migrants from Eastern European countries to Germany jumped over the eastern Länders to find a residence in the western part of the country, which offers better chances to find a job and higher wages. This is the efficient face of migration: it prevents overheating in local labour markets, helping to contain inflationary pressures.

Migrants decisions on where to settle are also based on the generosity of the welfare state. Part I of this book suggests that some European countries are acting as welfare magnets, distorting the composition of migrants (attracting more people who can claim benefits) and also altering somewhat their labour market arbitrage function. They often go where the welfare state is more generous, which does not necessarily correspond to the areas where labour is a more scarce factor. Welfare magnets may also affect the composition of migration flows, for example, by attracting those who are more likely to receive social welfare. These 'sorting effects' are discussed (and partly documented) in Part I of this volume.

There is some evidence that migrants are indeed receiving proportionally more social transfers than the native population in Europe. In particular, migrants tend to be over-represented among the pool of recipients of unemployment benefits and family allowances in most EU countries, as documented in Part I of this volume. Only part of these differences can be explained by the observable characteristics of migrants, that is, the number of dependent children, their marital status and skill level. In some of the European countries with the most generous welfare systems (Denmark, Belgium, The Netherlands, Austria, and France) there is evidence of 'residual dependency'; thereby non-EU citizens receive more social transfers than can be predicted on the basis of their characteristics. Put it another way, the very fact of being a non-EU citizen seems to (slightly, but significantly) increase the chance of being on welfare in these countries.

Under these circumstances, migration can be perceived as a tax on European immobile labour. Unfortunately, there are no data offering information on the propensity to move and on opinions about migrants. However, by combining ECHP data with information from the Eurobarometer survey, it is possible to isolate the characteristics of the less mobile component of the EU workforce and of those who declare themselves to be 'disturbed by the presence of citizens of another nationality'. The results of this exercise are displayed in Chart 2. They show that many characteristics which negatively affect the propensity to change residence—the fact of being older, less educated, and married—can also positively affect the probability of being 'disturbed' by migrants. Xenophobic attitudes towards migrants seem to go hand in hand with a low propensity to move.

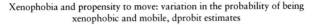

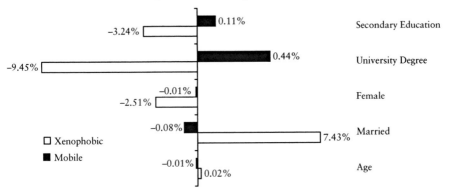

Chart 2. *Xenophobic attitudes towards migrants go hand in hand with a low propensity to move*

The policy response

Summarizing, European immobile workers oppose migration because they perceive it as a tax. More perhaps than the risk of job loss it is the burden on social security and public services at large (education, child care facilities, police, etc.) related to the inflow of migrants which drives these negative perceptions. There are certainly other determinants of xenophobia (e.g. cultural, ideological, and ethnic considerations), but economic factors would seem to play some role as well.

Put another way, while migration is needed because European workers are immobile, the immobility of Europeans makes them less keen to accept migrants. In order to break this vicious circle, three routes can be pursued: (i) restricting access to welfare by migrants, (ii) introducing selective migration policies, and (iii) delegating authority over migration to supranational bodies more capable of resisting pressures of public opinion.

Restricting access to welfare by migrants?

EU rules concerning access to welfare by EU citizens changing country of residence (within the EU) are inspired by the principle of *Equal Treatment* (stated by art 51 of the EC Treaty), which bans differential access to welfare by natives and EU foreigners. In the presence of significant differences in the generosity of welfare systems across Europe, the implementation of this principle is problematic, if not altogether impossible. Suppose, for instance that a worker having contributed to unemployment benefits for, say, 10 years and having consequently gained access to benefits for two years in case of job loss in country A moves to country B where unemployment benefits (replacing the same fraction of her earnings as in the country of origin) are offered for a person with the same contribution length only for six months at most. If the principle of equal treatment is interpreted as stating that the entire contribution record, the *stock* entitlement of the individual should be evaluated according to the rules in the country of destination, one would treat citizens coming from A less favourably than citizens of B (who always have the option to move to country A gaining potential access to a longer maximum duration of benefits).

Alternatively, one can interpret the equal treatment principle as stating that migrants should gain access to the welfare of the country of destination only on a flow, pro rata, basis. In other words, *past* contributions are rewarded as in country A (and should cover any residual claim of the individual concerning that period of her life), while *new* contributions (and taxes) paid in country B yield the same rights as for citizens of that country. This second, more restrictive, interpretation of the equal treatment principle reduces the incentives of migrants to exploit cross-country differences in the generosity of welfare systems. It also allows individuals to choose the welfare system, the combination of taxes and transfers, which they prefer. However, its enforcement is problematic. Difficulties arise for the defined benefit schemes, such as unemployment insurance and many occupational pension schemes. Even more serious problems arise for the non-insurance components of welfare systems, such as the unemployment assistance benefits offered to persons under long-term unemployment (the European plague) and social assistance, which is typically open-ended (in which case only the stock interpretation of the equal treatment principle is applicable).

Due to these enforcement problems, the equal treatment principle is often applied only in its *stock* version. This means that a more favourable treatment is offered to individuals moving from countries with a less generous welfare system to a country with a more generous system, whose immobile workers have to bear the costs of a larger social security budget. Hence, the economic sources of the opposition to migrants.

The Equal Treatment principle does not apply to non-EU citizens and the European Social Charter itself provides a preferential treatment to EU vs non-EU citizens also on these grounds. However, principles of 'fair' treatment of non-EU nationals, considerations related to the integration of migrants, and political economy factors often prevent Governments from applying different rules in terms of access to welfare to non-EU citizens. Also in this respect, the US experience is enlightening: as discussed in the second part of this volume, many US states found it hard, if not altogether impossible, to restrict access to welfare to non-US residents.

This suggests that restrictions to welfare access, if any are legitimate, should be possibly defined for all migrants, independent of their country of origin.

One of these restrictions is represented by the so-called *Origin Principle* (OP), which states that migrants should stay with the welfare system of the country of origin, that is, keep the contribution levels and entitlements of their original workplace. There are two problems with the OP. The first is that it may obstruct labour mobility in response to negative regional shocks on the part of EU-residents as they may bring with them entitlements which may not be adequate for the country of destination, particularly in the light of significant differences in the cost of living across EU countries and regions. From a macro perspective, this blocks an important channel of labour market adjustment in the presence of idiosyncratic shocks. From a microeconomic perspective, it prevents workers from insuring against labour market risk by taking advantage of being in a larger single market. The second problem is that the presence of workers paying lower contributions and receiving less transfers from the state (and partly the employers) increases competitive pressures on native workers. This is the problem faced by German authorities in the 'posted-worker case':[1] construction workers coming from relatively poor EU countries (e.g. Portugal) and non-EU countries were willing to work at wages significantly lower than natives, and lower than the German unemployment benefits.[2]

The Economic Advisory Board to the German Minister of Finance has recently proposed the introduction of another type of restriction to access to welfare by migrants, namely the so-called *Delayed Integration Principle* (DIP). This proposal assigns individuals to jurisdictions in terms of taxation, social insurance, and social assistance in the country of destination only after some waiting (or transitional) period. It is a thought-provoking idea, but is hardly enforceable and shares the same problems as the OP, that is, it further discourages work-related mobility of EU citizens and exerts competitive pressures on wages of natives which may backfire, as in the German posted-workers case.

Selective migration policies?

A more pragmatic way of coping with the problem of access to welfare by migrants is to restrict migration more than access to welfare itself. This means offering residence permits only to workers, individuals paying taxes and contributions in the country of destination. This is consistent with EU rules: the Treaty allows EU countries to deny residence permits to EU foreigners who cannot prove themselves able to finance their living and/or their families. This *Employment Principle* (EP), advocated also by the OECD Model Convention for the taxation of labour income, has the appealing feature of increasing incentives to work. This is not a minor advantage in presence of employment

---

[1] See Hunger (2000) for a thorough discussion of this case.
[2] As mentioned by Bertola *et al.* (2001), the issue was addressed in that case by introducing binding minimum wages for construction work in Germany, applicable also to foreign 'posted workers'.

rates which are currently too low to finance the ageing of the European population and Governments committed to raise employment to population ratios by roughly ten percentage points by 2010. As the Employment Principle is at odds with regulations which forbid some migrants—for example, asylum seekers—to work, it involves major revisions of migration policies in a number of EU countries.

Problems of enforceability apply also to this principle though. It can only be applied in determining conditions of access of migrants, as there is hardly any administration which can keep track of the employment record of all migrants. Applying the EP literally would mean repatriating the migrant and her family as soon as their capacity to generate revenues (hence pay taxes) in the country of destination is discontinued (e.g. by the fact of experiencing a spell of unemployment) and it is morally unacceptable—apart from political economy considerations—to 'get rid of the migrant' as soon as she/he is laid-off.

Therefore the EP principle does not entirely solve the problem. A better strategy may be to try and affect the composition of migrants, for example, by encouraging and/or allowing migration only of those workers who are less likely to be on the dole. As acutely noted by Dani Rodrik in the last section of this volume, the countries applying 'point systems' which select migrants on the basis, *inter alia*, of their skill level, typically display native populations more prone to accept migrants. Although there may be reverse causality involved here (countries more open towards migrants may be more favourable to point systems with respect to potentially stricter restrictions), this finding sheds some light on possible strategies for breaking the European vicious circle.

A European migration policy?

Selective migration policies—in terms both of conditioning residence permits to work and favouring skilled migration—have been recently endorsed by the so-called 'Süssmuth Commission', a group of experts asked by the German Government to put forward proposals for a new Immigration law. The Süssmuth report seems to be a major step toward more realistic migration restrictions in so far as it bravely abandons the hypocritic stance of formally allowing only 'temporary migrants' into Germany. Although well received by unions and employers' associations, it is not at all clear at the time of writing that the Süssmuth Report will ultimately become a stepping stone to a new migration law.

Other European countries are, instead, still stuck in the vicious circle of having formally overstrict migration policies, hence illegal migration and using ex-post amnesties to 'regularise' illegal migrants. Governments in these countries seem to be taken as hostages by voters who press for overstrict migration policies. Under these conditions there may be a strong case for delegating authorities to supranational bodies who are likely to be in a better position to pursue longer-term goals and resist pressures of public opinion to adopt policies leading to a vicious circle. This is, after all, the same principle that has been applied to monetary policy. The choice to delegate authority over monetary policy to independent central banks (and then to the European Central Bank) acknowledge the fact that Governments are not in the best position to pursue the longer-term goal of containing inflation. Similar considerations can also be made with respect to migration policies. Ulysses should be firmly tied to the mast in order to avoid being pulled out by the siren songs.

A case for stronger EC supranational power over migration policy can also be made based on considerations related to the enforcement of national legislations. How, after all, can national differences in immigration policies be reconciled with the idea of a Single Market for labour? Potential free-riding on border controls calls also for policies co-ordinated and co-funded at the EU level. As well documented in the second part of this volume, border controls are only effective when applied all along the borders. Otherwise, they just end up shifting pressure from one country to another. Finally, a EU-wide approach to migration policies can make it easier to reach agreements with sending countries conditioning migration quotas to the adoption of policies preventing illegal migration (in terms both of border controls and anti-poverty schemes).

If there are many reasons to advocate EU-wide migration policies, the consensus which can be gathered around EU-wide migration policies is rapidly fading away. According to the Eurobarometer survey support for European migration policies has been, since 1993, declining everywhere in the EU (with the only exception being the Netherlands) and there are already many countries where less than 50 per cent of the voters are against delegating authority to the EU on these issues (Chart 3).

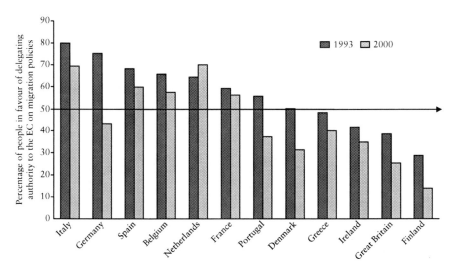

Chart 3. *Declining trend in the support for European migration policies*

We hope that this book can contribute to a more informed debate on these issues in Europe and to a sense of the urgency necessary on decisions concerning the type of migration policies which Europe needs and the level of Government which should adopt them.

Tito Boeri

Acknowledgements

Both studies were originally prepared for the third European conference of the Fondazione Rodolfo Debenedetti, which was held in Trieste in June 2001. This book draws much on the discussion in Trieste, which involved a qualified audience of academicians, professional economists, representatives of unions and employers' associations, industrialists, and policy-makers.

Needless to say, we are very much indebted to all those who attended that conference and contributed actively to the discussion. In particular, we wish to express our gratitude to Romano Prodi, President of the European Commission, who opened the conference with an influential speech on the scope of European migration policies and to Carlo Azeglio Ciampi, President of the Italian Republic for his message to participants.

We are most grateful to Carlo De Benedetti who paved the way for this event and introduced the topics of the Conference.

The American report was co-ordinated and funded by the William Davidson Institute at the University of Michigan Business School. We are most grateful to its Director, Jan Svejnar for the enthusiasm with which he participated in this project. Financial support from Assicurazioni Generali di Trieste is also gratefully acknowledged.

Special thanks go to Pietro Garibaldi, Mario Macis, Francesca Mazzolari, and Roberta Marcaletti who assisted in the organization of the conference and worked hard and skilfully in preparing the background material for this volume. We are also grateful to Giovanna Albano, Mauro Maggioni, and Giovanni Bono who contributed to the final stages of the preparation of the event.

Contents

Contents

List of Figures

List of Tables

List of Boxes

Contributors

Giuseppe Bertola, European University Institute, Florence and University of Turin, Turin, Italy

Olivier Blanchard, Massachusetts Institute of Technology, Cambridge, Massachusetts, USA

Tito Boeri, Fondazione Rodolfo Debenedetti, Innocenzo Gasparini Institute for Economic Research (IGIER), and Bocconi University, Milan, Italy

George Borjas, John Kennedy School of Government, Harvard University, Cambridge, Massachusetts, USA

Herbert Brücker, DIW (German Institute for Economic Research), Berlin, Germany

Michael Burda, Humboldt University of Berlin, Berlin, Germany

Gil S. Epstein, Bar-Ilan University, Tel Aviv, Israel

Riccardo Faini, Italian Ministry of Economics and Financial Affairs, Rome, Italy

Gordon Hanson, University of California at San Diego, San Diego, USA

Barry McCormick, University of Southampton, Southampton, UK

Dani Rodrik, John Kennedy School of Government, Harvard University, Cambridge, Massachusetts, USA

Gilles Saint-Paul, University of Toulouse, Toulouse, France

Giovanni Sartori, Columbia University, New York, USA

Kenneth Scheve, Yale University, New Haven, Connecticut, USA

Matthew Slaughter, Dartmouth College, Hannover, New Hampshire, USA

Antonio Spilimbergo, International Monetary Fund, Washington, DC, USA

Alessandra Venturini, University of Padua, Padua and University of Turin, Turin, Italy

Klaus Zimmermann, IZA (Institute for the Study of Labour), Bonn and DIW (German Institute for Economic Research), Berlin, Germany

PART I

MANAGING MIGRATION IN THE EUROPEAN WELFARE STATE

Herbert Brücker, Gil S. Epstein, Barry McCormick,
Gilles Saint-Paul, Alessandra Venturini,
and Klaus Zimmermann

1

Immigration and the EU

1.1. INTRODUCTION

The UN estimates that 2.5 per cent of the world's population—about 150 million people—live outside their country of nationality. The falling cost of information associated with both the rapid growth of third world urban populations and the expansion of the internet, appear likely to further enhance the world demand for overseas work. The net legal immigration rate for the EU, 1990–98, was 2.2 per 1000, compared with 3 for the US and almost nil for Japan. After peaking at over 1 million per year in the early 1990s, net migration to the EU declined over the past decade but is now rising again, and was over 700 000 in 1999.

Gross immigration flows into the EU over the decade 1989–98, per inhabitant, are similar to those into the US (Fig. 1.1). Whereas legal immigration into the US averaged about 1.0 million persons per annum, legal immigration into EU countries averaged 1.5 million per annum. Surveys suggest that 20 per cent of EU flows originate in other EU countries, so that legal immigration has averaged about 1.2 million per annum from non-EU countries. Illegal migration into the EU is estimated by Europol to be 500 000 per annum (European Commission, 2000), and since there is no incentive for EU residents to illegally migrate, these are almost entirely non-EU. Illegal immigration into the US is about 300 000 per annum (Borjas, 1999). Thus, total immigration into the US has been about 1.3 million, and that into the EU 31 per cent higher at about 1.7 million.[1] The population of the EU is 34 per cent larger than that of the US.

These EU migration flows occurred against a background of falling population growth and an increasing average age of the EU population. Between 1975 and 2000, the population of the EU15 grew from 349 to 375 million; however, the working age population (20–64) is beginning to decline, and is forecast to fall from 225 million in 1995 to 223 million in 2025. Whilst this is not a large decline, the number of elderly are expected to rise substantially: the share of population aged over 65 was 13 per cent in 1975, rose to 15.4 per cent in 1995, and is expected to reach 22 per cent of the population in 2025. As a result, net migration has become the primary influence on EU population

---

[1] This figure excludes an average flow of about 200 000 ethnic Germans per annum who moved from Communist bloc countries to Germany, but they are excluded from German migrant figures.

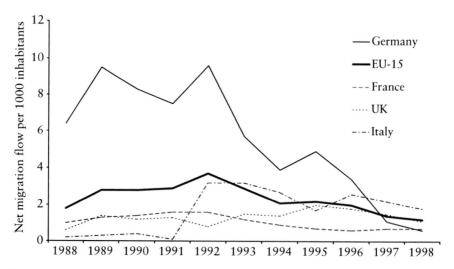

Figure 1.1. *Net migration flow of the EU and selected EU members, 1988–98*

growth, and there is extensive discussion regarding the role increased migration should play in resolving any problems brought about by a larger share of pensioners in EU populations. The traditional source countries of migration in Europe, however, experience similar trends of ageing: birth rates of the southern European countries are at par or even below those of the Northern Europe, and the Central and Eastern European countries that stand to be integrated in the enlargement process have even slower population growth since the demise of communism.

Whereas extensive job shortages in the 1950s and 1960s provided a background for the comparatively open-door policies towards international migration into the EU, since that time persistent unemployment has prompted the EU to gradually retreat behind policies which inhibit immigration from non-EU countries. Measures to facilitate mobility between EU countries have failed to increase the share of the EU population that live in other members states above 1.5 per cent so that a majority of the foreign nationals living in EU countries are non-EU citizens. While the overall macroeconomic picture in the EU is favourable, unemployment remains about 8 per cent and this casts a shadow over the willingness to accept further non-EU immigration, as well as heightening concern about the funding burden that further immigration will place given generous EU welfare benefit levels. Thus, as we shall document in Chapter 5, preferences regarding immigration are cautious, and generally give little support to policies which attract non-EU immigrants.

At present, the EU is contemplating enlargement to absorb ten candidate countries from Central and Eastern Europe. On a purchasing power parity (PPP) basis these countries have a GDP per head less than 40 per cent than that of the EU countries, and a population of 104 million, so that managing European migration requires a keen awareness of the human capital flows likely to be generated by this possible enlargement, and the implications of the various policy instruments that will influence these flows. Until the present, migration flows from these regions have primarily affected Germany and Austria, and if European migration policy is to be successful it will need to recognize that the various inflows we assess below do not, for several reasons, fall equally on all EU countries.

The patterns of European migration are missing from the literature largely due to the absence of unifying standards of registering and reporting immigration across European countries. In the remainder of this chapter, we start therefore with an overview of the quantity and national distribution of migration stocks and flows, the age and skill structure of immigrants, and the structure of employment, based on the fragmented information available from national and international sources. In Chapter 2 we investigate in depth the impact of European immigration policies on national origin and the human capital characteristics of migrants. In Chapter 3 we explore welfare take-up amongst immigrants and attitudes in three areas: unemployment benefits, health benefits, and pensions, discussing how a differentiated take-up for immigrants occurs and whether this arises from their separate observable characteristics such as youthfulness. In Chapter 4 the consequences of enlarging the EU to Central and Eastern Europe, that is, a group of countries which differ considerably from the present EU members regarding factor endowments and per capita income levels, are discussed. In Chapter 5 we analyse the attitudes of Europeans towards immigration and confront the attitudes with the facts about welfare dependency and labour market performance of migrants. In Chapter 6 we extend the policy debate by discussing the comparative economic implications for both host and origin country of a policy of accepting permanent immigration to fill a given number of positions, with one which rotates a larger number of temporary migrants through a similar number of positions. Finally, we draw conclusions for managing migration in the European welfare state against the background of our findings.

1.2. THE FOREIGN POPULATION IN EUROPE: BASIC FIGURES

The accumulation of immigration over time, and its importance relative to the native population, is usually measured by the share of either the foreign born population or foreign nationals. The more appropriate will depend on the problem to hand, but the careful application to Europe is made difficult by the lack of uniformity of country level surveys. Perhaps the primary difference is that German surveys collect information on nationality, but not location of birth, so that the foreign born measure of immigration is not available for unified EU statistics.

The different measures of the migrant population reflect different concepts of nationality. While the Southern European countries and Germany define citizenship by the *jus sanguinis* principle, which grants citizenship to all people who can prove that they descend from the same ethnicity, France and the United Kingdom define citizenship by the *jus solis* principle, which grants citizenship to all who are born in the country. Thus, as an example, the recent immigration of ethnic Germans from the former USSR or Poland is not reported as immigration of foreigners, while second or third generation migrants residing in Germany are still counted as foreigners. On the contrary, second generation migrants disappear from immigration records both in France and the UK when classified according to either foreign place of birth or foreign citizenship.

The primary consequence is that the EU basically gives measures of immigration based on nationality. Thus the EU statistics normally exclude naturalized immigrants from the 'foreign' population. It follows that the more rapidly an EU country 'naturalises' the immigrant body, the lower is the measured 'foreign' population. Since naturalization is itself a policy instrument, subject to change and country level variation, this measure presents difficulties of interpretation. The upshot of these measurement problems is twofold. First, the time series data for individual EU country's foreign populations are more readily interpreted than cross sectional comparisons between countries. Secondly, those countries with faster naturalization rates—which are not carefully documented, but probably include France and the UK—will tend to show lower immigrant populations.

1.2.1. *Main trends in the development of the foreign population*

Table 1.1 provides a summary of foreign populations in the EU and some other European countries, based on nationality. The exception is the UK, 1950–70, which is based on 'foreign birth'. The number of foreign nationals in the EU-15 amounted to some 18 million people in 1998. Almost one-fourth of the foreign residents in the EU are located in Germany, and around three-quarters in the 'big four', that is, France, Germany, Italy, and the United Kingdom. The share of foreign residents in the total population varied between 4 and 9 per cent in the western European countries—with the notable exception of Luxembourg—between 2 and 6 per cent in northern Europe, and around 2 per cent in the southern member states of the EU in 1998 (Table 1.2). Luxembourg, the outlier among the EU members, reports a foreigner share of around 30 per cent. This figure is, however, less outstanding if we compare it with other financial and industrial capitals in Europe such as Frankfurt and London, which achieve similar foreigner shares. Notice that naturalization rates are particularly low in Germany, such that foreigner shares of other receiving countries such as France and the UK are understated relative to Germany.

Table 1.1. *Foreign population in selected European countries, 1950–98*
(foreign population in thousand persons)

	1950	1960	1970	1980	1985	1990	1998
North Europe							
Denmark[a]	na	na	91.0	100.1	117.0	160.6	256.3
Finland	108.0	186.7	404.2	421.7	388.6	483.7	552.0
Ireland	na	na	na	82.0	79.0	80.0	111.0
Norway	16.0	25.0	76.0	82.6	101.5	143.3	165.1
Sweden	na	na	na	na	17.0	37.6	85.1
United Kingdom[b]	1576.3	2219.9	2904.3	1637.0	1731.0	1723.0	2208.0
West Europe							
Austria	849.0	na	605.0	na	304.4	456.1	737.3
Belgium	353.0	444.0	681.0	885.7	846.5	904.5	892.0
France[c]	1737.0	2170.0	2621.0	3714.0	3680.0	3596.6	3231.9
Germany	na	583.0	2509.0	4453.3	4378.9	5342.5	7319.6
Luxembourg	36.7	46.9	59.3	na	97.0	113.1	152.9
Netherlands	104.0	118.0	252.0	520.9	552.5	692.4	662.4
Switzerland[d]	278.0	570.0	1054.0	892.8	956.0	1163.2	1347.9
South Europe							
Italy	47.0	63.0	121.0	298.0	450.0	863.0	1250.2
Portugal	21.0	30.0	32.0	58.1	95.0	107.8	177.8
Spain	93.0	68.0	148.0	182.4	242.0	278.8	719.6
Total	5219.0	6524.5	11557.8	13328.6	14036.4	16146.2	19869.1
Memo item							
EU-15	4925.0	5929.5	10427.8	12353.2	12978.9	14839.7	18356.1

[a]1975.
[b]1950–70 refers to foreign-born population and Commonwealth and West Indies are included.
[c]Seasonal workers excluded.
[d]Incl. Algerians (20,000 in 1948 and 470,000 in 1968), 1985 estimated.

Notes: Data for 1950, 1960, and 1970 are derived from Census data. Foreigners are defined either by citizenship or by place of birth. The figures presented here refer to the definition by citizenship with the exception of the United Kingdom, where only data on the foreign born population value are available. Data for 1980–98 are derived from different national sources and refer to foreign citizens. They are derived from population registers for Austria, Belgium, Germany, Netherlands, Luxembourg, Denmark, Sweden, Norway, and Finland; from residency permits for Italy, Spain, and Portugal, from Labour Force Surveys for Ireland and United Kingdom, and from Census for France. If foreign born population is considered, the share for Netherlands goes up to 9.5, Sweden to 10.8, Norway to 6.1, and Denmark to 5.4. All figures refer to legal immigrants.

Sources: For 1950, 1960, and 1970 United Nations (1979) and Bonifazi and Strozza (2001), for 1980–98 SOPEMI (2000).

The country of origin mix has changed considerably over time. While the overwhelming share of foreigners in the western and northern EU countries stem from other EU-15 countries in the 1960s and 1970s, the share of EU foreigners has declined to around one-third of the foreign population or below in most EU countries in the 1990s (Tables 1.2 and 1.3). Note that this secular

Table 1.2. *Foreigner shares in selected European countries, 1950–98*

	\multicolumn{7}{c	}{Foreign nationals in % of total population}	\multicolumn{2}{c}{Share of EU-nationals in % of foreign population}
	1950	1960	1970	1980	1985	1990	1998	1950–70	1998
North Europe									
Denmark[a]	na	na	1.8	1.9	2.2	2.5	4.8	na	21
Finland	na	na	na	na	0	0.4	1.6	na	18
Ireland	na	na	na	2.4	1.9	2.2	3	na	77
Norway	0.5	0.7	2	2	2.4	2.6	3.7	na	46
Sweden	1.8	2.5	5	5	4.6	4.7	5.6	95	40
United Kingdom[b]	3.4	4.5	5.7	3	3.1	3.2	3.8	60	40
West Europe									
Austria	11	na	7	na	4	4.1	9.1	88	13
Belgium	4.3	4.6	7.2	8.9	8.5	8.6	8.7	85	63
France[c]	4.2	4.6	5.3	6.8	na	6.8	6.3	61	37
Germany	na	1.2	4.5	5.6	5.6	7.4	8.9	77	25
Luxemburg	9.9	13.2	18.4	na	26.5	26.3	35.6	53	87
Netherlands	1.1	1	1.9	3.6	3.8	3.9	4.2	66	29
Switzerland[d]	6.1	10.8	17.2	14.1	14.6	14.7	19	96	62
South Europe									
Italy	0.1	0.1	0.2	0.1	0.1	1.2	2.1	39	14
Portugal	0.2	0.3	0.4	0.6	0.9	1	1.8	26	27
Spain	0.3	0.2	0.4	0.5	0.6	1.1	1.8	60	41
Total	2.4	2.3	3.6	3.7	3.9	4.4	5.3	na	34[e]

[a]1975.
[b]1950–70 refers to foreign born population and Commonwealth and West Indies are included.
[c]Seasonal workers excluded.
[d]Incl. Algerians (20000 in 1948 and 470000 in 1968), 1985 estimated.
[e]Weighted average by authors.
See Table 1.1 for further notes and sources.

change in the country of origin mix is associated with increasing differences regarding per capita income levels, the distribution of income and human capital endowments between the countries of origin and destination (see Chapter 2 for an in-depth analysis).

The regional distribution of source countries varies widely across the main receiving countries (Tables 1.3 and 1.13), a fact which can be traced back to different historical patterns such as the colonial past and different phases of economic prosperity. The high percentage of immigrants from the EU in the stock of foreign population in France and Germany is mainly due to immigrants from South Europe, who are mainly unskilled, while in the UK the increase of EU citizens is mainly made up of skilled immigrants. Another difference to be noted is that the Asians in the UK are mainly from India and Pakistan, while in France immigration from south-east Asia is more important as immigrants come from Cambodia, Vietnam, Laos, and China together with Lebanon and above all Turkey.

Table 1.3. *Foreign population by national origin in selected EU countries*

	Germany			France			Italy			United Kingdom		
	In thousand persons		In % of total foreigners	In thousand persons		In % of total foreigners	In thousand persons		In % of total foreigners	In thousand persons		In % of total foreigners
	1991	1999	1999	1991	1997	1997	1991	1999	1999	1991	1998	1998
Europe	4856	5939	80.6	1662	1264	39.1	1987	487	38.9	950	na	na
EU	1487	1850	25.1	1312	1178	38.8	111	168	13.4	780	857	38.8
Other EEA[a]	252	na	na	34	23	0.7	19	na	na	35	na	na
CEECs[b]	550	2067	28.1	63	63	1.9	21	293	20.1	49	84.4	na
Africa	236	303	4.0	1633	1381	42.7	170	351	28.1	195	na	na
Maghreb	75	125	1.7	572	1160	35.9	62	220	15.4	10	14	na
America	160	199	2.7	73	75	2.3	64	173	13.8	278	na	na
USA/Canada	100	122	1.7	24	33	1.0	20	63	5.0	117	na	na
Other Americas	77	1	na	42	1	na	110	9	na	na	na	na
Asia	553	798	10.8	227	354	11.0	86	226	18.0	500	490	23.7
Australia/Oceania	8	10	0.1	2	3	0.1	3	4	0.3	68	na	na
Memo-item												
Non-EU countries	4395	5515	74.9	2285	1970	61.0	426	1082	86.6	1232	1350	61.2
Total foreign population	5882	7365	100.0	3597	3231	100.0	537	1250	100.0	2012	2207	100.0

[a] Other European Economic Area: Norway, Iceland, and Lichtenstein.
[b] Albania, Bulgaria, former Czechoslovakia, Hungary, Romania, former USSR, and former Yugoslavia.
Source: Eurostat Demographic Statistics.

Italy shares the Mediterranean model with France, in that Africans represent 20 per cent of total immigrants, as also the East European model with Germany because about 20 per cent of the immigrants come from Central and Eastern European Countries (CEEC). The low number of EU citizens is however unique and cannot be traced to its new found role as an immigrant country because it is not a characteristic of other south European countries.

France attracts a high share of foreigners from the Iberian countries, but this figure has stagnated since the early 1980s, while the share of foreigners from former colonies has been growing. In the northern EU the share of non-EU migrants from both the CEECs and developing countries has increased at the expense of immigration from the Nordic countries. In Austria the share of EU foreigners has declined relative to the share of foreigners from Turkey and Yugoslavia and, since the demise of socialism, the share of foreigners from the CEECs. In the UK the number of foreigners from Ireland and other EU countries has stagnated, while the number of foreigners from developing countries, namely from the New Commonwealth, is increasing. However, the UK also attracts a large number of immigrants from non-European Organisation for Economic Co-operation and Development (OECD) countries, especially from the USA. Finally, in the southern EU states we observe increasing immigration from African and Asian developing countries since the beginning of the 1980s.

To provide a historical picture to compare the European immigration record with the US, a direct comparison can be constructed using the UK and US census, and the data are summarized in Fig. 1.2. Two measures of 'foreign born' are given for England and Wales—both only a subgroup of those not born in those countries—so that we understate foreign born on the strict criterion. First, we include the Scots as natives, then both the Scots and Irish are counted as natives—not a characterization that many Irish or Scots would expect (or relish). As is well known, the US have remarkably high shares of foreign born during the mass migration period, but since the Second World War, there has been little difference between the scale of foreign born in the US, England, and Wales. Perhaps the most striking fact here is the remarkably low base of foreign born found in the US, for such a low population density country, in the 1955–85 period. As we have seen, the UK immigration experience, as best we can compare it, is by no means exceptional within Europe.

1.3. FOUR PHASES OF EUROPEAN MIGRATION

Only a few decades ago, Europe experienced mass out migration to the Americas, Africa, and Asia. According to Russel King (1993) 'about 55–60 million of people moved during 1820–1940 of whom 38 million went to the United States'. Meanwhile the picture has changed. After the Second World War Europe became one of the main receiving regions of the world. The annual net immigration rate into total Europe has increased continuously from −0.3 per 1000 in the 1950s to 1.3 per 1000 in the 1990s. In the EU it is, in the 1990s,

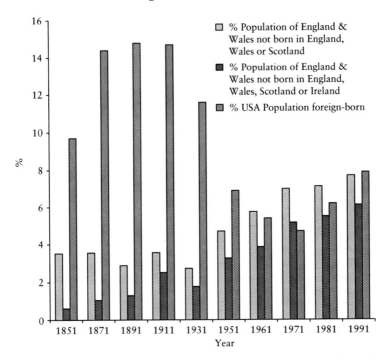

Figure 1.2. *Percentage of foreign-born in population: England & Wales, and USA*

Sources: UK census & US census.

at 2.2 per 1000 considerably higher than in the European average. As Table 1.4 shows, net migration rates vary considerably across countries and regions. In Western Europe, the main receiving area, the net migration rate has fallen after the first oil price crisis from 2.6 per 1000 in the 1960s to around 1.7 per 1000 in the 1970s and 1980s. However, following the demise of socialism, it increased to its historical peak of 4.7 per 1000 in the early 1990s. Conversely, Eastern Europe, after a period of intense migration mainly to Western Germany, ceased to be an area of large emigration after the construction of the Berlin Wall in 1961. Net emigration increased again from 0.7 per 1000 in the 1980s to 3.2 per 1000 in the 1990s. Southern Europe has changed its role from a net source to a net receiver of migration in the 1980s and 1990s (Table 1.3). Notice that the measured share of the foreign population is particularly understated due to a high share of migrants working illegally in the underground economy. Thus, both levels and growth rates of immigration in the southern EU members are underestimated by the official statistics.

What were the underlying forces that since the Second World War brought these foreigners to the EU? A sensible classification for the historical analysis is to distinguish four phases of post-war migration: the first begins immediately after the Second World War and ends in the beginning of the 1960s, the second

Table 1.4. *Migratory balance of Europe*

	1950–60	1960–70	1970–80	1980–90	1990–95
Migratory balance in thousand persons (annual average, rounded)					
North Europe[a]	−100.00	−10.000	0.000	30.000	60.000
West Europe[b]	290.000	420.000	280.000	300.000	840.000
South Europe[c]	−250.000	−270.000	40.000	30.000	120.000
CEECs[d]	−320.000	−110.000	−40.000	−90.000	−380.000
Total Europe	−220.000	30.000	280.000	280.000	640.000
Net migration per 1000 habitants (annual average)					
North Europe[a]	−1.3	−0.2	0.0	0.4	0.7
West Europe[b]	2.1	2.6	1.7	1.7	4.7
South Europe[c]	−2.7	−2.6	0.4	0.2	1.0
CEECs[d]	−2.9	−1.1	−0.4	−0.7	−3.2
Total Europe	−0.5	0.1	0.6	0.7	1.3

[a]Denmark, Finland, Iceland, Ireland, Norway, Sweden, and United Kingdom.
[b]Austria, Belgium, France, Germany, Luxembourg, Netherlands, and Switzerland.
[c]Greece, Italy, Malta, Portugal, and Spain.
[d]Albania, Bulgaria, Czechoslovakia, Slovakia, Hungary, Poland, Romania, East Germany, and former Yugoslavia (Bosnia-Herzegovina, Croatia, Macedonia, Slovenia and Yugoslavian Federation).
Sources: United Nations (1979, 1999) from Bonifazi and Strozza (2001), United Nations (1979).

phase lasts until the first oil price crisis 1973/74, the third starts with the end of full-employment in the mid 1970s and ends in 1989, and the third begins with the collapse of central planning in 1989. The first phase is characterized by the absorption of large migration flows caused by the disruptions of the Second World War and decolonization, the second by conventional economic migration, the third by restrained migration after the end of full-employment, and the fourth by the consequences of the dissolution of socialism (Zimmermann, 1995).[2]

1.3.1. *Forced migration after the Second World War and decolonization*

The number of people displaced by the Second World War was estimated at around 20 million, among them around 12 million Germans who had to leave Eastern Europe. Around 8 million of them migrated into Western Germany, together with another 2.6 million East Germans who moved there before the establishment of the Berlin Wall in 1961 (Zimmermann, 1995). Notice that the overwhelming shares of these population movements are not reported as international migration by the German statistics. In UK, we observe increasing immigration from the New Commonwealth after the Second World War,

---

[2] For a description of the history of European immigration after the Second World War see also Bonifazi and Strozza (2001), UNO (1979).

beginning with the Caribbean countries and, later, the Indian subcontinent. Nevertheless, the British government urged many former colonies to control emigration at source, such that total numbers are relatively moderate (Hatton and Wheatley-Price, 1999).[3] In France, more than one million Algerians of French origin have been repatriated after the independence of Algeria. Similar processes can be observed after the dissolution of colonies in Belgium, the Netherlands, and, several decades later, after the revolution in Portugal. Conversely, a non-negligible share of the European population emigrated in the first decade after the Second World War, basically to the Americas, such that the migratory balance of Europe was negative in the 1950s. However, the overwhelming share of migration took place within Europe, with the Western European countries being net receivers (Table 1.4).[4]

1.3.2. *Labour migration*

The second phase begins after full employment had been achieved in the western European economies in the beginning of the 1960s. Labour shortages induced some countries to open their labour markets or even to recruit foreign labour. The main source countries have been southern European countries (Italy, Greece, Portugal, Spain, Turkey, Yugoslavia) and North Africa (Morocco, Tunisia), the main countries of destination—France, Germany, UK, Switzerland, Belgium and the Netherlands. The total number of foreign born increased in Europe from around 4 million to 10 million people from 1950 to 1970 (Table 1.1). Total net migration from the South to the North can be estimated at around 5 million people at the same time (Zimmermann, 1995). The migratory balance of Europe turned into a positive one for the first time in this century.

Labour migration was mainly motivated by wage differences between the South and the North in Europe. European receiving countries applied very different approaches to recruit foreign workers. Germany preferred temporary labour migration and installed the so-called *guest-workers* programme. On the basis of bilateral agreements with the origin countries, workers were directly recruited in the source countries by German firms in co-operation with the Federal Employment Services. Work contracts and residence permits have been temporary. However, the temporary arrangements were not enforced, and as a result the guest-worker programme resulted in permanent migration. In contrast to Germany, immigration in Belgium, the Netherlands, the United

---

[3] Hatton and Wheatley-Price (1999) report a total net migration from the Indian subcontinent at 177,000, from Africa (without South Africa) at 73,000, and the Caribbean Commonwealth at 13,000 persons in the period 1965–74. Earlier figures are not available.

[4] The last column refers to the first 5 years of the 1990s, when the migration flows increased the most. In the second part of the 1990s, many emigrants went back to their country of origin, and in Germany and Austria the migratory balance became negative. For the 10 years the annual average would be lower for East, North, and West Europe.

Kingdom and France, went along with decolonization. As a consequence, immigrants or returning emigrants were basically permanent settlers and the new flows from the South were treated in a similar way. However, as soon as domestic unemployment increased, the more open continental countries tried to become more selective and to favour temporary migration. Altogether, the 1960s and early 1970s was the first time the European countries had actively pursued a policy of active labour recruitment. Since labour migration during this phase had, intended or not, largely a permanent character, it left its imprint in the structure of the foreign population of the EU until today.

1.3.3. *Restrained migration*

Most western European countries abruptly stopped recruiting foreign labour in the wake of the recession that followed the first oil-price shock in 1973. In the face of increasing and persistent unemployment, the EU and its members never readopted the policies of active labour recruitment in the 1960s. However, immigration did not halt. The main channels of immigration became family reunification and humanitarian immigration. Moreover, the foreign population increased substantially through natural population growth. Although several attempts had been made, return migration has been relatively low. Altogether, growth of the foreign population have been reduced by the policies of restrained migration relative to the 1970s, but the migratory balance of the Western European countries remained, at an annual rate of around 1.7 persons per 1000, positive in the 1980s and 1990s. Interestingly enough, net migration into total Europe increased during the phase of restrained migration, reflecting increasing numbers of migrants from developing countries.

The southern European countries, in the 1970s and 1980s, ceased to be emigration countries and little by little they became immigration countries for the neighbouring African countries and also for some countries in Asia and Latin America. The growth in per capita income in the southern European countries and the difficulties in reaching the rich countries in northern Europe made the South a satisfying second best destination for immigrants looking for better economic opportunities.

While at the beginning of the 1980s the percentage share of Africans and Asians in the stock of total immigrants in southern Europe was 9 per cent in Italy, 7.2 per cent in Spain, and 3 per cent in Greece, at the end of the 1980s their respective shares had grown to 32 per cent (16 per cent each group) in Italy, 14 per cent in Spain, 10 per cent in Greece and it remained at more or less the same level as before (43 per cent) in Portugal, but the numbers doubled.

1.3.4. *East–West migration after the end of communism*

The fourth phase of European migration began at the end of the 1980s, when the collapse of the former centrally planned economies of eastern Europe created a new source for migration in Europe. Eastern Europeans have a long tradition of emigration towards Europe, mainly into Germany, Austria, Switzerland, and France. Moreover, the gap in per capita income levels is currently higher than in the pre-Second World War period. While per capita GDP levels at purchasing power parities of the CEECs are estimated at around 50 and 60 per cent of those in the countries which today form the EU (Maddison, 1995), they are now estimated at almost 40 per cent for the accession candidates to the EU and below 30 per cent if they include the former USSR (World Bank, 2000).

Nevertheless, migration from the East has been fairly moderate in view of income differences. It started to increase with the political reforms in the mid-1980s and surged after the collapse of the Berlin wall in 1989. A peak was reached in 1993, and declined then to rather moderate numbers. Around 380 thousand people left Central and Eastern Europe p.a. on average in the first half of the 1990s, which corresponds to a rate of 3.2 per 1000 in the East (Table 1.4). An overwhelming share went to the EU countries. The cumulative net migration from the CEECs into the EU, between 1990 and 1998, can be estimated at around 2.6 million people (Table 1.5), while total foreign population numbers around 3 million people (Table 1.6). However, around 40 per cent of the migrants from the CEECs stem from the former Yugoslavia. Although a substantial community of Yugoslavs already existed in the EU before 1989, the wars in Croatia, Bosnia–Herzegovina, and Kosovo triggered a migration surge.

Table 1.5. *Cumulative net migration from the CEECs into selected EU countries,*
1990–98

	Total CEECs[a]		Accession candidates (CEEC-10[b])	
	In thousand persons	In % of total population	In % of foreign population	In thousand persons
Belgium	6	0.1	1.6	4.2
Denmark	8	0.8	17.2	5.9
Finland	31	0.6	40.8	10.9
Germany	2307	2.5	28.1	585.4
Luxembourg	1	na	na	1.2
Netherlands	24	0.3	6.9	14.4
Sweden	28	1.5	25.1	18.7
United Kingdom	4	0.1	4.3	1.3

[a]Albania, Bulgaria, Czech Republic, Hungary, Poland, Romania, Slovak Republic, former USSR, and former Yugoslavia.
[b]Bulgaria, Czech Republic, Estonia, Hungary, Latvia, Lithuania, Poland, Romania, Slovak Republic, and Slovenia.
Sources: EUROSTAT (2000), Boeri/Brücker (2001*b*), Hönekopp (1999), authors' calculations.

Table 1.6. *Foreign population from the CEECs in Europe, 1998*

	Total CEECs[a]			In thousand persons		
	In thousand persons	In % of total population	In % of foreign population	Former Yugoslavia[b]	Former USSR[c]	Accession candidates (CEEC-10[d])
Austria	na	na	na	na	na	103.0[e]
Belgium	15	0.1	1.6	1.1	2.9	11.2
Denmark	43	0.8	17.2	32.2	3.6	9.2
Finland	33	0.6	40.8	4.1	30.1	12.8
France	63	0.1	1.8	52.5	4.7	22.0[e]
Germany	2067	2.5	28.1	1353.3	254.0	547.8
Greece	47	0.4	28.9	5.9	22.4	20.1
Ireland	na	na	na	na	na	0.2[e]
Italy	293	0.5	37.3	85	5.7	55.8
Luxembourg	na	na	na	na	na	0.7[e]
Netherlands	47	0.3	6.9	32.9	5.1	11.3
Portugal	2	0.0	1.1	0.4	0.5	0.8
Spain	10	0.0	1.7	1.4	2.5	13.8
Sweden	131	1.5	25.1	4.1	6.7	26.4
United Kingdom	84	0.1	4.3	17.2	20.0	39.0

[a]Albania, Bulgaria, Czech Republic, Hungary, Poland, Romania, Slovak Republic, former USSR, and former Yugoslavia.
[b]Bosnia–Herzegovina, Croatia, FYR Yugoslavia (incl. Montenegro), Macedonia, and Slovenia.
[c]Azerbaijan, Armenia, Belarus, Estonia, Latvia, Lithuania, Georgia, Kazakhstan, Kyrgisia, Moldova, Russia, Tadschikistan, Turkmenistan, Ukraine, and Uzbekistan.
[d]Bulgaria, Czech Republic, Estonia, Hungary, Latvia, Lithuania, Poland, Romania, Slovak Republic, and Slovenia.
[e]Estimated on basis of employment figures.
Sources: EUROSTAT (2000), Boeri and Brücker (2000), Hönekopp (2000), authors' calculations.

Geography plays an important role in the distribution of migrants from the East across Europe: Austria and Germany receive the highest share of migrants. Austria is, with around 14 per cent of the migrants from the CEECs, the most affected country in per capita terms.[5] The share of foreigners has increased there from around 5 per cent in 1989 to 9 per cent in 1998. In absolute terms, Germany is, however, the largest receiving country. Around two-thirds of the foreigners from CEECs in the EU reside in Germany. The same relation holds for cumulative inflows since 1989. Moreover, Germany received large inflows of ethnic Germans (so-called 'Aussiedler') from the former USSR, Poland, and Romania, which are not covered by the immigration data presented here. The inflow of ethnic Germans totalled some 2 million persons in the 1990s, around 70 per cent of whom arrived between 1989 and 1993 (OECD, 2000, p. 63).[6]

Other countries close to the CEECs received notable inflows from there as well: Legal immigration from the CEECs into Italy numbered 41 000 persons

[5] Austria does not report foreign population figures by nationality. The figures are estimated on the basis of labour force survey data.
[6] The cumulated inflows of ethnic Germans from 1950 to 1998 are 3,924,000.

in 1993, a sum which amounts to around 70 per cent of total legal migration into Italy. The main source countries are the former Yugoslavia and Albania. In Greece the legal inflows from the East accounted for 22.1 per cent of total legal inflows, comprising mainly migrants from Albania and Bulgaria. The flows have affected countries in northern Europe too: Norway accepted 6200 immigrants from Bosnia–Herzegovina, 1700 from the former-Yugoslavia, and 300 from Poland in 1997, which together accounted for 34 per cent of their total immigration. Sweden accepted 20 700 immigrants from Bosnia–Herzegovina, 3300 from the former-Yugoslavia and 400 Poles, which in total make up 45 per cent of the total inflows. Even the more distant United Kingdom accepted 3500 immigrants from Poland, and 3500 from the Russian Federation, who in total represented 4 per cent of the 1994 inflows. Although France has a tradition of accepting immigrants from east European countries, it was not a favoured destination, only 6 per cent of total immigrants came from east Europe in 1993; 1100 Poles, 1000 Romanians and 4000 from the former-Yugoslavia.

Net migration from the CEECs into the EU and other western European countries ceased in the wake of the 1993 recession in continental Europe. In Germany, net migration rates of nationals from the CEECs became even more negative in the second half of the 1990s. In the course of this decline, destinations became more varied. As an example, the Romanian communities which were earlier concentrated in Germany are now spread around Europe, but, what is more important, many have returned home.

Altogether, the number of nationals from the Central and Eastern European countries residing in the EU is, with the exemption of the former-Yugoslavia, well below those of traditional source countries of European immigration. While 0.8 per cent of the population of the ten accession candidates from Central and Eastern Europe reside in the EU, around 5 per cent of the Greek population resides in other EU countries. The rather low shares of the population from the CEECs residing in the EU and other western European countries clearly reflect tight legal and administrative restrictions to immigration from the East. Thus, many observers expect a migration surge in the course of Eastern Enlargement of the EU. These possible consequences of free movement will be discussed in depth in Chapter 6.

Immigration in the 1990s is however not characterized only by inflows from Central and Eastern Europe. In UK, which has been almost not affected by the migration surge from the CEECs, the stock of foreign residents from traditional source countries has increased, at around 500 000, substantially. There was no change or even a slight decline in the foreign population in France, while Italy experienced an increase of 500 000, which is a historical peak for the newcomer among the receiving countries.[7] Illegal immigration, as we shall see in the next section, amends this picture.

---

[7] Greece unfortunately does not provide data on the total of its foreign population.

1.4. THE CHANNELS OF ENTRY

European migration of the 1960s and early 1970s was mainly driven by the demand for manual workers, which ceased after the first oil price crisis. The main receiving countries erected barriers to labour immigration after 1973, such that three other channels of entry became more important: family reunification, asylum applications, and illegal migration.

Even if European countries report immigration split by channels of entry at all, they do not apply uniform standards. Nevertheless, the available evidence indicates that the importance of family reunification has grown over time and is now the most important legal channel for immigration. According to the SOPEMI (2000), family reunification accounted for 50 per cent of the inflow in 1992 and 70 per cent in 1998. In the United Kingdom, 80 per cent of the foreign nationals who possess permanent residence status were accepted on the basis of their family ties. Inflows due to family reunion are not important only for old immigration countries but also for the new ones. In Italy, inflows of family members are already 40 per cent of total annual inflows (Table 1.7).

The number of asylum applications and other forms of humanitarian immigration has grown steadily since the early 1970s, and experienced a surge after the collapse of the Berlin wall in 1989. Table 1.8 displays the asylum applications for most European countries and, as a point of reference, the USA and Canada. Asylum applications in Europe tripled after the fall of the Berlin wall in 1989. Germany alone received twice the number of asylum seekers of the USA. After a peak at the beginning of the 1990s the number of asylum applications diminished, but it remained at a higher level than it had been during the previous decade. The main cause for the surge in asylum applications and other forms of humanitarian immigration were the Civil Wars in the countries of the former-Yugoslavia, but EU countries also received notable numbers from the transition countries in Central and Eastern Europe (Albania, Romania, former USSR). Moreover, the number of asylum seekers from Turkey (Kurds) and the trouble spots in developing countries (Afghanistan, Iraq, Zaire, Mali, Pakistan, Somalia, Sri Lanka, China) have increased in France, the UK, and Germany.

The fall in the number of applications for political asylum after 1993 can be explained with various reasons. The conditions for the entry and acceptance of asylum seekers have been tightened substantially in a number of other countries including Germany, France, and the UK (see Chapter 2), social benefits for asylum seekers and other humanitarian migrants have been reduced, and the economies of the transition countries started to recover.

Only a small share of asylum seekers are accepted—between 5 and 20 per cent of total applications. However, a much higher number of asylum seekers and refugees is tolerated in the receiving countries since they cannot be repatriated without risks to their personal safety. Nevertheless, the number of asylum seekers and refugees in the EU has been reduced by an active policy of

Table 1.7. *Immigration by main channels of entry, 1998 (in % of total immigrants)*

	Workers	Family reunification	Asylum seekers	Others[a]
Switzerland[b]	50	45	5	0
Sweden[c]	2	55	21	22
France[d]	21	55	10	16
Italy[e]	55	34	3	8
United Kingdom[f]	45	50	5	0
United States[g]	12	72	8	8
Canada[g]	55	29	13	3
Australia[g]	34	26	11	29

[a]Including students, visitors, etc. with the exception of Switzerland and UK. Totals do therefore not sum up to 100.
[b]OECD (2000), p. 258, reports in the text a different split for 1998 inflows—31% family reunion, 36% employment. We suppose the difference between the breakdown presented in p. 20 and in the table is due to the exclusion of seasonal workers.
[c]1997.
[d]France 1996, due to legalization in 1998.
[e]1999.
[f]Passengers excluding European Economic Area nationals in UK. The data only include certain categories of migrants: work permit holders, spouses and refugees. The category 'Workers' include Commonwealth citizens with UK ancestry.
[g]Inflows of permanent settlers 1998.
Source: OECD (2000); National Statistics for Italy (average 1998–99).

encouraging refugees to return home voluntarily, which led to an increased number of departures, particularly to Bosnia–Herzegovina and other countries of the former-Yugoslavia.

Although reliable figures are not available, there is mounting evidence that the number of illegal migrants residing in the EU has increased substantially in the 1990s. The total number of illegal entrants is estimated by Europol at 500 000 persons p.a. Countries with long sea borders which are difficult to patrol, especially in the south of Europe, experienced a surge in illegal immigration. Large shares of the informal sectors have increased incentives to illegal migration.[8] In traditional immigration countries, such as Germany, France, and the UK, the number of illegal migrants has increased in the wake of the fall of the Berlin wall. In Germany, different indicators, such as people stopped at the border and illegal migrants detected at their working places suggest that illegal migration has increased by between 150 and 300 per cent in the 1990s (Lederer, 1998). Although border controls have been tightened in recent years, the number of illegal entrants detected in the UK doubled from 7500 in 1994 to 14 300 in 1997.

[8] The importance of the irregular economy in the Mediterranean countries is highlighted by recent estimates of Friedrich Schneider: while the share of the informal sector is estimated in Italy between 16 and 28 per cent, in Spain about 23 per cent, in Portugal about 23 per cent, and in Greece at 29 per cent of GNP, the respective figures are 15 per cent in France and Germany, about 18 per cent in Denmark and about 10 per cent in Austria (Caritas, 2000).

Table 1.8. *Inflows of Asylum Applicants into selected OECD countries, 1980–99*

	1980	1985	1987	1989	1991	1993	1995	1996	1999	Average 1990–99	% asylum on inflows 1998–99[1]
Greece	1800	1400	6950	6474	2800	800	1400	1560	1500	2240	5.9
Portugal	1600	100	250	116	200	2090	450	269	300	550	9[b]
Italy	2450	5400	11 050	2240	27 000	1300	1700	675	33 400	9090	8.3
Spain[a]	1400	2350	3700	3989	8000	12 600	5700	4730	6400	8360	9.3[b]
France	18 790	28 809	27 568	61 372	50 000	27 600	20 400	17 405	30 900	29 720	21.5
Germany	107 800	73 850	57 400	121 318	256 100	322 600	127 900	116 193	95 100	187 960	31.5
The Netherlands	3200	5650	13 450	13 898	21 600	35 400	29 300	22 170	39 300	32 200	39.5
United Kingdom	9950	6200	5900	16 830	73 400	28 000	55 000	34 800	91 200	49 680	21
Austria	9300	5300	6000	8200	15 400	26 500	11 700	6991	20 100	12 960	[b]
Switzerland	3020	9700	10 900	24 425	41 600	24 700	17 000	18 001	46 100	28 250	37.7
Norway[a]	200	800	8600	4400	4600	12 900	1500	1800	10 200	5360	20
Sweden[a]	3000	14 500	18 100	30 000	27 400	37 600	9000	5800	11 200	24 500	68.7
USA[a]	26 000	16 600	26 100	101 700	56 300	144 200	154 500	128 217	42 500	99 070	15
Canada	1600	8400	35 000	19 900	32 300	21 100	25 600	26 120	29 400	27 920	16

[a]For Norway, Sweden, and USA data of the first column refer to 1983.
[b]For Portugal and Spain estimated inflows. Inflows for Austria not available.

1. Percentage ratio between average (1990–99) demand of asylum seekers to 1998 or 1999 total inflows.
Source: OECD, 2000, Trends in International Migration, Paris.

Several European countries have legalized substantial numbers of illegal immigrants in repeated amnesties in the post-war period (Italy has passed 5 amnesties, France 2, Spain 4, Portugal 3, and Greece 1). Moreover, considerable numbers of illegal immigrants have been legalized on an occasional basis. An overview on the regularization of illegal migrants in selected countries is provided in Table 1.14. In France, some 80 000 of the 143 000 applications for legalization were accepted, while the number of people deported and taken to the border reached 34 000 in the 1990s. Notice that the illegal presence of foreigners was always much higher than the number of foreigners who applied for a legal status. As an example, in Italy, it is estimated that the share of illegal migrants who do not participate in legalization varies between 20 and 61 per cent (Strozza and Venturini, 2001).

Illegal immigrants from outside the EU tend to come from those areas which also provide legal immigrants. The EU, of course, grants free movement to workers and persons with few restrictions, so there is no incentive for EU nationals to move about illegally. Table 1.8 highlights the importance of North African and Latin American countries for illegal migration in Italy, Spain, and Portugal. Illegal immigration has recently become more important in Greece and Italy. Notice that colonial ties and networks play a role in the different patterns of illegal migration in the individual receiving countries.

During the initial phase of immigration into Southern European countries, the most important channel of legal entrance was provided by amnesties offered to illegal workers. Little by little the institutions in charge of the management of immigration became more efficient, border controls more effective and the front door more open, such that we can expect that the number of illegal entrants will fall in the future. Illegality will remain a problem for the Southern European countries where the large underground economy attracts illegal workers, but the transition period in which legalization represented the main channel of entrance and an instrument to manage immigration is over. Illegal migration is likely to fall to a normal level caused by supply side considerations rather than by labour shortages and excess vacancies.

1.5. STYLIZED FACTS ON THE SOCIO-ECONOMIC CHARACTERISTICS OF MIGRANTS

The socio-economic characteristics of migrants living in the EU can be summarized by six stylized facts: (1) migrants are younger than natives, (2) the proportion of males is higher in the migrant population than in the native population, (3) migrants are concentrated in large cities, (4) the skill levels of migrants are below those of the native population, (5) their occupational status is below those of natives with comparable skill levels, and, (6), migrants are more than proportionally affected by unemployment. These summary 'facts', however, hide large differences between nationalities. The socio-economic characteristics of migrants and their performance in labour markets differ greatly between countries of origin. In general, we observe rather high skill levels and a better labour market performance of EU foreigners.

1.5.1. *Demographic patterns of European immigrants*

The average age of foreigners is well below that of nationals in the main receiving countries of the EU: while the share of the working-age population among EU nationals amount to two-thirds of the native population, the respective shares amount to between 75 and 80 per cent of the foreign population. Notice that the share of the 0–15 age groups is, among the EU foreigners, below that of the native population, while for the non-EU foreigners the converse holds true (Table 1.9). Not surprisingly, the age of the more recent immigrant cohorts is lower than that of the total foreign population. More than 65 per cent of the arrivals in Italy belong to the 19–40 age cohort, and more than 85 per cent of the arrivals in Germany and the UK are younger than 40 years. Even though the most recent immigrants are asylum seekers who move with their whole family, their average age is still about 30.

Although the majority of migrants in Europe are males, their shares differ widely between the receiving and source countries: the share of males among the foreign population is at around 65 per cent in Germany, 55 per cent in France and Italy, but only at 50 per cent in the UK. Among the source countries extraordinarily high shares of males can be observed among foreigners from the African continent and Albania, while the share of females among the foreigners from Central and Eastern Europe are substantially higher than among other foreigners. In some receiving countries the shares of females from Romania and the Philippines among the foreign population are above 50 per cent.

1.5.2. *Concentration in urban centres*

Migrants in Europe are concentrated in the urban areas, in particular in large cities, with few living in rural areas. This is important to note since additional migration is likely to enforce this trend further due to so-called 'net-work effects'. A high concentration of migrants not only reduces the costs of migration, it may also involve social costs in terms of social tensions and lower assimilation. As a consequence, local agglomeration of immigrant communities may shape attitudes toward migration in the native population.

In the UK, ethnic minorities have always been concentrated in certain urban areas. Forty-five per cent are located in Greater London, as compared to only 10 per cent of the white population. As a consequence, about 25 per cent of the 2001 London population is foreign born—up from 8 per cent in 1951. Other major areas of settlement are the Midlands and industrial areas in Lancashire and Yorkshire. The ethnic communities in many of these areas are often dominated by one particular group. For example Bangladeshis make up 23 per cent of the population of Tower Hamlets, Black Caribbeans make up 15 per cent of the population of Lambeth, while Indians predominate elsewhere

Table 1.9. Foreign population by age groups in the EU-15 and selected EU countries, 1999 (males and females in % of total population)

	EU-15	Austria	Belgium	Denmark	France	Germany	Netherlands	Sweden	United Kingdom
Nationals (years)									
0–14	17	16.7	17.9	17.4	19.5	14.8	18.7	18.3	20.2
15–24	12.3	11.4	12.2	11.5	12.7	10.4	11.9	11.6	11.7
25–49	36.2	37.8	36	36.5	36.3	36.6	39	33.7	35.7
50–64	17.9	17.9	16.7	18.7	15.6	20.5	17.2	18.4	17
65& +	16.6	16.3	17.3	15.8	15.8	17.7	13.2	18	15.3
15–64	66.4	67.1	64.8	66.8	64.6	67.5	68.1	63.8	64.5
Non-nationals: EU (years)									
0–14	11	11.8	9.7	13.2	8.6	15.3	12.9		6.3
15–24	10.3	8	9.8		6.4	12	8.8	9.1	11.9
25–49	46.1	54.7	48.3	53.6	43.7	46.7	52.6	52	42.9
50–64	21.5	13.6	18.7	22.7	25.4	20.8	19.5	29	22.3
65& +	11	12	13.5	7.4	15.8	5.3	6.2	9.8	16.5
15–64	77.9	76.3	76.8	79.4	75.8	79.4	80.9	90.2	77.1
Non-nationals: non-EU (years)									
0–14	21.4	27.3	24	35.1	17.7	23.8	23.3	32.3	14.2
15–24	15.2	13.7	17.4	13.1	13	16.7	17.5	10.6	13.2
25–49	47.2	48.7	44.9	38	46.8	43.8	46.8	41.1	56.5
50–64	12.5	8.3	10.9	8	17.3	13.3	10.6	9.9	9.4
65& +	3.7	2.1	2.8	5.7	5.2	2.4	1.9	6.2	6.8
15–64	74.9	70.7	73.2	59.2	77.1	73.7	74.9	61.6	79

Italy, Spain, Greece, and Portugal are omitted.

Source: Eurostat, Labour Force Survey 1999.

in London and in Midlands (Hatton, 1999). There is a similar pattern in France where 53.6 per cent of the foreigners are located in the Ile de France, 24.4 per cent in Paris, 10 per cent in Hauts de Seine, 9.6 per cent in Rhone-Alpes and 10.3 per cent in PACA (Le Bon, 1998 table f). In Italy 40 per cent of resident foreigners live in two regions, Lombardia and Latium, the city of Rome alone has 18 per cent of total legal stock of foreigners and Milan 14 per cent. The situation is changing and the importance of migrants in the north-east is growing, while it is declining in the centre and the north-west. Again, migrants are drawn to the large cities and to regions where the employment prospects are highest. In Germany, migration is concentrated on the large industrial and service centres. The number of foreign residents is highest in Frankfurt and Stuttgart with a foreigner share at around 30 per cent in the population. Note that shares of foreigners in employment are, at around 15–16 per cent, substantially lower, since the native employees tend to live in the suburban areas of these cities. High shares of foreign employees can also be observed in medium-sized cities in the south (Baden-Wurtemberg, Bavaria) and the north-west of Germany (Ruhrgebiet), where manufacturing industries are concentrated, while foreigner shares are relatively low in Berlin. As a consequence of the federalist structure of Germany, migration is more dispersed than in other receiving countries (Table 1.15).

1.5.3. *The skill structure of European immigrants*

Information about an immigrant's level of education should be taken with a lot of care: if they come from personal statements the level is generally overstated, while if it refers to the official recognition of foreign qualifications, the level is understated because many qualifications are not recognized. Nevertheless, we can derive a reasonable picture from the available evidence: in the main receiving countries of European immigration the skill levels of migrants are well below those of natives. European immigrants are in general more educated than third country nationals. In some immigration countries such as France, Belgium, Germany, and Luxembourg, which attracted large shares of manual workers from southern European EU members, the share of low-skilled migrants from EU were nevertheless high. The UK forms a notable exception: although it attracted large shares of foreigners from developing countries, the average skill levels of non-EU foreigners exceed those of natives. In many EU countries we can observe a polarization of educational levels of migrants, that is, their shares in the upper and the lower ends of the spectrum are higher than those of natives. A detailed discussion of the skill structure of migrants is provided in Chapter 4.

1.5.4. *Foreigners in the European labour market*

The occupation status of migrants lags behind their skill levels. In the main receiving countries such as Germany and France more than 70 per cent of the foreign employees, and only between 40 and 45 per cent of nationals are employed as manual workers either in manufacturing and agriculture or the service sectors. Interestingly, in the UK and some countries which recently experienced a migration surge—such as Austria—the share of foreigners in manual occupations is only slightly above those of natives. For the upper segment of occupations, the picture varies between countries: in several countries the shares of managers and professionals in total employment is higher among EU foreigners (Austria, UK) or equal (Belgium, Germany, Netherlands) with those of natives, while they are substantially lower in France. Non-EU foreigners are generally under-represented in these occupations in most EU countries. However, the UK and Denmark form a notable exception with high shares of foreign professionals in finance and other service sectors.

The pattern of sector of employment is similar: employment shares of migrants are well below those of natives in agriculture, while we observe extraordinarily high shares of foreign employees in manufacturing industries. As an example, in Germany, 51 per cent of the non-EU nationals and 45 per cent of the EU nationals are employed in manufacturing industries, while the share of nationals amount to 35 per cent. Similar patterns can be observed in the traditional receiving countries such as France, too. However, more and more migrants are employed in the service sectors, although their employment shares are well below those of natives (Tables 1.10 and 1.16).

Finally, the high share of migrants in manual low skill occupations is reflected in higher unemployment risks. While unemployment rates of EU foreigners are roughly in line with those of natives, the unemployment rates of non-EU foreigners are dramatically above those of nationals (Table 1.11). Although these figures have to be taken with a pinch of salt due to low response rates of the foreign population, they show nevertheless that in some countries unemployment risks of non-EU foreigners dramatically exceed those of natives. Figure 1.3 displays the ratio of the shares of foreigners in unemployment to their shares in the labour force: with the exception of the southern EU members, which attract rather small numbers of foreigners with relatively high skill levels, the unemployment rates of foreigners have been between 1.5 and 3 times higher than those of natives in 1998. There is a tendency for foreigners to be disproportionately unemployed in the high unemployment benefit countries.

The labour market performance of migrants has deteriorated over time relative to that of natives: in all EU countries we observe that the gap in unemployment rates between the native and the foreign population has increased between 1983 and 1995. As an example, in Belgium the unemployment rate of natives declined from 11 to 8 per cent between 1983 and 1995, while that of foreigners has increased from 22 to 23 per cent at the same time. Although in some countries unemployment rates of foreigners have fallen slightly along with the general recovery of the labour market, they decline less in these countries than those of the natives. Thus, foreigners are among the groups most affected by unemployment and their risks tend to increase relative to that of natives over time.

Table 1.10. *Employment of foreigners by sector in selected EU countries, 1995 (share of sector in % of total employment)*

	Austria	Belgium	Denmark	France	Germany	Netherlands	Sweden	United Kingdom
Nationals								
Agriculture	8	2.8	4.4	5	3.3	3.9	3.3	2.1
Industry	30.8	27.6	26.9	26.2	34.8	23.2	25.6	27.6
Services	68.6	69.6	68.7	68.8	61.8	72.9	71.1	70.2
Non-nationals: EU								
Agriculture	1.5	0.9	7.8	3	1.1	0.1	0.7	0.6
Industry	23.2	39.6	33.6	43.4	43.8	22	30.7	23.8
Services	75.3	59.6	58.5	53.6	55.2	77.9	68.6	70.3
Non-nationals: non-EU								
Agriculture	0.9	1.5	4.2	3.2	1.3	1.4	1.5	0.6
Industry	47.4	32.5	35.3	36.4	51.1	35	17.6	23.8
Services	51.7	66	60.6	60.3	47.6	63.6	80.9	75.6

Sources: Kiehl/Werner (1999); based on Eurostat Labour Force Survey, 1995.

Table 1.11. *Unemployment rates of nationals and non-nationals, 1996 (unemployment rate in %)*

	Nationals	Non-nationals	
		Other EU	Non-EU
Austria	4.3	na	9.5
Belgium	7.6	13.3	35.7
Denmark	5	na	16.4
France	11.4	10.5	30.5
Germany	8.2	8.8	18.9
Netherlands	3.4	3.3	18.5
Sweden	7.2	na	28.4
United Kingdom	6	7.3	11.5

Source: Eurostat Labour Force Survey, 2000.

1.6. THE IMPACT OF IMMIGRATION ON WAGES AND EMPLOYMENT OF NATIVES

Economies can adjust to changes in labour endowments in numerous ways. In the case of an isolated one-good economy, the labour markets bear the whole burden of adjustment. Most studies on the wage and employment impact of migration rely on this framework. We start therefore with an elaboration of this framework and discuss the findings of empirical studies on the labour market impact of migration. Then we proceed with a discussion on the implications of labour migration in a wider framework, which allows the adjustment through trade flows, in order to assess the implications of labour migration on native

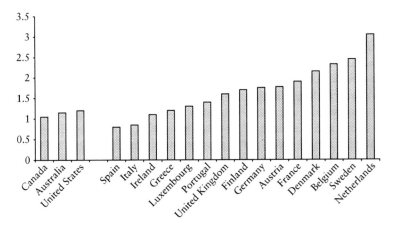

Figure 1.3. *Share of foreigners or the foreign-born in total unemployment relative to their share in the labour force 1995–98 average.*

Source: OECD, 2000, Trends in International Migration—Chart 1.12, p. 52.

welfare. Public concerns about the wage and employment impact of migration refer usually to the most simple case of an isolated economy, where only one good is produced, and the labour supply of natives remains fixed. In this case the labour market bears the whole burden of adjustment. Assume that a one-good economy produces with capital, high-skilled labour and manual workers, and that the production function is characterized by constant returns to scale technology. Capital and both types of labour are complements, while high-skilled labour and manual workers are imperfect substitutes. An additional supply of low-skilled labour will then raise the income of capital and reduce wages of low-skilled labour, while production expands. The impact of migration on high-skilled labour is ambiguous: the fall in wages for low-skilled workers may lead to the substitution of high-skilled workers by less-skilled ones, while the scale effect increases the demand for high-skilled labour. The total effects on income are positive in the receiving region, while aggregate income of those left behind in the sending region falls—at least if they are not compensated by remittances.

The result that immigration increases aggregate incomes of natives relies, however, on the assumption that labour markets clear. Assume that wages for manual workers are fixed by a monopolistic trade union above equilibrium levels, while wages for high-skilled labour are flexible. As a consequence, a part of the unskilled-labour force is unemployed and wages of skilled labour are below equilibrium levels. Individual employment is decided by a Harris–Todaro process (Harris and Todaro, 1970), that is, everyday a random draw is made to decide who is employed. If wages for unskilled labour remain constant, the immigration of unskilled labour simply increases aggregate unemployment, and, hence, reduces the average earnings of manual workers. Therefore aggregate welfare is reduced. If the trade union adjusts wages partially to the additional labour supply, the effects are ambiguous: production expands and the demand for, and hence, the wage for substitute skilled labour increases, while it depends on the scale of the wage response and the parameters of the model whether unemployment increases or not.

The different consequences of labour migration with full-employment and unemployment in a one-good economy have been illustrated by Bauer and Zimmermann (1997): under full employment, a calibration of a one-good model of the European economy gives welfare gain of 0.6 per cent of the EU's GDP if the workforce increases through immigration by 10 per cent, and all migrants are manual workers.[9] If the economy suffers, however, from unemployment and wages remain fixed, the losses amount to 6.5 per cent of the EU's GDP (Box 1.1). Thus, if we follow the one-good model, European immigration policies were well-advised to reject the immigration of manual workers after the first oil-price shock in 1973—at least if those policies had been enforced properly.

1.6.1. Empirical findings

A number of papers assess the impact of migration on native employment and wages in various European countries. Most of these studies rest explicitly or implicitly on the one-good framework. They rely either on a cross section of regions or branches, and use variations in the immigrant density in order to identify the impact of migration on wages or other variables of interest such as employment opportunities. All these studies suffer from an endogeneity problem, since migrants usually select themselves into prosperous regions or branches, such that simple regressions between migrant density and wages yield spurious results (Friedberg and Hunt, 1995; Borjas, 1995a). Moreover, if migration decisions of natives respond to labour immigration, the estimated results are also distorted. Estimating in first differences circumvents these problems only partially, since expectations on wage growth may affect migration decisions too. Many estimates rely therefore on the instrumental variable technique, in order to control for the endogeneity of migration decisions. However, the choice of suitable instruments is controversial, such that a good deal of uncertainty surrounds the results.

Following the seminal paper of Grossman (1982), one branch of the literature estimated the elasticity of complementarity of different types of labour in a production function framework. In general, these studies find rather low elasticities: as an example, Gang and Rivera-Batiz (1994) estimate for the skill composition of workers from Turkey, Portugal, Spain, Italy, and Ireland that in Germany an increase of foreign workers from the respective nations by 10 per cent will cause in the worst case a loss of 0.5 per cent of native wages, and in the best case a gain of 0.1 per cent of native wages in Germany. Similar

[9] Note that these gains are below those calibrated for the USA by Borjas (1995b): the maximum net gain is calculated at 2.4 per cent of the US GNP there.

Box 1.1. *A calibration of the impact of labour migration on welfare of natives*

The possible implications of labour migration on welfare in the EU-15 have been calibrated for a one-good economy with a constant return to scale technology by Bauer and Zimmermann (1997). Production technologies are approximated by a Cobb–Douglas function, where the shares of manual workers have been estimated at 26.7 per cent, of non-manual workers at 45.3 per cent, and of capital at 29 per cent. Immigrants differ with regard to their skill composition, but bring no capital. Potential gains from immigration depend, hence, on the skill composition of migrants. In order to calibrate the quantitative impact of migration on native welfare, two cases are conceived: in the first case labour markets are in equilibrium, while in the second case the economy suffers from unemployment of unskilled labour.

In the first case an immigration of 10 per cent of the EU's labour force (13.6 million workers) affect a minimum gain of 0.1 per cent of the EU's GNP at a share of 40 per cent of manual workers among the migrants, while these gains increase to 0.34 per cent of the EU's GNP if all migrants are skilled, and to 0.6 per cent if all migrants are unskilled. The actual share of manual workers among the migrant workforce in the EU is around 60 per cent. This would imply a gain of around 0.15 per cent of the EU's GNP. Note that these are rather small numbers. However, migration has a considerable impact on the distribution of incomes: if 100 per cent of the migrants are manual workers, their native counterparts lose 3.1 per cent of the EU's GNP, while they will gain 3.7 per cent of the EU's GNP if all migrants are non-manual workers.

In the second case, under consideration of unemployment, the picture changes: assume first that only non-manual workers immigrate and wages of unskilled workers remain constant. Unemployment is, hence, reduced and the gains from immigration could increase up to 8.6 per cent of the EU's GNP. In the converse case, if only manual workers immigrate and wages are held constant, losses from migration can increase up to 6.5 per cent of the EU's GNP. Thus, although the immigration of manual workers enhances welfare of natives in labour market equilibrium with full employment, it may reduce welfare if less skilled labour is plagued by unemployment (ibid., p. 96).

results have been obtained by Bauer (1997): an increase of foreign workers by 10 per cent will induce in the worst case a wage loss of 0.2 per cent for low-qualified native workers.

Another branch of the literature estimated wage equations based on panel and household survey data sets, which allow the controlling for individual characteristics. The findings of these studies depend heavily on the choice of instrumental variables. The upper limit is provided by a study of DeNew and Zimmermann (1994) based on data from the German Socio-Economic Panel (GSOEP), which estimates that an increase in the share of foreigners by 10 per cent will induce a loss of almost 4 per cent of native wages. This implies, that an increase in share of foreigners by one percentage point in the 1990s, that is, from 8.5 to 9.5 per cent, would have caused loss of 4.1 per cent in native wages in Germany. Against the background of considerable differences between the OLS and the instrumental variable estimates, the authors warn the reader that their results may be affected by the choice of unsuitable instruments. Indeed, a series of follow-up studies find much lower wage effects in the range from the studies reported above (Haisken-DeNew and Zimmermann, 1995; Haisken-DeNew, 1996; Bauer, 1998). In a study on Austria, Winter-Ebmer and Zweimüller estimated wage effects of a 10 per cent increase of the foreigner share in an interval of −0.5 and 0.5 per cent (Winter-Ebmer and Zweimüller, 1996). In recent literature increasing doubts about the use of instrumental variables have evolved. Since no instruments could be identified which pass the statistical tests on validity, wage equations have been estimated in first-differences without instrumental variables (Gavosto *et al.*, 1999; Trabold and Trübswetter, 2001). Interestingly enough, these studies find small, but positive effects of migration on native wages.

1.6.2. *Does one migrant replace one native worker?*

The finding that immigration does not have notable effects on native wages is not *per se* surprising. If the European system of wage determination involves wage compression, one could expect on the basis of the one-good framework sketched above that labour markets adjust by increasing unemployment to the influx of foreign labour. However, there is little evidence that immigration involved higher unemployment. In one of the very few macroeconometric studies, Gross (1999) found, on the basis of a Keynesian-disequilibrium model, no evidence that migration had increased unemployment rates in France. A number of studies which refer to regional differences in unemployment rates come to similar results: doubling immigration into a German region affects an increase in the unemployment rate of natives of 0.2 percentage points (Pischke and Velling, 1997). Similar results have been obtained by Hatizius (1994) for Germany, and Winter-Ebmer and Zweimüller (1996) for Austria. Trabold and Trübswetter (2001) find even declining unemployment probabilities with an increasing density of foreigners in Germany. In Italy, Venturini and Villosio (2002) as well find mainly a positive or nil effect of immigration on the probability for natives to find either a new job or first job searchers to exit from unemployment. However, these findings are affected by the same endogeneity problems as the estimations of the wage effects of immigration. Moreover, there is some evidence that a greater number of foreigners is partially absorbed by an out-migration of natives (Trabold and Trübswetter, 2001).

In summary, we would concur that '(...) there is little evidence for displacement effects due to immigration. This is true in particular for unemployment rates' (Pischke and Velling, 1997, p. 604).

1.6.3. *Other adjustment mechanisms*

Thus, there is not much empirical evidence that supports the prediction of the one-good models that the immigration will reduce either wages or employment of natives. Although a considerable amount of uncertainty surrounds the empirical findings, other channels for adjustment should be considered. Immigration need not affect wages and employment if the assumption of a closed economy is relaxed: in the standard case of trade theory, the Heckscher–Ohlin–Samuelson (HOS)-model, factor prices depend on the prices of traded goods but not on factor endowments. An influx of manual workers is completely accommodated by increasing exports of labour intensive goods and decreasing exports of capital or human capital intensive goods and a shift in the output-mix (Rybczynski effect). Thus, migration affects welfare and income distribution neither in the host nor in the home country if the assumptions of the standard case of trade theory hold. If the standard assumptions are relaxed, (that is, if we allow for the specialization of countries in different technologies, factors which are immobile between sectors, sectors which produce non-tradable goods), migration may affect factor prices, for a detailed discussion Venables, 1999; Trefler, 1997. It remains therefore an empirical question as to whether economies adjust to an increasing supply of labour by changing the output-mix and the composition of traded goods or by a change in factor prices and employment.

1.7. THE IMPACT ON THE LABOUR MARKET PERFORMANCE OF MIGRANTS

As we have seen in the previous section, the change in factor endowments induced by labour immigration had only a negligible impact on wages and employment of natives in host labour markets if at all. However, migration may affect welfare in host countries by other channels. In this section we review the empirical literature on the labour market performance of migrants in order to address the question: what have been the consequences of the (self-)selection of migrants on their labour market performance, and, hence, do their risks depend on welfare?

The labour market performance of migrants lags well behind that of natives and has deteriorated in most EU countries over the last decades. The following facts characterize the situation: firstly, the share of unemployed in the migrant population is higher than that of the native population (Table 1.11). Secondly, studies in Denmark, Sweden, and Germany provide evidence that migrants remain longer than natives in unemployment spells (Hansen, 2000; Pederson, 2000; Schmidt, 1997). Thirdly, EU-foreigners are less affected by unemployment than non-EU foreigners, in some cases even less than natives (see Table 1.11 again). The 'some' holds true for unemployment risks of OECD foreigners relative to non-OECD foreigners.[10] Fourthly, the gap between the unemployment rates of migrants and those of natives has increased (OECD, 1998; Pederson, 2000) (Table 1.12).

---

[10] The unemployment data for OECD foreigners resemble largely the data for EU foreigners in the European Household Survey Panel and is therefore not reported here.

Table 1.12. *Unemployment rates of natives and foreigners in selected EU countries, 1983–95 (unemployment rate in %)*

	1983	1985	1987	1989	1991	1993	1995
Belgium							
Nationals	10.8	10.5	10.2	7.2	6.1	7.1	8.1
Total foreigners	21.9	22.6	24.7	22	18	19.4	23.4
EU-foreigners	19.2	19.8	21.7	17.4	15.1	14.6	17.4
Netherlands							
Nationals	11.3	9.8	9.4	8	6.6	5.7	6.5
Total foreigners	24.5	27.1	24.9	26.6	25.2	19.6	23.5
EU-foreigners	16	15.4	14.4	11.8	12	8.1	11
Denmark							
Nationals	9.6	7.7	5.9	8	8.9	10.4	6.8
Total foreigners	19	14.8	15.2	17.5	19.1	28.1	18.1
EU-foreigners	8.1	8.2	11.3	7.7	15.8	19.7	7.2
France							
Nationals	7.4	9.6	10.2	9	8.7	10.8	11.2
Total foreigners	14.5	18.5	19	17.8	16.7	20.6	21.7
EU-foreigners	11.2	12.2	11.7	10.2	9.5	11.5	10.5
Germany							
Nationals	6	6.4	6.3	5.4	5.1	7.1	7.5
Total foreigners	11.3	12	12.5	9.3	8.4	13.3	15
EU-foreigners	9.7	9.7	9.6	6.7	4.8	7.9	9.4
United Kingdom							
Nationals	11	11.3	10.9	7.3	8.4	10.1	8.5
Total foreigners	13.9	15.1	13.2	9.8	12.2	16	14.3
EU-foreigners	11.2	14	12.3	9	10.5	11.9	11

Source: Kiehl/Werner (1999). *Data source*: Eurostat Labour Force Survey 1983–95.

A large amount of literature on the labour market performance of migrants in Europe has meanwhile evolved which sheds some light on the causes of the deteriorating labour market performance of migrants. In a nutshell, the findings can be summarized as follows: firstly, earnings and unemployment experience of migrants are closely related to their human capital characteristics: migrants with higher education, better language proficiency[11] earn more and are less likely to be unemployed.[12] In the German case, there exist moreover some evidence that the high concentration of guest workers on employment sectors which are

---

[11] Language abilities, and especially writing proficiency, improve the earnings position of migrants considerably (Dustmann, 1993).
[12] See for UK: Blackaby, Leslie and Murphy (1997), Blackaby, Drinkwater *et al.* (1997); Blackaby, Clark *et al.* (1994), Hatton and S.W. Price (1999); for Sweden: Carling *et al.* (1996); Hansen (1999); for Denmark: Pederson (2000); for Germany: Schmidt (1997); Dustmann (1993); Dustmann and Schmidt (1999); Fertig and Schmidt (2001), for Switzerland: Golder (1998), Golder and Straubhaar (1999).

subject to severe structural changes, contributed to their relatively high labour market risks (Dustmann, 1993). Some studies conclude that differences between native and migrant labour market performance can be exclusively attributed to differences in observable human capital characteristics (e.g. Schmidt, 1997), while others provide some weak evidence that unobservable characteristics such as 'ability' may have affected labour market performance (Hansen, 2000). Moreover, studies on the labour market performance of first- and second-generation ethnic minorities in the UK reveal that their unemployment risks are higher than those of whites of equal human capital characteristics (Blackaby *et al.*, 1997; Wheatley Price, 1998). Secondly, earnings and employment probabilities of refugees and other humanitarian migrants lag behind those of other foreigner groups. Note that this holds true also for countries that open their labour markets for humanitarian migrants immediately after arrival, for example, Denmark (Pederson, 2000) and Sweden (Hansen, 2000).

Thirdly, mixed patterns of labour market assimilation of migrants have been observed across Europe: the prediction from human capital theory, that the age-earnings profile of first-generation migrants is steeper than that of natives is backed by a number of studies in UK, Denmark, and Sweden. Moreover, the unemployment risk of migrants declines with the time after arrival. However, the German evidence on labour market assimilation is more fragile: a number of studies found that earnings of migrants from the guest worker generation lag persistently behind those of demographic equivalent native workers (Dustmann, 1993; Schmidt, 1997). Moreover, the employment risks for migrants of the guest worker generation do not decline with the duration of stay. In contrast, the labour market performance of ethnic Germans, which immigrated immediately after the Second World War, has converged to those of native born.

As a consequence of all this, the poor labour market performance of migrants in continental Europe is traced back in the literature basically to a change in the skill composition of recent migrant cohorts. This in turn is conjectured to result from an increasing number of migrants from non-EU countries which utilize the channels of family reunification and asylum and refugee laws for immigration. Thus in Sweden, Hansen (2000) observes that unemployment varies between migrant cohorts after controlling for arrival time and that increasing employment risks correspond to declining skills of recent cohorts involved by increasing numbers of tied movers and refugees. In Denmark, large differences in labour market performance have been found between migrants from the Nordic countries, other EU members, and the Americas at the one end, and migrants from Turkey and Pakistan at the other end of the spectrum. Refugees and tied movers are particularly affected. However, the poor labour market performance of recent migrant cohorts is not only a result of their skill composition, but also of unfavourable labour market conditions at their time of arrival (Pederson, 2000). In Germany, distinct differences in the labour market performance of the cohorts of ethnic Germans, which immigrated after the Second World War, and the guest worker generations, have been found after controlling for the duration of stay (Schmidt, 1997). Moreover, the cohorts of ethnic Germans immigrated after the fall of the Berlin wall perform poorly relative to the post-Second World War cohorts. However, no large differences between different cohorts of migrants from the traditional source countries of guest worker migration have been found. Golder and Straubhaar (1999) report for Switzerland that the shift in the country of origin mix toward Portugal, Turkey, the former Yugoslavia and other non-European countries in Switzerland was associated with a less favourable skill profile and a higher age of immigrants, which corresponds again to lower earnings and higher unemployment risks of these cohorts. In contrast to the experience in continental Europe, we can observe a better labour market performance of the more recent migrant cohorts in UK relative to the older ones, which reflects again a change in the human capital composition (Hatton and Wheatley Price, 1999).

Altogether, the distinct gap in the labour market performance between natives and migrants is mainly caused by observable human capital characteristics. Unobservable factors such as migrant 'ability' seem to play no or only a minor role. Moreover, it is important to note that it is not country of origin *per se*, but differences in the skill composition of migrants that affects their labour market performance.

1.8. CONCLUSIONS

The empirical evidence from EU countries is that immigration had at most a very small impact on wages and employment opportunities of natives. These empirical findings are in accordance with the predictions of standard trade models, which state that open economies adjust by a shift in the composition of the output mix rather than by wages or employment to an increasing supply of labour. The negligible impact of migration on wages and employment of natives does not mean that migration did not affect host labour markets. However, more detailed knowledge about the ways in which the European economies have adjusted to the influx of foreign labour awaits further research.

The labour market performance of migrants is largely determined by their human capital characteristics. While the relatively high-skill levels of intra-EU migrants translate into a relatively favourable labour market performance of EU foreigners, the converse holds true for non-EU foreigners, mainly those stemming from the 'European periphery': their labour market performance lags persistently behind natives. Notice that this is not only a result of human capital endowments and the distribution of incomes in the country of origin. The relatively low skill composition of migrants has been enforced by restricting migration from these countries basically to the channels of family reunification and humanitarian migration.

1.9. APPENDIX

Table 1.13. *Inflows of immigrants by national origin in selected EU countries, 1998*

	Germany		France		Italy		United Kingdom	
	In thousand persons	In % of total immigration	In thousand persons	In % of total immigration	In thousand persons	In % of total immigration	In thousand persons	In % of total immigration
Europe	437.9	7.2	15.0	22.8	55.6	38.8	72.0	38.7
EU	150.6	24.5	6.4	9.7	9.2	6.4	61.0	32.8
Other EEA[a]	4.7	0.8	0.6	0.9	0.7	0.5	1.0	0.5
CEECs[b]	225.5	36.6	3.2	4.9	45.6	31.8	4.0	2.2
Africa	33.5	5.4	35.8	54.5	49.7	34.7	17.0	9.1
America	29.5	4.8	5.4	8.2	16.1	11.2	19.0	10.2
USA/Canada	17.0	2.8	2.4	3.7	1.4	1.0	16.0	8.6
Other Americas	12.5	2.0	3.0	4.6	14.7	10.3	2.0	1.1
Asia	105.9	17.2	9.3	14.2	21.4	14.9	56.0	30.1
Australia/Oceania	2.3	0.4	0.1	0.2	0.3	0.2	22.0	11.8
Memo-item:								
Non-EU countries	462.0	75.1	59.4	90.4	133.9	93.5	125.0	67.2
Total foreign population	615.3	100.0	65.7	100.0	143.2	100.0	186.0	100.0

[a]Other European Economic Area: Norway, Iceland, Lichtenstein.
[b]Albania, Bulgaria, former Czechoslovakia, Hungary, Poland, Romania, former USSR, former Yugoslavia.

Source: Eurostat Demographic Statistics.

Table 1.14. *Recent regularizations of illegal migrants in Southern European countries by main countries of origin*

Italy

I	1987–88	II	1990	III	1996	IV	1998	%
Morocco	21.7	Morocco	49.9	Morocco	42.3	Albania	39.4	18.10
Philippines	10.7	Tunisia	25.5	Albania	34.9	Romania	23.4	10.70
Sir Lanka	10.7	Senegal	17	Philippines	29.9	Morocco	22.4	10.30
Tunisia	10	Ex-Yugoslavia	11.3	China	14.9	China	19.1	8.80
Senegal	8.4	Philippines	8.7	Peru	14.9	Nigeria	11.6	5.30
Ex-Yugoslavia	7.1	China	7.1	Romania	10	Senegal	10	5.00
Other	50.1	Other	68.3	Other	102.1	Other	91.7	42.40
Total	118.1		217.7		249		218.747	100

Spain

I	1985–86	II	1991	III	1996	IV	2000
Morocco	7.9	Morocco	49.2	Morocco	7		
Portugal	3.8	Argentina	7.5	Peru	1.9		
Senegal	3.6	Peru	5.7	China	1.4		
Argentina	2.9	Dominican Rep.	5.5	Argentina	1.3		
UK	2.6	China	4.2	Poland	1.1		
Philippines	1.9	Poland	3.3	Dominican Rep.	0.08		
Other	21.1	Other	34.7	Other	7.8		
Total	43.8		110.1		21.3		126.9

Portugal				Greece		France	
I	1992–93	II	1995	I	1997–98	I	1997–98
Angola	12.5	Angola	9.3	Albania	239.9	Algeria	12.5
Guinea-Bissau	6.9	Cape-Verde	6.9	Bulgaria	24.9	Morocco	9.2
Cape-Verde	6.8	Guinea-Bissau	5.3	Romania	16.7	China	7.6
Brazil	5.3	Brazil	2.3	Pakistan	10.8	D.Rep.Congo	6.3
San Tome'	1.4	Pakistan	1.7	Ukraine	9.8	Tunisia	4.1
Senegal	1.4	China	1.6	Poland	8.6	Other	11.3
China	1.4	San Tome'	1.5	Other	58.9		
Other	3.5	Other	6.5				
Total	39.2		35.1		369.6*		77.8

*Granted a white card as a first step to getting a green card.

Source: OECD, 2000, Trends in International Migration.

Table 1.15. *The share of foreign employees in
selected German cities, 1997*

Employment district[a]	Foreign employees in % of total
Stuttgart	16.3
Munich	15.7
Frankfurt	15.5
Cologne	12.5
Berlin	10

[a]Employment districts include suburban regions.

Source: Federal Employment Services (Bundesanstalt für
Arbeit), special provision.

Table 1.16. *Occupational status of foreign employees in selected EU countries,
1995 (in % of total employment)*

	Austria	Belgium	Denmark	France	Germany	Netherlands	United Kingdom
Nationals							
Armed forces	0.3	1.1	0.6	0.5	1.4	0.6	0.6
Managers	7.7	10.4	6.5	7.9	6.1	12.6	14.9
Professionals	9	18.5	12.2	10.6	12	14.5	14.7
Technicians	13.8	10.2	16.8	17.4	19.7	18.2	8.3
Clerks	15.2	17	12.7	14.9	13.8	13.3	16.6
Service worker	11.9	10	13.6	14.1	12	10.7	15.6
Farmer/agricultural worker	6.3	2.6	1.8	1.2	5.1	2.4	3.4
Craft worker	18.9	13.4	12.6	13.3	18.3	10.8	12.7
Assembler	8.7	8	8.2	10.5	7.1	7.3	8.5
Basic occupation	8.1	8.8	7.3	8.5	6.8	9.5	11.5
Non-nationals: EU							
Armed forces	0	0.1	0.7	0.2	0.2	0	0
Managers	15.8	15	11.9	5.4	9.2	11.3	18.8
Professionals	23.8	11.4	20.1	6.4	8.8	16.5	21.4
Technicians	21.4	10	20.6	6.3	11.4	16.1	6.8
Clerks	9.1	11.2	11.6	5.5	8.1	12.8	11.9
Service worker	11.5	9.8	15	17.6	9.3	13.4	8.7
Farmer/agricultural worker	1.5	1	0.9	0.1	3.1	0.8	7.5
Craft worker	8.3	20.2	6.6	29.4	19.6	12.6	8.3
Assembler	6.1	10.7	10.3	15.1	12.3	9.2	5.8
Basic occupation	2.5	10.7	5	8.9	19.1	16.6	2.7
Non-nationals: non-EU							
Armed forces	0	0.7	0.3	2.5	0.1	0	0
Managers	2.4	12.4	9.4	7.4	3.3	7.1	16.8
Professionals	3.2	7.6	17.4	5.7	5.1	7.6	19.6
Technicians	5.5	3.5	11.2	5	8.1	7.9	6.9

Table 1.16. *(Continued)*

	Austria	Belgium	Denmark	France	Germany	Netherlands	United Kingdom
Clerks	3	6.8	5.4	5.8	5.4	7.3	10.2
Service worker	8.4	12.7	14.8	17.9	13.3	12.2	7.2
Farmer/agricultural worker	0.1	1.7	1.3	0.1	3.9	0.8	1.7
Craft worker	28.8	16.2	11.1	20.8	26.5	14.7	8.5
Assembler	18.1	14.1	11	19.4	15.7	18.3	7.8
Basic occupation	30.6	24.3	20.8	9.8	18.6	22.8	25.6

Source: Kiehl/Werner (1999); based on Eurostat Labour Force Survey, 1995.

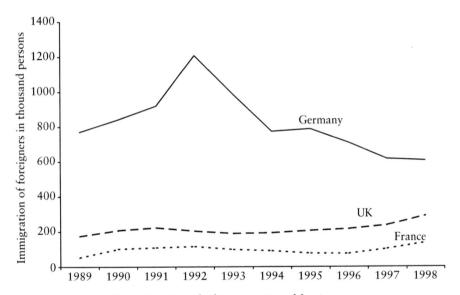

Figure 1.4. *Trend of immigration of foreigners*

2

European Immigration Policy and the Selection of Immigrants

2.1. INTRODUCTION

Immigration policy is about the selection of migrants, and whether intended or not, affects the costs and benefits from international migration. In Europe, many regulations concerning the influx of foreigners have been delegated to the authority of the European Union. These regulations fit uneasily with the free movement of EU citizens that is a fundamental feature of the 'Single Market' in the 15 member Union. Although a comprehensive set of regulations has evolved at the EU level, which aim to protect EU households against discrimination in other member states, the mobility of the population among the present EU members is low: no more than 1.5 per cent of the EU's population reside in other member countries. Most foreigners living in the EU countries—at around 3.2 per cent of the community's population—stem from non-EU countries.

The reduction of barriers to labour mobility in the EU has, since 1973, gone hand in hand with the establishment of increasing restrictions to the immigration from non-EU countries. Since the first oil price crisis in 1973, family reunification, humanitarian migration, and illegal migration have become the main channels for migration in many member states. As a consequence of the 'Single Market' principles, the protection of labour markets against an influx of workers from non-EU countries has meanwhile been instituted at EU levels. However, European immigration policies are far from being consistent: the two main legal channels for the immigration of non-EU nationals—family reunification and rules designed for humanitarian migration—remain under the authority of the individual states.

This chapter reviews research on the implications of European immigration policies for the structure of migration during the post-war period. The consequences of enlarging the EU to a club of countries with relatively low per capita incomes are addressed in the next chapter. As a basis for further analysis, we start with an overview of the polices that govern immigration within and into the EU. We then discuss the possible implications of these policies within the selection and self-selection framework of migration theory. On this basis we analyse how European immigration policies have actually affected the country of origin mix and the skill composition of migrants. Finally we summarize our findings.

2.2. THE RULES OF EUROPEAN
IMMIGRATION POLICIES

Before proceeding to the empirical analysis, an overview of the cornerstones of European immigration policies will be instructive in order to establish the institutional background. Post-war immigration to the countries which now form the EU has been regulated both at the level of the community and at the national level. Around the core of the free movement of labour, a large set of regulations has evolved at EU level which cover the equal treatment of workers, the eligibility to welfare benefits and external border control. While the barriers to the mobility of workers and other persons have been removed step by step in a continuously growing union of countries, barriers against labour immigration for non-EU nationals have been established in most member states after the first oil price crisis in 1973. These policies have also been instituted at EU levels. In the EU of today, we can distinguish basically four policy areas, which regulate migration within and into the EU: (i) rules which govern the free movement of workers and other persons in the Common Market and their access to national welfare benefits, (ii) rules which govern labour immigration and family reunification from non-EU countries, (iii) the regulation of humanitarian migration (asylum seekers, refugees), and (iv) the co-ordination of external border control after internal borders have been removed in the 'Schengen' area.

2.2.1. *Integrating labour markets in the European community*

The foundation of a Common Market in Europe was based on the idea that integration of all four markets, that is, the markets for goods, services, capital, and labour, would enhance welfare of all members of the community. The Treaty of Rome, which established the then European Economic Community (EEC) in 1957, defines the free movement of workers, consequently, as one of the four fundamental freedoms of the 'Single Market'.[1] It took, however, another ten years until the free movement was granted to the citizens of the community (see Box 2.1).

The free movement of workers started in a community of six countries with a joint population of 185 million persons and relatively homogenous per capita GDP levels,[2] and has been extended step by step to the 15 members

---

[1] Art. 48–51, EEC Treaty.

[2] Measured in purchasing power parities, the GDP per capita of Italy, the poorest country among the six founding Members, was at 90 per cent of the community average in 1968 (author's calculations based on Maddison, 1995). However, large regional disparities in income levels induced notable migration flows from Italy to other founding Members of the community in the 1960s.

Box 2.1. *Immigration policy of the EU*

1957	'Treaty of Rome' (EEC-Treaty): Art. 48 defines the free movement of workers as a fundamental freedom of the 'Single Market'.
1968	Full free movement of workers for the six founding members of the EEC (Belgium, France, Germany, Italy, Luxembourg, and the Netherlands).
1968	Completion of the 'Customs Union'.
1971	Accession of Denmark, Ireland, and UK; no transitional period for free movement.
1981	Accession of Greece; transitional period for the free movement of workers.
1985	'Schengen'—Agreement on border control (Schengen I).
1986	Accession of Portugal and Spain; transitional period for the free movement of workers.
1986	'Single European Act': Establishment of the legal framework for the 'Single Market'.
1988	Greece: transitional period for free movement expires.
1990	'Social Charter'. The free movement of workers is granted in Art. 1.
1990	'Schengen'—Application Convention on border control (Schengen II).
1992	Portugal and Spain: transitional period for free movement expires.
1992	Completion of the 'Single Market': unrestricted right for provision of services, self-employment, and establishment of firms. Mutual recognition of education degrees.
1992–97	'Europe Agreements' with ten countries from Central and Eastern Europe.
1995	Accession of Austria, Finland, and Sweden; no transitional periods for free movement.
1998	'Treaty of Amsterdam' (EU-Treaty): Art. 38–48 defines again the free movement of workers and persons as a fundamental freedom of the Single Market.
2000	Inclusion of Bulgaria, Latvia, Lithuania, Romania, and Slovakia into accession negotiations, candidate status for Turkey.
2001	The European Commission proposes transitional periods of $5 + 2$ years for the free movement of labour for the CEEC-10, no transitional periods for Cyprus and Malta.

---

of the present EU with a joint population of some 375 million persons. Moreover, in 1990 the free movement was extended to the members of the European Economic Association (EEA), which today comprises Iceland, Liechtenstein, and Norway with a joint population of almost 5 million persons. As a rule of thumb, the citizens of the relatively rich countries have been entitled to free movement immediately after accession, while transitional periods have been agreed in the cases of countries with relatively low income levels.

The free movement of workers entitles citizens of the community to work in other member countries and to reside there. More specifically, the free movement of workers comprises the following rights: (i) to seek employment in other EU countries, (ii) to move there for the purpose of employment seeking, (iii) to reside in other EU countries for the purpose of employment, (iv) to remain in other EU countries after the completion of employment if the household is able to finance its living out of its own means.[3]

The right to seek employment implies in practice that EU citizens can stay in other member states for at least three months. A recent statement of the European Supreme Court states that a time span of six months and, in reasonable cases, even more is appropriate. Employed persons are automatically entitled to a residence permit. France, Germany, Italy, and Spain decided to demand no residence permit for employed EU citizens in July 2000.

The *acquis communautaire*, that is, the common set of legal rules in the community, requires the equal treatment of all EU citizens with regard to employment, occupation, remuneration, dismissal and other conditions to work.[4] Moreover, the legal framework of the EU attempts to reduce barriers to labour mobility through the mutual recognition of education, degrees and the harmonization of education systems. Finally, several obstacles to the establishment of businesses, self-employment, and the supply of services in other member countries were removed during the declaration of the 'Single Market' on 1 January 1993.

EU foreigners are, in principle, entitled to the same set of welfare benefits, and obliged to pay the same taxes and social contributions as natives (see Box 2.2). However, the immigration of EU foreigners can be rejected if they cannot prove that they are able to finance their living out of their own means. This holds true also for family reunification. Moreover, the member states are entitled to withdraw residence permits if a foreign household relies on social assistance. In practice, however, social assistance and other welfare benefits are granted to EU foreigners similar to natives in many EU countries after a certain period of stay.

Although 'welfare shopping' of newly arrived migrants is partly ruled out by the *acquis communautaire* and the legislation of the member states, differences in social security and tax systems still affect the benefits and costs of international migration across the member states. On the one hand, entitlement to welfare benefits affects both the incentives for return migration of those whose earnings fall under the level of social assistance and the self-selection of migrants with regard to their prospective social risks. On the other hand, complex rules for the taxation of claims against pay-as-you go and capital financed pension schemes may involve double taxation or double tax exemptions for migrants (see Box 2.2).

---

[3] Art. 39 (1), EC Treaty. The general principles have been translated into practice by the Regulation 1612/68 (EEC) on the free movement of labour and the Directive 68/360 (EEC) on the abolition of barriers to travel and residence of EU citizens in other member states.

[4] Art. 39 (2), EC Treaty.

Box 2.2. *Eligibility of EU foreigners to welfare benefits*

The legal framework of the EU, the *acquis communautaire*, does not aim to harmonize social security schemes, but to avoid migrant workers being penalized in the field of social security. In general, the eligibility of EU foreigners to welfare benefits is governed by the legal principle of 'equal treatment' (Art. 51 EC Treaty; Art. 42 EU Treaty). The principle of 'equal treatment' requires that EU foreigners should enjoy the same protection by the social security systems as natives. As a consequence, a number of regulations demand that claims against social insurance are portable and that they can be set off against each other. This holds true for pension schemes, disability benefits, health care, unemployment benefits, family benefits, etc. In principle, it does not matter whether social benefits are financed by social insurance contributions or by taxes.[5] However, benefits that are not financed by social insurance contributions are paid at the place of residence and cannot be exported.

According to the rules of the *acquis communautaire*, the payment of social benefits should follow the principle of equivalence, that is, that claims against social insurance should be granted if similar contributions have been made or similar claims exist in home countries. However, many obstacles to the mobility of labour remain since social security systems are not harmonized in the EU. As an example, different rules for taxing pension schemes are applied in the EU, that is, some countries exempt contributions and capital gains but not tax benefits, while others exempt benefits but not tax contributions and/or capital gains. As a consequence, in some cases the change of a social security system involves double taxation, while in other cases double tax exemptions (EC, 2001).

Several provisions in the legislation of the EU and its member states are designed to protect national social security systems against welfare shopping: nationals from other EU countries are only admitted if they can prove that they are able to finance their living out of their work or other financial means. Job seekers are not entitled to any welfare benefits in the host country. Claims against social insurance such as unemployment benefits are only accepted after certain periods of payment. This also holds true for family reunification.[6] Although the EU and the member states attempt to protect social security systems against the immigration of welfare seekers, workers from other EU countries and their families are in practice entitled to the same set of social welfare benefits as natives once they have been employed in another EU country for a certain period of time. Residence permits are only withdrawn in exceptional cases.[7]

---

[5] Art. 42 EU Treaty demands the co-ordination of social insurances and other social security systems. The basic rules for the portability of claims against social security systems for employed persons, self-employed persons and their families are defined in the Regulation 1408/71 (EEC) and Regulation 574/72 (EC).

[6] Moreover, in some member states the national legislation explicitly rules out that social assistance is paid to those who emigrated for the purpose of seeking welfare benefits. See, for example, the German social legislation, namely §120 of the Federal Social Assistance Law (BSHG).

[7] For an in-depth description of the legal rules which cover the eligibility to welfare benefits see Beirat beim Bundesminister der Finanzen (2001) and Sinn *et al.* (2000).

Altogether, barriers to the mobility of labour and persons have been removed within the EU to an extent which goes far beyond those in other regional trade areas. Nevertheless, the share of EU foreigners residing in other member states is at 1.5 per cent of the EU's population, rather small and fairly stagnant (see Chapter 1). The low level of labour mobility across the EU relative to that within countries is probably indicative that national differences in culture, language, and institutions still affect the efforts to integrate EU labour markets.

2.2.2. *Restricting immigration from non-EU countries and preferential treatment of EU citizens*

The main source of foreigners in EU countries are still non-EU countries. The influx of these foreigners has been regulated mainly at national levels during the post-war period. After full employment had been achieved in the mid-1950s, many central and northern European countries actively recruited manual workers from the Mediterranean countries (e.g. the 'guest worker' system in Germany). The policy of active labour recruitment ceased immediately after the first oil price shock in 1973, although labour immigration from non-EU countries still plays a role (see Chapter 1).

Family reunification has been one of the key channels for immigration of non-EU nationals into the EU since the barriers to labour immigration were raised in the wake of the oil price shock in 1973. Although the criteria for admitting migrants through family reunification differ among the individual countries, all member states allow family reunification in one way or another (see SOPEMI, 2000, for a review). Note that the combination of high barriers to labour immigration and relatively low barriers to family reunification had a long-lasting impact on the composition of migration from non-EU countries (see below).

The legal framework of the EU reflects the protective policies of its member states: the *acquis communautaire* explicitly demands a preferential treatment of EU citizens *vis-à-vis* non-EU citizens in the labour markets. Labour from outside the community can only be hired if it is proved that the position cannot be occupied by EU nationals or by non-EU nationals who already possess a residence permit in the respective country.[8] Temporary work permits can be granted to non-EU citizens if a position is offered to a specific person with specific skills and the position cannot be filled with employees from domestic and EU labour markets. Seasonal workers, border commuters and key personnel from non-EU countries can be admitted under restrictive conditions. Thus, the legislation of the EU demands discrimination between EU and non-EU nationals regarding entry to the labour market of the community. However, these regulations hardly form a binding constraint to the member states, since it confirms only common practice in the member states.

---

[8] Regulation 1612/68 (EEC) and 569/90 (EC).

Although the EU imposes several restrictions on its members with regard to the admission of workers from non-member countries, immigration from outside the EU remains basically under the authority of the individual members. It is explicitly stated in a General Declaration to the 'Single European Act', which establishes the Single Market, that 'nothing in these provisions shall affect the right of member states to take such measures as they consider necessary for the purpose of controlling immigration from third world countries'. Thus, immigration policies *vis-à-vis* third countries remain under the domain of national policies. Non-EU foreigners are, consequently, excluded from the free movement: residence and work permits cannot be transferred to other EU countries.[9]

The legislation of the EU does not explicitly regulate the access of third-country nationals to welfare benefits, but it demands 'fair treatment' for workers and other persons from non-EU countries. This implies that basic rules for integrating workers from EU countries into social security schemes also apply to nationals from non-EU countries. However, individual member states are free to withdraw residence permits if non-EU foreigners rely on social assistance.

2.2.3. *Admitting humanitarian migrants*

Although all member states of the EU signed the 1951 Geneva Convention on refugees, asylum and refugee policies differ largely across the individual EU countries. Both, the rules of admitting asylum seekers and refugees, as well as the practices of how to proceed with non-accepted asylum seekers and refugees are not yet harmonized in the EU. Nevertheless, one common feature in all EU countries is that only few applications for political asylum and refugee status are accepted (see Chapter 1). Many humanitarian migrants are however tolerated in EU countries, even though their applications for asylum or refugee status have been rejected (see Box 2.3).

Although the share of forced migrants among asylum seekers and other applicants for humanitarian migration is higher than the official statistics suggest, legal rules defined for humanitarian migration have nevertheless been used as a channel for large scale economic migration. As we have seen in Chapter 1, the number of asylum seekers and other humanitarian migrants has increased as conditions for labour immigration have tightened. The number of asylum applications experienced a surge in the early 1990s and concentrated on few immigration countries. Germany was particularly affected: a historical peak of 440 000 asylum seekers was reached there in 1992.

As a consequence, Germany and many other EU countries have tightened the legal and administrative rule for admitting asylum seekers and other

---

[9] However, non-EU foreigners with a residence permit in a member state can move freely to other EU countries for a period of up to three months.

Box 2.3. *What is a humanitarian migrant?*

For an understanding of the phenomenon of humanitarian migration it is helpful to distinguish three types of forced migrants: the activist, the target, and the potential victim. The first is a political agent who is primarily persecuted because of his or her political activities. The target has not contributed or caused his or her persecution, other than by belonging to an ethnic, religious, or other type of group. The last category, the potential victim, comprises those who are not especially targeted for persecution, but are nevertheless fleeing from threats against their safety which are induced by Civil Wars and other social catastrophes (Boswick, 1997; Zolberg *et al.*, 1989). The first type of forced migration is usually covered by political asylum laws, for example, Art. 16 of the German basic law. The second type is protected under the Geneva Convention and may stay in a host country even if their asylum applications are rejected. The third type is neither captured by national asylum laws nor by the Geneva Convention, but comprises nevertheless the largest share of forced migration. As an example, most of the refugees from the Civil Wars in former Yugoslavia are not entitled to asylum or to the Geneva Convention definition of refugee status. However, as in the cases of the civil wars in the former Yugoslavia or Uganda, many of these humanitarian migrants have been tolerated in EU member states. This helps to explain why many humanitarian migrants were not repatriated, although they are not accepted as asylum seekers or refugees in EU countries.

---

humanitarian migrants significantly. The measures applied are similar: accelerating the processing of applications, rejecting work permits, reducing social assistance for applicants, paying social assistance in the form of vouchers, and preventing the entry of humanitarian migrants. All these measures are aimed at, and have resulted in, limiting entries to the respective countries and shortening the duration of stays. In particular, policies to reject the entry of humanitarian migrants have proved to be efficient in the German case: after the amendment of Art. 16 of the German basic law, asylum seekers can be rejected if they arrive from a 'safe country'. Moreover, asylum seekers arriving at an international airport are kept in the transit area and their immigration is rejected if their application is proved as 'manifestly unfounded' (see Boswick, 1997, for an analysis). These restrictive measures have reduced asylum applications in Germany to one quarter of the 1992 figure, while the number of applications has increased in other member states such as the UK and the Netherlands. Nevertheless, similar measures as in Germany have already been applied by the other EU members or are discussed there (see the SOPEMI, 2000, report on the developments in the individual member states and other OECD countries).

Thus, although large numbers of refugees have been tolerated in Germany and some other EU countries during the Civil Wars in the former Yugoslavia, it can hardly be denied that asylum and refugee laws have been tightened significantly throughout the last decade. This is hardly surprising, since national asylum and refugee policies tend to penalize the generous countries in the community, such that a 'race to the bottom' is unavoidable if migrants contrast different national rules. A common European asylum and refugee policy is on the agenda of the EU, but has not yet brought many results. The competence of the European Community for a common asylum and immigration policy has been established for the first time in the Treaty of Amsterdam, but it does not go much beyond an information mechanism on national policies. In the Dublin Convention from 1990, twelve EU members agreed on a common procedure for asylum seekers, which addresses, *inter alia*, the question of how to deal with multiple asylum claims. The content of asylum claims remain, however, unaffected by this agreement. Finally, the European council declared at the Tampere summit in 1999 that 'the separate but closely related issues of asylum and migration call for the development of a common EU policy'. In a recent Communication by the European Commission to the European Council and the European Parliament it is proposed that rules on the recognition and content of asylum and refugee status should be harmonized at EU levels. Moreover, a refugee fund, which should compensate individual member states for the burden of humanitarian immigration, is under discussion (EC, 2000).

2.2.4. *The Schengen Accords: Controlling external borders and combating illegal migration*

As a consequence of the Single Market, a subset of the EU members decided to establish a region without internal border controls, known as the 'Schengen' area. The first Schengen Accord was signed in 1985, and a second one in 1990. The objective of the Schengen initiative is to abolish the internal borders of the signatory states, to create a single external border where immigration checks are carried out in accordance with a unique set of rules, and to harmonize rules regarding visas and asylum applications. As a consequence, a set of measures such as the co-ordination of policies, customs, judiciary, and the development of a common information system have been adopted. The Schengen Accord has meanwhile been signed by all EU members, except the UK and Ireland. The later countries participate, however, in many aspects of the Schengen Accord, except the abolition of border controls.

Although the Schengen Accord is a milestone in reducing the barriers to mobility of persons within the EU, it has a more limited impact on the integration of labour markets. Non-EU foreigners permitted to reside in a member country are allowed to travel within the Schengen area, but they are not allowed to reside or work in other EU countries. Moreover, asylum seekers and refugees are usually not allowed to leave the country (or even the region) of residence. Thus, Schengen is basically about organizing efficiently the external control of borders in a community which has abolished its internal borders for the transport of goods and movement of people. It certainly has an impact on combating illegal migration, but it does not affect the national authority to regulate the immigration of workers and persons.

The two cornerstones of post-war European immigration policies are the removal of barriers to mobility for the members of the EU and its predecessors, and the establishment of barriers to labour immigration from non-EU countries after the first oil price shock in 1973. However, in contrast to the integration of goods markets, the EU's policy toward the integration of labour markets remains partial: while the barriers to intra-EU mobility of labour have been removed, the entry of non-EU migrants to EU's labour markets is still regulated by the individual member states. Free movement is consequently denied to non-EU citizens residing in the EU. Thus, although we can observe several attempts to harmonize rules of admitting third world country nationals, it is premature to speak about a common immigration policy of the EU, except in that policies attempt to protect host labour markets against immigration from non-EU countries in one way or another.

2.3. SELECTION AND SELF-SELECTION OF MIGRANTS

In a nutshell, the principles of European immigration policies can be summarized by two imperatives: (i) remove the barriers to mobility of labour for the club of rather rich countries with relatively homogenous factor endowments, and (ii) protect labour markets of the club members against an additional labour supply from non-club members. These policies not only had an impact on the quantity of migration flows, but also on the human capital characteristics of migrants.

A simple, but systematic way to tackle the question how immigration policy may affect the composition of migrants has been proposed by Borjas (1987), relying on the Roy (1951) model: under the assumption, that the costs of migration are a constant share of wages, the self-selection of migrants is determined by the distribution of incomes in the country of origin relative to the country of destination. For a given structure of incomes in the host country, the net benefits for migration are higher for individuals with high abilities and skills if the income distribution is more equal in the country of origin than in the country of destination, and vice versa. Thus, removing the barriers to immigration *vis-à-vis* a country with a lower inequality of income relative to the country of destination yields a more 'favourable' skill composition of migrants, while the removal of barriers to immigration *vis-à-vis* a country of a higher inequality of earnings results in a less 'favourable' self-selection of migrants (Borjas, 1987).

However, two qualifications are needed. Firstly, the terms 'favourable' and 'unfavourable' self-selection suggest a normative judgement, which might be misplaced. In the models of trade theory, factor movements which are motivated by differences in factor prices increase welfare in the receiving country or region. Thus, the movement of unskilled labour into a country in which high-skilled labour is relatively abundant may increase aggregate welfare. Secondly, the self-selection model, as is sketched here, is only a special case of a more general human capital model of migration (Chiswick, 2000). If we relax the assumption that the costs of migration are a constant proportion of wages for all types of migrants, then the composition of migrants is not only determined by the inequality of incomes in the country of origin relative to the country of destination, but also by the structure of migration costs. As a consequence, the picture becomes more complex.

Consider the following cases: firstly, if all or a part of the migration costs are equal for all types of migrants (e.g. out-of-pocket costs for transport and communication), then migration yields, *ceteris paribus*, higher net returns for the high-skilled relative to the low-skilled. Secondly, if abilities to minimize migration costs are related to the labour productivity of individuals, then net returns for the high-skilled are again higher than those of the low-skilled, all other factors equal. Thirdly, if employers in the home countries know the true productivity of migrants, while employers in the host countries do not, then the relative wage of a high-skilled migrant is, *ceteris paribus*, in the host countries below his or her wage in the home country. This may result in adverse selection, that is, that the negative self-selection of migrants induce employers in host countries to reduce wages for immigrant workers, which reduces the skill levels of migrant cohorts further, and so on (Kwok and Leland, 1982; Katz and Stark, 1986; Stark, 1991). Finally, if liquidity constraints of migrants and their families are (negatively) correlated with education and labour productivity, then migrants tend to be, *ceteris paribus*, favourably self-selected.[10] Notice that all these cases rely on relative, not absolute income differentials.

Against this background, we expect that the immigration policies of the EU and its members has affected the composition of migrants in different directions:

1. *Selective migration barriers.* The rationale to remove barriers to migration within the EU while establishing barriers to immigration *vis-à-vis* third countries is to affect the mix in the countries of origin. If implemented efficiently, this policy should have increased migration from countries with a relatively low inequality of earnings and reduced it from countries with a relatively high inequality of earnings, and, hence, raised the skill composition of migrants.

2. *Channelling migration from third countries.* Establishing barriers to labour immigration *vis-à-vis* non-EU countries has increased the importance of

---

[10] It is, however, also possible to construct the reverse case: individuals may emigrate in order to escape from liquidity constraints in rural areas or poor countries. Even small chances for success may motivate the emigration of risk-averse individuals if liquidity constraints are present (Stark, 1991). Thus, if a positive correlation between liquidity constraints and skills exist, then liquidity constraints favour the emigration of the low-skilled. It is however reasonable that ability of migrants increases with liquidity constraints, since their prospective returns of migration are higher.

the channels of family reunification, humanitarian migration and, presumably, illegal migration for migrants from there. All three channels tend to increase incentives for migration of relatively low-skilled workers (e.g. Chiswick, 2000). Thus, the impact of protecting EU labour markets is ambiguous: on the one hand, it may have increased the skill composition of migrants by reducing migration from countries with relatively high earnings inequality, while it has, on the other hand, affected the skill mix of migrants from these countries unfavourably.

3. *Labour market integration in the EU.* Reducing the costs of migration can work in both directions, that is, increasing the net benefits of migration for either the high-skilled or low-skilled workers. In general, all measures which reduce the costs of transferring human capital (e.g. harmonization and acceptance of education degrees, language training, etc.) increase net benefits of migration for the high-skilled relative to the low-skilled, while reducing out-of-pocket costs such as transport increase the net benefits of migration for the low-skilled relative to the high-skilled. At the balance, the large set of measures implemented by the EU to reduce information costs and the mutual recognition of education degrees, etc. should have favoured the migration of high-skilled workers relative to the low-skilled within the EU.

4. *Eligibility for welfare benefits.* Redistributing incomes and increasing the eligibility of foreigners to welfare benefits tend to increase migration incentives of the low-skilled relative to the high-skilled. However, the impact of welfare benefits on the selection of migrants is ambiguous: if the risks of migration increase with the accumulation of human capital, insuring migrants against social risks such as unemployment may increase incentives to migrate for high-skilled workers relative to the low-skilled. Thus, the impact of improving the access of EU citizens to welfare benefits in host countries may have, at the balance, improved incentives for high-skilled workers of EU countries to migrate.

5. *Temporary migration.* Immigration policies in many, but not all, EU countries favour temporary migration. If a complementarity between country specific and internationally transferable human capital exists, temporary migrants (guest workers, sojourners) tend to be less skilled than permanent migrants. Thus, temporary migration restrictions reduce both the incentives for the high-skilled to migrate, and incentives for those who emigrated to invest in country specific human capital (Chiswick, 2000). Moreover, if temporary migration arrangements are not properly enforced such as the guest worker arrangements in Germany, they may have a long-lasting impact on the skill composition. However, restricting the duration in the country of destination may not reduce incentives to migrate for high-skilled professionals whose human capital can be transferred internationally with low costs. Moreover, low-skill temporary immigration may increase welfare in host countries—at least if they manage to enforce return migration (see Chapter 6).

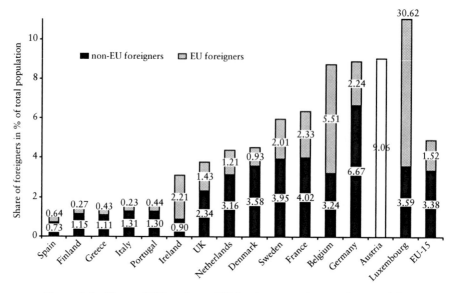

Figure 2.1. *Share of EU and non-EU foreigners in the population of the EU members, 1998*[11]

Source: Eurostat (2000), own calculations.

2.4. HOW DID EUROPEAN IMMIGRATION POLICY AFFECT THE COUNTRY OF ORIGIN MIX?

At first glance, European immigration policies have been unsuccessful in affecting the mix in the national origin of migrants. Since the early 1970s, when the free movement of workers was introduced for the founding members and barriers to the immigration from non-EU countries were established, the share of EU citizens residing in other member countries stagnated at around 1.5 per cent of the EU's population.[12] At the same time, it can be estimated that the share of foreigners from non-EU countries residing in the EU has increased from around 1.5 to 3.3 per cent of the EU's population.[13] As a consequence, more than two-thirds of the foreign population residing in the EU stem from non-EU countries in 1998 (Fig. 2.1).

This development can be illustrated with the German example: the number of citizens residing in Germany, from the present EU members, increased slightly from 1.6 million in 1970 to 1.84 million in 1998, while the number of non-EU foreigners increased from 1.4 million to 5.5 million at the same time. The change in the mix of the country of origin led to the average PPP-GDP per

---

[11] Note that cross-country comparisons are distorted by different national concepts of citizenship and different naturalization rates, see Chapter 1.

[12] These figures refer to the population of the present EU-15 members.

[13] Own estimates, based on Eurostat (2000) and national sources.

capita of the source countries of German immigration declining from around two-thirds to around one-third of the German level between 1961 and 1998 (Table 2.1). This is basically a result of increasing shares of the traditional countries of origin for guest worker recruitment at the European periphery (Turkey, Yugoslavia) at the expense of EU members.

Similar trends can be observed in many other EU countries (see Chapter 1). As a consequence, developing countries and low-income countries at the European periphery are the countries of origin for between 40 and 70 per cent of the migrants in the main immigration countries of the EU now (Table 2.2).

The most important countries of origin, which cover around two-thirds of the migrants from non-EU countries, are portrayed in some further detail in Tables 2.3 and 2.4: GDP per capita levels measured in purchasing power parities vary in these countries usually between one-tenth and one-third of those in the EU-15, while industrial wages at current exchange rates vary between 5 and 25 per cent of those in the EU-15. Moreover, the Gini-coefficient for the distribution of per capita incomes is significantly higher than in most EU countries.

The rather low levels of per capita incomes of the main countries of origin are closely related to relatively low education levels, in particular in secondary and tertiary education (Table 2.4).

However, the properties of the transition countries in Central and Eastern Europe differ somewhat from this picture: although their PPP-GDP per capita and wage levels are only slightly above those of the other main immigration countries, the inequality of earnings is, in most cases, well below, and education levels are well above those of the traditional source countries of EU immigration. However, all measures of earnings inequality in transition countries have to be taken with a pinch of salt, since the distribution of incomes underlies rapid changes in the course of transition and measurement problems may distort results. Moreover, qualitative studies indicate that actual education levels in Central and Eastern Europe fall short of those indicated by formal indicators such as school enrolment rates (Boeri and Keese, 1992; Boeri, 2000). Nevertheless, relative to their income levels the CEECs possess a well educated population and a low inequality of earnings.

Many econometric studies provide evidence that differences in per capita GDP levels or wages are the main factor which affect migration within and into the EU and its member states, although labour market conditions, institutional variables, language, distance, and unobservable country characteristics also play a role (Rotte and Vogler, 1998; Fertig, 1999; Boeri and Brücker, 2001a; Brücker, 2001). It is however important to note that the number of migrants from countries with relatively low income levels in the EU (and other OECD countries) has tended to grow, while absolute incomes in these source countries has also tended to increase. This phenomenon can be traced back to a number of causes, *inter alia* to the relaxation of liquidity constraints.[14] As a consequence,

---

[14] For a discussion see Faini and Venturini (1995).

Table 2.1. *Germany: Change in country of origin mix, 1961–98 (foreign population by country of origin)*

	1961		1967		1970		1980		1990		1998	
	In thousands	In % of total	In thousands	In % of total	In thousands	In % of total	In thousands	In % of total	In thousands	In % of total	In thousands	In % of total
EU-15	451.7	65.8	946.6	52.4	1586.7	53.3	1836.6	41.2	1661.772	31.1	1844.243	25.0
Southern Europe[a]	283.8	41.4	814.8	45.1	1216.4	40.9	1207.6	27.1	1093.63	20.5	1235.02	16.8
European periphery[b]	32.1	4.7	508.7	28.2	997.0	33.5	1749.4	39.3	2384.471	44.6	3289.176	44.7
Other OECD	33.4	4.9	83.2	4.6	99.9	3.4	131.5	3.0	36.912	0.7	202.571	2.8
Central and Eastern Europe[c]	34.9	5.1	97.0	5.4	113.4	3.8	124.9	2.8	371.927	7.0	826.82	11.2
Developing countries	134.1	19.5	171.2	9.5	179.5	6.0	610.9	13.7	887.45	16.6	1203.023	16.3
Total	686.2	100.0	1806.7	100.0	2976.5	100.0	4453.3	100.0	5342.532	100.0	7365.833	100.0
Average PPP-GDP per capita of countries of origin[d]												
In US$	na		6.505		7.860		5.313		5.897		7.391	
In % of Germany	na		63.51		65.87		0.35		31.26		33.56	

[a]Greece, Italy, Portugal, Spain.
[b]Cyprus, Iceland, Malta, Turkey, (former) Yugoslavia.
[c]Albania, (former) Comecon members.
[d]1967–90: 1990 Geary-Khamis Dollars based on Maddison (1995); 1998: World Development Indicators (2000).

Source: Federal Statistical Office, Maddison (1995), World Bank (2000), author's calculations.

Table 2.2. *Country of origin mix for selected EU countries, 1998 (foreign population by country of origin)*

	Belgium		France		Germany		Italy		Luxembourg		Sweden		UK	
	In thousands of total	In %	In thousands of total	In %	In thousands of total	In %	In thousands of total	In %	In thousands of total	In %	In thousands of total	In %	In thousands of total	In %
EU-15	560.6	63.0	1321.5	36.7	1844.2	25.0	211.7	23.9	127.9	89.6	178.2	48.3	805.5	38.0
Southern Europe[a]	300.5	33.7	1124.6	31.3	1235.0	16.8	27.9	3.2	76.9	53.9	13	3.5	163.3	7.7
Other OECD	18.2	2.0	56.9	1.6	202.6	2.8	23.6	2.7	na	na	51.5	14.0	237.2	11.2
Central and Eastern Europe[b]	11.6	1.3	63.0	1.8	826.8	11.2	11.6	1.3	na	na	131.1	35.6	84.4	4.0
European periphery[c]	92.3	10.4	250.2	7.0	3289.2	44.7	7.8	0.9	na	na	19.1	5.2	81.6	3.8
Developing countries	210.7	23.7	1905.0	53.0	1203.0	16.3	629.9	71.2	na	na	146.7	39.8	911.9	43.0
Total	890.4	100.0	3596.6	100.0	7365.8	100.0	884.6	100.0	142.8	100.0	526.6	100.0	2120.6	100.0

[a]Greece, Italy, Portugal, Spain.
[b]Albania, (former) Comecon members.
[c]Cyprus, Malta, Turkey, (former) Yugoslavia.

Source: Eurostat (2000).

Table 2.3. *Key income indicators in main countries of origin and the EU-15*

	Foreign citizens (in thousands)		PPP-GDP per capita, 1998[a]		Labour cost per worker in manufacturing, 1995–99[b]		Gini-coefficient[c]
	Population	In the EU-15	In US$	In % of EU-15	In USD	In % of EU-15	
Main countries of origin							
Turkey	63 500	2635[f]	6594	31.1	7958	29.6	41.5
former Yugoslavia	22 600	2019[f]	4005	18.9	na	na	na
Morocco	29 100	1141[e]	3188	15.0	3391	12.6	39.5
Algeria	29 900	658[e]	4595	21.7	6242	23.2	35.3
Poland	38 654	414[e]	7543	35.6	1714	6.4	32.9
USA	268 033	353[d]	29 240	137.9	28 907	107.6	40.8
former USSR	291 667	321[e]	6180	29.2	1528	5.7	48.7
Tunisia	9300	285[e]	5169	24.4	3599	13.4	40.2
India	979 700	193[e]	2060	9.7	1192	4.4	37.8
Pakistan	131 600	146[e]	1652	7.8	3099	11.5	31.2
Romania	22 526	142[e]	1360	6.4	119	0.4	28.2
Present EU members							
Austria	8068	215[d]	23 145	109.2	28 342	105.5	23.1
Belgium	10 170	139[e]	23 622	111.4	24 132	89.8	25.0
Denmark	5275	81[e]	23 855	112.5	29 235	108.8	24.7
Finland	5132	133[e]	20 641	97.4	26 615	99.0	25.6
France	56 652	365[e]	21 214	100.1	na	na	32.7
Germany	82 012	280[e]	22 026	103.9	33 226	123.6	30.0
Greece	10 487	434[e]	13 994	66.0	15 899	59.2	32.7
Ireland	3661	479[f]	17 991	84.9	25 414	94.6	35.9
Italy	57 461	1 216[e]	20 365	96.1	35 138	130.7	27.3
Luxembourg	418	11[e]	38 840	183.2	na	na	26.9
Netherlands	15 567	281[e]	22 325	105.3	39 865	148.3	32.6
Portugal	9934	289[e]	14 569	68.7	7577	28.2	35.6
Spain	39 299	477[e]	15 960	75.3	8475	31.5	32.5
Sweden	8845	76[e]	19 848	93.6	29 043	108.1	25.0
United Kingdom	58 185	444[f]	20 314	95.8	23 843	88.7	36.1
EU-15	371 166	4918[g]	21 200	100.0	26 876	100.0	
Memo items							
CEEC-10	104 690		8007	37.8	na	na	

[a]GDP per capita in purchasing power parity.
[b]Gross monthly wages in manufacturing industries.
[c]Years 1994–98. Note that gini-coefficients in transition countries underly rapid changes and may underly measurement error.
[d]Without Ireland.
[e]Without Austria and Ireland.
[f]Without Austria.
[g]Reporting countries only.

Sources: Worldbank (2000); Eurostat (2000*a*), Eurostat (2000*b*), authors' calculations.

the trend of increasing differences in per capita income levels between the host countries in the EU and the countries of origin may continue.

2.4.1. *Did the free movement of workers in the EU increase migration?*

A first look at the statistics does not support the view that integration into the EU and the introduction of free movement had an impact on migration: in case of the introduction of free movement for the southern EU members we observe

Table 2.4. *Key education indicators for main countries of origin and the EU-15*

	Gross school enrolment rates figures refer to 1997 unless otherwise indicated		
	Primary	Secondary	Tertiary
Main countries of origin			
Algeria	108	63	13
Bulgaria	99	77	41
Czech Republic	104[b]	99[b]	23[b]
former Yugoslavia	69	62	22
Hungary	103[b]	98[b]	25[b]
India	100	49	7
Morocco	86	39	11
Pakistan	40	14	4
Poland	96[b]	98[b]	24[b]
Romania	104[b]	78[b]	23[b]
Russian Federation	107	96	46
Slovak Republic	102[b]	94[b]	22[b]
Tunisia	118	64	14
Turkey	107	58	21
Ukraine	102	94	42
Present EU members			
Austria	106[b]	77[b]	18[b]
Belgium	103[b]	146[ab]	57[b]
Denmark	102[b]	121[b]	46[b]
Finland	99[b]	116[b]	71[b]
France	106[b]	111[b]	52[b]
Germany	102[b]	104[b]	45[b]
Greece	94[b]	95[b]	43[b]
Ireland	104[b]	116[b]	40[b]
Italy	101[b]	94[b]	43[b]
Netherlands	107[b]	137[ab]	50[b]
Portugal	128[b]	106[ab]	38[b]
Spain	107	122[b]	53
Sweden	106[b]	137[ab]	49[b]
United Kingdom	115[b]	133[ab]	50[b]
Memo items[b]			
High income countries	103	106	58
Middle income countries	114	70	15
Low income countries	93	42	5

[a] Incl. training for unemployed.
[b] 1996.

Source: World Bank (2000), authors' calculations.

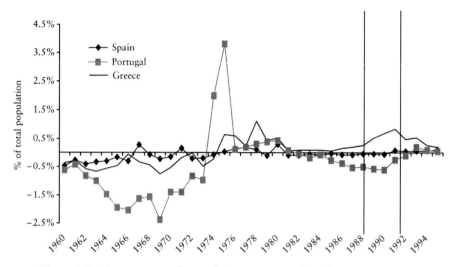

Figure 2.2. *Net migration flows of Greece, Portugal, and Spain, 1960–94*
(negative sign = net emigration, positive sign = net immigration)

Source: Boeri and Brücker *et al.* (2001*a*), based on Eurostat (1987).

a net immigration rather than a net emigration of nationals with the exception
of Portugal (Fig. 2.2).

However, it is premature to draw from this descriptive evidence the conclusion that the free movement of workers in the EU and the establishment of
external restrictions had no quantitative impact on the migration of workers
and other persons in the EU. The counterfactual question, what would have
been the quantity and country structure of immigration if the EU had not
introduced free movement, cannot be answered by simply looking at actual
migration figures. Econometric studies indicate that the introduction of free
movement had increased migration within the EU slightly. The free movement
of labour increases both, the absolute level of migrants as well as the elasticity
of migration with regard to income differences. As an example, the long-run
share of migrants from Turkey residing in Germany would be between 0.5 and
0.8 percentage points higher in case of free movement for the current difference
in per capita income levels (see Chapter 3, Brücker, 2001; Boeri and Brücker,
2001*a*; similar results are presented by Flaig, 2001). Thus, although these figures should be treated with caution, the free movement of workers seems to
contribute at least somewhat to labour mobility in the EU.

2.5. HOW DOES NATIONAL ORIGIN AFFECT THE SKILL COMPOSITION OF MIGRANTS?

The selection and self-selection models discussed above predict that the skill
composition of migrants is affected by the mix in the countries of origin, or,

more precisely, by differences in distribution of incomes between the countries of destination and origin. An indication of the skill composition of migrants can be provided on the basis of the European Community Household Panel (ECHP), which applies an international comparable classification of education levels in its questionnaire (see Chapter 4 and Annex for details). Unfortunately, the response rates are too low for an analysis of the skill composition of migrants by detailed country samples. However, the sample allows classification of migrants in EU foreigners and non-EU foreigners, which provides some interesting insights on the consequences of national origin on the skill mix of migrants (Figs 2.3 and 2.4). Note that all figures should be interpreted with caution, since all information depend on self-classification, which tend to bias skill levels of foreigners upwards.

Within the EU, countries with relatively low education levels of natives— that is, Portugal, Spain, Greece, Ireland, Italy—receive migrants with high-skill levels from other EU countries. However, the share of EU foreigners in these countries is, with the exception of Ireland, at between 0.2 and 0.6 per cent of the population almost negligible (see Fig. 2.1, again). Interestingly enough, in many—but not all—EU countries with high education and income levels, education levels of EU foreigners are almost at the same levels as natives or even

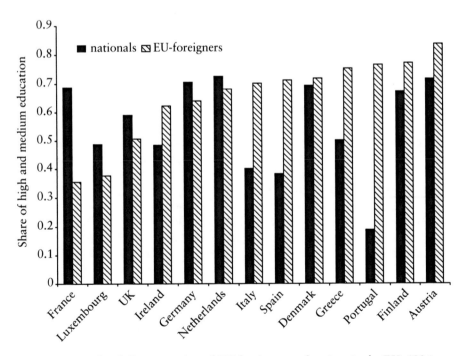

Figure 2.3. *The skill composition of EU foreigners and natives in the EU, 1996*

Source: European Community Household Panel.

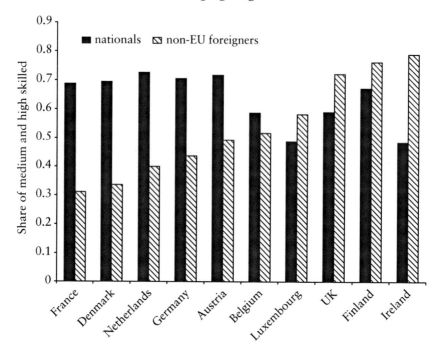

Figure 2.4. *The skill composition of non-EU foreigners and natives in the EU, 1996*[15]

Source: European Community Household Panel.

slightly above (Austria, Germany, Netherlands, Denmark, and Finland). Note that in some of these countries (Germany, Austria) the main countries of origin of EU foreigners are in the south of the EU. Finally, we observe a distinct gap in education levels between natives and EU foreigners in France and Luxembourg, which recruited notable shares of their workforce in Iberian countries and Italy. The skill composition of EU foreigners in these countries is roughly in line with that of the countries of origin.

Although these data should be interpreted with caution, there seems to be little evidence for an unfavourable selection of skills in intra-EU migration. At least in the German case, factors which induce a favourable selection of EU migrants with regard to their skill composition seem to affect the composition of migrants. While we can observe in some cases a Heckscher–Ohlin pattern of migration, that is, that low-skilled EU foreigners move to countries with a high share of high- and medium-skilled labour, and EU countries with relatively low education endowments receive high-skilled migrants, the rather high skill levels of EU migrants in Germany and some other receiving countries does not exactly fit well into that pattern.

---

[15] Foreigners are defined by citizenship and not by immigrant status.

The average skill composition of non-EU foreigners is well below that of EU foreigners, but we observe a polarization at the upper and the lower ends of the skill distribution, which are basically determined by differences in the source country mix: on the one hand, in France, Denmark, the Netherlands, Germany, and Austria the overwhelming share of the migrants from non-EU countries belongs to the low-skilled category. This reflects low human capital endowments in the countries of origin. On the other hand, in Ireland and Finland the high skill levels of non-EU migrants reflect relatively high skill levels in the countries of origin—the USA in the Irish case, and the CEECs in the Finnish case. The main outlier is the UK: it managed to attract non-EU foreigners with skill levels above those of natives, although three-quarters of this group stem from developing countries.[16]

2.5.1. *Has the skill composition of foreigners deteriorated over time?*

There is neither evidence that the skill composition of foreigners in the EU has significantly improved nor that it has declined during the last few decades. Unfortunately, there is no historical data for the EU such as the Censuses in the USA, every ten years, which allows a comparison of the skill composition of migrant cohorts over time. Instead we have to rely on the information of recent surveys, which differentiate between immigrants by their date of arrival. Since immigrants may increase education levels after arrival and return migration may affect the skill composition of the remaining immigrants, this gives only a crude picture. In many countries the share of low-skilled among the recent immigrant cohorts, that is, those which immigrated during the last 10 years, relative to those who immigrated more than twenty years ago, has declined (Belgium, France, UK, and less significantly in Austria, Luxembourg, and the Netherlands). However, with a few exceptions, the skill composition of the newly arrived immigrants is only slightly above that of the older ones. In Spain, Italy, and Portugal, that is, those countries which receive notable migration flows from Africa and other developing countries, the shares of low-skilled among the newly arrived cohorts has been above those of the older ones or the same. However, these groups are insufficiently covered by the ECHP there, such that we have no reliable information on the skill composition of non-EU foreigners in these countries (Table 2.5).

A number of studies has analysed educational attainments of immigrants in host countries, in particular of second generation immigrants and ethnic minorities. We can observe mixed trends across individual EU countries: based on microcensus surveys, Riphahn (2000) found evidence that educational attainments of second generation migrant cohorts born between 1956 and 1974

---

[16] Notice that foreigners are defined by citizenship and not by immigrant status, such that these figures reflect the more recent immigration.

Table 2.5. *Share of individuals with low education levels*

	Total population	By citizenship			Native born	By immigration status			
		Nationals	EU foreigners	Non-EU foreigners		Foreign born years since immigration			
						All	0–9	10–20	20+
Ratio of low education relative to group total									
Netherlands	0.2773	0.2742	0.3181	0.6007	na	na	na	na	na
Austria	0.2931	0.283	0.1635	0.5075	0.2916	0.183	(0.13)	(0.08)	0.2807
Germany	0.3013	0.2945	0.3596	0.5633	na	na	na	na	na
Denmark	0.3123	0.3056	0.2816	0.664	0.3013	0.4371	0.55	0.3726	0.3745
Finland	0.3258	0.3273	0.2285	0.2373	0.326	0.3049	0.4427	(0.5766)	(0.235)
France	0.4077	0.3119	0.6453	0.6892	0.3911	0.5217	0.4435	0.5204	0.5398
UK	0.4094	0.4097	0.4933	0.2781	0.4859	0.3162	0.179	0.3291	0.351
Belgium	0.4126	0.4126	na	0.4831	0.3918	0.3912	0.224	0.4505	0.4261
Greece	0.4975	0.4988	0.2473	0.3727	0.5075	(0.2586)	(0.1704)	(0.2599)	(0.3257)
Ireland	0.5117	0.5154	0.3768	0.21	0.5173	0.3669	0.3279	0.4262	0.3516
Luxembourg	0.5469	0.5123	0.6233	0.4177	0.5225	0.5888	0.4894	0.4559	0.7165
Italy	0.5983	0.5991	0.2978	(0.3592)	0.5933	(0.4366)	(0.3458)	(0.4081)	(0.4638)
Spain	0.6163	0.6177	0.2875	(0.3687)	0.6227	(0.537)	(0.4236)	(0.2429)	(0.3187)
Portugal	0.8106	0.812	(0.2347)	(0.4995)	0.8198	(0.442)	(0.4742)	(0.4988)	(0.4855)

Figures in brackets are affected by low response rates.

Source: European Community Household Panel.

tend to *diverge* from those of natives: the gap in educational degrees between second generation migrants and natives increases with the later born cohorts. Interestingly enough, these trends reflect a change in the country of origin mix of second generation cohorts. After controlling for country of origin, the significant difference in cohort effects disappears (Riphahn, 2000, p. 9). In contrast to Germany, educational attainments of foreigners in the UK have improved: early migrant cohorts tend to be less qualified than later migrant cohorts, and first generation migrants tend to be less qualified than second and third generation migrants (Hatton and Wheatley Price, 1999). Moreover, there is evidence that the younger members of ethnic minorities have attained higher educational attainments than whites (Berthoud and Modood, 1997).

Altogether, the size and structure of immigration within and into the EU is largely, but not exclusively, driven by differences in factor endowments. As a general rule, EU members with higher per capita incomes and higher endowments of physical and human capital received a higher share of migrants, and among the migrants, in many cases, a higher share of manual workers. The converse holds true for the EU members with lower per capita income and a higher share of less-skilled workers in their labour force. However, the skill composition of migrants does not always follow a Heckscher–Ohlin pattern: on one hand, we observe that in most countries with highly skilled natives, the skill composition of foreigners is relatively low (Austria, Denmark, France, Germany, and the Netherlands). But on the other hand, the UK attracted a high share of skilled labour inflows although their main sources of foreign labour from outside the EU are developing countries. Moreover, in some countries such as Germany and Austria we observe that skill levels of foreigners originating in the EU and the CEECs[17] are high—even relative to natives in the host countries. Finally, immigration from Africa and other developing countries is increasing in the Southern EU members, which will tend to reduce the average skill composition of immigrants over time.

The skill composition of migrants in the EU seem to reflect differences in factor endowments between the countries of destination and origin, but migrants tend in general not be unfavourably self-selected with regard to their skill composition: within the EU, migrants are at least as highly qualified as the average native in the countries of origin. In particular, in Germany and some other countries we observe a skill composition of EU foreigners which is high relative to that of natives in their home countries, while France and Luxembourg receive EU migrants with a skill composition which is roughly in line with that of natives in their home countries. We do not have enough information to evaluate the skill composition of the population in the countries

---

[17] Note that in case of the CEECs education is high and earnings inequality is in most countries still low, such that this observation fits pretty well in the self-selection framework. However, earnings inequality tend to increase rapidly in the CEECs such that the skill composition of migrants from there may deteriorate over time.

of origin in the case of non-EU foreigners properly, but the information we have tends to indicate that migrants are again favourably self-selected.

2.6. CONCLUSIONS

Post-war immigration policies of the EU and its member states have brought paradoxical results: on the one hand, removing barriers to labour mobility within the EU was not associated with increasing immigration. On the other hand, the share of foreigners from non-EU countries has doubled since the early 1970s, despite immigration policies at national and EU levels designed to protect labour markets against non-EU immigration. This has coincided with a drift towards a higher share of non-EU immigration that arises from family unification and refuge seekers. Thus, it may be in these areas that EU member states will need to adjust policy if immigration objectives are to be achieved.

Increasing immigration from non-EU countries has involved a substantial shift in the mix of the countries of origin toward low-income countries at the 'European periphery' (i.e. Turkey, former Yugoslavia) and developing countries. The gap in per capita GDP levels between the main immigration countries in the EU and the countries of origin has, with some exceptions, increased substantially during the post-war period. The relatively low per capita incomes of the source countries are associated with relatively low human capital endowments, and, as a consequence, low education levels of non-EU foreigners. There is, however, no evidence that they are unfavourably self-selected relative to the average skill composition in the countries of origin, and indeed the converse appears to hold true.

The shift in the country of origin mix reflects large and persisting differences in per capita income levels between the EU and the source countries of migration. Increasing levels of absolute incomes in the source countries have presumably relaxed liquidity constraints, while falling transport and communication costs and network effects have reduced the costs to migrate. These factors cannot be affected much by immigration policies. Nevertheless, immigration policies have contributed to the skill composition of migrants. In many continental European countries—namely Germany, France, Denmark, and Sweden—labour immigration was reduced to small numbers after the first oil price crisis in 1973. The three main channels for migration there—family reunification, humanitarian immigration, and illegal immigration—have systematically selected migrants with relatively low human capital, and poor labour market prospects: family dependants of manual workers, refugees from regions with political unrest such as Yugoslavia, eastern Turkey and a number of developing countries, and migrants working in grey sectors of the economy that provide low returns to human capital. Conversely, we observe in the UK, where the mix between labour immigration and the other channels is relatively balanced, a favourable selection of migrants from non-EU countries.

Although the share of EU citizens in the foreign population of the EU member states stagnates, introducing free movement has nevertheless had an impact on intra-EU labour mobility: econometric studies have demonstrated, that the share of EU foreigners would have been lower without removing the barriers to migration in the Common Market. Stagnating shares of EU foreigners are basically a consequence of the relatively small and declining differences in per capita incomes among the EU member states.

In many—but not all—receiving countries EU foreigners are favourably self-selected, that is, their skill levels are above average skill levels of natives in home countries. Although we have no hard evidence, it appears that the removal of barriers for the transfer of human capital, the protection of EU workers against discrimination, and the insurance of accumulated human capital by the welfare systems, has enforced the favourable self-selection of EU migrants at the margin. However, the low mobility of labour and persons between the Member States indicates that the EU citizens either do not yet regard EU labour markets as integrated, or have high non-pecuniary valuations of their own communities.

Altogether, policies that aimed to protect host labour markets against labour immigration have contributed to an unfavourable selection of migrants regarding their skill composition. Ironically, against the background of the empirical knowledge about the labour market implications of migration, it looks as if the high emphasis on protecting labour markets was misplaced: empirical studies find at best minor effects of labour migration on wages and employment opportunities of natives (see Chapter 4). Nevertheless, policies that would have promoted 'economic' migration at the expense of the other channels would have improved the skill composition of migrant cohorts and their labour market performance without involving large effects on wages and increased risk of unemployment for natives.

3

Welfare State Provision

In the previous chapter we explored EU immigration policy and how the structure of this policy influences the types of immigrants the EU receives. In this chapter we examine the comparative use by migrants of various branches of the welfare state in different EU countries and the influence of the welfare system on the selection of a destination economy. In particular, we ask: Do migrants take into account the generosity of the welfare system when choosing a host country? Does this put a strain on the financing of the welfare state? Does it adversely affect the distribution of skills in the host country's economy? These are politically sensitive issues. In this chapter we explore the sort of insights that can be obtained from economic analysis. We then use data for the EC countries to examine the empirical evidence regarding welfare dependence amongst immigrant workers.

Only a few studies have yet analysed the causes of welfare dependency of migrants in Europe. A number of studies focus on Germany[1] (Frick *et al.*, 1996; Riphahn, 1998; Bird *et al.*, 1999; Fertig and Schmidt, 2001; Sinn *et al.*, 2001), some recent evidence is available on Sweden (Hansen and Lofstrom, 1999). In all three countries welfare dependency ratios have increased in absolute terms and relative to the native population. As an example, in Germany the share of foreigners among welfare recipients[2] numbered 8.3 per cent in 1980 and 23.5 per cent in 1996, while the share of foreigners in the population has increased from 7.2 to 8.9 per cent at the same time (Riphahn, 1998). A part of this increase can be traced back to higher numbers of asylum seekers and refugees, which are not or only under restrictive conditions permitted to work. In Sweden we observe similar trends (Hansen and Lofstrom, 1999; Pederson, 2000).

The main findings of the literature on welfare dependency of foreigners can be summarized as follows. First, the higher probability of migrant households relative to native households to depend on social assistance and related welfare programmes is basically a result of their human capital and other

---

[1] The major part of the German literature relies on household panel survey (German Socio Economic Panel, GSOEP), one study on the microcensus data (Fertig and Schmidt, 2001). The Danish study relies on administrative data which records the full population, the Swedish data on a longitudinal data set which comprises one per cent of the population.

[2] We use the term welfare synonymous to social assistance. In Germany the social assistance consists of two parts, general income support and support under special circumstances (handicapped, elderly care).

socio-economic characteristics: all German studies find that foreigners are equally or even less likely to depend on welfare than natives once the data is controlled for observable characteristics. Lower education, a lower age of the household head and a higher number of children of migrants relative to native households are the prime factors that contributed to the higher welfare dependency of foreign relative to native households (Frick *et al.*, 1996; Bird *et al.*, 1999; Riphahn, 1998; Fertig and Schmidt, 2001). The higher welfare dependency of foreign households relative to their native counterparts is, not surprisingly, closely related to the weaker labour market performance of adults in the foreign households relative to the native households. Moreover, foreigner households are not more likely to claim benefits for which they are eligible than native households (Bird *et al.*, 1999). Bird *et al.* (1999, p. 17) conclude that 'immigrants are more likely to be in the circumstances that would lead any household—German or native—to claim benefits more frequently'. The same differences in socio-economic characteristics explain the higher welfare dependency ratios of foreign relative to native households in the Swedish studies (Hansen and Lofstrom, 1999). In contrast to the German studies, it has been found in Sweden that the high welfare participation of migrant households is, beyond socio-economic factors, affected by unobservable characteristics of migrant households (Hansen and Lofstrom, 1999). As we shall see, our evidence for other European countries is more in line with these Swedish studies, although for Germany it fully confirms the findings of the above mentioned studies.

Secondly, in contrast to evidence from the US (e.g. Borjas and Hilton, 1996), the European studies find evidence that foreigners tend to assimilate out of welfare assistance. In Germany, welfare dependency declines with the duration of stay of migrant households, all other factors being equal (Fertig and Schmidt, 2001; some weak evidence is also provided in Riphahn, 1998). Strong evidence for the hypothesis that migrants tend to assimilate out of welfare has been found also in the Swedish case. Nevertheless, it is not predicted that welfare dependency ratios of migrants and natives will tend to converge (Hansen and Lofstrom, 1999).

Thirdly, welfare usage of non-humanitarian migrants is well below that of humanitarian migrants in Sweden. Non-humanitarian migrants tend, however, to assimilate more rapidly out of welfare than other migrants (Hansen and Lofstrom, 1999).

3.1. BASIC THEORY

Standard economic analysis holds that migration choices depend on the distribution of income.[3] This is illustrated in Fig. 3.1. On the horizontal axis is the skill level of a given individual. On the vertical axis is his income net of

---

[3] See Borjas (1987).

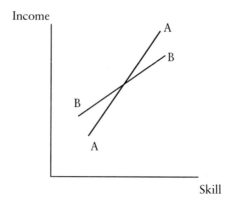

Figure 3.1. *Country choice as determined by relative distribution of income*

migration costs. The AA line represents the individual's income in his or her home country. The BB line is income in the host country, net of the cost of migrating.

As Fig. 3.1 is drawn, the slope of AA is greater than that of BB. This means that the source country is assumed to be more unequal than the recipient country. This would be typical when dealing with migration from a 'poor' to a 'rich' country (for example, the steeper slope of the poor country may simply come from the scarcity of skilled labour there). As Fig. 3.1 makes clear, those who will migrate to the skilled country are workers with a skill level below a critical threshold. *Alternatively*, Fig. 3.1 may represent the choice by a pool of migrants *between two host countries*, one more egalitarian than the other, in which both the lines AA and BB represent income net of migration costs. It then says that the least skilled migrants will select the most egalitarian country, while the most skilled go to the inegalitarian one.

How is this analysis changed when one deals with the welfare state? Suppose that the migrant has to choose between two destination countries that only differ by their welfare system. In particular, suppose that, as displayed in Fig. 3.2, country 1 does not have any assistance system, while country 2 has a minimum guaranteed income which is financed by a tax on labour income. Accordingly, the schedule corresponding to country 2 has a horizontal portion corresponding to this guaranteed income, and above that level it is below the schedule for country 1 because of the taxes needed to finance the welfare system.

As drawn in Fig. 3.2, workers with a skill level below a certain threshold will select country 2 and they will indeed be on welfare; those above that threshold will select country 1. Therefore, the welfare state contributes to bias the composition of migrants towards low-skill types who are more likely to get benefits.

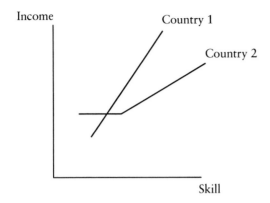

Figure 3.2. *Locational decisions under welfare minima*

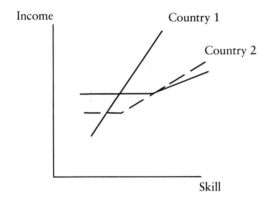

Figure 3.3. *Impact of more generous benefits in the most generous country*

An increase in the generosity of benefits is represented in Fig. 3.3. It lifts the income floor upward while reducing net income at high skill levels because of the extra taxes needed to finance the increase in the welfare minimum. This increases the skill level below which one selects country 2, thus increasing the number of migrants in country 2 and reducing it in country 1 (Fig. 3.3).

In contrast, if country 1 introduces a guaranteed income then this will not attract any migrants as long as it is below that of country 2 (Fig. 3.4). Therefore, in the most generous countries, immigration acts as a multiplier which boosts the response of the number of claimants to an increase in the generosity of benefits. This effect is not present in the less generous countries.

The above analysis predicts that in the most generous countries migrants will have characteristics that make them more likely to be on welfare. However, after controlling for these characteristics, immigrants are not more nor less likely to be on welfare than natives. The literature on migration has however

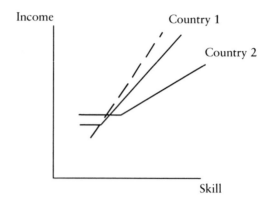

Figure 3.4. *Impact of an increase in benefits in the least generous country*

noted the importance of networks in determining migration decisions. If belonging to a given network affects the migration decision, then migrants can be less or more likely to be on welfare than natives even controlling for their characteristics. For example, if migration is mediated by networks of employers and family members who are already in the host country and have a job, then the cost of migration is likely to be lower if one comes to work than if one comes to be on welfare. This makes migrants more likely to work relative to natives with the same characteristics. If, on the other hand, there exists networks of people who have good information about how to get benefits, the converse will occur. This will also occur if there are specific adaptation costs (language, etc.) associated with migration, which makes it more likely that a migrant will end up on welfare.

Another complication is the effect of age. The cost of migrating increases with age, while its benefits fall with age. Therefore we expect migrants to be younger on average than the source population, and presumably also the host population. This makes them less likely to be on pensions and therefore migration tends to ease the problem of financing pensions, at least temporarily. We return to that important point below.

Also, the above analysis assumes that the labour market clears. If there is involuntary unemployment, and if it is unevenly distributed across skill levels, then the migration decision will not be based on the distribution of wages, but rather on the distribution of permanent income, which has to be adjusted in order to reflect expected unemployment spells. This is illustrated in Fig. 3.5, where the distribution of permanent income is more unequal than that of wages because it is assumed that the incidence of unemployment is higher at the low end of the distribution of income. The difference between the two slopes is larger:

(1) the more unemployment is concentrated at the bottom of the distribution of income;

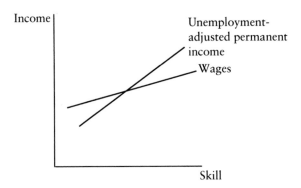

Figure 3.5. *Adjusting the income profile for unemployment*

(2) the lower the unemployment benefit (UB) ratio;

(3) the more the migrant population is likely to enter the host country labour market as unemployed job seekers. This may not however be the typical case as much migration is the result of employers' overseas recruiting activities;

(4) the more the migrant population is likely to be ineligible, as new entrants, for unemployment benefits. This is typically the case for unemployment insurance but not for assistance.

To summarize, the existence of involuntary unemployment at the bottom of the distribution of income is likely to reduce the attractiveness of countries with generous welfare systems, although we do not typically expect it to entirely offset the basic economic mechanisms described at the beginning of this chapter. Insofar as native workers are able to claim welfare benefits and to work in an informal (illegal) sector, then some employers may prefer to hire in the informal market. The larger is this sector of illegal employment the greater may be the opportunities for illegal migrants to work in the economy. This secondary consequence of the welfare system may act to support a higher level of illegal immigration.

3.2. AN EMPIRICAL ANALYSIS: COMPARING MIGRANTS WITH NATIVES

The central prediction of the theory outlined above is that countries with more generous welfare systems will attract migrants disproportionately likely (relative to natives) to be dependent on welfare. In other words, migrants' characteristics (such as human capital) are more elastic to taxes and benefit than natives' characteristics, because migrants are self-selected to be more mobile. Typically, we should expect migrants' differential dependency on welfare to be entirely explained by differences between their characteristics and those of natives. This is what is implied by the above theoretical analysis and the previous empirical findings for Germany that are reported in the introduction. However, to the extent that some of the characteristics are unobservable and that there are specific effects associated with migration, it is also possible that *controlling for their observed characteristics*, migrants have a different exposure to welfare than natives. Thus, our empirical analysis will proceed in two parts. First, we shall compare the characteristics of migrants with those of natives and impute their predicted welfare dependency. Second, we shall analyse the specific consequences of migrant status as such for welfare dependency, defined as *residual welfare dependency*.

We now empirically investigate the phenomena analysed in the previous section using the European Community Household Panel (ECHP). This survey is a standardized annual longitudinal survey carried out in the European Union since 1994. All current EU member states, with the exception of Sweden, are represented. Austria and Finland joined only in wave 2 (1995) and 3 (1996) respectively.

The data are collected separately at the national level by 'National Data Collection Units'—'NDUs', either National Statistical Institutes (NSIs) or research centres depending on the country. The questionnaire and procedures are fairly standard across countries, but there are differences, mainly in sample selection and anonymization (whereby some countries have stricter requirements by law, as for example Germany). Comparability is ensured by Eurostat guidelines which are followed by NDUs.

The interviews took place mostly in the calendar year following the survey year (1994 for the first survey, relating to 1993, etc.). Only the first three waves (1994, 1995, and 1996) are currently available. In the first wave a sample of some 60 500 households, that is, approximately 130 000 adults aged 16 years and over were interviewed in the then 12 member countries. In wave 2, EU-13 samples totalled some 60 000 households and 129 000 adults. In wave 3, 14 samples included some 61 000 households and 131 000 adults.[4]

3.2.1. *Measuring migrant status*

The first step consists of defining immigrant status. There is no ideal way of doing it, so we have considered two possibilities.

The first one is to define an immigrant as a non-citizen of the country one is considering. As it turns out that migrants from other EU countries are quite similar with natives, we found it more informative to define a migrant as non-citizen of the European Union. Consistent with this definition, we consider an EU citizen as native even if she/he lives in another EU country. The problem

---

[4] For a detailed description of the ECHP methodology and questionnaires, see 'The European Community Household Panel (ECHP): Volume 1—Survey methodology and implementation' and 'The European Community Household Panel (ECHP): Volume 1—Survey questionnaires: Waves 1–3'—Theme 3, Series E, Eurostat, OPOCE, Luxembourg, 1996.

with this definition of migrant is that it does not identify the country of origin and may be subject to bias due to cross-country differences in naturalization laws. Furthermore, this criterion reduces the number of people classified as immigrants, thus reducing the number of observations in relevant cells. This problem is aggravated by the fact that sampling is biased in favour of EU citizens. For example, in Italy, there are only 6 observations out of more than 17 000 where the respondent is not an EU citizen.

Alternatively, one can use information on the country of birth as a proxy for immigrant status. Here, the source of bias is misclassification as immigrants of 'true nationals' born abroad for whatever reason. Such misclassification may be a serious source of bias for countries which have former colonies such as France, the UK, Belgium, and Portugal. However, as Table 3.1 makes clear, this increases the number of observations classified as immigrants.

Another issue is that non-EU citizens have reduced welfare eligibility compared to EU citizens, which makes it difficult to extrapolate our results to the EU enlargement process.

In Table 3.1, we only report results associated with the first criterion. Results using the second criterion were qualitatively similar, and are available from 'Fondazione Debenedetti' upon request.

In reading the results, one should be cautious that there are not many observations of non-EU citizens in the panel.

3.2.2. *Migrants' average welfare dependency*

The first thing we do is to look at the raw figures of non-EU citizens vs EU citizens welfare dependency. Table 3.2 reports the proportion of people who are on unemployment benefits in 11 countries. Roughly speaking, one can decompose these countries into two groups: those where non-EU citizens'

Table 3.1. *Comparison between the two measures of immigrant status (1st wave of the panel)*

Country	% EU	% EU born
Germany	97.8	na
Denmark	98.0	97.1
Netherlands	99.3	na
Belgium	97.0	93.9
France	97.2	92.3
UK	98.1	94.6
Greece	99.1	na
Spain	99.6	98.9
Portugal	98.9	98.0
Luxembourg	na	95.8
Ireland	na	98.7

Table 3.2. *Welfare dependency of EU citizens and migrants from non-EU countries*

Country	% receiving UB		% receiving old age pension		% receiving family benefits	
	EU citizens	Non-EU migrants	EU citizens	Non-EU migrants	EU citizens	Non-EU migrants
Germany	6.96	8.57	na	na	na	na
Denmark	13.0	37.5	21.0	3.1	19.7	25.0
Netherlands	6.7	13.7	18.8	3.9	19.6	27.5
Belgium	10.7	17.4	21.1	15.0	24.5	25.6
France	7.7	12.6	22.8	10.0	15.3	32.0
UK	2.8	3.4	26.8	3.45	20.1	20.7
Greece	2.2	1.4	23.6	21.4	3.8	5.7
Spain	6.5	4.9	15.8	4.9	1.7	4.9
Portugal	2.2	0.0	24.6	18.2	18.8	9.09
Austria	5.3	14.2	21.0	3.0	23.9	32.0
Finland	15.4	47.1	18.4	5.7	22.4	22.6

dependency is not significantly higher, sometimes even lower, than EU citizens: Germany, the UK, Greece, Spain, and Portugal, and those where it is significantly higher than natives and sometimes very high indeed: Denmark, the Netherlands, Belgium, France, Austria, and Finland.

Far fewer non-EU citizens are on pensions than EU citizens, which is probably mostly due to their younger age and their propensity to retire in their native country. In fact, in many countries the absolute number of respondents who are both non-EU citizens and on old-age pensions is quite small: 3 in Finland, 4 in Portugal, and 2 in Spain, the UK, the Netherlands, and Denmark. In other words, for these countries the panel is quite inappropriate to deal with this issue.

Finally, dependency on family benefits is reported in the last column of Table 3.2. It is typically comparable to that of natives except in the Netherlands, France, and Austria where it is much higher. In Greece, Spain, and Portugal, the results have to be interpreted with caution because of the small number of relevant observations.

These differences come from the complex interactions of many factors. The first thing to look at, in light of the discussion of Section 3.1, is migrant's characteristics as compared to natives.

3.2.3. *Migrants' characteristics*

What are the characteristics of immigrants? The following tables compare them to the non-immigrant population by education, age, sex, and marital status. As will become clear, non-EU citizens' characteristics differ substantially from those of EU citizens, in a way which itself varies across countries.

In Table 3.3 we look at the characteristics of migrants. In particular, the first column looks at the sex ratio. In many cultures, males migrate first, and the

Table 3.3. *Characteristics of natives and migrants*

Country	% of males		% of married people		% of people not having completed secondary education		% of people with college degree		Average age		Average number of children	
	EU citizens	Non-EU migrants	EU citizens	Non-EU migrants	EU citizens	Non-EU migrants	EU citizens	Non-EU migrants	EU citizens	Non-EU migrants	EU citizens	Non-EU migrants
Germany	48.5	47.1	70.4	82.1	28.8	50.0	20.5	15.0	48.1	39.5	0.51	1.05
Denmark	48.8	51.6	55.8	71.9	40.0	54.7	30.7	31.3	47.7	39.9	0.53	1.00
Netherlands	46.8	49.0	68.6	72.6	27.4	50.0	17.6	22.9	46.8	39.1	0.62	1.27
Belgium	46.6	30.8	65.4	66.2	36.2	46.8	28.3	14.2	47.9	45.4	0.62	0.74
France	47.7	51.4	61.9	71.5	42.4	64.9	18.2	11.0	47.3	43.7	0.57	1.67
UK	47.1	51.7	65.3	81.0	45.2	29.8	22.7	43.9	49.0	40.3	0.61	1.46
Greece	47.5	38.6	71.2	78.6	61.2	51.4	15.3	21.4	46.9	47.5	0.50	0.57
Spain	47.7	41.5	66.0	58.5	68.9	41.5	15.1	29.3	49.7	42.4	0.53	0.87
Portugal	47.2	54.6	69.7	40.9	87.3	52.4	3.7	23.8	49.9	43.6	0.56	0.91
Austria	47.3	48.7	65.6	77.7	31.8	39.6	6.11	18.27	48.3	37.7	0.69	1.04
Finland	49.4	58.5	67.5	75.4	33.1	20.8	29.7	47.2	46.9	39.5	0.66	0.7

rest of the family joins thereafter if it is decided to settle for a long time in the host country. Thus we would expect the sex ratio to be biased toward males for non-EU relative to EU citizens. This is significantly true in France, the UK, Portugal, the Netherlands, and Denmark, but not in Germany, while non-EU citizens are mostly females in Greece, Spain, and Belgium (with an abnormally low sex ratio in Belgium). Here, a note of caution is necessary: given the low proportion of non-EU citizens in the sample, for smaller countries the results are not very stable across waves of the survey.

The second column of Table 3.3 looks at marital status, and shows that migrants are typically more likely to be married than natives, except in Portugal and Spain, while in Belgium the likelihood is the same. Being single presumably reduces the cost of migration, which would account for a lower marital status ratio for non-EU citizens, but on the other hand it makes it less likely to encounter economic hardship, which reduces the need to migrate.

The third column of Table 3.3 looks at the low end of the skill distribution. It shows that there are striking disparities across countries regarding the educational levels of non-EU citizens *vis-à-vis* EU citizens. Typically, European countries can be classified into two groups. In the first group, migrants are substantially less educated than natives. This group includes Germany, Denmark, the Netherlands, Belgium, and France. In the other group, which comprises the UK, Greece, Spain, and Portugal, migrants are more skilled than the average citizen.

Note the order of magnitude of the effect: in Germany, the proportion of migrants who have not completed secondary education is almost twice as large as for natives, and in France 50 per cent higher.

Is this pattern confirmed when one looks at the top of the skill distribution? As shown in the fourth column of Table 3.3, educational comparisons between natives and migrants are more favourable to the latter when one looks at the top rather than at the bottom of the educational ladder. Denmark and the Netherlands now join the group which benefits from better educated non-EU citizens (with the above mentioned caveat that the results are less robust for smaller countries because of sample size), while France, Germany, and Belgium remain in group 1.

One may argue that differences in the educational levels of non-EU citizens vs EU citizens across European countries reflect differences of the quality of manpower in source countries, which for historical reasons are allocated differently across recipient countries. In order to investigate this possibility, we have computed the average characteristics of African-born migrants to various destination countries.[5] This is a way of controlling for the geographical origins of migrants, although admittedly there is large heterogeneity among African countries—but finer disaggregations are not possible because they would reduce the number of relevant observations by too much. If one compares the

---

[5] This was done using wave 1 of the survey.

two main recipients of African migrants, namely France and the UK, we still get a pattern similar to the third column of Table 3.3: in France, 33 per cent of Africans have not completed secondary education, vs 18 per cent in the UK.

Turning now to age, the fifth column of Table 3.3 shows that migrants are on average substantially younger than natives. The age difference ranges from −0.6 years in Greece to 10.6 years in Austria. This result is not surprising and is explained by the existence of return migration as well as the greater demographic dynamism of source countries. It suggests that at least in the medium run, non-EU citizens significantly alleviate the financing problems of the pension system.

Finally, the sixth column of Table 3.3 looks at an important determinant of welfare entitlement, namely the number of children. The variable used is the number of children living in the same household, and it is much higher for migrants than for natives, with a difference ranging from 14 per cent in Greece to 192 per cent in France. This is explained by the migrants' cultural background and some of their characteristics such as age and education, but it is possible, in the line of the logic exposed in the theoretical section, that there is systematic self-sorting of migrants according to the generosity of family benefits; that is, migrants with more children may systematically choose more generous countries. Because of this sorting effect, migrants' fertility may be more responsive to family benefits than natives'.

3.3. IMPLICATIONS FOR THE WELFARE STATE

The above evidence suggests that migrants have personal characteristics that make them substantially different from natives. This in turn affects their expected relationship with the welfare state. In particular, one may expect the following:

1. In all EU countries, immigrants should be less likely to be on old-age and health benefits because they are younger.
2. In Germany, Denmark, the Netherlands, and France, immigrants are more likely to be on unemployment benefits and welfare assistance because of their reduced earnings capacity. In the UK, Greece, Spain, and Portugal, the contrary should occur.
3. In all countries, migrants are more likely to be on family benefits because they have more children; their greater likelihood of being married has more ambiguous predictions, since it may reduce their access to benefits associated with single parenthood.

In this section, we analyse the differential welfare dependency of migrants compared to natives. We distinguish between two concepts. First, we estimate the dependency that a probability model, over the whole population would predict on the basis of migrants' characteristics. Second, we estimate 'residual' dependency, that is, the difference between their actual dependency and their predicted one. This is a measure of the extent to which migrant status increases (or reduces) dependency on a given programme, everything else equal.

In particular, in Section 3.3.1, we report econometric estimates of the determinants of welfare dependency for three programmes: unemployment benefits, family benefits, and pensions. This allows us to estimate the impact of non-EU migrant's characteristics on their predicted welfare dependency, and to compare it with EU citizens. In Section 3.3.2, we empirically estimate residual dependency for each of the three programmes, and discuss various economic interpretations of residual dependency.

3.3.1. *The determinants of welfare dependency*

In order to assess which individual characteristics make it more likely for non-EU citizens to be on welfare, we estimate a probit model explaining the likelihood of being on one of three types of benefits: pensions, unemployment, and family.[6] We report our results for each type of benefit.

3.3.1.1. *Unemployment benefits*

Probit results predicting the effect of individual characteristics on the probability of being on unemployment benefits have been run for each wave of the panel and the coefficient values are fairly robust across waves, while their significance varies. Table 3.4 summarizes the results, with two stars indicating significance at the 5 per cent level and one star at the 10 per cent level.

These coefficients capture the cumulated effect of individual characteristics on both incidence and eligibility. These two aspects vary greatly across countries. Hence, variables such as sex and marital status may come up with a positive significant coefficient in some cases, and a negative one in other instances. On the other hand, variables like education that are strongly negatively correlated with incidence and have little impact on eligibility systematically come out with a negative significant coefficient.

With these empirical results in hand, we can find out whether non-EU citizens' characteristics make them more likely, on average, to be on unemployment benefits. The results are summarized in Table 3.5, which compares the estimated probability of being dependent on unemployment benefits for a 'typical' EU citizen (i.e. a representative individual with each explanatory variable set to the average of this group) with that of a representative non-EU immigrant worker. Note that because of the nonlinearity of the probit model, the predicted probability of welfare dependency of such an 'average' individual is not equal to the average proportion of respondents on UB.

---

[6] We have also looked at sickness benefits, but our results implied insignificant predicted and residual effects of migrant status on sickness benefit dependency. Therefore, we drop them from this chapter in order to better focus the discussion.

Table 3.4. *Econometric determinants of UB dependency*

Variable/Country	Germany	Denmark	Netherlands	Belgium	France
Sex = male	−0.05	−0.22**	0.07*	−0.24**	−0.02
Married	−0.2**	−0.2**	−0.26**	−0.136**	−0.14**
Age	−0.014**	−0.045**	−0.006*	−0.015**	−0.00
Experience	0.00	0.018**	−0.006*	−0.01**	0.03**
Tertiary education	−0.076	−0.406**	−0.187**	−0.583**	−0.23**
Secondary education	0.03	−0.24**	−0.144**	−0.134**	0.05
Number of children	−0.00	0.048*	−0.00	0.06**	−0.01

	UK	Greece	Spain	Portugal	Austria	Finland
Sex = male	0.28**	0.11*	0.36**	0.05	0.25**	−0.06
Married	−0.06	0.11	0.18**	0.167**	−0.18**	−0.07
Age	−0.007	−0.006	−0.00	−0.009**	−0.021**	−0.027**
Experience	−0.01	−0.017**	−0.017**	−0.003	0.00	−0.00
Tertiary education	−0.14	−0.5**	−0.48**	−0.94**	−0.53**	−0.45**
Secondary education	−0.06	−0.3*	−0.323**	−0.267**	−0.287**	−0.21**
Number of children	−0.04	0.01	0.034*	−0.03	−0.005	−0.03*

Table 3.5. *Migrants vs natives predicted dependency*

Country	EU	Non-EU	Difference
Germany	0.05	0.06	0.02
Denmark	0.11	0.18	0.07
Netherlands	0.06	0.08	0.02
Belgium	0.09	0.11	0.02
France	0.06	0.07	0.00
UK	0.02	0.03	0.01
Greece	0.02	0.02	0.00
Spain	0.05	0.05	0.00
Portugal	0.01	0.01	0.00
Austria	0.05	0.07	0.02
Finland	0.14	0.17	0.03

Overall, the excess predicted dependency of migrants is typically positive but small, with the exception of Denmark. For countries of group 2 as defined above, it is substantially smaller than the actual difference, suggesting migration-specific effects play a big role in explaining this difference.

These small predicted differences come from different factors. In France for example, the educational level of non-EU citizens is lower than that of EU citizens, mostly because there are fewer people with secondary education. But secondary education has little impact on UB dependency. In the UK, migrants are better educated than natives, but education overall has a low impact on UB dependency. In Spain, the higher educational level of migrants tends to reduce their UB dependency, but their lower experience tends to increase it, so that the net effect is zero.

3.3.1.2. *Old-age pensions*

We now turn to old-age pensions. This programme is different from UB in that it is only likely to fall upon individuals older than a certain age. For this reason we run our regression explaining the likelihood of being on old-age pension by limiting the sample to respondents older than 50. Furthermore, we enrich the specification in order to capture a complex dependence of eligibility on age. That is, we introduce age dummies to the regression that are defined as follows:

$$D50 = 1 \quad \text{if } 50 \le \text{age} < 55, \quad 0 \quad \text{if not}$$
$$D55 = 1 \quad \text{if } 55 \le \text{age} < 60, \quad 0 \quad \text{if not}$$
$$D60 = 1 \quad \text{if } 60 \le \text{age} < 65, \quad 0 \quad \text{if not}$$
$$D65 = 1 \quad \text{if } 65 \le \text{age} < 70, \quad 0 \quad \text{if not}$$

Observations for which all these dummies are equal to zero therefore correspond to respondents older than 70. The main econometric coefficients of interest are summarized in Table 3.6.

Table 3.6. *Econometric determinants of old-age pension dependency*

Variable/Country	Denmark	Netherlands	Belgium	France	UK
Sex = male	−0.108	0.7**	0.657**	0.699**	0.016
Married	−0.065	−0.425**	−0.356**	0.083	−0.017
Tertiary education	0.047	0.369**	0.146	−0.1	0.474**
Secondary education	0.163	0.116	0.245**	−0.06	0.133*
Experience	0.015	0.009**	−0.026**	−0.033**	0.014**
Number of children	−0.523	−0.11*	−0.116	−0.09*	−0.1
D50	−3.92**	−5.37**	−3.42**	−4.22**	−2.94**
D55	−3.76**	−4.42**	−2.17**	−3.15**	−2.45**
D60	−2.71**	−3.38**	−0.92**	−1.45**	−1.48**
D65	−1.77**	−1.59**	−0.3**	−0.4**	−0.5**

	Greece	Spain	Portugal	Austria	Finland
Sex = male	0.709**	1.66**	0.29**	0.52**	−0.07
Married	−0.029	−0.036	−0.111**	−0.054	0.056
Tertiary education	0.163*	−0.089	−0.095	−0.007	0.19*
Secondary education	0.0676	0.043	−0.039	0.12*	0.0658
Experience	−0.017**	−0.022**	−0.003	−0.003	0.033**
Number of children	0.0114	0.02	−0.144**	−0.094**	−0.025
D50	−3.31**	−4.23**	−2.91**	−2.92**	−3.96**
D55	−2.58**	−3.36**	−2.40**	−1.68**	−3.24**
D60	−1.81**	−2.09**	−1.86**	−0.742**	−2.33**
D65	−0.719**	−0.724**	−0.604**	0.037	−1.04**

Not surprisingly, the age dummies have a monotonic profile and are very significant in all countries. But other variables often show up significant, with a somewhat surprising sign.

Our results have to be interpreted with more caution than for other welfare benefits, because the determinants essentially reflect past labour market history of natives and this makes it difficult to extrapolate the results to migrants and to the future. For example, the male dummy often comes out significant and with a positive sign, which probably reflects the greater workforce attachment—and therefore greater pension rights—of males *in the past*. But increased female participation over time should ideally lead us to pick up a lower value for this coefficient.

Similarly, the younger age distribution of non-EU citizens in a cross section would typically lead us to predict a lower welfare dependency; but migrants will eventually reach retirement age, and on top of that a substantial fraction will be naturalized and therefore counted as EU citizens. Thus the cross-sectional determinants of pension dependency tend to overstate the differences between non-EU and EU citizens in predicted pension dependency, relative to a true dynamic perspective.

Another issue is that there are not many non-citizens in this subsample, so that our results are not very stable.

Despite these caveats, let us proceed and look at what this econometric model predicts for migrants vs natives pension dependency.

As Table 3.7 makes clear, the non-EU citizens' predicted pension dependency is virtually nil relative to EU citizens. This is because even if one limits oneself to this age group, they are overwhelmingly below 60, which is far from being the case for natives. The predicted values are thus simply capturing the wide differences between the two populations in terms of the cross-sectional age distribution at a point in time.

This suggests that in the mid-1990s, in most European countries non-EU citizens generate transitory, but substantial gains in easing the financing of the pension system.

Table 3.7. *Predicted dependency of migrants vs natives*

Country	EU	Non-EU	Difference
Denmark	0.60	0.04	− 0.56
Netherlands	0.51	0.00	− 0.51
Belgium	0.47	0.01	− 0.46
France	0.55	0.00	− 0.55
UK	0.65	0.14	− 0.50
Greece	0.45	0.06	− 0.39
Spain	0.21	0.06	− 0.15
Portugal	0.48	0.08	− 0.40
Austria	0.49	0.08	− 0.41
Finland	0.50	0.33	− 0.17

3.3.1.3. Family benefits

We now turn to the determinants of family benefits. Here we expect the number of children to play an important role, and eligibility to be strongly and non-linearly related to that variable. Consequently, as we did for age in the case of pensions, we enrich our specification by adding dummies representing different intervals for the value of this variable. These dummies are defined as follows:

$$D1 = 1 \quad \text{if } n \text{ children} = 1$$
$$D2 = 1 \quad \text{if } n \text{ children} = 2$$
$$D3 = 1 \quad \text{if } n \text{ children} = 3 \text{ or } 4$$
$$D5 = 1 \quad \text{if } n \text{ children} = 5 \text{ or } 6$$
$$D7 = 1 \quad \text{if } n \text{ children} \geq 7$$

The reference case for which they are all equal to zero therefore corresponds to zero children in the household. The coefficients of the regressions are summarized in Table 3.8. Whenever a cell is empty, the corresponding variable was dropped because of multicollinearity.

Table 3.8. *Econometric determinants of family benefits*

Variable/Country	Denmark	Netherlands	Belgium	France	UK
Sex = male	−2.91**	2.33**	−1.30**	−0.487**	−2.53**
Married	−0.078	−0.328**	0.423**	0.096**	0.114*
Age	−0.0046	0.026**	−0.003	0.00	−0.013
Tertiary education	0.276**	0.08	0.115*	0.023	−0.039
Secondary education	0.175*	0.187**	0.139*	0.083*	−0.05
Experience	−0.01	−0.0183**	−0.01**	−0.0088*	−0.0077
D1	2.95**	2.54**	1.31**	1.38**	2.13**
D2	2.81**	2.55**	1.25**	1.88**	2.29**
D3	2.96**	2.62**	1.22**	1.96**	2.49**
D5	2.66**	2.25**	1.27**	1.92**	2.87**
D7	—	0.783	0.68	1.39**	3.22**

	Greece	Spain	Portugal	Austria	Finland
Sex = male	−0.938**	−0.146**	0.947**	−0.013	−2.78**
Married	0.0149	−0.005	0.546**	0.124**	0.237**
Age	0.012**	−0.001	−0.007**	0.001	−0.004
Tertiary education	−0.543**	−0.409**	0.213**	0.192**	0.096
Secondary education	−0.424**	−0.342**	0.119**	0.02	0.045
Experience	0.001	−0.004	−0.009**	−0.002	−0.012
D1	0.542**	0.7**	1.19**	1.18**	2.49**
D2	0.472**	0.791**	1.27**	1.23**	2.52**
D3	1.39**	1.20**	1.3**	1.24**	2.56**
D5	2.56**	—	1.44**	1.32**	2.77**
D7	—	1.66**	2.59**	0.77	3.43**

Table 3.9. *Predicted dependence on family benefits*

Country	Pred. EU	Pred. non-EU	Diff.
Denmark	0.028	0.057	0.029
Netherlands	0.056	0.210	0.154
Belgium	0.157	0.170	0.014
France	0.074	0.191	0.118
UK	0.041	0.189	0.148
Greece	0.016	0.018	0.002
Spain	0.007	0.010	0.003
Portugal	0.122	0.165	0.043
Austria	0.198	0.301	0.102
Finland	0.050	0.070	0.020

With respect to the number of children, the predicted positive dependence is observed, although one may distinguish between countries where the probability is not increasing in the number of children (Denmark, Netherlands, Belgium), and those where it is. In some cases the coefficient is lower when the number of children increases (e.g. D2 vs D1 in Greece), perhaps reflecting a lack of time to devote to claiming benefit.

With respect to education, in many countries (Denmark, Netherlands, Belgium, Portugal, Austria, and to a lower extent France and Finland), the dependence is 'regressive' in that a better education increases the probability of earning family benefits. This may be due to better information about these benefits or a more flexible allocation of time which may make it easier to claim the benefit. This dependence is likely to lower migrants' expected dependency, at least partially offsetting the effect of the number of children.

Finally, whenever marital status comes out significant, it is positive, while in most cases female respondents are more likely to declare being on such benefits than males, with the noticeable exceptions of the Netherlands and Portugal.

The predicted dependency is summarized in Table 3.9. Migrants' excess dependence on benefits ranges from 0 to 15 percentage points. Note that the discrepancy with actual data is large in some cases, reflecting the greater vulnerability of this prediction to nonlinearities. For example, in Denmark, sex has a strong effect on family benefit dependency, and the 'average sex' person for which this indicator is about 0.5 is predicted to be much less dependent than the population as a whole, where it is equal to 0 for 50 per cent of the people and 1 for the remaining 50 per cent.

3.3.2. *Residual dependency*

The preceding tables give us the predicted welfare dependency of migrants' *characteristics*. That is, they tell us the effect on the welfare state of fictitious perfectly 'integrated' migrants, that would have overcome any specific shock associated with migration, would evolve in the same networks as similar natives, would have the same preferences regarding work, leisure, and job search, and would not suffer any discrimination in labour markets.

In this section, instead, we ask the following question: is migrant status associated with any *excess* dependency? That is, would a non-EU citizen with a given set of characteristics be more or less likely to be dependent on unemployment benefits than a EU citizen with identical characteristics?

In order to answer this question and to see whether any difference is statistically significant, we have run the probit regressions explaining welfare dependency while adding a dummy equal to one for non-EU citizens and to zero for EU citizens. We have again done so for the three programmes we have looked at: unemployment benefits, family benefits, and pensions.

Before reporting these results, however, it is worth discussing what mechanisms may lie behind the existence of residual dependency.

3.3.2.1. *Sources of residual dependency*
Residual dependency is defined as the difference between actual migrants' dependency as predicted on the basis of their individual characteristics and the actual proportion of migrants under a given welfare scheme. Such residual dependency may result from various sources:

1. *Self-selection.* As argued above, countries with generous welfare systems will attract migrants with relatively low earnings. If earnings depend not only on individual characteristics but also on some unobservable individual ability component, then this component's average value will typically be lower for migrants than for natives, because it is conditional on the migrant having elected the generous country as a destination, that is, on the migrant having an earnings capacity lower than a certain threshold.[7] Self-selection would then lead to positive residual welfare dependency of migrants. It may also lead to negative welfare dependency in some cases. For example, if being in good health makes it easier to bear migration costs, then migrants will be less likely to be paid sickness benefits than natives with similar characteristics.

2. *Migration-specific effects.* Immigrants may suffer from specific shocks such as psychological trauma, language problems, etc., which make them more likely to be on welfare controlling for their individual characteristics. One may also think of specific effects going in the other direction: welfare entitlement may be more sensitive to literacy in the destination country's language than getting a low-skill job, in which case there will be negative welfare dependency.

3. *Discrimination.* If employers discriminate on the basis of ethnicity then some migrants may have trouble finding jobs and may end up on welfare. Note, though, that this supposes that bureaucrats who allocate welfare payments do

---

[7] Formally, earnings capacity is $y = Xb + e$, where X is a vector of individual characteristics and e unobservable ability. If y^* denotes the migration threshold, then the expected value of e for migrants is $E[e/Xb + e < y^*]$, which is lower than the unconditional expectation of e.

not discriminate, or at least that they discriminate less than employers. If the contrary occurs, then one will observe negative residual dependency.

The discrimination hypothesis is plausible in light of anecdotal evidence and legal cases of racial bias, although at the statistical level it is not straight-forward to distinguish it from network effects.[8]

4. *Network effects.* The importance of co-ethnic ties in locational and occupational choice has been documented.[9] Specific networks of immigrants may develop in order to get jobs, which will generate negative residual dependency.[10] On the other hand, some ethnic groups may have access to networks that are less well connected than natives, and this phenomenon may be compounded by urban ghettos; this will again generate positive residual welfare dependency. It is also conceivable that networks may develop for access to welfare benefits, which will yield positive dependency.

5. *Non-portability of entitlements.* If entitlements are not transferable across countries then non-EU citizens will have lower entitlements than EU citizens of similar characteristics, which will generate negative residual dependency of non-EU citizens. We expect this phenomenon to be particularly salient for *pensions.* But migrants may also have reduced eligibility for other programmes because of their past labour market history and/or reduced legal access to benefits.

6. *Reduced wages.* Phenomena which reduce the wages of immigrants may also reduce their employment rate and therefore increase their welfare dependency. This is because they have lower incentives to look for a job, for example. Beyond discrimination, an important contributing factor may be reduced access to public jobs.

3.3.2.2. *Unemployment benefits*
We now turn to the empirical results, starting again with unemployment benefits. Table 3.10 reports the probit regression on the migrant status dummy when it is added to the set of explanatory variables. In Denmark, the Netherlands, France, Austria, and Finland, being a migrant clearly has a positive and significant impact on unemployment benefit dependency, while this is not true in Germany, the UK, Greece, and Spain.[11]

The last column expresses this residual dependency in terms of the increment of an 'average' person's probability of being on UB if he or she is a migrant, in percentage points.

---

[8] See Richard (2001) for an analysis of differential unemployment incidence across ethnic groups in the French case.

[9] See Borjas and Bronars (1991) and Casella and Rauch (1997).

[10] For example Richard (2001), in the case of France, finds that migrants of Portuguese origins have a lower probability of being long-term unemployed than native French, while the contrary is true for migrants of North African origins, which may be interpreted as evidence of discrimination but also as a network effect.

[11] Results for Portugal are unavailable because of multicollinearity problems.

Table 3.10. *Econometric determinants of residual migrant UB dependency*

Country	Coefficient	z-statistic	Excess Prob. (%)
Germany	0.07	(0.48)	0.97
Denmark	0.613**	(3.55)	15.6
Netherlands	0.412*	(1.8)	6.6
Belgium	0.204**	(2.1)	3.6
France	0.359**	(3.3)	5.6
UK	0.08	(0.24)	0.4
Greece	−0.19	(−0.47)	−0.6
Spain	−0.09	(−0.28)	−0.8
Portugal	na		
Austria	0.481**	(3.79)	7.1
Finland	0.876**	(4.97)	27.4

3.3.2.3. *Old-age pensions*

We have also looked at old-age pensions, adding the migrant status dummy to the probit regressions. We have only kept those countries for which the number of observations of migrants on old-age pension is not trivial, that is, Austria, Greece, France, and Belgium. For all these countries, the dummy coefficient is not significantly different from zero, indicating that there is no residual effect on pensions.[12] This is somewhat not surprising, as eligibility depends only on age and not on economic outcomes, although one could possibly have expected a negative coefficient because of portability and eligibility problems.

3.3.2.4. *Family benefits*

Finally, turning to family benefits, we find positive residual effects in France and Spain, although they are only significant at the 10 per cent level, while there is a negative significant residual effect in the UK (see Table 3.11).

3.3.3. *How persistent is welfare dependency?*

The above analysis suggests that there is residual dependency of migrants on unemployment benefits in Belgium, Denmark, the Netherlands, Finland, Austria, and France. There is no such residual dependency in other countries and for other welfare programmes the evidence is much more mixed.

One may ask: how persistent is migrants' residual UB dependency? If it is associated with the specific shocks of the migration itself, one may expect it to vanish with time. On the other hand, Western European countries are well known for long unemployment duration and duration dependence of exit rates,

---

[12] In Denmark and the UK, there is a significant negative residual effect, and in Portugal, a significant positive one. Note however that there are very few relevant observations in these cases.

Table 3.11. *Residual migrant family benefit dependency*

Country	Coefficient	z-statistic
Germany	na	
Denmark	−0.256	(−0.8)
Netherlands	−0.188	(−0.7)
Belgium	−0.06	(−0.5)
France	0.187*	(1.9)
UK	−0.75**	(−2.5)
Greece	0.199	(0.7)
Spain	0.63*	(1.9)
Portugal	−0.54	(−1.4)
Austria	0.03	(0.3)
Finland	−0.065	(−0.23)

so that there may be some irreversibility associated with such excess UB dependency.

To know more about that, we have run probits explaining UB dependency on individual characteristics and migrant status, while distinguishing between migrants who arrived less than 5 years before the survey date and those who arrived before. The results (not reported) imply that there is no significant difference between the two types of migrants. Consequently, the residual UB dependency of migrants seems to be quite persistent and not to vanish with the length of stay in the host country.

3.4. ARE CROSS-COUNTRY DIFFERENCES IN MIGRANT SELECTION RELATED TO DIFFERENCES IN THE WELFARE SYSTEM?

If as suggested above, excess welfare dependency of migrants is due to their greater responsiveness to the generosity of benefits, then in a cross section of countries we should expect this excess dependency to be larger in countries with more generous benefits. Turning now to consider this relationship, let us bear in mind that since we do not have many countries, our results have to be interpreted with caution.

Let us start from unemployment benefits where our results are most clear-cut, since they indicate a positive predicted and residual dependency in a well-identified group of countries. The OECD (1995) has defined a summary measure of benefit entitlement which is increasing in the generosity of unemployment benefit systems. For 1996, this summary measure is reported in Table 3.12.

Then, if we split our sample of countries in two groups, those where the proportion of migrants with less than secondary education is higher than that of natives (group 1), and those in the opposite case (group 2), it turns out that the average measure of UB generosity is 58 for group 1 and 45 for group 2. This

Table 3.12. OECD *summary measure of benefit entitlement*

Country	Summary measure (1996)	Group
Germany	54	1
Denmark	81	1
Netherlands	69	1
Belgium	59	1
France	55	1
United Kingdom	51	2
Spain	49	2
Portugal	47	2
Greece	20	2
Austria	30	1
Finland	59	2

Source: Martin (1996), OECD.

Table 3.13. *Share of GDP spent on family benefits*

Country	Fam. benefit, 1993, % GDP
Germany	1.34
Denmark	1.61
Netherlands	1.19
Belgium	2.25
France	2.27
United Kingdom	na
Spain	0.27
Portugal	na
Greece	0.12
Austria	2.24
Finland	na

Source: OECD Statistical compendium, 2000.

is only mild evidence, however, as a regression of the relative proportion of migrants with less than secondary education on the generosity measure yields a positive coefficient, but only significant at the 15 per cent level.[13]

Similarly, migrants' residual dependency on unemployment benefits is correlated with the generosity measure, as evidenced in Table 3.12. A regression of

[13] The *t*-statistic is 1.64.

residual welfare dependency on the generosity measure yields a positive coefficient, on the margin of significance (12 per cent).

With respect to family benefits, it is much more difficult to obtain a synthetic measure of generosity. However, the OECD reports the fraction of GDP spent on family benefits for 8 of our 11 countries. This crude measure is summarized in Table 3.13.

Using as a dependent variable the ratio between the last and next-to-last columns of Table 3.3, i.e. between the average number of children in immigrant and in EU households, we again find a positive correlation between this generosity measure and the relative number of children of migrants. However, this correlation is quite weak and insignificant.

3.5. CONCLUSIONS

There are large differences across European countries with respect to the composition of the migrant population and their welfare dependency. To some extent, these differences seem to be correlated with the generosity of the welfare state in a way consistent with the economic mechanisms described at the start of the chapter, although the evidence is not very strong. One consequence is that as far as unemployment benefits are concerned, increased migration may increase pressure on this programme in the most generous countries, but not in the least generous ones. The effect is typically moderate, since its order of magnitude is the product of the proportion of immigrants—a few percentage points—times the excess UB dependency of migrants—a few percentage points too. But in some countries like Denmark and the Netherlands, this latter component is quite large, suggesting the most generous countries may act as welfare magnets.

Despite big differences in characteristics, in many cases a lot of the excess dependency of migrants is residual, one might have expected this component to go away with time. But we did not find any evidence of that: residual welfare dependency seems fairly persistent.

Our evidence on residual dependency is at variance with the literature mentioned in the introduction, which has ascribed most of the differential welfare dependency of migrants to their characteristics. Here, despite the fact that their characteristics are quite different from those of natives, in many countries they do not explain a large share of their welfare dependency, either because of conflicting effects of various characteristics or because the link between observable characteristics and welfare is not very strong. In contrast, residual effects are strong in countries with generous welfare systems. These differential effects are consistent with the possibility of discrimination but their correlation with welfare generosity suggests that sorting and/or network effects may also be at work.

The differential fertility rate of migrants is also likely to put pressure on family benefits, although there is much less evidence of systematic sorting of migrants with many children into the most generous countries.

On the other hand, the much lower age of migrants tends to ease the financing of the pension system for a long transitory period. In wave 3 of the European Household Panel Survey virtually no non-EU citizen had characteristics such that he or she would claim a pension. This is not surprising since eligibility is due to past labour market history which is unchanged when one migrates.

Overall, our findings are broadly consistent with the view that welfare benefits distort the composition of migrants, both in terms of their observable and unobservable characteristics; while the effects are quantitatively moderate, some of the most generous countries seem to act as welfare magnets.

What are the consequences of the above findings for the design of EC migration policies? One may split this question in two parts. First, what are the implications for policy *vis-à-vis* non-EU migrants? Second, what are the implications for policies regarding intra-EU migration?

As for the first question, one may be concerned with the fact that the country where immigrants enter may differ from the destination country and may generate excess migration. If the cost of controlling migration entirely falls upon the entry country, while the benefits accrue to the destination countries, then countries which have less generous benefits, and therefore are less likely to end up as a destination country, have a reduced incentive to control migration. In fact, one way for them to reduce their stock of migrants may, paradoxically, be to give citizenship to them, since it will facilitate their move to other EU countries. That is, a logical implication of free movement within the EU is that, in order to reduce these externalities, immigration and naturalization policies be in the hand of the EU as a whole rather than individual member states.

As for the second question, the prospect of EU enlargement to poor countries may increase migration pressures to the countries with the most generous welfare state. In order to mitigate such pressure, it may be desirable to condition the entry of accession candidates upon the introduction of minimal social insurance of those countries. EU transfers to these countries could be used to finance the set-up cost of their social safety net.

4

Immigration and the Extension of Free Movement to Eastern Europe

This chapter explores the likely impact of enlargement on the levels of migration into the current EU countries. In past enlargement rounds, the EU has extended the free movement of labour to countries with similar per capita incomes and factor endowments. Even in the case of the Southern Enlargement, differences in income levels were moderate compared with the gap in per capita income levels that the EU will face in the context of the eastern rounds. Figure 4.1 displays the population and PPP-GDP figures of the EU-15, the ten accession candidates from Central and Eastern Europe[1] (CEEC-10), and a set of other countries, which may apply for accession in the future. Turkey already possesses a candidate status. The total population of all ten accession candidates from Central and Eastern Europe amounted to 104 million persons in 2000 and that of the southern EU countries (Greece, Spain, and Portugal) 59 million at the time of their accession. While per capita PPP-GDP levels of Greece, Spain, and Portugal have been between 60 and 70 per cent of average levels in the EU at the time of their accession, the average GDP of the ten candidate countries from Central and Eastern Europe was in 1999 less than 40 per cent of average GDP in the EU-15 at purchasing power parities, and at 15 per cent at current exchange rates. The differences in per capita GDP levels between the EU and the CEECs are associated with marked differences in factor endowments and factor costs: the book value of the capital stock in the ten candidate countries is reported at 10 per cent of those of the EU-15, the incremental capital output ratio (ICOR) is substantially lower than that of the EU, and wages number around 10–15 per cent of those in the EU (Boeri and Brücker, 2001b, table 1). Differences in per capita income levels and factor endowments between the EU and other potential accession candidates are even higher (Fig. 4.1).

Against this background, there are mounting concerns in the EU member states that the extension of the free movement will involve a mass migration

[1] Bulgaria, Czech Republic, Estonia, Hungary, Latvia, Lithuania, Poland, Romania, Slovakia, and Slovenia. All ten CEECs are involved in the accession negotiations at the present, but many observers expect that at least Bulgaria and Romania will not participate in the first accession round. We exclude Cyprus and Malta from our discussion here, since these rather small countries are characterized by per capita GDP levels similar to many EU members.

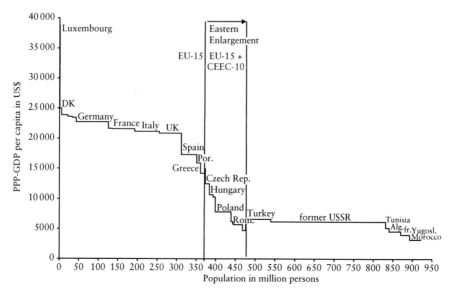

Figure 4.1. *Population and PPP-GDP in the EU and potential accession candidates, 1999*

Source: Own calculations based on World Bank (1998) and Eurostat (2000).

from the East into the countries and regions adjacent to the CEECs, and will affect employment and wages of natives there. As a consequence of these concerns, the present EU and its member states pursue with regard to the free movement a prudent enlargement policy. If the European Council at the Göteborg summit follows the proposal of the European Commission, then the free movement of workers will be suspended for the first five years after accession, and, after a review of the labour market conditions in the present member states, for another two years. Moreover, individual member states can ask for a further prolongation of the transitional period if they fear labour market disruptions. This implies that the introduction of the free movement is postponed for the CEECs at least until 2010, presuming that the first countries will accede in 2005. During the transitional period, each member state can admit workers from the CEECs. These workers will benefit from equal treatment under the *acquis*.

How will the extension of the free movement to countries with low per capita income levels affect welfare of natives in the present EU? We address two questions in this section: firstly, we ask whether introducing the free movement will indeed involve a mass migration wave. Secondly, we assess briefly the implications of migration from the East on labour markets in the affected countries of the EU. The alternatives to the prudent enlargement policy of the EU are discussed in the final chapter.

4.1. WILL EASTERN ENLARGEMENT SWAMP EU LABOUR MARKETS?

Incentives to migration will be stronger than in past enlargement rounds. Accession candidates border countries which possess income levels above the EU average, and, perhaps most importantly, present immigration from the CEECs is rather low: at present, around 840 000 nationals from the CEECs reside in the EU, this is roughly 0.8 per cent of the population in the CEECs. The number of employees from the CEECs working in the EU can be estimated at around 300 000 workers, including commuters and the full-time equivalent of temporary employment. These rather moderate figures reflect tight restrictions on labour mobility. It seems therefore reasonable that the migration potential from the East—in contrast to Southern enlargement—has not yet been exhausted.

Numerous studies, starting with Layard *et al.* (1992), have tried to reduce uncertainty as to the migration potential from the East. These studies apply basically three approaches: opinion polls, extrapolations from South–North migration, and multivariate analysis of past migration episodes in econometric models.

Opinion polls face several methodological problems: firstly, they provide only information on the supply side, that is, on the propensity of workers to migrate, but not on the demand side, that is, on the ability of labour markets to absorb an additional labour demand. Secondly, it is not known whether somebody who reveals in an opinion poll a general propensity to migrate has indeed serious intentions to move. Thirdly, migration from the East is largely a temporary phenomenon, such that the share of the population which will move to another country and perhaps return within a certain *period* of time is much higher than the share of the population which will live in a foreign country at a given point of time.[2] Thus, although opinion polls provide interesting qualitative information on the structure of migration, it is hard to draw any quantitative conclusions about the migration potential from them.

The extrapolation exercises take as reference the migration flows from the southern European countries to the western and northern European countries in the 1950s and 1960s, and the migration of Mexicans to the US in the 1970s and 1980s (Layard *et al.*, 1992; Lundborg, 1998; Bauer and Zimmermann, 1999). These studies conclude that no less than 3 per cent of the population in the CEECs will migrate to the West, which corresponds to an immigration of

---

[2] As an example, around 200 000 temporary workers from the CEECs have been employed per annum in Germany with an average duration of stay of three months for the last five years. Under the (unrealistic) assumption, that each worker from the CEECs has been employed in Germany only once, this figure corresponds to a total immigration of one million workers in five years. However, only 40 000 temporary workers from the CEECs have been employed in Germany at each point of time on average during this period.

around 200 000 people p.a. for all CEECs (including the former USSR) or 130 000 persons from the Czech Republic, Hungary, Poland, and Slovakia (Hönekopp, 1999). However, these studies do not control for differences in incomes differences and unemployment in the countries of destination and origin, nor for differences in the institutional conditions to migrate.

A number of econometric studies have tried to exploit the information provided by post-war migration episodes in western Europe to assess potential migration after enlargement has been introduced. Needless to say, these studies suffer from various methodological problems, too. The main problem is that the estimates are based on migration episodes which differ in several respects from those of East–West migration. Moreover, there exists great heterogeneity in the propensity to migrate between countries, which creates a number of estimation problems (see Fertig and Schmidt, 2000, Alecke *et al.*, 2001, for a discussion).

The estimates presented here rely on a time-series analysis of migration to Germany (where, in 1998, two-thirds of the migrants from CEECs settled) from 18 European countries of origin in the period from 1967 to 1998.[3] The empirical model we used was inspired by Hatton (1995).[4] In line with other approaches, it assumes that migration is an investment in human capital, whose returns are determined by expectations regarding future income (Sjaastad, 1962). Expectations of income in the country of destination are conditioned by the opportunity to find a job in its labour market. Following Harris and Todaro (1970), the average employment rate serves as a proxy for the individual probability to find a job. Individuals are heterogeneous, that is, they differ in their preferences and human capital characteristics which are relevant for migration. As a consequence, the propensity to migrate declines the higher the share of the population which already lives abroad. For a given differential in per capita incomes and other relevant variables, the stock of migrants will eventually reach a steady state, where its growth is solely determined by the natural rate of population growth and the rate of regularizations. This does not rule out the possibility that chain- or network effects affect migration positively. But in the long run these effects are dominated by declining preferences to migrate in the population. The adjustment of migration stocks to its steady state levels is modelled in terms of an error-correction mechanism. Note that the error-correction mechanism imposes less restrictions on the data than other dynamic models do (see Box 4.1 for technical details).

The dependent variable in the model is the annual change in the ratio of the stock of migrants to the home population in per cent. Four sets of

---

[3] The model presented here relies largely on the model presented in Boeri and Brücker (2001). Nevertheless, several changes have been applied: the interaction between institutional variables such as the free movement and guest-worker recruitment is considered, more freedom is allowed in the error correction mechanism and more recent data are used.

[4] See Fertig (1999) for a first application of the Hatton model to a panel of European countries.

Box 4.1. *Description of the migration model*

The model estimated here relies on the assumption that a dynamic equilibrium between the stock of migrants, or more precisely, between the share of the population which resides in the foreign countries, and the economic variables such as the difference in the log of per capita incomes and the employment rates, exists. Migration stocks do not adjust immediately to changes in the economic variables. We model the adjustment process to the equilibrium levels in the form of a simple error-correction mechanism, which imposes less restrictions on the data than other dynamic models. For a derivation of the adjustment process from a model which takes explicitly the formation of expectations into account, see Hatton (1995). The model we estimated has the form

$$
\begin{aligned}
\Delta mst_{ht} = {} & \alpha_h + \beta_1 \Delta \ln(y_f/y_h)t + \beta_2 FREE \cdot \Delta \ln(y_f/y_h)_t + \beta_3 GUEST \cdot \Delta \ln(y_f/y_h)_t \\
& + \beta_4 \Delta \ln(e_f)_t + \beta_5 \Delta \ln(e_h)_t + \beta_6 \ln(y_f/y_h)_{t-1} + \beta_7 FREE \cdot \ln(y_f/y_h)_{t-1} \\
& + \beta_8 GUEST \cdot \ln(y_f/y_h)_{t-1} + \beta_9 \ln(e_f)_{t-1} + \beta_{10} \ln(e_h)_{t-1} + \beta_{11} \cdot FREE \\
& + \beta_{12} \cdot GUEST + \beta_{13} mst_{ht-1} + \sum_n \beta_{13+n} \Delta mst_{ht-n},
\end{aligned} \tag{4.1}
$$

where mst_h denotes the ratio of the stock of migrants to the population in the home country in per cent, w_f and w_h represent wages, and e_f and e_h the employment rate, in the foreign (host) and the home country respectively, $FREE$ and $GUEST$ are two dummy variables that cover the free movement of labour within the EU and guest-worker recruitment agreements between the foreign and the home country, respectively. The term α_h denotes the country specific fixed effects. Thus, we considered both, the level effect of free movement and guest-worker recruitment and their interaction with the income variables. The number of lags for the dependent variable has been chosen by different information criteria.

The model is estimated with the seemingly unrelated regression technique in order to account for an uneven distribution of the variance across the sample and correlation in the error terms caused by common shocks. Our tests suggests that both are present in our data. Note that coefficient for the lagged dependent variable may be distorted in dynamic panel models with fixed effects. Simulation studies have, however, shown that we have to expect in our data set only moderate distortions.

Note that the migration stock and the wage and employment variables enter the model as levels as well as rates of change. The first variables determine a dynamic equilibrium relation between the migrant stock and the income and wage variables in the long run, while the changes in the variables determine the response of migration to short-term fluctuations of the explanatory variables. The equilibrium stock of migrants can be derived from eqn (4.1) if we set all changes as null. The model specified in eqn (4.1) presumes that a dynamic equilibrium relation holds for the stock of migrants and the wage and employment variables. In technical terms, the variables have to be 'co-integrated', that is, the estimation of the model in eqn (4.1) requires that the variables have to satisfy certain statistical properties (Engle and Granger, 1987). Indeed, we found a co-integration relationship for the variables in eqn (4.1). The results from the statistical tests and the descriptive statistics are available from the authors on request.

variables are used:

(1) the difference of the PPP-GDP per capita between the host and the home country as a proxy for the differential in real wages (regressions 1 and 2 in Table 4.1). In further regressions, the GDP at current exchange is used in order to analyse the sensitivity of results to different income variables (regressions 3 and 4);
(2) the employment rate (1-unemployment rate) in the home and the host country as proxy for employment opportunities;
(3) the lagged ratio of the stock of migrants to the home population;
(4) dummy variables, which capture the institutional conditions to migrate such as guest-worker recruitment before 1973 and free movement of labour in the EU.

Furthermore, we include two dummy variables for the civil war in the former Yugoslavia and the repatriation of refugees and some dummy variables for breaks in the statistics (1974, 1983, 1990). In a variant of the model we analyse the interaction of the institutional dummies with the income variables (regressions 2 and 4).

The results are reported in Table 4.1. The coefficients of the level variables are highly significant and have the expected signs: the difference in per capita income levels and the employment rate in the host country have a significant positive impact on migration, while the employment rate in the home country has a negative impact. However, the impact of the employment rate in the home countries is, as expected, smaller than the impact of the employment rate in the host country. Note that the coefficients for the income variable are substantially lower in the models which use the GDP per capita at current exchange rates than in the models which use the GDP per capita at purchasing power parity. Both, guest-worker recruitment and the free movement, have a significant positive impact on migration (see regressions 1 and 3). However, the impact of the free movement is much smaller than the impact of guest-worker recruitment. The interaction of the institutional dummies with the income variables brought, not in all cases, significant results (see regressions 2 and 4). The variables in differences have, with the exception of the income variable in the first regression, the expected signs and are significant, too. The results turned out to be robust to changes in the time period (e.g. 1968–90) and to changes in the country sample (e.g. the five southern European countries, exclusion of Yugoslavia, etc.).[5]

The model is estimated with fixed effects which capture all constant factors that may affect migration, such as distance, language, culture, and long-term differences in the quality of life across countries. For a forecast of potential migration from the CEECs an explanation of the country specific effects is needed. We 'explained' the fixed effects in a second regression with the

---

[5] The results are available from the authors on request.

Table 4.1. *Estimation results for the error-correction model; dependent variable, Δmst; observations, 30; panel observations, 540*

Variable	PPP-GDP				GDP at current exchange rate			
	Regression (1)		Regression (2)		Regression (3)		Regression (4)	
	Coefficient	t-statistics	Coefficient	t-statistics	Coefficient	t-statistics	Coefficient	t-statistics
$\Delta\ln(y_f/y_h)_t$	−0.006	−0.369	0.140***	5.419	0.007	1.171	0.023**	2.171
$FREE*\Delta\ln(y_f/y_h)_t$			−0.244***	−8.448			−0.070***	−5.063
$GUEST*\Delta\ln(y_f/y_h)_t$			−0.779***	−4.070			−0.015	−0.166
$\Delta\ln(e_f)_{t-1}$	0.749***	3.809	0.700***	3.456	0.806***	4.500	0.697***	2.938
$\Delta\ln(e_h)_{t-1}$	−0.427***	−10.218	−0.348***	−7.372	−0.479***	−11.389	−0.437***	−8.892
$\ln(y_f/y_h)_{t-1}$	0.045***	8.285	0.056***	9.489	0.039***	9.186	0.022***	4.534
$FREE*\ln(y_f/y_h)_{t-1}$			0.009	1.291			0.029***	6.774
$GUEST*\ln(y_f/y_h)_{t-1}$			−0.005	−0.189			0.010	0.781
$\ln(e_f)_{t-1}$	0.262***	3.371	0.201***	2.453	0.218***	3.141	0.182**	2.037
$\ln(e_h)_{t-1}$	−0.145***	−8.863	−0.143***	−7.227	−0.156***	−9.024	−0.160***	−7.389
mst_{t-1}	−0.126***	−18.087	−0.127***	−15.430	−0.128***	−18.570	−0.112***	−15.475
Δmst_{t-1}	0.416***	17.391	0.407***	15.732	0.414***	17.672	0.391***	14.909
$FREE$	0.003**	2.404	0.001	0.684	0.004**	2.767	−0.010***	−4.031
$GUEST$	0.128***	18.963	0.134***	10.674	0.137***	18.822	0.146***	9.415
$CIVIL\ WAR$	0.574***	12.286	0.538***	10.733	0.539***	11.488	0.596***	13.212
$REPATRIATION$	−0.088	−1.308	−0.104	−1.411	−0.119*	−1.741	−0.100	−1.471
Log likelihood	1530		1526		1511		1501	
Forecast indicators (dynamic forecast in sample)								
RMS error	0.165		0.159		0.167		0.166	
RMS percentage error	0.307		0.290		0.322		0.298	
Theil's U	0.054		0.052		0.055		0.055	
Bias proportion	0.000		0.001		0.000		0.000	
Variance proportion	0.001		0.001		0.001		0.000	
Covariance proportion	0.999		0.999		0.999		1.000	

Table 4.1. (*Continued*)

Variable	PPP-GDP				GDP at current exchange rate			
	Regression (1)		Regression (2)		Regression (3)		Regression (4)	
	Coefficient	*t*-statistics	Coefficient	*t*-statistics	Coefficient	*t*-statistics	Coefficient	*t*-statistics
Memo item: unweighted statistics								
Adjusted R^2	0.742		0.745		0.744		0.740	
Standard error of residuals	0.067		0.067		0.067		0.067	
Autocorrelation: estimated ρ	0.076		0.062		0.089		0.099	
F-test: (H_0: pooled model vs. H_1: fixed effects)			5.44***				10.95***	
LM-test (H_0 = homoskedasticity vs. H_1: groupwise heteroskedasticity)			108***				113***	
LR-test (H_0: groupwise heteroskedasticity vs. H_1: heteroskedasticity + groupwise correlation)			814***				813***	

Notes: ***, **, * null hypothesis is rejected at the 1%-, 5%-, 10%-level, respectively.

Human Development Index (HDI), which should capture long-run differences in the quality of life, and two dummy variables which capture the geographical location of the source countries in Europe (*WEST* and *NORTH*).[6] Note that the ranking of the HDI is almost constant over time. The results in Table 4.2 point to the fact that around 50 per cent of the variance in the fixed effects can be explained with these variables.

The results of these estimates have been used for the simulation of potential migration flows from the CEECs to Germany under a set of different assumptions. Needless to say, all these simulations should be treated with great caution and give just broad indications as to the magnitude of the actual migration potential. In our baseline scenario, the number of foreign residents in Germany who have come from the CEECs is estimated to grow at around 220 000 initially if the free movement was introduced for all ten candidate countries in 2002. This number increases to around 300 000 persons, but declines within one decade to 50 000 persons p.a. (see Fig. 4.2). The migration stock will grow at around 140 000 persons on average in the first decade. The long-run migration stock is reached at some 2.2 million residents from the CEEC-10 after around 15 years, which will then decline in the course of converging per capita incomes (Fig. 4.3(a)). Note that these figures refer to residents. The share of employees in the total number of residents can be estimated at around 35 per cent. If the regional distribution of migrants in the EU remains constant after enlargement, the baseline scenarios implies that the stock of migrants from the CEEC-10 will grow at some 335 000 persons initially and that, in the long run, some 3.5 million nationals from the CEEC-10 will reside in the EU-15.

In the baseline scenario, a convergence of per capita PPP-GDP levels to the average per capita PPP-GDP at a rate of 2 per cent p.a. is assumed; the 1999 unemployment rates in Germany and the CEECs are assumed to remain unchanged; the population projections rely on the World Bank (2000) scenario. All results apply to the estimates based on PPP-GDP as an income variable.[7] The estimates based on the GDP at current exchange rates bring only slightly higher results (see Figs 4.2 and 4.3(a)).

In two other scenarios, different rates of convergence and employment have been applied. Firstly, we have assumed that per capita GDPs of the CEECs will converge at a rate of 3 per cent p.a., that the unemployment rate of Germany will be at 10 per cent, and that the unemployment rates of the CEECs will be at 5 per cent over the period. This yields an initial increase of some 175 000 residents p.a. and a long-run stock of some 1.9 million residents. Conversely, a convergence rate of 1 per cent, an unemployment rate of 5 per cent in Germany, and an unemployment rate of 15 per cent in the CEECs yield an initial increase of some 250 000 and nearly 2.5 million residents in the long run (Fig. 4.3(b)).

---

[6] The dummy-variable *WEST* has a value of 1 for Portugal, Spain, UK, and Ireland, and of 0 otherwise; the dummy-variable *NORTH* has a value of 1 for Denmark, Sweden, and Norway, and of 0 otherwise.   [7] The baseline scenario is based in regression 2.

Table 4.2. Estimation results for the fixed effects from the regressions 1–4; observations, 18

Variable	Regression (1)		Regression (2)		Regression (3)		Regression (4)	
	Coefficient	t-statistics	Coefficient	t-statistics	Coefficient	t-statistics	Coefficient	t-statistics
Constant	1.294***	3.270	1.252**	3.206	1.260***	3.198	1.2028***	3.350
Human Development Index	-1.243**	-2.815	-1.199**	-2.752	-1.210**	-2.752	-1.1513**	-2.875
WEST	-0.111**	-2.025	-0.119**	-2.185	-0.122**	-2.227	-0.1210**	-2.425
NORTH	-0.098*	-1.734	-0.099*	-1.776	-0.091	-1.620	-0.0878	-1.707
R^2	0.591		0.596		0.590		0.617	
Adjusted R^2	0.503		0.509		0.502		0.535	
Standard error of regression	0.090		0.089		0.090		0.082	
F-statistic	6.737		6.874		6.707		7.512	

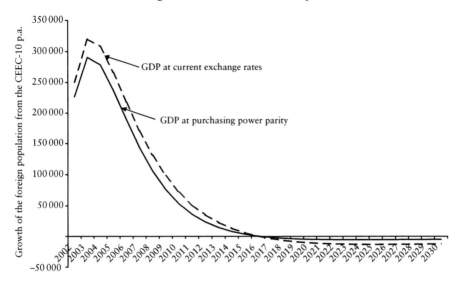

Figure 4.2. *Annual growth in the number of residents from the CEEC-10 in Germany*

Finally, we have simulated different accession scenarios. To postpone the free movement until 2010, as is planned by the European Commission, will reduce the migration potential only by small numbers: introducing the free movement for all ten CEECs will reduce initial net migration by around 10 000 persons (Fig. 4.4). This can be traced back to the rather moderate rate of convergence. However, if Bulgaria and Romania are excluded from the first accession round, then initial net migration will decline from some 220 000 persons to around 130 000 persons.

These simulations illustrate the consequences of different enlargement policies and give a clue as to the order of magnitude involved by extending the free movement to the CEECs, but should not be understood as an accurate forecast of actual migration flows and stocks. Interestingly enough, our results are roughly in line with the estimates which are based on the extrapolation of South–North migration (Layard *et al.*, 1992; Bauer and Zimmermann, 1998). There are, of course, findings that point either to lower or higher numbers, an example for the first case is Fertig and Schmidt (2000), one of the latter is Sinn *et al.* (2000).[8] Altogether, we can draw three conclusions from our estimates: first, it is a reasonable guess that free movement will involve a migration of 2 and 4 per cent of the population from the CEECs into the present EU in the long run. Secondly, the adjustment of the migration stock to the income differential will take time. Thus, average net migration rates will hardly exceed

---

[8] The differences are due to different methodologies and assumptions, which we cannot discuss in detail here.

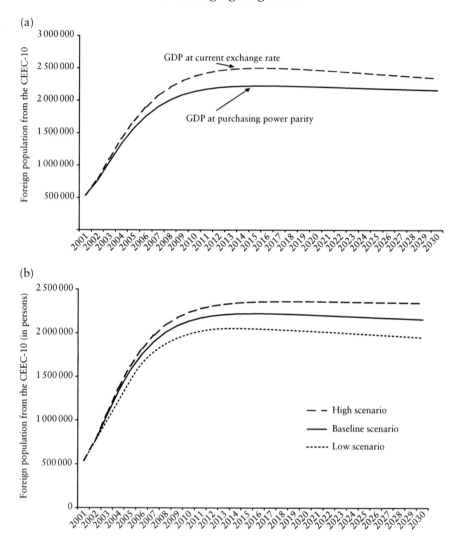

Figure 4.3. *(a and b) Scenario of the number of residents from the CEEC-10 in Germany*

200 000 persons in Germany and 300 000 persons in the EU-15 in the first decade after introducing the free movement. However, immediately after the introduction of the free movement, migration rates can be higher. Moreover, they are expected to vary widely with the business cycle. Thirdly, postponing the free movement will not reduce the migration potential by large numbers, if we base our expectations on realistic assumptions as to the pace of convergence of per capita incomes.

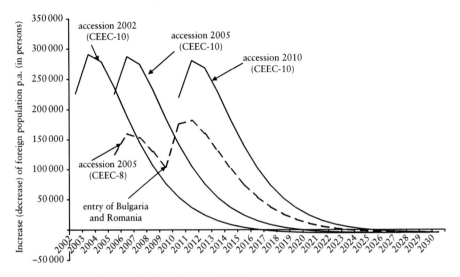

Figure 4.4. *Simulation of different accession scenarios*

4.2. WHAT ARE THE CONSEQUENCES FOR EU LABOUR MARKETS?

Migrants from the CEECs at present concentrate in countries and regions adjacent to the CEECs: around 80 per cent of the migrants from the CEECs living in the EU reside in Germany and Austria, and this pattern seems to be stable over time. However, not all border regions are affected. Migrants from the CEECs tend to move into prosperous regions with above average growth rates of GDP and employment, and a high density of working places. Conversely, border regions with high unemployment rates, low wage growth, and a low population density receive only negligible numbers of migrants. As an example, the share of migrants from the CEECs in the population and employment of Eastern Germany amounts only to one-third of the German average, while the shares in the border regions in Bavaria and lower Austria are at around three times the country averages in Germany and Austria. Border commuting is at present negligible, with around 6000 workers in Austria and Germany. It will, however, increase notably if free movement is introduced. Recent estimates based on the East–West migration between both parts of Germany estimate potential border commuting at around 95 000 (Alecke *et al.*, 2000). If the migration forecasts cited above hold true, the share of workers from the CEECs will altogether increase to around 7–12 per cent of employment in the most affected regions of the present EU.

These are substantial but not unacceptable inflows into the border regions. Against the background of the empirical findings on the wage and employment impact of labour migration, it is unlikely that the affected regions and countries will adjust by reducing wages or increasing unemployment, as predicted by one-sector, closed economy models. Conversely, it is likely that the affected regions and countries will absorb the migration surge by increasing production and adjusting the output mix. Preliminary evidence from the border regions in Austria and Germany confirms this view: employment and production grows there at above the country average, and changes in the output mix (e.g. increasing shares of wood processing) can be observed (Huber and Hofer, 2001).

Notice that the CEECs form a specific group of countries: on the one hand, per capita income levels are not much above those of the main source countries of the foreign population in the present EU. On the other hand, human capital endowments are much richer than in countries at comparable income levels. Moreover, incomes have been relatively equally distributed in the past, although inequality is increasing rapidly. Recent migrants from the East tend to be more qualified than natives in the host countries, according to labour force survey data (Hönekopp, 1999; Boeri and Brücker, 2001). However, these figures should be taken with a grain of salt, since temporary migrants with—presumably—lower qualifications are systematically underreported. Moreover, the skill level of migrants from the East may deteriorate with the increasing earnings inequality in the East. Nevertheless, the average skill composition of migrants from the CEECs will be, in any case, higher than that of other non-EU foreigners. As a consequence, migrants from the East will probably perform better in labour markets and are less likely to depend on welfare than the recent migrant cohorts in Europe.

5

European Attitudes Towards Immigrants

5.1. ATTITUDES TOWARDS MIGRANTS IN THE CONTEXT OF ECONOMIC CONDUCT AND PERFORMANCE

This chapter is concerned to examine the attitude of the EU native population towards immigration together with their self-reported racist feelings, and the relationship of these attitudes to unemployment, the scale of immigration and welfare take-up. We shall discuss later attitudes and sentiments towards migrants and foreigners which vary quite widely across countries. They may arise from racial antipathy or may be associated with economic fears about conditions in the labour market, the costs of generosity to migrants of the welfare state, and in particular an individual's own economic perspective. They may also be related to the success and degree of assimilation of foreigners in society and the labour market. Since success in the destination is affected by personal characteristics, it is also important how migrants are selected into the host country.

Racial prejudice is one important element of behaviour against migrants and can be fuelled from various sources. It typically arises from the natives' personal insecurity and fear for the future, caused for instance by a fear of loss of national characteristics. Racial attitudes can also derive from a taste for cultural homogeneity. Europeans have a strong preference for a continuation of traditional cultural differences between some European communities, which is potentially lost if immigration is high. Ethnic origin is frequently the basis for racial prejudice and discrimination, and the degree to which these happen depends on how dissimilar immigrants are culturally and ethnically from the native population.

Racism and xenophobia can be related to economic concerns about the development of society, the labour market, and the welfare state. Migrants can be considered to be a threat to the native population in that their presence could increase unemployment and depress wages. It is also sometimes conjectured that migrants rely more heavily on welfare payments and hence are often seen as exploiting the welfare system (we have discussed these concerns in Chapter 3).

Consequently, those natives that are directly affected by competition from migrant workers are more likely to exhibit racial prejudice. However, it is also possible that natives are jealous of migrants' good performance in the labour market and society, and it is this that causes the negative feeling.

Migration policy is partly responsible for the characteristics of the immigrants a country receives, and thus influences their economic performance and that of the economy as a whole, and as well as how immigrants are perceived by the native-born population. If migration policy takes into account labour market needs, migrants are more likely to perform well in the labour market, assimilate quickly and contribute to the development of the economy. If non-economic motives dominate the selection of migrants, it is less likely that they perform well in the economy. Their skills may be less transferable to the host country, and consequently labour market assimilation is more difficult. This all implies that the choice of a migration policy should be expected to have an impact on the sentiments of natives towards foreigners.

Native workers can be affected by immigrants either through payments needed for the welfare system or through their effects on the labour market. If immigrants are substitutes for a group of natives, the natives may suffer from depressed wages or a rise in unemployment. However, if they are complements, natives will benefit. For example, it may be argued that low-skilled immigration is likely to benefit native high-skilled workers, while high-skilled migration may benefit native low-skilled workers. If some labour markets are in excess demand, immigration of those workers does not harm natives, but brings benefits. As long as migrants bring no capital with them, native capital owners will gain from migration. As a consequence, it is not unlikely that sentiments towards immigration are likely to depend on labour market status, education, and type of skills.

There are only few contributions in the economic literature. An early paper is by Gang and Rivera-Batiz (1994), who investigate the effect of foreign workers on the employment status of German citizens and whether attitudes toward immigrants are related to the labour status of natives or to prejudice and ethnic bias. Dustmann and Preston (2000a,b) deal with similar issues in the British context and also investigate the local context and the role racial attitudes have and how they are generated. Fertig and Schmidt (2001) study the welfare dependence of migrants in Germany and contrast the actual figures with the German natives' perception of migrants welfare dependency. Bauer *et al.* (2000) compare native sentiments of migrants across various OECD countries and contrast the perceived variance to different migration policies.

It is clear from this discussion that social and economic concerns may be interrelated. To suggest some basic structure for the analysis, this chapter will further investigate the attitudes using survey data similar to previous contributions in the literature. To begin with an instructive example, we consider country aggregates of survey responses on concerns about migration and unemployment. Unemployment is often seen as a major problem associated

with immigration, and hence one would expect to see a high positive association between the worries over unemployment and the worries over immigration
in population surveys.

The 1997 Eurobarometer survey contained various questions on the attitudes of Europeans toward immigrant populations. The question asked was:
'I am going to read out a list of some of the big political and social issues of our
time. Could you please tell me which three are you most worried about?'
Among the potential answers were 'unemployment in Europe' and 'immigration'. Excluding Luxembourg and Greece, Fig. 5.1 contains the aggregate
responses in the remaining 13 member states of the EU concerning the worries
expressed over unemployment and immigration.

The message provided by Fig. 5.1 is compelling: By no means is there a clear-
cut relationship between both concerns. To the contrary, the variables seem to
exhibit no interaction at all. There appear to be four distinct groups of countries. The group with least worries about migrants and unemployment contains
the United Kingdom, Ireland, and the Netherlands. Danish respondents have
been the only ones expressing serious concerns about migrants and little concern about unemployment, and hence form their own group. Finland, Portugal,
and Spain do not have serious concerns with migration, but worry about
unemployment, and form the third group. The fourth group contains the
remaining countries: Austria, France, Italy, Belgium, Sweden, and Germany.
Here, worries are relatively high about both migrants and unemployment.
Germans worry most about unemployment, although the German unemployment rate ranks in the middle of all European countries. Denmark is the

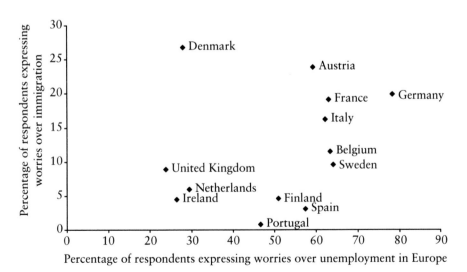

Figure 5.1. *Main political and social worries of our time: percentage of respondents
mentioning immigration or unemployment in Europe*

country in which concerns about migration are highest, while the Danish foreign population share ranks only middle amongst the EU member states. This is another observation that suggests that fears and facts are not necessarily related.

In Section 5.2, we first investigate the occurrence of racism. Section 5.3 studies attitudes towards migrants and their determinants in more detail. Section 5.4 deals with the interaction of migration policies and sentiments.

5.2. RACISM AND CONCERNS ABOUT UNEMPLOYMENT AND IMMIGRATION

The 1997 Eurobarometer survey contained a question on racism: 'Some people feel they are not at all racist. Others feel they are very racist. Would you look at this card and give me the number that shows your own feelings about this? If you feel you are not at all racist, you give a score of 1. If you feel you are very racist, you give a score of 10. The scores between 1 and 10 allow you to say how close to either side you are.' Although only few people said that they are 'very racist', the overall level of racism and xenophobia was worrying. Nearly 33 per cent of those interviewed openly described themselves as 'quite racist' or 'very racist' (4–10 scores).

The percentage of those reporting some racist feelings (who scored 2–10 in the survey) in 1997 are graphed against the 1996 OECD standardized unemployment rates (see Fig. 5.2), and against the 1996 foreign population share (see Fig. 5.3). Judging from Fig. 5.2, there is no indication of a positive relationship between the actual experience of unemployment and the share of

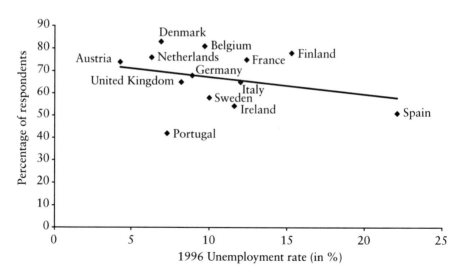

Figure 5.2. *Percentage of respondents reporting racist feelings by 1996 unemployment rate*

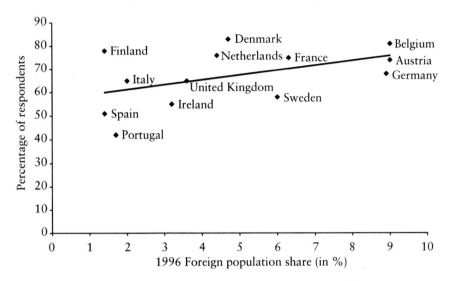

Figure 5.3. *Percentage of respondents reporting racist feelings by 1996 foreign population share*

reported racist feelings in the various countries. To the contrary, the line in Fig. 5.2 is negatively sloped, although the slope is not statistically significant.

Portugal and Spain seem to be outliers, with the lowest level of racist feelings, probably because there are few foreigners in the country. Figure 5.3, however, shows the expected positive relationship between the foreign population share and the reported racist feelings.

To examine this more formally, an illustrative regression across the EU countries was run. Self-reported racism in 1997 was explained by the 1996 unemployment rate, the 1996 foreign population share, and the mean real GDP growth rate over the 1991–96 period. The result of the regression analysis is contained in column 1 of Table 5.1. It shows that this approach has hardly any explanatory power and the regression coefficients are never close to significance. This implies that racism is unrelated to the central economic variables of the debate, at least at this level of analysis.

The study by Dustmann and Preston (2000a) provides a deeper analysis of racial attitudes at the micro level. Based on data for white respondents from England contained in the British Attitude Survey using various years between 1983 and 1991, they estimate a multi-stage factor model, where they compose attitudes towards further immigration through the three channels: welfare, labour market, and racial issues. In this analysis, various racial indicators and their determinants are examined. We will report their findings in some detail.

Dustmann and Preston (2000a) use three different questions in the survey as measures of racial prejudices: (i) Self-rated prejudice against minorities: 64 per cent of respondents are 'not prejudiced at all'. (ii) Acceptability to inter

Table 5.1. *Racism and concerns about unemployment and immigration*

	I	II	III
	Self-reported racism	Concerned about unemployment	Concerned about immigration
1996 Unemployment rate	−0.24 (0.94)	2.02 (0.84)	−0.19 (0.57)
1991–96 Mean GDP growth	−2.56 (2.69)	−6.75 (2.54)	−0.07 (1.70)
1996 Foreign population share	1.84 (1.41)	5.41 (1.38)	1.06 (0.92)
Self-reported racism	—	−0.63 (0.30)	0.26 (0.20)
Constant	65.57 (16.77)	58.44 (24.79)	−8.49 (16.57)
Adjusted R^2	0.09	0.64	0.28

Notes
I: if respondent declares some degree of racist feeling, = 0 otherwise.
II: if respondent considers unemployment in Europe to be one of the three most important political and social issues of our time, = 0 otherwise.
III: if respondent considers immigration to be one of the most important three political and social issues of our time, = 0 otherwise.
Source: Eurobarometer 1997, own calculations. Standard deviations in parentheses.

ethnic marriage of a relative with a person of Asian or West Indian origin: 48 per cent would 'not mind', and (iii) Acceptability of a suitable ethnic minority superior at work of Asian or West Indian origin: 64 per cent would 'not mind'. Racial attitude probit regressions using these indicator variables show that racial hostility is positively associated with ethnic concentration at the county level; at the individual level, hostility seems to be lower for low income groups, females, Catholics, young people, and for the highly educated. Neither the unemployment rate at the county level nor individual unemployment experience have a significant impact on hostility measures.

As we have seen in Fig. 5.1, worries over unemployment and immigration measured in the 1997 Eurobarometer survey are uncorrelated. Are there any general observations we can make concerning the potential economic forces that are driving theses worries? Are they related to the size of ethnic groups in the country or to the degree of measured racism? It is instructive to first consider some figures. There is some positive relationship between the foreign population share in 1996 and the worries expressed in 1997 concerning immigration and unemployment (see Figs 5.4 and 5.5).

We find a linear upward trend between the foreign population share and expressed worries over immigration (see Fig. 5.4). Countries where worries over immigration are particularly high given the observed foreign population share (measured by the line in the figure) include Italy, Denmark, France, Austria, and Germany. Figure 5.5 exhibits a U-shaped relationship between the foreign population share and the expressed worries over unemployment in Europe. Four distinct groups show up. First, a group with low foreign share but large worries over unemployment including Italy, Spain, Finland, and Portugal.

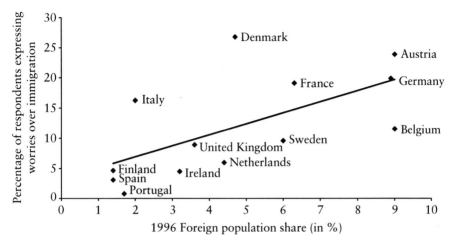

Figure 5.4. *Percentage of respondents considering immigration to be an important issue by 1996 foreign population share*

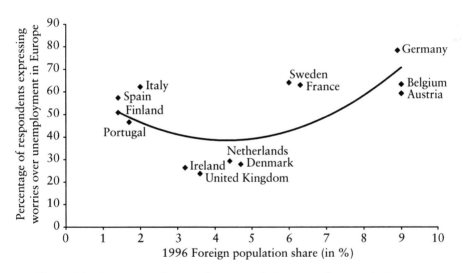

Figure 5.5. *Percentage of respondents considering unemployment in Europe to be an important issue by 1996 foreign population share*

Second, a group with low unemployment concerns and a medium foreign share including Ireland, the United Kingdom, the Netherlands, and Denmark. Then, a group with very large worries over unemployment but medium foreign population share consisting of Sweden and France; and finally there is a group of countries (Germany, Belgium, and Austria) with very high worries over unemployment and high levels of the foreign population share.

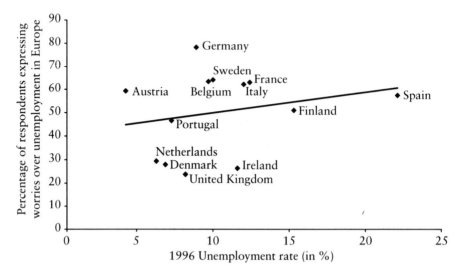

Figure 5.6. *Percentage of respondents considering unemployment in Europe to be an important issue by 1996 unemployment rate*

The expressed worries concerning unemployment in Europe are largely unrelated with the foreign population share, and hence not shown here. Figure 5.6 exhibits these worries against the actual OECD standardized unemployment rates in 1996. A positively sloped line fits well along the responses measured in Portugal, Finland, and Spain, who can be considered responding 'average' given the size of the actual unemployment problem. Low concerns about unemployment are found for the Netherlands, Denmark, the United Kingdom, and Ireland. Large worries over unemployment are found in Austria, Belgium, Sweden, Italy, France, and especially Germany.

Table 5.1 contains two regressions explaining the concerns towards unemployment and immigration by the actual unemployment rate in 1996, the mean real GDP growth in 1991–96, the 1996 foreign population share and the degree of self-reported racism in the particular country. We find that the worries about unemployment can be explained by these variables. The larger the previous unemployment rate and the foreign population share, and the lower past growth was, the higher are these worries. More racist countries are less worried about unemployment. In contrast, not even racism seems to have an effect.

To conclude, there is some evidence that the presence of foreigners or ethnic minorities may cause racial tensions. While this is less visible in the cross-country comparisons among the EU member states, it is quite clear at the local level. General economic conditions like economic growth and country level unemployment play no role, as is true for the local unemployment rate and the individual unemployment experiences. Education plays a positive role in moderating ethnic hostility, perhaps because it may make economic arguments more accessible to those educated, or education attracts those more inclined to think in such terms. It is also important to note that concerns over unemployment are affected by economic factors, the size of the foreign population, and the degree of racism, but concerns over immigration are not. Hence, further analysis of attitudes towards foreigners is needed, and is discussed in Section 5.3.

5.3. DETERMINANTS OF ATTITUDES

Various studies have examined the determinants of sentiments towards migrants. Before we go deeper into the microeconomics of these exercises, we examine again the cross-country evidence using data from the 1997 Eurobarometer survey. Responses on the following questions have been utilized:

'Our country has reached its limits; if there were to be more people belonging to these minority groups we would have problems.' (The boat is full!)
'People from these minority groups abuse the system of social benefits.' (Abuse welfare system.)
'The presence of people from these minority groups increases unemployment in our country.' (Cause unemployment.)

The feeling that the boat is full can be reached through different channels, for example, this can result from racism, through the view that ethnic minorities abuse the welfare system or that they cause labour market problems, where the most prominent labour issue is unemployment. Figure 5.7 exhibits the

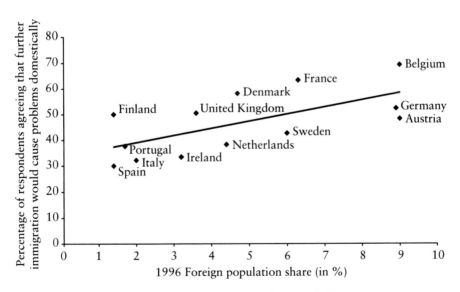

Figure 5.7. *Percentage of respondents agreeing that people from minority groups abuse the system of social benefits by 1996 foreign population share*

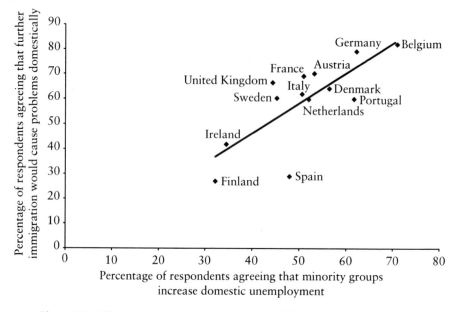

Figure 5.8. *Views on immigration: domestic problems and unemployment*

cross-country relationship between the 1996 foreign population share and the percentage of respondents agreeing that people from minority groups abuse the system of social benefits. The attitude that migrants constitute a problem given a particular size of the foreign population is above normal in Finland, the United Kingdom, Denmark, France, and Belgium. Figure 5.8 contains the same investigation for the attitude that minority groups increase domestic unemployment. Again, there is a positive correlation, but the countries above the regression line are now different from the ones before (Portugal, Italy, Spain, the Netherlands, and Germany are new), only Denmark and Belgium belong to the group of states with relatively strong fears of job losses.

Figures 5.9 and 5.10 exhibit the 1997 responses that the boat is full against the 1996 foreign population share and the 1996 unemployment rate. The fear that minorities create unemployment is positively related to the relative size of the foreign population, but negatively related to actual unemployment. The first relationship looks quite stable, while the latter and more surprising finding stems from three 'outliers', namely Ireland, Finland, and Spain. However, even without them, it would be impossible to derive a positive relationship between a perceived unemployment threat of minorities and actual unemployment.

Figure 5.8 plots the views that 'further immigration would cause problems domestically' against the frequency of the response that 'minority groups increase domestic unemployment'. The graph suggests that these variables are well contrasted indicating that the 'boat is full' mentality comes from a strong feeling that future migrants would cause native unemployment. This interaction

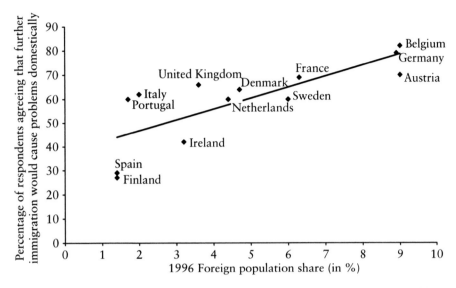

Figure 5.9. *Percentage of respondents agreeing that further immigration would cause problems domestically by 1996 foreign population share*

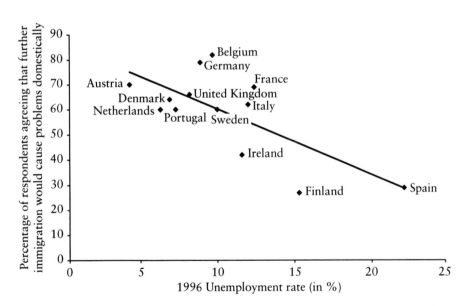

Figure 5.10. *Percentage of respondents agreeing that further immigration would cause problems domestically by 1996 unemployment rate*

Table 5.2. *Abuse of welfare and cause of unemployment*

	IV	V
	Immigrants abuse social security system	Immigrants push up unemployment
1996 Unemployment rate	0.16 (0.69)	−0.47 (0.81)
1991–96 Mean GDP growth	−1.42 (2.07)	−1.84 (2.44)
1996 Foreign population share	1.90 (1.12)	1.93 (1.33)
Self-reported racism*	0.45 (0.24)	−0.21 (0.29)
Constant	8.50 (20.17)	64.25 (23.87)
Adjusted R^2	0.50	0.06

Notes
*In regression IV, self-reported racism if respondent agrees that people from minority groups abuse the system of social benefits, = 0 otherwise.
In regression V, self-reported racism = 1 if respondent agrees that the presence of people from these minority groups increases domestic unemployment, = 0 otherwise.
Source: Eurobarometer 1997, own calculations. Standard deviations in parentheses.

is more fantasy than fact, in that it is unrelated to past unemployment (see also Fig. 5.10).

Some regression exercises shed more light on these findings. Table 5.2 contains two regressions explaining the responses concerning the abuse of the social security system and the perception that minorities create unemployment by previous unemployment, past real average growth, the previous foreign population share and self-reported racism. It turns out that these variables hardly explain the 'unemployment threat' concerns. In the case of the perceived abuse of the social security system, the estimated coefficients have the expected signs, but it is only for the foreign population share, and self-reported racism variables that the received standard errors are more reliable. We conclude that it is difficult to explain the measured attitudes across countries simply by using this proxy for racism, the relative foreigner share, and the macroeconomic differences.

Table 5.3 investigates the 'boat is full' mentality. To what extent can we explain the sentiments that further immigration would cause problems domestically? Column 1 employs the same regressors as the previous regressions, namely past unemployment and real growth, foreign population, and self-reported racism. The estimated coefficients for racism and growth are clearly non-significant. The relative foreign population size has a positive impact, while the unemployment rate seems to have a negative effect. The latter, somewhat surprising finding, is consistent with the graphical analysis outlined above. Whether this is an artefact or the result of the belief that immigrants might help to fight unemployment cannot be solved at this stage.

Column 2 of Table 5.3 concentrates on the hypothesis that the antipathy to immigration is based on three effects: racism, the threat of unemployment, and

Table 5.3. *Further immigration would cause problems domestically, the boat is full!*

	VI	VII	VIII
	The boat is full!	The boat is full!	The boat is full!
1996 Unemployment rate	−1.58 (0.79)	—	−1.17 (0.56)
1991–96 Mean GDP growth	−2.26 (2.37)	—	—
1996 Foreign population share	3.54 (1.29)	—	2.22 (0.94)
Self-reported racism	−0.19 (−0.28)	0.07 (0.39)	—
Immigrants push up unemployment	—	1.02 (0.35)	0.67 (0.24)
Immigrants abuse social security	—	0.37 (0.43)	—
Constant	76.27 (23.10)	−14.71 (23.38)	26.76 (14.15)
Adjusted R^2	0.65	0.55	0.81

Notes: Regressions VI, VII, and VIII: self-reported racism = 1 if respondent agrees that further immigration would cause problems domestically, = 0 otherwise.

Source: Eurobarometer 1997, own calculations. Standard deviations in parentheses.

welfare concerns. The explanatory power of the regression is low, and only the estimated parameter for unemployment concerns provides a decent size and significance. It supposes that a combination of the significant variables of the two first regressions as shown in column 3 works best. The explanatory power is large, and the foreign population share and unemployment concerns show a positive and significant effect, while the previous unemployment rate remains negative and significant.

There have been a few studies which investigated these issues using micro survey data and the appropriate micro-econometric techniques. The relevant literature includes Bauer *et al.* (2000), Dustmann and Preston (2000*a*), Fertig and Schmidt (2001) and Gang and Rivera-Batiz (1994). We deal with these studies in three steps. First, we deal with the unemployment concerns migrants often face, which also play a decisive role in the public debate about immigration policies. Second, there is the conjecture that migrants exploit the welfare system of the host country, an issue that is finding rising interest in the public debate. Third, there is the attitude towards further immigration. In Germany and other European countries there are attempts to change the immigration policies to allow more qualified immigrants in. Hence, the extent that perceptions of natives depend on economic motives or on racist feelings is of interest. While racism is difficult to fight, it might be possible to convince a wider public of the potential positive effects of immigration.

A popular presumption is that migrants are substitutes for the native-born workers and are depressing wages, displacing natives, and causing unemployment. This presumption is behind most public worries and has generated demand for tighter regulation of immigration. However, there are many reasons to believe that migration can be beneficial even in the face of unemployment in the host country (Zimmermann, 1995). For example: in the cases where they are complements to local workers in production, if there is excess demand for workers or if migrants bring capital with them.

Gang and Rivera-Batiz (1994) were the first to study both the effect of immigration on natives and the attitudes towards foreigners shown by individuals in various labour market situations using individual data for Germany from the 1988 Eurobarometer survey. They first examine whether there is an effect on the probability of native employment for those who are in the labour market, from foreign presence in the labour market after controlling for differences in schooling, labour market experience and demographic characteristics. Foreign presence is measured in two ways: first, by an objective measure which is the actual percentage of population in the region; and secondly by a subjective measure using the respondents' self-report of foreign presence using the survey question 'are there many, a few or no people of another nationality who live in your neighbourhood?' They find that foreign presence (measured by the objective variable) has a positive (although not significant) effect on native employment, while the subjective measures show a negative and significant result. Naturally, it is difficult to judge whether this difference in findings results from the better quality of the individual evaluations or that they are biased by misperceptions.

When asked whether 'foreigners increase our unemployment', the proportion of German respondents answering 'no' was 71 per cent while the overall response rate in the European Economic Community in 1988 was 67.7 per cent, while the Netherlands had a response of 73.4 per cent, France 64.2 per cent, and the United Kingdom 67.4 per cent. When analysing these data for Germans at the individual level studying the question whether 'foreigners increase our unemployment', Gang and Rivera-Batiz (1994) find no significant impact of employment status or gender. However, for education they estimate a highly significant negative effect parameter.

Among many questions on natives' sentiments towards migrants, Bauer *et al.* (2000) also study whether 'immigrants take jobs away' using the micro responses in 12 OECD countries provided in the 1995 International Social Survey Programme. This data provides some information about the different perceptions people had about migrants across OECD countries in 1995. In the United Kingdom, about half of the native population felt that immigrants take jobs away, closely followed by the United States. Spain, New Zealand, Ireland, Italy, Austria, and Germany rank in the middle at around 40 per cent. At the other end of the spectrum were Sweden, where only about 16 per cent reported that they feel threatened by migrants in the labour market. Similarly low findings to Sweden were received for the Netherlands, Norway, and Canada. Cross-country regressions using the micro data and employing country-specific fixed effects suggest that negative attitudes rise with age, are higher for females, and lower if married or better educated. Being unemployed also seems to increase significantly the probability that a person thinks that immigrants take jobs away.

Dustmann and Preston (2000), while having no comparable question available, construct their own variable measuring job insecurity from various survey responses on perceived labour market conditions. The data is again from the British Attitude Survey using various years between 1983 and 1991. They find that perceptions of job insecurity are strongest among poorer, older, female, manual workers with low or medium education, and experience of unemployment. However, only the effects of age, income, rank, and gender are strongly statistically significant. While not directly comparable to the results provided by Gang and Rivera-Batiz (1994) and Bauer *et al.* (2000), they are nevertheless largely consistent in interpretation. This is not surprising, if one accepts that migrants may contribute to job insecurity.

A recent study by Fertig and Schmidt (2001) investigates the claim that migrants are a burden to the welfare state, or are at least perceived to be so. Using German Microcensus data from 1995 to evaluate the actual welfare take-up and the 1996 ALLBUS survey to examine the individual sentiments, they also distinguish between first and second generation migrants. According to the ALLBUS data, 36 per cent of the natives disagree, 21 per cent are indifferent, and 43 per cent agree when asked whether 'foreigners are a burden for the social security system'.

The issue of welfare dependence of foreigners was already studied by Riphahn (1998). Using micro data from the German Socio-Economic Panel for the 1984–96 period, she reports a detailed pattern of welfare dependence for foreigners and natives. The paper asks whether the welfare dependence of foreigners is due to their exogenous characteristics or due to behaviour such as benefit take-up. The estimation finds that foreign households are no more likely to depend on welfare, once exogenous characteristics are accounted for. The most sizeable effects on the risk of welfare dependence show up when the unit is a single parent household, the household head is female and has a large number of children. The estimates show that between natives and foreigners there are significant differences in the effects of the number of children, the household's residence in a large town, and whether the household head is of retirement age on welfare dependence. The general result of Riphahn (1998) that the estimated differences in the dependence on social assistance payments between foreigners and natives suggest a statistically significant and substantially lower risk of foreigners depending on these benefits, is clearly at odds with the reported perception in the ALLBUS opinion survey reported in Fertig and Schmidt (2001).

The study by Fertig and Schmidt (2001) uses a much larger sample from the German Microcensus data and largely confirms the findings of Riphahn (1998). To explain welfare dependence, they use a number of different regressors on the household level (e.g. married, children), the individual level (e.g. age, gender, education, training, employment status), city size and various sets of variables to characterize first and second generation migrants in the sample. Married respondents are substantially less likely to be on welfare than single adults, and single adults with children are somewhat more likely to receive welfare benefits. Number of children also has a positive impact on the probability of welfare dependence. East Germans are less likely to be on welfare than west Germans, probably the result of other public support programmes. Age plays a significant role, with welfare dependence more likely for younger people. Females and inhabitants of big cities are more likely to be on welfare; a higher education and more training, however, has a strong negative impact on benefit take-up. First generation migrants have a clearly lower welfare dependence than natives, while second generation migrants are closer to native Germans although some foreigner groups such as Turks and citizens from other EU countries are still significantly higher.

Since the attitude towards migrants and native ideas about the welfare take-up of foreigners is in contrast to what we see in the evidence from the Riphahn (1998) and Fertig and Schmidt (2001) studies, it is worth studying the determinants of the individual responses on the attitude question. Fertig and Schmidt (2001) do this using the ALLBUS 1996 survey and the responses to the statement 'foreigners are a burden on the social security system'. Again, various individual characteristics have been employed as explanatory variables for the political opinion and the share of foreigners in the region. Older people, east Germans, females, the less educated and right wing respondents living in an environment with a low share of migrants all agree more with this statement. However, being unemployed or currently fearing a job loss show no significant estimated coefficients.

This chapter has provided a review of various results that contradict popular beliefs about welfare take-up by migrants and job losses caused by foreigners. It is interesting to examine whether it is possible to separate racist feelings from concerns about unemployment (or job insecurity) and welfare dependence. Dustmann and Preston (2000) have tried to do so using a multistage factor model and a sample of English white respondents from the British Attitude Survey. In the first stage, they determine the factors: racist behaviour (race), job insecurity (jobs) and welfare concerns (welfare) using various indicators and a larger number of regressors. In the second stage, they study the impact of those factors on the expressed opinions towards further immigration. Then, they are able to separate the findings for different educational levels and different ethnic origins of the migrants. Results for manual and non-manual workers are also presented.

These findings confirm that both welfare and labour market concerns matter for the expressed opinion towards further immigration, but racially motivated concerns are the most important factors. Since the data allows us to distinguish between attitudes towards different origin groups, the nature of the bias can be explored more deeply. All three factors (race, jobs, and welfare) play a larger (and negative) role for Asians and West Indians, while it is less strong for Europeans. The fourth region (Australia and New Zealand) is hardly explained by any of these factors. The dominant racial factor is especially strong for West

Indian and Asian populations. A further important finding of the study is that there are no relevant effects of labour market and welfare concerns of low skilled or manual workers on the attitude against further immigration. To the contrary, Dustmann and Preston (2000) find that welfare and labour market concerns are more closely related to an attitude against further immigration for non-manual workers and for the more educated.

5.4. ATTITUDES AND MIGRATION POLICY

A recent contribution by Bauer *et al.* (2000) has examined various measures of natives' sentiments and their relationship to migration policies across 12 OECD countries. They found some evidence that the design of an immigration policy may be important for the prospect of immigrant assimilation, or labour market success, and hence for the development of sentiments of natives towards immigrants. They start with the observation that current immigration policies give priority to particular groups of people, and these preferences vary greatly across the major receiving countries. Whereas Canada and New Zealand focus on the selection of immigrants following the needs of their labour markets, other countries either favour the immigration of family members of former migrants, such as the US, or on ethnic groups, such as ethnic Germans from the former USSR in Germany, or citizens of the Commonwealth in the UK. In Sweden, Norway, and the Netherlands the majority of new immigrants typically consist of refugees and asylum seekers.

Economic theory suggests that immigrants from countries that are similar to the host country, with respect to economic development, the schooling system, language and culture, assimilate well into the labour market. This is probably due to a rapid transferability of the human capital they accumulated in their home country. In addition, the migration motive is important for the labour market success of immigrants. Empirical studies on the assimilation of migrants in different countries (see also Bauer *et al.*, 2000) have shown that the country-of-origin and the migration motive are among the most important determinants of the labour market success of migrants. In particular, it has been shown that the success of immigration policies selecting migrants on the basis of their skills, such as in Canada and New Zealand, seem to be successful, not primarily because they attract the most skilled migrants from a given country, but because they alter the mix of countries which immigrants come from. It has also been shown that nearly all significant receiving countries recently experienced a decline in the quality of immigrants, as measured by the wage differential on arrival between immigrants and natives. In all cases, the decrease in the quality of migrants comes together with a significant change in the country-of-origin mix of the immigrants.

Finally, even though all countries face a decline in the quality of migrants, an assimilation of immigrants to natives can be observed only in those countries that select immigrants on the basis of their labour market characteristics.

It is difficult to separate the extent to which the sentiments of the population are in line with policy or policy is in line with sentiments. There are at least indications that immigration policies affect natives' sentiments of immigrants. Analysing individual data from 12 OECD countries, Bauer *et al.* (2000) find evidence suggesting that natives in countries selecting immigrants on their skills are more likely to think that immigrants are generally good for the economy than those in countries which receive mainly asylum seekers and refugees. Natives in Canada and New Zealand, however, are more concerned that immigration negatively affects their own labour market situation, whereas in countries that receive mainly non-economic migrants, natives are mostly concerned about increasing crime rates. Socio-economic characteristics of the respondents such as education, gender, and employment status do not seem to explain the major differences in the perception of immigrants across countries. The results indicate, however, that the relatively more educated have a more positive view of immigrants.

Previous parts of this chapter have found that ethnic hostility or racism is visible in various European countries. However, its strength is hardly related to economic determinants like unemployment. Insofar as pressure against further immigration is fuelled by racism, and not by concerns about the misuse of welfare measures and the threat of unemployment, it is not surprising that worries about unemployment and immigration are unrelated. A clear-cut result is that the claims that migrants are a burden on the welfare state and a threat to the labour market shows up in the measured opinions, but they are nevertheless unfounded if one relies on applied research. Foreigners hardly affect the employment status of natives, at least not negatively. Welfare dependence of immigrants is lower than for natives as soon as one controls for the individual characteristics. Attitudes towards migrants are affected most effectively by education.

All these have interesting policy implications. Policy-makers are typically concerned about re-election, and hence must be interested in the emotions of voters caused by immigration. There are two important channels by which re-election might be affected: first, there are social tensions caused by ethnic rivalry and other negative social externalities such as crime. It will be hard to fight racist feelings, although better education may be useful as a long-run measure. However, there is hope that the other driving forces behind the pressure against migration can be better addressed: the observed fears, that migrants would take away jobs is not supported by empirical evidence. The fear of potential abuse of the generous EU welfare system is not without grounds for concern—as we have seen in Chapter 3—but should be addressed administratively, and explained with appropriate perspective. The more information that is provided to the public about this, the more likely it is that this will be understood by a larger part of the population. It is also useful to select economic immigrants better in order to avoid negative signals in the labour market and the social security system. Second, immigration can improve the economic conditions in a country. Migrants take jobs which natives refuse to do, they are often complements to natives or they enter in market segments which have an excess demand for labour. Hence, they increase production and create further employment among natives. Since the popularity of a government depends largely on its economic success, a well-chosen migration policy will be effective also in a political sense. For example, European governments might be able to increase their popularity by means of a migration policy that relies more on the respective country's labour market needs. Popularity might increase further by such a policy since social tensions may decline with a relatively higher proportion of labour migrants.

It is also important to realize that any humanitarian policy can be costly in an economic sense. However, by reducing negative attitudes towards immigrants in the native population through a migration policy that stresses the economic needs of the receiving country, the government may also be able to increase the number of admitted humanitarian immigrants without a higher risk of not being re-elected.

6

Contracted Temporary Migration

6.1. INTRODUCTION

Our analysis of EU migration policy in Chapter 2 gives little attention to the comparative implications of temporary vs permanent immigration to the EU and the policy institutions which might accompany temporary migration. In view of the population density of the host regions and cities of western Europe, their current foreign born proportions, and the various social tensions which, as we have noted in Chapter 2, are associated with present institutional arrangements towards immigration, we consider in this chapter the possibility of host countries in the EC adopting policies to facilitate contracted temporary immigration. This immigration differs from temporary migration as it currently occurs in the EC in that the contracted wages and other conditions may differ from those of host country workers. This increases the demand for temporary migrants, and enables employers to offset the higher non-wage costs of employing temporary migrants and assisting the government with ensuring return to the origin country. This would enable affluent EC countries to ensure the rotation of migrant employees in temporary migrant positions, which has been considered key to the success of such policies,[1] and to expand temporary employment without exposure to permanent immigration. Such a policy brings costs and benefits that may be compared to those arising from permanent immigration.

A flow of permanent legal immigrants brings both benefits and costs to the host country. At certain times, the host country may consider that the costs outweigh the benefits: the integration of immigrants may be slow and social tensions may exist; the economy may be depressed and unemployment high amongst the existing labour force; the level of illegal immigration may be considered to be excessive; and, the level of anticipated family unification immigration may be high. More recently, the terrorist attacks in America have raised security issues. In these situations the host country may wish to create additional flexibility in both the numbers and skills of migrants by substituting temporary immigration for permanent immigration. This alters the pattern of costs and benefits for both the origin and host countries. The distribution of benefits and costs

---

[1] See Zimmerman (1995).

between potential migrants will also be changed if a large number of migrants experience short spells of temporary overseas employment, rather than a smaller number living overseas permanently.

Contracted temporary migration of high- and low-skilled workers benefits the local firms in the host country because the firms gain access to skilled and/ or unskilled workers who are needed for production. Contracted temporary migrants have a specific contract between the employer and the migrant, thus the contracted worker cannot move from one employer to another. How are firms affected by employing temporary rather than permanent migrants? First, temporary workers will have to leave the host country after a certain time period and thus, the employer may have to incur costs to train new workers. However, this may not be a major additional cost if permanent migrant workers change jobs and are replaced by others in the different life cycles of a job. It will also be a minor cost if migrants supply general human skills not firm-specific ones. Second, workers' incentives to invest in firm-specific human capital will be lower if they anticipate a shorter spell at the contracted firm than other workers do. However, if contracted temporary workers are unable to invest in general human capital in the origin country due to training opportunities being unavailable, this may encourage such investment at higher rates than permanent migrants in the host country. Depending on the work context, this may increase or reduce the effort of the temporary migrant provided to the employer. In many situations, where workers are providing well-defined professional services such as computer programming, or unskilled work, rotating temporary labour would be similar to having permanent migrants.

As well as the degrees of freedom it gives the authorities, and the consequences for employers, there are other aspects to this policy. Consider the position with regard to the origin country. The migrants who immigrate to the EC, are frequently highly skilled workers in their home country who may provide skill spillover and other externalities in their origin countries. Their migration may therefore reduce the welfare of the local population. Temporary workers will, most probably, return to their family[2] in their home country after a certain period of time, and frequently with a higher human capital that was obtained in the host country. This incremental human capital may itself possess positive economic externalities for the home country and affect the quality of future migrants to the EC, and the terms of trade between the home country and the EC (this proposed policy is, of course, not a substitute to trade policies between the LDC and the EC. However, it may well be complementary policy to such trade policies).

Corporate partnerships between EC and Third-World firms might emerge on a substantial scale, allowing worker exchanges. This could enrich a large

---

[2] With permanent migration the issue of family reunion is likely to arise. However, with temporary migration this problem does not exist. There is, of course, no guarantee that migrants will return to the origin country for more than a brief period.

number of temporary migrants and their countries of origin, rather than allowing benefits to a smaller number of permanent migrants to settle in the EC. There is a small literature[3] which documents how returnees from international migration contribute through various channels to development in the origin country—remitted savings, entrepreneurship and increased business investment, enhanced skills, and the accumulation of information. A policy of rotating workers through temporary overseas jobs will increase dramatically the impact of overseas work experience on the typical LDC economy.

If the migrants are skilled, their migration may impose a further cost on the origin country workers. Instead of the home country becoming economically 'close' to the EC, the home country may drift away as a result of this 'brain drain' of the skilled workers (see for example Beine *et al.*, 2001). This has macro- and microeconomic effects on the host country and on the terms of trade with the EC (of course this policy is not meant to be a substitute for trade policies). There is the mixed possibility of the origin country becoming a talent-poor and persistently low GDP per head region, rather than one with the potential to fully participate in world development. A policy which facilitates temporary contracted migration rather than permanent migration to enter the EC may therefore *also* benefit the sectoral balance and long-term potential growth in the home country.

Illegal migration is a phenomena that many countries would be happy, at least to some extent, to demolish. Many of the illegal migrants return home after a given period in the host country. Enabling contracted temporary migration may well decrease the number of illegal migrants that intended to enter illegally for a given period of time. The reason for this is that the migrants that would have entered illegally now may enter the host country as temporary contracted workers and stay the period of time they were intending to stay as illegal migrants.

However, temporary worker policies also raise a variety of economic problems. In the first place one has to consider what will happen if the policy cannot be enforced and the temporary workers stay in the host country illegally. It is not clear what mechanism should be used in order to force the temporary workers to return home at the end of the period. Moreover, when a contracted temporary migrant enters one country he/she may decide to migrate to a different country within the EC and ask for asylum. Thus, enabling workers to enter the EC as temporary contracted migrants may well open up new possibilities for asylum seekers. They may enter the EC legally and then go from a country that has low welfare benefits to a country with high welfare benefits. In this way the migrants can increase their probability of receiving asylum.[4] We will now consider the different options the authorities have and

---

[3] This literature, which deserves further contributions includes, for example, Ilahi (1999), McCormick and Wahba (2000, 2001), Swamy (1981), Russell (1986), and Cornelius (1990).

[4] Laws must be established so that the workers would not be able to do so.

the consequences of having temporary workers in the host country. Moreover, a policy must be supported by the local population and not only by the local employers.

6.2. IMPLEMENTING CONTRACTED TEMPORARY MIGRATION POLICY

Economic studies of illegal immigration have considered how border controls and apprehending migrants internally can be used to control illegal presence (see, for example, Ethier, 1986; Jahn and Straubhaar, 1995; Zimmermann, 1995; Hillman and Weiss, 1999a). Here we consider compliance with immigration laws when people enter a country legally for purposes of temporary employment, and where there is, at the same time, no credible and effective internal detention mechanism should a foreign worker decide to switch to illegal unemployment and overstay the permissible contractually specified time period. Since entry into the country takes place legally, border controls are of no relevance to our study, nor is there a role for internal detention under the circumstances we are considering.

The circumstances, which we are investigating, arise when a legal employer has been granted a permit to bring in a foreign worker for a designated period of time, after which the foreign worker is obliged to depart. The intention of the government policy is for guest workers to be temporary guests, to be replaced in a revolving pool of temporary foreign workers. The foreign workers, however, receive job offers on a secondary market, and can accept an offer of illegal employment if they so wish. In legal employment, workers are obliged to return home at the end of the specified contractual period, whereas in illegal employment there is no such effective restriction on the length of stay. By making the transition to illegal employment, the foreign intended temporary workers would be transformed to illegal permanent immigrants (see Hillman and Weiss, 1999b).[5]

The question which we wish to consider is whether governments can expect to be successful in enforcing a temporary stay, when the source of illegal immigration is those who have entered the country legally under the terms of contracted temporary migration employment.

In Israel in the 1990s, for example, the purpose of contracted temporary migration guest-worker programmes were a result of sector-specific labour shortages: temporary migrant workers have been nurses and providers of old-age care from the Philippines, building construction workers from Romania, agricultural workers from Thailand, and other specialized services from Russia and the Ukraine (catering principally for other foreign workers). The purpose of such workers could also be for reasons of worker exchange between the EU

---

[5] The transition to becoming an illegal migrant is more likely if the migrant is younger with no family obligations in the home country.

and the Third-World firms. The latter would present a policy of enriching a large number of temporary migrants and their origin countries, rather than settle a smaller number of permanent migrants in the EC.

Foreign workers arrive in a country under short-term employment contracts. The intention of temporary stay is reflected in families left behind, and in the local employer often taking responsibility for housing, health care, and other services during the temporary stay. Yet, some foreign workers may well prefer not to return home as the alternative income and life standard in the home country are well below that of the host country (moreover, they may not have ties such as families and different assets that tie them to the home country).

One way of trying to ensure that the migrants return to their home country is a bond that is forfeited if a worker does not leave as determined by the employment contract. Ideally, the migrant worker would post the bond. A credible bond may, however, be beyond the migrant worker's means, and also there are jurisdictional and convertible-currency impediments to having immigrant workers make payments conditional on the issuance of temporary work visas. It is therefore usual for the bond to be paid by the employer who has requested the foreign worker (we will return to ways and means of imposing some sort of a bond on the worker himself at a later time). The procedure in Israel and Greece is to set a bond on the employer rather the on the worker himself. This type of a bond shifts the departure enforcement from the government to the employer (see Epstein *et al.*, 1999 for a detailed description).

How the legal employer acts depends on the opportunities facing the foreign worker. If foreign workers can leave legal employment for illegal employment more or less freely, the legal employer confronts the problem of devising incentives that pre-empt or inhibit the transition to illegal employment. When governments choose not to deport illegal immigrants, legal employers indeed confront a compromise of contractual rights. They have paid the bond to bring in a foreign worker. They cannot, however, prevent the foreign worker, once present in the country, from making the switch to illegal employment, and if the foreign worker makes the switch, the legal employer loses the value of the bond.

This problem for a legal employer arises in a society where all residents, including intended temporary workers, are free to exercise choice of employment. The problem does not arise in those countries where the relation between employer and temporary immigrant worker can verge on indentured service or near slavery, and where foreign workers can be confined to the housing complex of the family to whom they are bonded, or to the domain of physical control of the business enterprise to which they are legally subject. In these countries the penalty for absconding from the legal employer can be harsh, and a policy, which assigns responsibility to employers for departure of migrant workers, can be effective. We are concerned, however, with circumstances where all employment, including that of foreign workers, is *de facto* voluntary, in the sense that, should a foreign worker choose to leave a legal employer, the costs of seeking out and deporting the absconded worker are too high to warrant the enforcement activity, by either the legal employer or the government. The legal employer then forgoes the bond, and incurs the cost of replacing the lost worker with a new legal migrant worker (which entails a new bond). The new worker may, however, likewise decide to become illegal. In this process, a pool of illegal immigrants is created, contrary to the intentions of the contracted temporary migration programme.

It is important to note that under such circumstances it is not clear why an employer would employ a legal migrant and not just employ an illegal one. Some employers have no choice but to employ legal workers. This may be a result of tax constraints, the visibility of the employment relationship, the cost of being caught or simply for moral reasons as it is not moral to employ an illegal worker.

The contracted temporary migration programme allows the import of legal workers and thus the legal workers provide the pool for a population of illegal immigrants. However, the illegal market is, in practice, not organized to provide continuous market job offers. Advertising for illegal workers cannot take place because of the illegal nature of the job offer. Legal workers accordingly tend to receive random job offers from prospective illegal employers which they can accept or decline. Legal employers are, however, aware of the incentives that confront the foreign worker, and can therefore be expected to make allowance in their wage payments for the likelihood that their legal workers will receive illegal job offers. Employers who have chosen to employ illegal workers could alternatively have chosen to bring in legal workers. If illegal employers are indifferent to importing legal workers themselves and employ other legal workers, the wage for illegal employment is *ceteris paribus* greater than for legal employment, since the legal employer incurs the cost of the bond while the illegal employer does not. The wage premium for illegal employment makes illegal offers attractive for migrant workers. A move to illegal employment before the end of the legal contractual period has another advantage for the foreign worker, who can thereby avoid having to return home. Should the worker still be with his legal employer when the permissible stay expires, the legal employer will redeem his bond by ensuring exit of the worker from the country. There are, on the other hand, offsetting benefits when a worker chooses to remain legal. Life is easier, and also the freedom of legal residence facilitates accumulation of human capital, which is rewarded in the legal wage contract. All aspects considered, the position of the legal employer is, however, not advantageous, for job offers can be expected to arise when the worker, for whom the bond has been posted, leaves to accept illegal employment.

6.2.1. *Legal workers and illegal jobs*

Legal immigrants can enter the country under the contracted temporary migration policy. However, illegal immigrants also enter the host country in order to increase their income in relation to their earnings in their home country. Both the legal and illegal migrants are related to each other. The legal temporary workers are granted entry to host countries in order to work in specific assigned jobs. These jobs are limited by law. Since such workers aim to maximize earnings during the period spent in the host country, there is an incentive for them also to take on jobs which are not allocated to them legally (working overtime, weekend, holidays, etc.).

Illegal workers entering host countries (Ethier, 1986; Borjas, 1994) cannot find jobs as easily as legal workers and tend to use the existing networks generated by the local migrants (legal and illegal) to find jobs. In this process, both legal and illegal migrants gain specific human capital, thereby increasing their incomes over time. These can include on-the-job training as well as learning the language. Legal immigrants may work in both legal and illegal jobs; therefore their designated wage is higher than that of illegal migrants, who are restricted to illegal jobs. The increase in specific human capital, and, hence income, for both legal and illegal immigrants enables both groups to employ newly arrived illegal immigrants with low specific human capital. Naturally, illegal immigrants turn to the local network for help.

By specializing in certain fields or professions, such as home health care, cleaning and educating children, illegal immigrants may substitute for the legal immigrants at home. Such assistance enables the legal immigrants to devote more time to increasing their earnings. Immigrants generally prefer to employ migrants from their own country as they come from a similar environment, culture, and language, enhancing network externalities (Marks, 1989; Church and King, 1993; Carrington *et al.*, 1996; Chiswick and Miller, 1996). Therefore, a sub-economy is emerging whose sole purpose is to provide services for migrants. Much of this economy is illegal. In Malaysia and Israel, for example, temporary migrant workers, both legal and illegal, employ illegal migrants (see Epstein, 2000).

6.2.2. *Contracted temporary migrants and illegal migration*

A major concern of EU countries is the presence of illegal migrants. The question we address here is whether contracted temporary legal migrants will increase or decrease illegal migration. There are two conflicting effects. Those migrants who seek temporary employment in the host country will prefer to be temporary legal migrants rather than illegal migrants. This will lead to a lowering of the stock of illegal migrants. Conversely, the migrants who wish to stay permanently in the host country may use the contracted temporary migration policy in order to enter the host country and then overstay their permits and become illegal migrants. In other words, when the contract expires, the contracted legal temporary migrants have to decide whether to return home or stay illegally in the host country. Becoming illegal may be better financially for the migrant than returning to the home country where the income is relatively low. The policies set by the authorities should take this into consideration and should be set such that they decrease the incentives of the contracted temporary migrants to stay in the host country and not return home. Policy instruments (such as forced saving) that accomplish this goal will be presented in Section 6.3.

To conclude this section of the chapter we could say that any contracted temporary migration policy must insure that: (1) temporary workers leave at the end of their legal time period; (2) the interaction between legal and illegal migrants is minimized, and (3) legal migrants are given strong incentives to avoid illegal activities.

6.3. POLICY INSTRUMENTS

We now consider four different public policies that may have an effect on the three main issues stated above. The policies we will consider are: (1) imposing a bond on the legal employer, (2) taxing legal migrants' earnings, (3) imposing a penalty on local employers caught employing illegal migrants, and (4) forced savings, whereby migrants are compelled to save part of their legal earnings, which they would lose if deported as a result of being caught working illegally.

We now consider briefly the implication of each of these different policies. The analysis presented here is based on the papers by Epstein *et al.* (1999) and Epstein (2000).

6.3.1. *Imposing a bond on the legal employer*

The bond, we consider, is one the employer pays at the time of the entry of the temporary worker. When the immigrant leaves the host country legally at the end of the time permit, the employer will receive his bond back from the authorities. If the immigrant does not leave the country legally at the end of this time period, the employer will forfeit the bond.

Epstein *et al.* (1999) show how the bond affects the wage differential between legal and illegal employment of migrant workers, and thereby the incentives for transfer from legal to illegal employment. An increased bond is an additional cost imposed on legal employers. This additional cost of employing legal immigrants increases the legal wage, since there is an increased incentive for legal employers to attempt to forestall the departure of legal workers to illegal employment. The value of a bond is complementary to the legal wage; and a higher legal wage is *ceteris paribus* a greater attraction to remain legal.

Still, if migrant workers desire to remain longer than the permissible period, they will wish to avoid being with their legal employer at the end of their period of legal contractual employment. Both the government and the legal employer have an interest in ensuring that the worker returns home. The intention of the government is expressed in the policy of temporary admission to the country, while the legal employer does not wish to forfeit his bond. Despite the government's intentions, the legal employer can find his position quite *precarious.* If his legal workers are still with him at the end of the legal period of employment, *it is only* because they will have rejected an illegal offer which, in retrospect, they should have accepted (as earnings in the host country on the legal and illegal market are higher than that of the home country). Also, if the worker leaves the legal employer just before he is to be deported, the employer has paid twice—once via the higher second period wage, and again via the forfeited bond. A policy of intended temporary foreign workers appears inevitable therefore to the creation of a population of illegal immigrants. The question is only the size of the illegal population.

It has been shown therefore that even with a completely inelastic legal demand, a bond is effective in decreasing illegal employment (by increasing the wage offered in legal employment and thereby reducing the probability that a legal worker will make the transition to illegality by accepting an illegal job offer).

6.3.2. *Taxing legal migrants' earnings*

Given that the demand for legal migrants is not inelastic, the net income of the migrants working on the legal market will decrease as a result of imposing an income tax on the legal migrant's earnings. This, of course, will also affect the income on the illegal market. However, its impact will be stronger on the legal market than on the illegal market. Thus, taxing the legal immigrants' earnings increases the probability that the immigrants will accept an offer of work on the illegal market. This will affect the timing when the legal migrant will be willing to accept an offer on the illegal market. As the tax rate increases, the benefit from staying on the legal market decreases and thus the migrant will tend to move to the illegal market leaving his legal employer. This will occur earlier than in the case where the tax rate is low, thus increasing the probability of the legal immigrant staying on the illegal market working for local employers, when his legal permit expires. The number of illegal migrants will increase therefore and the time spent on the legal market will decrease. Taxing legal immigrants' earnings also affects the number of illegal migrants the legal migrants can employ. As the tax rate increases, both the legal and illegal net earnings will decrease. As the effect of the taxes on the legal earnings are stronger, the difference between the legal and illegal earnings will decrease. This will then decrease the incentive of the legal migrant to employ an illegal migrant and will increase the time spent on the illegal market by the legal migrant.

6.3.3. *Imposing a penalty on local employers caught illegally employing migrants*

Imposing a penalty on the local employers employing an illegal worker will decrease the earnings of the immigrants on the illegal market. It will, however, also have the same type of effect on the earnings of the legal workers as both markets are tied together. However, the effect of such a penalty will be stronger on the illegal market than on the legal markets. Thus, such a policy will increase the time the legal employee works legally for the local employer before he decides to move to the illegal market. As stated above, it is not always easy to find jobs on the illegal market and it is not clear if the illegal worker will receive an offer quickly enough to ensure that it would be worth his staying illegally in the host country. Therefore, such a penalty, on average, will decrease the number of migrant workers staying illegally in the host country.

Imposing a penalty on local employers caught employing illegal migrants also has an effect on the time the legal worker spends working on illegal jobs parallel to the time spent on the legal market. Such a penalty would increase the proportion of time spent by the legal migrant on the legal market and decrease the number of illegal migrants they employ.

6.3.4. *Forced savings*

Forced savings is the case where the migrants are compelled to save part of their legal earnings, which they would lose, if deported. This could be seen as a lump sum of money paid by the employer to the local worker when he departs legally from the host country. It could be implemented by the employer paying part of the employees' earnings to the government (such as social security payments)[6] and when the worker leaves the host country legally he/she will receive this lump sum of money. The recourse of the legal employer for offering his legal workers a lump-sum payment at the end of the legal period of employment transfers the bond to the migrant worker. The deferred payment to the migrant worker makes switching to illegality less attractive and increases the likelihood that the worker will still be legal when the period of permissible stay expires. Moral hazard nonetheless intrudes on the interests of the legal employer and the government when they coincide. The legal employer can gain, when the opportunity arises, by compelling his workers to move to illegal employment after the accumulated value of deferred wage payments exceeds the value of the bond. The intent of the bond is then nullified, via a reversal of the employer's incentives. If workers anticipate such opportune behaviour, the bond will remain with the legal employer. Then, the vulnerability of the legal employer, because of defection to illegal employment, is also the source of the government's vulnerable policy.

Therefore the cost, of not leaving the country legally, is transferred from the employer to the employee. This will increase the probability that the legal

---

[6] In order to decrease the costs to the local employer, the deferred payments of the low-skilled workers should be relatively lower than those of the high-skilled workers.

worker will leave the host country legally and will decrease the illegal population of migrants.[7]

If a migrant wishes to stay illegally in the host country he/she would want to leave the legal employer as soon as possible before he/she has accumulated forced savings. The reason for this is that as forced savings increase over time, the cost of becoming illegal also increases with time in the host country.

Imposing a policy whereby the legal migrant 'saves' also affects the time the legal migrant will work on the illegal market parallel to his work on the illegal market. Such savings increases the cost if caught and thus reduces the time spent on the illegal market. If in addition to the penalty of employing an illegal migrant, he loses his savings, if caught employing an illegal migrant, we would then see a reduction in the number of legal migrants employing illegal migrants.

There are two parties that have a strong influence on determining whether the worker will decide to become illegal or not: the worker himself and the employer via the wages he/she offers. The combination of a bond and forced savings puts the responsibility that the worker will leave the host country legally on both the employer (via the bond) and on the worker (via forced savings). As stated above, if the migrant wishes to stay illegally in the host country he/she will leave the employer 'as soon as possible'. However, if the legal migrant becomes an illegal migrant then the employer will lose the bond posted. Therefore, in equilibrium the legal employer will offer a wage contract whereas, over time the migrant's wages will increase. This will decrease the probability that the immigrant will want to become illegal (see Epstein *et al.*, 1999). We could think of a combination that integrates the bond with the forced savings: let the bond set by the employer be the forced savings of the worker. Thus, the temporary contracted migrant will receive the bond on his/her legal departure. The main problem with such a proposal is that by doing so, while there is still an incentive for the migrant to stay legally in the host country, the employer's incentive that the migrant leaves legally decreases as he will not receive the bond even if the worker leaves legally.

We, therefore, conclude that forced savings together with a bond imposed on the employer which he/she will receive when the worker leaves legally, increases the probability that the worker will leave the host country legally. The policies, each by themselves, are focused on a different aspect of the responsibility of the migrant leaving legally. The forced savings places the responsibility on the migrant while the bond imposes the responsibility on the employer.

---

[7] A contemporary migrants policy together with forced savings could also be used in the case of a request for asylum. While the 'migrant' in the host country is waiting for a decision regarding obtaining an asylum, the authorities could contract the worker to an employer so that the worker will have a job during this time period. The forced saving and the money earned by the 'migrant' increase the probability that the worker will leave the country legally in the case that the authorities refuse to provide him/her with asylum.

6.4. THE EC AND THE CASE OF ISRAEL

In this section we describe the situation in a few EC countries. We then describe the case of Israel where the employment of foreign temporary workers has been implemented successfully in the past few years. Finally, we compare the case of Israel and the EC countries.

6.4.1. *The EC*

The EC countries employ temporary foreign (non-EC) workers. Different countries in the EC design different policies with regard to the employment of the foreign temporary workers. The temporary workers in the EC can be divided into two main groups: highly skilled workers and seasonal workers (or as defined in the UK 'working holiday makers'). The majority of the temporary workers in the EC countries in 1999 are seasonal workers rather than highly skilled workers. Fifty-seven per cent of the workers in France and 84 per cent in Germany are seasonal workers while approximately 51 per cent in the UK are working holiday makers and seasonal agricultural workers (if we consider the short-term permit holders also as seasonal workers then the percentage increases to 72). In most countries temporary workers are limited to work for the employer from whom they have received the permit. Moreover, in most cases they usually have no possibility of changing their status from temporary to permanent workers (the UK is an exception where highly skilled workers can change their status to permanent workers after working for four years as temporary workers).

Comparing 1992 to 1996, 1997, 1998 and 1999 (see Table 6.1) we see that there has been a rather large change in the number of foreign temporary workers in different countries in the EC. The number of temporary workers during the last four years has been more or less the same. Moreover, in Germany and France the number of entry permits for temporary workers is more or less equal to the stock of migrants (and in some cases even higher). Thus, the temporary workers seem to be leaving the country legally rather than staying illegally in the host country.

In order to understand the different policies in different countries we now present a more detailed description of three countries: France, Germany, and the United Kingdom. The statistics described below with more detailed data are summarized in Table 6.1. In France there were 13 400 temporary workers in 1999. Of these 2800 were highly skilled workers (employees on secondment and researchers) while 7600 were seasonal workers. Most of the temporary workers are students holding passports from America, Canada, Brazil, Algeria, Poland, and Russia. If domestic workers are available for the jobs which the temporary workers are applying for, then there may be grounds for refusal of a permit to work in France. All workers are restricted to work in the jobs for which they have obtained the permit. The responsibility of obtaining the work

Table 6.1. *Temporary workers in thousands and in percentage of entries*

	1992	1996	1997	1998	1999
France					
Employees and secondment	0.9	0.8	1.0	1.2	1.8
	2	*7*	*9*	*12*	*15*
Researchers	0.9	1.2	1.1	1.0	1.0
	2	*10*	*10*	*10*	*8*
Seasonal workers	13.6	8.8	8.2	7.5	7.6
	32	*77*	*75*	*73*	*62*
Beneficiaries of provisional work permits	2.8	2.8	2.6	2.2	3.1
	7	*24*	*24*	*21*	*25*
Total	18.1	13.6	12.9	11.8	13.4
	43	*118*	*117*	*115*	*110*
Germany					
Workers employed under a service contract	115.1	45.8	38.5	33.0	40.0
	28	*17*	*13*	*12*	
Seasonal workers	212.4	220.9	226.0	201.6	223.4
	52	*84*	*79*	*73*	
Trainees	5.1	4.3	3.2	3.1	3.7
	1	*2*	*1*	*1*	
Total	332.6	271.0	267.7	237.7	267.1
	81	*103*	*94*	*86*	
United Kingdom					
Long-term permit holders (one year and over)*	12.7	19.1	22.0	25.0	30.6
Short-term permit holders*	14.0	17.0	20.4	23.5	21.8
Working holiday makers	24.0	33.0	33.3	40.8	45.8
Trainees	3.4	4.0	4.7		
Seasonal agricultural workers	3.6	5.5	9.3	9.4	9.8
Total	57.6	78.7	89.7	98.8	107.9

*Long- and short-term permits are now dedicated to highly skilled workers or those where skills are in short supply.

Notes: Figures in *Italic* represent the percentage of the category over the number of entries of permanent workers. Totals in the table may differ from those which can be calculated on the basis of the displayed figures because of rounding.

Source: OECD, Trends in International Migration, 2001.

permit is imposed on the employer rather than the worker. In the case of seasonal workers, the requirement to obtain a permit falls on the employer while the workers themselves must hold a temporary residence permit valid for the period of employment. In France, there are no quotas set for highly skilled workers while in the case of seasonal workers, under certain bilateral agreements such as with Morocco and Tunisia, quotas do exist. Seasonal workers are limited by age and must be between the ages of 17 and 50. Highly skilled workers are limited for nine months of work with a possibility of renewal, for a further nine months. On the other hand, the maximum duration of seasonal workers is 6 months while there is also, in some cases, a minimum duration period (for example: 4 months for workers from countries like Morocco and Tunisia).

In Germany there were 267 100 temporary workers in 1999 divided into two main groups: workers employed under contract for services (40 000) and seasonal workers (223 400). The employment of a temporary worker can be arranged only under bilateral agreements made by Germany with the home country of the workers. In some cases, the employer of the worker in the home country must also approve such employment (especially in the case of workers employed under contract). The workers must be at least 18 years old and hold a working permit. The availability of domestic workers can affect the employment of seasonal workers. However, it will not affect the employment of workers employed under contract. On the other hand, there are quotas for service workers while there are no quotas for seasonal workers. Germany also limits the duration of the workers' stay: workers employed under a contract for services are employed for a maximum of 2 years (3 in some exceptional cases) and seasonal workers are limited to 3 months per year.

United Kingdom also permits the employment of temporary workers and sets similar restrictions to those described above. In 1999 there were 107 900 temporary workers in the UK divided into three main groups: long-term permit holders (30 600), short-term permit holders (21 800)[8] and working holiday makers (45 800). Highly skilled workers need work permits while seasonal workers are not required to have such permits. The highly skilled workers can change employers under specific conditions. The availability of domestic workers can affect the possibility of employing seasonal workers while it has no effect on the highly skilled workers. Seasonal workers must be unmarried, aged between 17 and 27 and have sufficient finances to return home after the holiday. There are no quotas set for temporary workers in the UK. Highly skilled workers are authorized to stay in the UK for up to 4 years while renewals are possible, subject to the same conditions as when first accepted. Renewal permits normally do not exceed 36 months. Holiday workers, on the other hand, are limited to 2 years without the possibility of renewal.

6.4.2. *The case of Israel*

Until the 1990s the Israeli economy relied on foreign workers who came to work in the morning and went home at the end of the day. This situation was very convenient, as the country did not need to import foreign workers

---

[8] Both long-term and short-term permits are now dedicated to highly skilled workers or those where skills are in short supply.

permanently or for temporary stays in Israel. These foreign workers were Arabs who came to work in the Israeli cities from the Gaza Strip and the West Bank. During the late 1980s and the early 1990s the workers became a threat to the Israeli population, as it was difficult to distinguish between Arab terrorists and workers whose only objective was to work. As the number of Israeli casualties increased and the various methods of protection did not succeed in stemming the number of terrorist attacks, the Israeli authorities decided to decrease the number of Arab workers working in the different Israeli cities (for example, in order to decrease the probability that a worker could be a terrorist, at different periods of time, the Israeli authorities allowed only married workers above the age of 35 to work in Israeli cities). The decrease in the number of Arab workers working in the Israeli cities, and lack of workers for other reasons, caused a shortage in specific sectors. The authorities thus decided to permit the import of temporary workers for a certain period of time.

To minimize the number of temporary workers deciding to stay illegally following the termination of the legal permit, the Israeli authorities decided to implement a policy under which an employer who received approval to import temporary workers could do so for a period of 5 years but had to renew the permit after 2 years. After the 5 years the worker must leave the host country for at least one year before he can return to the host country. The reason for insisting that the worker must leave Israel for one year is the high probability that the employer will not hold the job for the foreign worker for that period of time and thus may employ a local or different worker. If the foreign worker returns to Israel after a year it is as a result of the economical situation of the country. The employer would place a bond of around Euro 1250 for each worker imported, returnable when the legal temporary worker leaves the host country. If the worker left the legal employer and became an illegal migrant then the legal employer would forfeit the bond. The legal foreign workers receive high-level modern health care paid by the employer. In many cases, if a foreign worker becomes illegal and needs health care then either the worker pays it him/herself or, in the case where the worker cannot afford it, the government pays (however, then the authority will know that the worker is illegal and he/she will be deported).

The bond that was imposed on the employer shifted the responsibility, of the workers leaving the country legally, from the government to the employer. As described above, the incentive of the legal immigrant to stay illegally in Israel decreased as a result of this policy. However, many temporary workers still stayed in Israel illegally after their legal employment terminated. As we can see from Table 6.2 the estimated proportion of legal and illegal workers were more or less identical in 1995 and 1996 (56 100 legal temporary workers in 1995 and 47 000 illegal workers; in 1996 the number of workers increased, the legal to 85 200 and the illegal to 74 000). Over time, as a result of this market failure, when employers lost their bond as a result of legal migrants staying illegally in Israel, the employers started contracting an agreement whereby legal temporary workers would receive part of their income when they left the host country. A different agreement used was that of workers posting a bond, in his/her host country, in favour of the new employer, before entering Israel. This ensured that he/she would leave Israel at the end of the period agreed. As we can see from Table 6.2 this new policy rapidly decreased the growth of temporary workers staying illegally in Israel on the termination of their legal agreement.

This brings about the question regarding the duration of legal and illegal workers in Israel. Table 6.3 presents the duration distribution of legal and illegal workers in Israel in 1999. It is clear from the table that most of the legal and illegal workers depart from the country within 2 years. For the legal workers this is a direct result of the contract between the workers and the employers (which is dictated, in many cases, by law). The percentage of illegal workers staying in Israel over 2 years is around 10 per cent. In general we could say that most legal and illegal workers leave inside 2 years while a small proportion of illegal workers stay in Israel over this period of time. We should note that many of the illegal workers were legal before becoming illegal. Thus, the duration of an illegal worker's stay, which includes the time spent as a legal worker, is longer and is around 4–5 years. With high probability we could say

Table 6.2. *Estimated number of illegal foreign temporary workers in Israel 1995–99 (thousands)*

Year	Source	Total legal foreign temporary workers	Estimated total illegal foreign workers
1995	CBS	56.1	47
1996	CBS	85.2	74
1997	Rasuth	64	76
1998	Rasuth	80.5	88.6
1999	Rasuth	67.2	79.3

Source: CBS, The Israeli Central Bureau of Statistics; Rasuth, The Israeli Ministry of Labor and Welfare.

Table 6.3. *Duration of legal and illegal workers in Israel in 1999 (in per cent)*

Period in months	Legal	Illegal
1–6	7.6	1
7–12	45.8	52.1
13–24	44.2	37.1
25+	2.4	9.8
Total	100.00	100.00

Source: Bar Tzuri (2001).

that workers who have spent over 4 years in the country without leaving to visit their home country (illegal workers cannot re-enter after departing) would prefer to stay permanently in Israel. However, as we can see, the number of such workers is less than 10 per cent out of the stock of illegal workers.

6.4.3. *The EC and Israel*

The main outstanding difference between the EC and Israel is that most temporary workers in the EC are seasonal workers coming to work for short periods of time (a few months) while in Israel the temporary workers come for a longer period of time (5 years). Moreover, the temporary workers in Israel are mostly low skilled while in EC countries the per cent of low-skilled temporary workers is lower than in Israel. The low-skilled foreign workers in Israel receive health care financed by the employer. This is not always the case in the EC.

The low-skilled workers' income in Israel increases the welfare of the families left in the home country through the transfers sent back by the worker. Thus, the long period of employment of foreign temporary workers in Israel (5 years) enables both the local employer and the workers to take full advantage of the temporary worker policy. This long period of time decreases the costs for both sides and increases their welfare.

One main difference between Israel and the EC is that when a contracted temporary migrant enters one country he/she is in the EC and may decide to migrate to a different country within the EC and ask for asylum. This may open up new possibilities for asylum seekers: the migrants enter the EC legally and then go from a low welfare country to a high welfare country. In this way the migrants can increase their probability of receiving an asylum. A bond together with forced savings could decrease this phenomena to some extent as a worker moving to a different country within the EC is leaving illegally his/her employer and thus the worker will lose his/her forced savings and the employer will lose the bond posted when the worker entered the country.

Even though there is pressure by employers, Israel does not have any policies to permit temporary highly skilled workers in the country. Highly skilled temporary workers are conceived by the Israeli authorities as a threat to the local highly skilled workers, threatening the income and employment of the local population.

Comparing the temporary foreign worker policy in the EC and Israel seems to reveal three main pillars that enable the implementation of a successful policy: (a) a relatively long period of time that the worker can stay in the host country; (b) the ability to make sure that the workers leave at the end of the period; and (c) the low threat to the local population. The first pillar decreases the cost for both sides and increases efficiency. The second pillar is aimed at decreasing the possibility of creating an illegal migration. The third pillar determines what type of workers are allowed under such a policy. Should these workers be high- or low-skilled workers? Should the policy be pre-empted only for certain professions? The answer to these questions must be determined individually by each country. Choosing the right type of workers will decrease the threat to the local population and will thereby receive political support both from the employers and the local population.

These three pillars seem to be the basic framework for a successful temporary foreign worker policy. Such a policy will enable an increase in the local population's welfare and increase the welfare of the temporary workers and their family in the home country.

6.5. CONCLUSIONS

While many workers migrate only temporarily, and the benefits to both origin and host economy may depend on the duration of stay in the host economy, little policy analysis has been given to the choice between temporary and permanent migrants. We have presented the basis of a framework for accepting temporary contracted workers under which the workers will enter the host country for a given period of time and at the end of that period return home to the host country. Under quite weak assumptions this policy could benefit both the host and the home country of the migrant. The fact, that the workers are temporary, decreases the political resistance in the destination country to a high level of immigration—as for example, has occurred in Switzerland. One of the main questions this raises is how to implement such a policy.

Drawing upon evidence from the policy carried out in Israel and in the different EC countries it would seem that the successful implementation of a temporary foreign worker policy has three requirements: (a) a relatively long period of time for the worker to stay in the host country; (b) the ability to make sure that the workers leave at the end of the period; and (c) the low threat to the local population. The third requirement determines the types of workers to be allowed to enter the host country. The latter will depend on the economic needs of each of the countries in question. This will increase the political support for such a policy both from the employers and from the local population (see Epstein and Hillman, 2000; Tapinos, 1999).

The second requirement seems to be the most difficult to implement. As presented above, and given the experience in Israel, a bond could be undertaken to make sure that the temporary legal worker will return to the origin country. There are two types of bonds: (1) a bond imposed on the employer, and (2) a bond imposed on the worker. The bond imposed on the employer transfers the responsibility for the worker leaving the host country at the end of the period, from the authorities to the employer. This policy does not always work and as we can see from the case of Israel, the total number of illegal immigrants, staying after completing their legally permitted time, increased over time. The second possibility is imposing a bond on the legal migrant. The legal migrant may not have many assets and as such it would be difficult to impose such a bond on him. However, the possibility of 'forced savings', under which the worker is required to save part of his income and receive it only if he leaves legally (such as social security and medical care), seems to be a more efficient policy to decrease the number of migrants that remain after their legally permitted period. Thus, the combination of forced savings together with a bond imposed on the employer will increase the number of immigrants leaving the country legally.

A temporary contracted workers' policy could be considered, at first, in the form of seasonal workers which already exists in many countries and thus the countries would only have to increase the number of permits for such workers.

7

Managing European Immigration

7.1. OPENING EU LABOUR MARKETS

The political backdrop in Europe provides a clear message that a 'window' has opened to promote changes in European migration policies. The European Council, meeting at Tampere in October 1999, determined that a common EU policy on 'asylum and migration' was called for. The complex and wide ranging impact of immigration policy over social, economic, legal, and cultural areas were considered to undermine reliance on a piecemeal individual country approach to legislation as anticipated in Article 63 of the EC Treaty. Furthermore, the Commission reviews the 'zero migration' policies of the past twenty years—mindful of the co-existence of illegal immigration, estimated by Europol at 500 000 persons per annum, and growing skilled labour shortages—and considers that channels for legal immigration to the Union should now be made available for migrants. The not inconsiderable political threats to this 'open doors' approach appear to be the consequences of an imminent serious recession and the aftershock of the terrorist attacks on America. Assuming these obstacles are surmountable, what should be the commonly agreed objectives and policy proposals of EU migration policy? We are mindful that migration policies go beyond the immediate issues of the grounds for admission to the EU to include policy against racism, towards assimilation, etc., but in this context we have nevertheless limited our discussion to the more narrow task of policy towards migration flows. We have organized our response by examining migration policy under the channels for migration: Eastern enlargement, family unification, asylum for refugees, illegal migration, and economic migration.

7.2. EASTERN ENLARGEMENT

It is unlikely that Eastern enlargement will have significant effects on employment and income distribution in the affected regions. However, there is a high degree of uncertainty as to the actual outcome of introducing the free movement: migration from the CEECs has been restricted so far. Enlargement policies have to take into account this uncertainty, since introducing the free movement is an irreversible decision.

The policy proposal of staggered integration by the EC will, however, neither reduce this uncertainty nor mitigate the adverse implications on labour markets. First, given the slow speed of convergence, the migration potential from the East will decline only by marginal numbers until 2010. Moreover, by simply postponing migration, little can be learned about the actual migration potential from transitional periods. As a consequence, the EU will stand roughly at the same square in 2010. Second, migration will be channelled, according to statements of the member states (see, e.g. Schröder, 2000), mainly by temporary work permits during the transitional period. Temporary work permits may mainly select low-skilled migrants. This may have, as in the case of guest-worker recruitment, long-term implications for the skill composition of migrants which are enforced by chain migration. As a consequence, transitional periods may have an adverse impact on the skill composition of migrants from the East.

In contrast to this proposal, quota arrangements and safeguard clauses have three advantages: First, they can help to reduce uncertainty on the size of actual migration. If properly designed, utilization rates of quotas provide information on the propensity to migrate. They can be lifted if application rates show that they are not filled up. Both, quotas and safeguard clauses can be easily monitored through work permits. Second, they reduce migration pressures after the end of the transitional period. In contrast to simply postponing migration, the migration potential is reduced step by step if quotas or safeguard clauses are applied. This allows a smooth adjustment. Third, they are either neutral for the selection of migrants (safeguard clauses) or they can affect the skill composition of migrants favourably, for example, when quotas are allocated by point systems which take human capital characteristics into account.

The introduction of the free movement may have adverse implications on the sending countries and regions. The outflow of labour, in particular of high-skilled labour, may reduce welfare of those left behind. Although fears of a 'brain drain' are exaggerated, compensatory policies of the EU should address the sending rather than the receiving regions. Instead of preventing migration, compensatory measures such as allocating some means from the structural and cohesion funds to the education sector in the CEECs will help to increase welfare on both sides.

7.3. FAMILY UNIFICATION

About half of the migration into EU countries arises from the right of those settled in the EU to bring dependants to live with them. This proportion is likely to rise if migration policies are successful. This right is subject to qualifying criteria such as non-dependence on public funds. The share of family unification migration is even greater in the US, comprising 72 per cent of permanent settlers in 1998. The extent to which the flows in this channel of immigration will continue to rise in the EU will have a major influence on the direction of legal inflows: the unanticipated acceleration in the US of legal immigration in the 1990s is partly due to the emphasis on family ties to persons living in the US as the factor that determines whether a visa applicant is admitted, and the increased tendency for migrants in the past decades to come from low or middle income countries. The incremental recent migration into the EU is also primarily from low and middle income countries, and it would be unsurprising if a similar pattern of rising family unification migration occurs in the EU. In the UK, family unification migration rose by 20 per cent in 1999 and 15 per cent in 1998.

Although there is evidence that family unification has contributed to welfare dependency in some EU countries, the case for restricting such migration is contentious. Policies supporting family cohesion and the nurturing of children lie at the heart of EU social policy, and a change in this area is not recommended. However, EU countries should consider the incentives for immigrant destination choice provided by differing national policies towards family criteria for entry, and in particular that towards siblings. As with other areas of immigration policy the case for a common EU policy is strong. The importance of family unification migration in the EU may well be in setting a baseline of unexceptionable migration that together with the internal social constraints on immigration—described in Chapter 4—will limit the acceptability of migration through other channels.

7.4. DEVELOPING A COMMON EUROPEAN ASYLUM AND REFUGEE POLICY

European Union member states are signatories of the 1951 Geneva Convention which 'provides for access to work as a direct individual right stemming from the status of refugee and cannot be made dependent on an economic needs test'.[1] The choice of the countries of destination by humanitarian migrants is, similar to other forms of migration, affected by economic benefits and costs.[2] National standards with regard to asylum and refugee policies differ widely, and, as a consequence, humanitarian migrants are extremely unequally distributed across individual countries in the EU as well as the rest of the world. Moreover, empirical evidence suggests that the labour market performance of humanitarian migrants lags behind those of other foreigners and that they depend on welfare in a disproportionate fashion (Hansen, 2000; Pederson, 2000). As a result, national standards of admitting asylum seekers and refugees have been tightened in several EU countries, among them the most affected country, Germany. Further measures to restrict the admission of humanitarian migrants are under discussion in several member states (Section 4.1). Thus, the national regulation of humanitarian migration is producing a 'race to the

---

[1] Communication from the Commission to the Council and the European Parliament on a Community Immigration Policy, 2000, p. 12.
[2] See Rotte and Vogler, 1998, for empirical evidence.

bottom'. The combination of an unchanging policy towards the scale of family unification, and the expected Eastern enlargement, are likely to reduce the scale of economic and humanitarian migration that EU residents will wish to accept. Insofar as an economic migrant category 'door' is opened to potential EU immigrants then the EU might simply give preference to those coming with humanitarian cases, or vary the economic places by skill according to the scale of humanitarian migration in that skill category.

As long as the EU members and their constituencies rely on the same set of norms, the policy solution is straightforward: agree on a common set of rules for admitting asylum seekers and refugees into the EU, co-ordinate the implementation of the rules, and share the costs of humanitarian migration equally, for example, by a fund for asylum seekers, refugees, and other humanitarian migrants. This will internalize costs and prevent countries with more generous policies being penalized. Against the background of large differences in national standards, the policy problem is to agree on a common set of norms to guide European asylum and refugee policies. A set of minimum standards, which are partially financed at the European level, while national policies remain free to admit further non-financed humanitarian migrants, may be a first step in the right direction toward a common European asylum and refugee policy.

The administrative costs of large fluctuations in the number of asylum seekers that accompanies the present non-coordinated outcomes are very large as the UK is finding—post 1998—with more than twice as many asylum seekers presently entering the UK than the US. These dramatic fluctuations reduce the demand for asylum in the host country, and make a humanitarian policy less popular. The EU countries may need to reach an agreement on which refugees should be protected, but this should not be insuperable.

This co-ordination concerning refugees within the EU might also strengthen the influence of the EU on immigration policy in the other affluent countries. This is not unimportant from the EU viewpoint. Despite very slow population growth, Western Europe remains one of the most densely populated areas of the world, with high marginal congestion costs in comparison with most of the other OECD countries that might absorb refugees.

7.5. ECONOMIC AND ILLEGAL MIGRATION

The EU, with other OECD countries, will experience a secular shift in the demographic structure of its population in the next decades. Low fertility rates and increasing life expectancy will substantially increase dependency ratios, that is, the ratio of the non-working age population to the working-age population. Figure 7.1 displays the general trend on the basis of the demographic scenario of the World Bank: the dependency ratio will start to increase from levels of slightly below 50 per cent in the present EU after 2010, and tend to converge to levels of above 80 per cent around four decades later. This scenario relies, as any other demographic scenario, on a set of strong

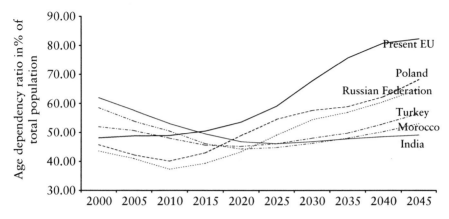

Figure 7.1. *Ageing in the EU and in a sample of immigration countries*

Source: World Development Indicators, 2000; own calculations.

assumptions, and presumes that migration has only a minor impact on population growth.[3] The general demographic trend holds for all EU members. Germany and the southern European countries are, due to extraordinarily low fertility rates, particularly affected.

There is an extensive debate concerning whether it makes sense to manage the demographic structure of societies. Whereas a large number of authors are critical (e.g. Coleman, 1992; OECD, 1991), others argue that immigration can help to provide time for the economic system to adjust (Börsch-Supan, 1993; Straubhaar and Zimmermann, 1993). Generational accounting exercises indeed demonstrate that, after setting off the net present value of claims and contributions to social security systems, the native population will receive a net gain (Bonin, 2001). The electorate, which as we found in Chapter 5 is unsympathetic to policies to facilitate immigration, might also be offered a democratic choice between an older retirement age and greater immigration.

The contribution of migration to mitigate demographic pressures on the welfare systems will nevertheless be in any case limited: following a recent study of the UN (UN, 2000), an average net migration of around 1.4 million people is needed between 1995 and 2050 to maintain a stable share of the working-age population in the EU (2005–10: 550 000 p.a., 2010–50: 1.6 million p.a.). It is unlikely that a net migration of this size can be achieved, since ageing is a global phenomenon: in Figs 7.1 and 7.2 we have displayed the dependency ratios and the share of those aged 20–35 in the male population, that is, the share of individuals which have the highest propensity to migrate, for a representative sample of the main source countries of non-EU foreigners.

---

[3] The World Bank presumes that net migration will decline: starting from 0.8 per thousand of the EU's population in the period 2000–05, it declines to 0.4 in 2006–10, 0.2 in 2010–15, 0.1 in 2015–25 and then to zero.

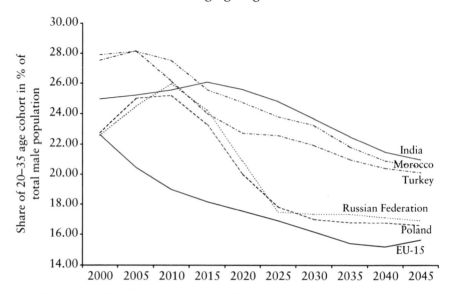

Figure 7.2. *Share of the 20–35 age cohort in the male population for the EU-15 and main source countries, 2000–45*

Source: World Development Indicators, 2000; own calculations.

In source countries with relatively high human capital endowments, that is, the Central and Eastern European countries, we observe a similar pattern as in the EU, with one interesting exception: dependency ratios tend to decline until 2010, since relatively large cohorts reach the working age until this time. After a peak in 2010, the decline in birth rates after transition can be felt and the demographic structure converges to that of the EU (see Coleman, 1993, for a detailed discussion). In contrast, in source countries with relatively low human capital endowments, we observe falling dependency ratios until 2025. The share of the young cohorts in the working-age population tend to fall from 2010 onwards, but they are nevertheless substantially higher than those of the EU and the CEECs. Thus, the shares of the age cohorts with high propensity to migrate tend to fall in countries with relatively high human capital endowments, but remain high in countries with relatively low human capital endowments. As long as education does not improve in these countries substantially, the supply of unskilled labour will therefore tend to increase relative to skilled labour.

As a consequence of the demographic challenge, the opening of EU labour markets to non-EU immigrants is under discussion in the EU[4] and its

---

[4] The formulation of a Common Immigration policy is demanded in Art. 63 of the Treaty of Amsterdam from 1997, without stating a specific time schedule. The European Council asked the European Commission to elaborate policy proposals, see, for example, the recent Communication of the European Commission (EC, 2001). A comprehensive proposal is, however, still missing.

member states.[5] The demographic challenge is, however, not the only reason to revise 'zero' labour immigration policies. As we have seen in the previous sections, an emphasis upon family unification and humanitarian migration has not given proportionate representation to highly skilled immigration. Economic migration provides an opportunity to balance the skill composition of migrants. Whatever the reasons are, a revision of the policy of 'zero' labour immigration is now on the EU agenda.

Laissez-faire vs selective immigration policies. Complete *laissez-faire* is not a political option, but it forms the implicit counterfactual to all policy proposals. In an economy without externalities or international remittances, the laissez-faire approach yields the optimal allocation of labour across countries. However, migrants who pay taxes and contribute to social security systems also receive social benefits and consume goods which are provided by public means. As a consequence, a selective migration policy, which attempts to increase the social benefits from migration by admitting migrants from which it expects that their social contribution exceeds social costs, can increase welfare in the host countries relative to a laissez-faire approach.

Selecting high-skilled vs less-skilled workers. In the closed-economy framework, the benefits from migration increase if factor endowments of immigrants are complementary to those of natives. Thus, a country with a high-skilled labour force benefits more from the immigration of relatively low-skilled labour and vice versa—at least if low-skilled labour does not suffer from unemployment. However, in addition to the adverse effect on the income distribution of EU natives, the post-war immigration episode provides rich evidence that unemployment and welfare dependency risks are closely related to the skill levels of migrants. These welfare risks tilt the comparative EU country benefits of migration towards migrants with favourable skill endowments. Moreover, the demand for unskilled labour has declined continuously due to factors such as skill-biased technological change. As a consequence, most OECD countries pursue an immigration policy that favours high-skilled workers, and the EU countries appear poised to recruit extensively university level immigrants to enable economic growth to continue without wage inflation or increased wage inequality.

Point systems vs auctions. For an immigration policy which explicitly addresses the selection of migrants, there are basically two mechanisms to organize the allocation: point systems and auctions. Point systems have been adopted in Canada, Australia, and more recently, in Switzerland. The immigration commission of the German government has recently proposed a similar system. Point systems may improve the allocation significantly relative to

---

[5] In Germany, a council of experts under the head of Rita Süssmuth has been commissioned by the federal government to provide proposals for a revised immigration policy. The Süssmuth report proposes *inter alia* the provision of 40 000 work permits p.a. to non-EU foreigners (FR, June 29, 2001).

policies which channel migration by family reunification and other non-economic mechanisms. Point systems are relatively easy to implement, but have a series of deficiencies: (i) the criteria of the system may distort an efficient allocation, since they need not match actual demand on host labour markets, (ii) even if an efficient allocation is achieved initially, time lags between the allocation and the actual landing of migrants may distort the selection, (iii) point systems cannot address unexpected events such as recessions (Bauer and Zimmermann, 2000). Auctions can allocate work and residence permits either to migrants or to firms. At first glance auctions are quite appealing, because an auction selects migrants or firms according to their abilities and needs and their willingness to pay. However, they have two main drawbacks: first, selecting migrants by auctions may yield an unfavourable selection, since high-skilled migrants may move to countries which have no auctions in place. If firms auction for migrants, transaction costs are high. Moreover, the allocation is difficult to monitor and to enforce. Thus, for practical reasons, a favourable composition of migrants with regard to their skills and other human capital characteristics is probably best achieved by an allocation using a points system.

Overall, opening EU labour markets to immigration from non-EU countries is a chance to favourably affect the composition of the EU labour force with regard to their skills and other human capital characteristics. This does not imply that labour immigration should be restricted solely to high-skilled workers, but immigration policies should balance the skill characteristics of economic and 'family' migrants in a way that assures that future immigrants will not depend on welfare in disproportionate fashion and strengthen incentives to invest in country specific and other human capital. However, the extent to which a given intake of skilled economic migrants into the EU will balance less skilled migrants from other categories, may well vary between EU countries, so that for language reasons such a policy may reflect more favourably on the UK, than say, France.

The scale of illegal immigration and refugee arrivals (together, about 700 000 p.a.) into the EU reduces the issue of whether to attract 150–250 000 high-skill migrants to rather modest proportions. Arguments regarding the mitigation of the costs of illegal and refugee migration are very important to the EU and contribute to us advancing a further proposal.

7.6. TOWARDS A CO-ORDINATED POLICY WITH COUNTRIES OF ORIGIN

There are two economic reasons which suggest that the EU should cease to pursue unilateral policies towards migration from low/middle income countries of origin: (1) the costs of high (500 000 per annum) illegal flows and the gains from policies to induce efficient policing, and (2) the costs of refugee migration. The origin countries may value the remittances and reductions in unemployment which accompany unskilled migration, but would wish to adopt policies to mitigate the externality costs that result from skilled worker/entrepreneur migration. It is in the interests of both recipient and origin countries that skilled labour is employed where, net of all non-pecuniary considerations, it is most productive. The origin countries are likely to be concerned that skilled labour should gain overseas experience and savings, but return after a brief period, on the grounds that such workers generate externalities of various kinds and are thus net contributors to the country. The essence of the agreement would provide a framework within which the EU compensates the origin country (assumed middle or low income) for the estimated mean externalities lost by skilled workers' migration, but would reduce the sum with 'fines' arising from illegal flows and violations of domestic human rights standards, partly measured by refugee flows. This is intended to produce a pool of income to origin least developed countries (LDCs), and to encourage origin countries to assist with policies to control illegal outflows.

To implement this, the EU might determine 'skill' by the earnings of migrants in the EU country concerned, and given a base line of (say) mean EU earnings, repatriate x per cent of the individual's tax payments above the tax contribution of a household earning the mean income in that country—along the lines of the brain drain tax as discussed by Bhagwati. Against this income the EU would deduct fines for illegal immigrants, and refugee flows (Sample surveys could be used to gauge tax contributions in order to safeguard invasion of individual migrant's privacy). The partnership with origin countries might prompt the view that permanent migration of skilled workers should be limited to a quota below the laissez-faire level, and a policy institution sought to preserve some of this gain from skilled migration. We have discussed in Chapter 5 how a rotation of temporary migrants allows potentially more workers to acquire savings and skills to use in the origin country, than with permanent migrants who, evidence suggests, gradually lose contact with their origin country. The implementation of such a policy framework would require careful preparation, but by working in partnership with a group of LDCs, this would be a quite different political contract to the 'guest worker' programmes of the 1960s, and instead should be partly viewed as part of the EU international development programme.

The OECD countries presently aim, through foreign aid, various charities, the World Bank and other institutions, to enable LDCs to gradually reach Western living standards. If the talent pool is substantially eroded by unilateral policies prompting a race to hire and assimilate LDC talent, the more realistic future for these countries may at best be a slower growth and at worst, be a permanently lagging region within a world economy in which the US and EU become increasingly dominant. The political, social, and economic implications of this may prove much more costly to unpack than the plunder of third world resources during the colonial period, and reinforce the case for co-operative policies towards immigration and balanced economic development.

Comments

MICHAEL BURDA

Europe is best described as a tribal mosaic. It consists of a great many individual sociological identities, peoples living alongside each other, each identifying more or less exclusively with one of a great many parallel histories. Given this backdrop, it seems no accident that Europe was the cradle of the Western nation-state. Because that notion has been frequently abused—and because Europeans continue to treat its ethnic minorities poorly, even to this day— Europe has been a traditional *source* of migration, to the United States and Canada, to South America, and to Oceania.

Not surprisingly, institutions of Europe have grown up around this 'culture of immobility' and have been designed not only to support it, but also to defend it—in typical tribal fashion—against outsiders. This attribute has been strengthened by selection, to the extent openness and tolerance have genetic origins with more open and tolerant individuals seeking like individuals and accommodating cultural constellations abroad. Just as tribes are wont to take care of their own, it was natural that a social safety net developed in Europe as an expression of national *solidarity*. In a tribal culture, or in a small village, this type of solidarity can only emerge when common cultures, histories, and traditions admit it.

In a globalized world, a tribal existence is anachronistic and potentially dangerous, raising prospects of social conflict, violence, and war. Yet, given this historical backdrop of exclusion, Europe has now become a *sink* for immigration. This is hardly surprising: continental Europe saw a later industrial maturation, now reaching or even exceeding levels of GDP per capita in the US. In contrast to much of the previous century, Europe looks largely democratic and is governed, for the most part, by rule of law. For most of its civilized part, the risk of war has been banished, and prosperity abounds. A persistent shortage of unskilled labour characterizes even the poorest EU economies. In the spirit of integration, intra-EU borders have attained the characteristic of Swiss cheese.

Given all these facts, it is not difficult to conclude that Europe is fundamentally different from the United States. In their impressive report, Brücker *et al.* illustrate this point in both expected and unexpected ways. While the US and Europe exhibit striking similarities with respect to the sheer volume of migrants, we learn that xenophobic tendencies are significantly higher in Europe. Because, Europe does not yet want to face its 'immigration problem' openly, it receives an inferior selection of low-skilled illegals and refugees, lowering the potential gains it might reap from opening its borders. At the same time, it remains difficult to pin down purely economic reasons for policy paralysis in Europe, nor is it easy to explain Europe's reticence to accept migrants, since the obvious economic candidates do not seem to work.[1]

It could be that the authors have not worked hard enough on this aspect. For my thinking, the report is short on an overall framework for the economics of migration. For me—and for a great deal of others who have thought about the subject—migration is an investment, with all of the attributes of an investment, or even a human capital investment (Sjaastad, 1962). As such, it is imperative to use concepts related to investment decisions to understand migration, to understand the limitations of forecasts made using data from the past, and maybe even to understand the different reception migrants have received in Europe compared with other parts of the world. Let me explore some of the implications of this old but neglected idea.

First, migration represents an investment for the migrant; that is obvious enough. The fact that migration has occurred indicates—abstracting from refugees to some extent—that the investment was worth it; it met the criteria of positive expected net present discounted value, at least *ex ante*. Migration is also an investment for the receiving country, although the immediate gains may be difficult to identify in the first instance.[2] This 'investment' must include the political and efficiency costs of distributional conflict resulting when shifts occur in supply and demand for production factors. These subtle conflicts are exacerbated if labour markets are distorted, and if an increased social safety net burden increases distortionary taxation.

Second, migration represents an investment for the receiving country. Otherwise what appears to be xenophobia could simply be a reflection that the receiving country has lost something (in per capita terms). Everyone knows that migrants bring observable and unobservable attributes which can make their contribution increasingly attractive to the host economy, for example, if they raise the national endowments of other factors, or if there are positive external effects. Human and financial capital—if not physical capital!—are transportable and may be part of a joint package. At the same time, it may be difficult to attract the right migrants, as recent policy discussions in Germany have illustrated, and as the well-known work of Borjas using the Roy model shows. Unless these effects are quite large, however, it is likely that *per capita* GDP (*including* the migrants) will decrease as an immediate short-run outcome of large migration flows, and will require an increase in savings (forgone consumption) or borrowing from abroad to recover the old growth path of

---

[1] Similarly, it is difficult, if not impossible, to explain violence against foreigners in Eastern Germany using economic covariates; see Krueger and Pischke (1997).

[2] To a crude first-order approximation which we know as the Solow decomposition, all national output gains from migration are captured by the migrants. Let $y = f(x_1, x_2, \ldots, x_n)$ describe production of output y in the host country using factors x_i, and assume that market distortions are fully absent. Log-linearization holding factor prices constant gives the change of production resulting from a small change in x_j as $\Delta \ln y = \alpha \Delta \ln x_j$ all of which is paid to the incoming factor. Constant factor prices are likely, however, to obtain only in small, unspecialized open economies.

physical, and especially infrastructural capital stocks. In the immediate short run, migration inflows can thus alter the national economic image of a nation, in the same way that it can alter its cultural *Leitbild* (to use an ugly German word). It would have been nice to see what the bounds are on this economics for the receiving country.

One aspect I missed acutely was some mention of the investment aspect—if any—for *sending* economies. In the 1960s, the notion of 'brain drain' was of central interest, that the loss of elites could hamper development in the developing world. How times have changed: the present report sketches policy options for an imperial EU, optimizing its intake of migrants without regard to the damage it may inflict on the rest of the world. The sending countries, including some potential EU accession countries, will lose a sizeable chunk of their tax base, productive factors, and shrink in absolute size. In the absence of some pretty subtle arguments, it is reasonable to expect that if an aggressive migrant recruitment policy is a good idea in the West, it will be a bad one for the East. 'Beggar thy neighbour' is the first reaction I have: it is one thing to vacate large regions of Poland, Slovakia, the Ukraine, and Romania, and it is another to take their programmers, engineers, doctors, and especially their entrepreneurs.

The harms might be undone if migrants return after some period of time and contribute once again economically to the country of origin. Sadly there was no coherent discussion of return migration in this paper. The gross flows between Turkey and Germany are much larger than the net changes in resident population, and some discussion of the age structure of return migrants would have been illuminating. Table 7.1 shows that even in the shrinking *Bundesländer* of East Germany there are positive gross flows; older people, frustrated migrants, and hopefully the talented homesick are returning in large numbers. Why did not the report address this issue in the international context? Certainly some persistent questioning of interior ministries would have yielded information on this score. Even if return migration is significant, the loss of people in the youngest and most productive years may stunt growth in the source country in ways which are not well understood.

Table 7.1. *Population of selected German states since unification*

	1990	1995	1998	% Change
Age 25–40				
Bavaria	2745.2	3052.9	2963	7.9
Hessia	1388.6	1535	1487.6	7.1
Mecklenburg	479.7	444.6	411.5	−14.2
Saxony	1053.8	1013.7	971.2	−7.8
Age > 65				
Bavaria	1723.1	1854.2	1894.8	10.0
Hessia	892	949	965.2	8.2
Mecklenburg	209.1	226.6	248.1	18.7
Saxony	749	768.9	783.9	4.7

Source: Statistisches Bundesamt.

Naturally, the central question is whether this report be used to assist future EU immigration policy. The econometric evidence—both the estimates and the forecasts—certainly reflects a lot of hard work. Good consistent data on migration flows are not easy to come by. Yet, the price for this data quality is that the estimates involve only Germany, and strictly speaking, represent evidence only for this not particularly representative European country. This is a rather severe limitation indeed. Econometric evidence is problematic for a plethora of reasons, and even if we want to use it for policy I would like to have seen at least one other country considered—Denmark and Sweden certainly maintain very good information on migrants.

In addition, a number of other estimation issues and specification issues arise. The Lucas critique looms large in this application, since the estimates are conducted under a different policy regime. After accession we will see many policy measures which enhance substitutes for migration, such as trade integration and capital mobility. How can expectations be adequately modelled in such a setting? What is the role of growth prospects at home? In a related context, I have shown (Burda, 1995) that the option value of waiting may be large in the migration context; under these conditions high and variable growth at home will actually keep migrants at home. Is there any way one could quantify these aspects, perhaps using information from the sending country? Another question involves confidence intervals, which are likely to be very large in this exercise. How much of the variance in the forecasts is due to parameter uncertainty, and how much to variance in the exogenous factors? It would be interesting to see the relative importance of some of the dummy variables such as civil war or the country-specific dummies, since a proper forecast must assign some probability to the event that another conflict erupts in the Balkans, or a crisis arises in Algeria. To cover themselves on these problems, the authors could have looked at more even studies and examples—the dynamics of Portuguese, Italian, and Spanish cases with respect to Germany would have proved useful.

Overall, the report tackles a huge problem of great contemporary importance. I think a bit more attention to the relevant theoretical literature might have helped in drawing clearer policy implications as well as designing the empirical specification. I realize that the brief is to explore the interaction of social policy with migration. Yet, for precisely that reason, the theory of migration needs to be taken seriously in attempting to understand the tribal aspects of Europe and its social safety net, in contrast to 'friendlier' countries with fewer public goods at stake—US, Canada, Australia for example.

RICCARDO FAINI

This is a thoughtful and well-written essay. Not only does it break new grounds in the analysis of European migration. It also provides an impressive array of data and institutional information, as well as a comprehensive and insightful survey of existing empirical evidence. It will be of considerable interest to migration specialists, policy-makers, and economists.

The main messages of the paper can be summarized as follows:

1. Migration flows toward Europe are on the rise and are quantitatively large.
2. Attitudes in Europe toward migrants have grown increasingly hostile.
3. At first blush, such attitudes are difficult to rationalize. There is indeed little evidence that migration has a significantly negative impact either on wages or on unemployment. At the same time, though, the paper offers some new evidence showing that migrants make a disproportionate use of the European welfare system, particularly of unemployment and family benefits.
4. European migration policies are misguided. First, they have been ineffective in stemming the increase in migration flows. Second, while closing the front door of legal workers migration, they have virtually neglected the side door of family reunification and the back door of illegal immigration.[3] Both family reunification and illegal migration are skewed toward unskilled migrants, a fact that has exacerbated the negative impact of migration on the labour market and the welfare system.
5. Migration policies need to be thoroughly reformed. First, Europe must abandon the zero migration policy and acknowledge that it has become a major destination of international labour flows. Second, migration policies must be reformed with a view to encouraging skilled workers to move to Europe. The new approach to migration policy, however, should not penalize sending countries by fostering a further brain drain from poor regions. According to the paper, a system of contracted temporary migration that penalizes migrants for overstaying their visa could be designed so as to achieve all such objectives.

What is proposed therefore is nothing less than a radical overhaul of the European approach to migration. The point that in the past migration policies have been largely misguided is well taken. The zero migration policy that was adopted in Europe after 1974, in the wake of the first oil shock, in an effort to close the doors to further labour inflows and encourage return migration, has been a fiction that has, quite perversely, encouraged illegal and unskilled migration. I would only add in this respect that such a policy may have backfired also by lowering rather than increasing the propensity of migrants to return to their home country. Indeed, in a relatively free regime, returning migrants always retain the option of migrating again to the host country. However, if mobility is severely restricted, this option is no longer there, or at least has become much more costly. Under these circumstances, therefore, migrants may be loath to return home for fear of being unable to work again in the host country. A highly restrictive stance to migration can therefore induce temporary migrants to become permanent migrants. Similarly, it provides an

---

[3] I have borrowed this terminology from Thomas Straubhaar.

unintended incentive for single migrants to bring their family to the host country.

Despite its merits, the broad policy proposal of the paper raises many questions. Let me focus on the main ones.

First, the emphasis is exclusively on migration policies. The paper therefore neglects the possibility that other policies may have a significant, and perhaps unintended, impact on migration. Consider for instance trade policies in industrial countries. By restricting the flow of imports precisely in those sectors where developing countries have a comparative advantage, such policies act to discourage labour absorption in sending countries and to foster the demand for unskilled labour in host countries. On both counts, therefore, restrictive trade policies in key sectors such as agriculture and textiles and clothing tend to increase migration pressures. There are also additional more subtle effects. European agricultural policies are geared to keep domestic prices stable. Excess supply of agricultural goods is systematically unloaded onto the world markets. For such commodities, therefore, fluctuations in world prices will be substantially larger. If agricultural producers in sending countries are risk-averse, they will be more prone to migrate to Europe, where prices are significantly more stable. To sum up, trade liberalization could well be a palatable alternative (or at the very least an essential complement) to the proposed approach to migration policy.

Second, it is not clear whether and how the proposed approach of a contracted temporary migration skewed toward skilled workers will actually work; (1) the suggested forced saving scheme—where migrants pay higher social security contributions that are then refunded to them if they do not overstay their visa—may boost the incentive for legal migrants to move at an early stage to the underground economy, (2) while the proposed scheme worked well in Israel where it was designed to attract unskilled migrants, its effectiveness in a European context where the main objective should be to raise the skill content of migrants is much less obvious, (3) European migration policies in the sixties have highlighted the pitfalls of schemes that rely on temporary workers to fill permanent posts.

Third, the global implications of such a scheme needs to be thoroughly investigated. The imposition of tight limits on unskilled migration would, if it was ever effective, strongly undermine the convergence process between capital-rich and capital-poor countries. Conversely, the emphasis on skilled migration would deprive sending countries from their most skilled and talented workers. The authors are well aware of these problems. They propose a scheme where the bias toward skilled immigrants should be more than offset by the temporary nature of such flows. In their view, this should benefit all the parties involved: the host country, the migrants (which would acquire further skill during their temporary stay abroad), and the sending country (which would benefit both from remittances and from return migration of skilled workers). The success of this scheme hinges on the assumption that skilled migrants could be prompted to return home. This is by no means granted. Skilled migrants typically tend to move with their own family. Their ties to the home country weaken over time, as demonstrated by the finding that the propensity to remit is a decreasing function of the skilled content of the stock of migrants (Faini, 2001). Overall, if the proposed scheme of contracted temporary skilled migration was not successful in promoting the early return of skilled migrants, it could well aggravate existing economic imbalances between the industrial and the developing world.

A final note. The basic premise of the paper is that migration is large and on the rise. However, this is not true, at least by any historical standards (Aghion and Williamson, 1998). The truth is that in many respects migration is the grand absentee of the globalization process. At the beginning of the twentieth century, for instance, migration flows played a crucial role in fostering factor price and income convergence between capital-rich and capital-poor countries. Similarly, during the 1950s and the 1960s, migration was a key factor in the process of European economic integration. In both episodes, absolute and relative numbers were significantly larger than those seen in the present globalization phase.

The debate on the new international economic order fell out of fashion more than two decades ago. It can still be said, however, that a world economy where unskilled migration flows are no longer there to foster North–South convergence, where only skilled migration is encouraged depriving therefore, sending countries of their most skilled talents, where perhaps even trade liberalization is restricted along regional lines in a way that excludes the poorest countries is somewhat less than a truly global economy.

References

Aghion, P. and Williamson, J. (1998), *Inequality, Growth and Globalisation*, Cambridge: Cambridge University Press.

Alecke, B., Huber, P., and Untiedt, G. (2001), 'What a Difference a Constant Makes—How Predictable are International Migration Flows?', in OECD, *Migration Policies and EU Enlargement, The Case of Central and Eastern Europe*, Paris, pp. 63–78.

——and Untiedt, G. (2000), Determinanten der Binnenwanderung in Deutschland seit der Wiedervereinigung—Eine makroökonometrische Analyse mit Paneldaten für die Bundesländer und den Zeitraum 1991 bis 1997, Volkswirtschaftliche Diskussionsbeiträge 309, University Münster.

Bar Tzuri, R. (2001), 'Foreign Workers Without permit in Israel', 1999, Rasuth—The Israeli Ministry of Labor and Welfare.

Bauer, T. (1997), 'Lohneffekte der Zuwanderung', Eine empirische Untersuchung für Deutschland, Mitteilungen aus der Arbeitsmarkt- und Berufsforschung, 30, 652–6.

——(1998), 'Arbeitsmarkteffekte der Migration und Einwanderungspolitik'. Eine Analyse für die Bundesrepublik Deutschland, Physika, Heidelberg/New York.

——Dietz, B., Zimmermann, K., and Zwintz, E. (2001), 'German Migration: Development, Assimilation and Labor Market Effects', in K. Zimmermann (ed.), *European Migration*, Oxford Economic Press (forthcoming).

——Lofstrom, M., and Zimmermann, K.F., (2000), 'Immigration Policy, Assimilation of Immigrants and Natives' Sentiments Towards Immigrants: Evidence from 12 OECD-Countries', *Swedish Economic Policy Review*, 7, 11–53.

——and Zimmermann, K.F. (1997), 'Looking South and East, Labour Markets Implications of Migration in Europe and LDCs', in O. Memedovic, A. Kuyvenhoven, W.T.M. Molle (eds.), *Globalisation and Labour Markets. Challenges, Adjustment and Policy Responses in the EU and the LDCs*, Dordrecht/Boston/London: Kluwer, 75–103.

——and—— (1998), 'Causes of International Migration: A Survey', in C. Gorter, P. Nijkamp, J. Poot (eds.), *Crossing Borders: Regional and Urban Perspectives on International Migration*, Ashgate, Aldershot *et al.*, 95–127.

——and—— (1999), 'Assessment of Possible Migration Pressure and its Labour Market Impact Following EU Enlargement to Central and Eastern Europe', IZA Research Report no. 3, IZA, Bonn.

——and—— (2000), 'Immigration Policy in Integrated National Economies', IZA Discussion Paper no. 170, IZA, Bonn.

Beine, M., Docquier, F., and Rapoport, H. (2001), 'Brain Drain and Economic Growth: Theory and Evidence', *Journal of Development Economics*, 64, 275–89.

Berthoud, R. and Modood, T. (1997), 'Ethnic Minorities in Britain', Policy Studies Institute, London.

Bertola *et al.* (2001), 'EU Welfare Systems and Labour Markets: Diverse in the Past, Integrated in the Future?', in G. Bertola, T. Boeri, and G. Nicoletti (eds.), *Welfare and Employment in a United Europe*, Cambridge, MA: MIT Press.

Bird, E.J., Kayser, H., and Frick, J.R. (1999), 'The Immigrant Welfare Effect, Take-up or Eligibility?' IZA Discussion Paper no. 66, IZA, Bonn.

Blackaby, D.H., Clark, K., Leslie, D.G., and Murphy, P.D. (1994), 'Black–White Male Earning and Employment Prospects and the 1970s and 1980s', *Economic Letters*, 46, 273–9.

—— Leslie, D.G., and Murphy, P.D. (1997), 'Explaining Racial Variations in Unemployment Rates in Britain', *The Manchester School*, 97, 1–20.

—— Drinkwater, S., Leslie, D.G., and Murphy, P.D. (1997), 'A Picture of Male and Female Unemployment among Britain's Ethnic Minorities', *Scottish Journal of Political Economy*, 44, 182–97.

Boeri, T., Brücker, H. *et al.* (2001*a*), 'The Impact of Eastern Enlargement on Employment and Labour Markets in the EU Member States', Europäische Kommission, Brüssel.

—— and Brücker, H. (2001*b*), 'Eastern Enlargement and EU Labour Markets, Perceptions, Challenges and Opportunities', *World Economics*, 2(1), 49–68.

—— (2000), *Structural Change, Welfare Systems, and Labour Reallocation. Lessons from the Transition of Formerly Planned Economies*, Oxford: Oxford University Press.

—— Burda, M., and Köllö, J. (1998), 'Mediating the Transition: Labour Markets in Central and Eastern Europe', CEPR, Forum Report of the Economic Policy Initiative no. 4, New York *et al.*

—— and Keese, M. (1992), 'Labour Markets and the Transition in Central and Eastern Europe', *OECD Economic Studies*, 18, 133–63.

Bonifazi, C. and Strozza, S. (2001), 'Le migrazioni internazionali in Europa dagli anni cinquanta ai nostri giorni', in N. Acocella, E. Sonnino (eds.), *Movimenti di popolazione e di capitale in Europa*, Roma: Carocci editore.

Bonin, H. (2001), 'Fiskalische Effekte der Zuwanderung nach Deutschland, Eine Generationenbilanz', IZA Discussion Paper 305, IZA, Bonn.

Borjas, G.J. (1985), 'Assimilation, Changes in Cohort Quality, and the Earnings of Immigrants', *Journal of Labor Economics*, 3, 463–89.

—— (1987), 'Self-Selection and the Earnings of Immigrants', *American Economic Review*, 77, 531–53.

—— (1994), 'The Economics of Immigration', *Journal of Economic Literature*, 32, 1667–1717.

—— (1995*a*), 'The Economic Benefits from Immigration', *Journal of Economic Perspectives*, 9, 3–22.

—— (1999), 'Immigration and Welfare Magnets', *Journal of Labor Economics*.

—— and Bronars, S.-G. (1991), 'Immigration and the Family', *Journal of Labor Economics*.

—— and Hilton, L. (1996), 'Immigration and the Welfare State, Immigration in Means-tested Entitlement Programs', *Quarterly Journal of Economics*, 111, 575–604.

—— and Trejo, S.J. (1991), 'Immigrant Participation in the Welfare System', *Industrial and Labor Relations Review*, 44, 195–211.

—— (1999), 'Immigration and Welfare Magnets', *Journal of Labor Economics*.

Börsch-Supan, A. (1993), 'Immigration and the Social Pension System', mimeo, University of Mannheim.

Boswick, W. (1997), Asylum Policy in Germany, in: P. Muss (ed.), *Exclusion and Inclusion of Refugees in Contemporary Europe*, Utrecht University, Netherlands, 53–77.

Brücker, H. (2001), 'Die Folgen der Freizügigkeit für die Ost-West-Migration', Schlussfolgerungen aus einer Zeitreihenanalyse der Migration nach Deutschland, 1967 bis 1998, Konjunkturpolitik, *Applied Economics Quarterly*, Beiheft 52, 17–54.

Burda, Michael, C. (1995), 'Migration and the Option Value of Waiting', *Economic and Social Review*, 27 (October 1995), 1–19.

Caritas (2000), 'Immigrazione Dossier Statistico', Anterem Roma.

—— (1999), 'Immigrazione Dossier Statistico', Anterem Roma.

—— (1998), 'Immigrazione Dossier Statistico', Anterem Roma.

—— (1997), 'Immigrazione Dossier Statistico', Anterem Roma.

Carling, K., Edin, P.A., Harkman, A., and Holmlund, B. (1996), 'Unemployment Duration, Unemployment Benefits, and Labor Market Programs in Sweden', *Journal of Public Economics*, 59(3), 313–34.

Carrington, W.J., Detragiache, E., and Vishwanath, T. (1996), 'Migration with Endogenous Moving Costs', *American Economic Review*, 86, 909–30.

Casella, A. and Rauch, J.-E. (1997), 'Anonymous Market and Group Ties in International Trade', CEPR DP 1748.

Chiswick, B.R. (1978), 'The Effects of Americanisation on the Earnings of Foreign Born Men', *Journal of Political Economy*, 86, 897–921.

—— (1980), 'The Earnings of White and Coloured Male Immigrants in Britain', *Economica*, 47, 81–7.

—— (1982), 'The Employment of Immigrants in the United States', in W. Fellner (ed.), *Contemporary Economic Problems*, 1982, American Enterprise Institute, Washington, DC.

—— and Miller, P.M. (1996), 'Ethnic Networks and Language Proficiency among Immigrants', *Journal of Population Economics*, 9, 19–35.

—— (2000), 'Are Immigrants Favorably Self-Selected? An Economic Analysis', IZA Discussion Paper no. 131, IZA, Bonn.

Church, J. and King, I. (1983), 'Bilingualism and Network Externalities', *Canadian Journal of Economics*, 26, 337–45.

Coleman, D. (1992), 'Does Europe Need Immigrants? Population and Workforce Projections', *International Migration Review*, 26, 413–61.

Coleman, D.A. (1993), 'Contrasting Age Structures of Western Europe and Eastern Europe and the Former Soviet Union: Demographic Curiosity or Labor Resource?', *Population and Development Review*, 19(3), 523–55.

Cornelius, W. (1990), 'Labour Migration to the United States: Development Outcomes and Alternative in Mexican and Co-operative communities', Commission for the Study of International Migration and Co-operative Economic Development, Washington, DC.

Del Boca, D. and Venturini, A. (2001), 'Italian Migration', in K. Zimmermann (ed.), *European Migration*, Oxford Economic Press (forthcoming).

DeNew, J. and Zimmermann, K.F. (1994), 'Native Wage Impacts of Foreign Labour: A Random Effects Panel Analysis', *Journal of Population Economics*, 7, 177–92.

—— and —— (1995), 'Wage and Mobility Effects of Trade and Migration', CEPR-Discussion Paper no. 1318, London.

Desai, M., Kapur, D., and McHale, J. (2001), 'Sharing the Spoils: Taxing International Human Capital Flows', mimeo.

Dustmann, C. (1993), 'Earnings Adjustments of Temporay Migrants', *Journal of Population Economics*, 6, 130–56.

—— (1994), 'Speaking Fluency, Writing Fluency and Earnings of Migrants', *Population Economics*, 7, 133–56.

Dustmann, C. (1996), 'Return Migration: The European Experience', *Economic Policy*, 22, 213–42.

—— and Schmidt, C.M. (1999), 'The Wage Performance of Immigrant Women, Full-Time Jobs, Part-Time Jobs, and the Role of Selection', IZA Discussion Paper no. 233, Bonn.

—— and Fabbri, F. (1999), 'Language Proficiency and the Labour Market Performance of Immigrants in the United Kingdom', Paper presented at the European Economic Association annual conference, Santiago de Compostela, September.

—— and Preston, I. (2000a), 'Racial and Economic Factors in Attitudes to Immigration', IZA Discussion Paper no. 190, Bonn.

—— and —— (2000b), 'Attitudes to Ethnic Minorities, Ethnic Context, and Location Decisions', *Economic Journal*, 111(470) (April 2001), 353–73.

Engle, R. and Granger, C.W.J. (1987), 'Co-integration and Error Correction: Representation, Estimation and Testing', *Econometrica*, 55, 251–76.

Epstein, G.S. (2000), 'Labor Market Interactions Between Legal and Illegal Immigrants', *Review of Development Economics* (forthcoming).

—— and Hillman, A.L. (2000), 'Social Harmony at the Boundaries of the Welfare State: Immigration and social Transfers', IZA DP no. 168. Forthcoming also on *Journal of Public Economics* (2002), 'Unemployed Immigrants and Voter Sentiment in the Welfare State'.

—— —— and Weiss, A. (1999), 'Creating Illegal Immigrants', *Journal of Population Economics*, 12(1), 3–21.

Ethier, W. (1986), 'Illegal Immigration: The Host Country Problem', *American Economic Review*, 76, 56–71.

European Commission (2000), 'Communication from the Commission to the Council and European Parliament on a Community Immigration Policy', COM 757/2000, Brussels.

Eurostat (1987), 'Demographic Statistics', Eurostat, Luxembourg.

—— (1995), Migration Statistics.

—— (2000), 'Yearbook 2000', Eurostat, Luxembourg.

—— various years, Demographic Statistics.

Faini, R. and Venturini, A. (1993), 'Trade, Aid and Migration, Some Basic Policy Issues', *European Economic Review*, 37, 435–42.

—— and —— (1994), 'Migration and Growth: the Experience of Southern Europe', Working Paper C.E.P.R. no. 964.

—— (2001), 'Development, Trade, and Migration', Annual Bank Conference on Development Economics, Europe.

Fertig, M. (1999), 'The Economic Impact of EU-Enlargement: Assessing the Migration Potential', Discussion Paper no. 964, Department of Economics, University of Heidelberg.

—— and Schmidt, M. (2000), 'Aggregate-Level Migration Studies as a Tool for Forecasting Future Migration Streams', Discussion Paper no. 324, Department of Economics, University of Heidelberg.

—— and Schmidt, C.M. (2001), 'First- and Second-Generation Migrants in Germany— What Do We Know and What Do People Think', in R. Rotte (ed.), *Migration Policy and the Economy–International Experience*, mimeo.

Fischer, P.A. and Straubhaar, T. (1996), 'Migration and Integration in the Nordic Common Labour Market', Nord, 2/1996, Copenhagen.

Flaig, G. (2001), 'Zur Abschätzung der Migrationspotentiale der osteuropäischen EU-Beitrittsländer', Konjunkturpolitik, *Applied Economics Quarterly*, Beiheft 52, 17–54.

Frick, J., Büchel, F., and Voges, W. (1996), 'Sozialhilfe als Integrationshilfe für Zuwanderer in Deutschland', *DIW-Wochenbericht*, 63(48), 767–75.

Friedberg, R.M. and Hunt, J. (1995), 'The Impact of Immigrants on Host Country Wages, Employment and Growth', *Journal of Economic Perspectives*, 9, 23–44.

Gang, I. and Rivera-Batiz, L. (1994), 'Labour Market Effects of Immigration in the United States and Europe, Substitution vs. Complementarity', *Journal of Population Economics*, 7, 157–75.

—— and Rivera-Batiz, F.L. (1994), 'Unemployment and Attitudes Towards Foreigners in Germany', in G. Steinmann and R.E. Ulrich (eds.), *The Economic Consequences of Immigration to Germany*, Physica-Verlag Heidelberg, 121–54.

Garson, J.P., Moulier-Boutang, R., Silberman, R., and Magnac, T. (1987), 'La Substitution des Autochthones aux Etrangers sur le Marché du Travail dans la CEE', European Commission, Brussels.

Gavosto, A., Venturini, A., and Villosio, C. (1999), 'Do Immigrants Compete with Natives?' *Labour*, 13(3), 603–22.

Gaytán-Fregoso, H. and Lahiri, S. (2000), 'Foreign Aid and Illegal Immigration', *Journal of Development Economics*, 63, 515–27.

Golder, S.M. (1998), 'On the Employment Performance of Immigrant Workers: An Empirical Analysis for Switzerland', Discussion Paper 74, Institute for Economic Research, Haue, Haue.

Golder, S.M. and Straubhaar, T. (1999), 'Empirical Findings on the Swiss Migration Experience', IZA Discussion Paper no. 40, IZA, Bonn.

Gross, D. (1999), 'Three Million Foreigners, Three Million Unemployed? Immigration and the French Labour Market', IMF Working Paper no. 99/124, IMF, Washington, DC.

Grossman, J.B. (1982), 'The Substitutability of Natives and Immigrants in Production', *Review of Economics and Statistics*, 64, 596–603.

Haisken-DeNew, J. (1996), 'Migration and Inter-Industry Wage Structure in Germany', Springer, Berlin/Heidelberg/New York.

—— and Zimmermann, K. (1995), 'Wage and Mobility Effects of Trade and Migration', University Munich, Department of Economics, Discussion Paper 95–24.

—— and —— (1999), 'Wage and Mobility Effects of Trade and Migration', in M. Dewatripont, A. Sapir, K. Sekkat (eds.), *Trade and Jobs in Europe, Much Ado about Nothing?*, Oxford University Press, pp. 139–60.

Hansen, J. (2000), 'The Duration of Immigrants' Unemployment Spells: Evidence from Sweden', IZA Discussion Paper no. 155, IZA, Bonn.

—— and Lofstrom, M. (1999), 'Immigration and Welfare Participation: Do Immigrants Assimilate Into or Out-of Welfare?' IZA Discussion Paper no. 100, IZA, Bonn.

Hanson, G.H. and Slaughter, M.J. (1999), 'The Rybczinski Theorem, Factor Price Equalization, and Immigration: Evidence from U.S. States', NBER Working Paper no. 7074, NBER, Cambridge, MA.

Harris, J.R. and Todaro, M.P. (1970), 'Migration, Unemployment and Development, A Two-Sector Analysis', *American Economic Review*, 60, 126–42.

Hatizius, J. (1994), 'The Unemployment and Earnings Effect of German Immigration', Applied Economics Discussion Paper 165, Oxford Institute of Economics and Statistics, Oxford.

Hatton, T.J. (1995), 'A Model of U.K. Emigration, 1870–1913', *Review of Economics and Statistics*, 77(3) (August 1995), 407–15.

—— and Price, S.W. (1999), 'Migration, Migrants and Policy in the United Kingdom', IZA Discussion Paper no. 81, IZA, Bonn.

Hillman, A.L. (1994), 'The political economy of migration policy', in H. Siebert, J.C.B. Mohr, P. Siebeck (eds.), *Migration: A Challenge for Europe*, Tubingen.

—— and Weiss, A. (1999a), 'Beyond International Factor Movements: Cultural Preferences, Endogenous Policies and the Migration of People: An Overview,' in R. Faini, J. de Melo and K.F. Zimmermann (eds.), *Migration: The Controversies and the Evidence*, Cambridge: Cambridge University Press, 76–91.

—— and —— (1999b), 'A Theory of Permissible Illegal Immigration', *European Journal of Political Economy*, 15(4), 585–604.

Hönekopp, E. (1999), 'The Impact of Migration', Background Report to 'The Impact of Eastern Enlargement on Employment and Labour Markets in the EU Member States', mimeo, Institut für Arbeitsmarkt- und Berufsforschung (IAB), Nuremberg.

Huber, P. and H. Hofer (2001), Preparity Report, Teilprojekt 9: Auswirkungen der EU-Erweiterung auf den österreichischen Arbeitsmarkt, in Peter Mayerhofer, Gerhard Palme (eds.), Preparity – Strukturpolitik und Raumplanung in den Regionen an der mitteleuropäischen EU-Außengrenze zur Vorbereitung auf die EU-Osterweiterung, Vienna, 2001.

Hunger, A. (2000), 'Temporary Transnational Labour Migration in an Integrating Europe and the Challange to the German Welfare State', in M. Bommes, and A. Geddes (eds.), *Immigration and Welfare*, London: Routledge.

Hunt, J. (1992), 'The Impact of the 1962 Repatriates from Algeria on the French Labor Market', *Industrial and Labor Relations Review*, 45, 556–72.

Jahn, A. and Straubhaar, T. (1995), 'On the Political Economy of Illegal Immigration'. Paper presented at CEPR workshop on Illegal Immigration, Thessaloniki, September.

Katz, E. and Stark, O. (1984), 'Migration and Asymmetric Information', *American Economic Review*, 74, 533–4.

—— and —— (1986), 'Labor Mobility under Asymmetric Information with Moving and Signalling Costs', *Economic Letters*, 21, 89–94.

Krueger, Alan, B. and Jorn-Steffen Pischke (1997), 'A Statistical Analysis of Crime Against Foreigners in Unified Germany', *Journal of Human Resources*, 32, 182–209.

Kwok, V. and Leland, H. (1982), 'An Economic Model of the Brain Drain', *American Economic Review*, 72, 91–100.

Ilahi, N. (1999), 'Return Migration and Occupational Change', *Review of Development Economics*, 3, 170–86.

ILO (1997), International Migration Statistics, Geneva.

Layard, R., Blanchard, O., Dornbusch, R., and Krugman, P. (1992), *East–West Migration. The Alternatives*, Cambridge, MA: MIT Press.

Lebon A. (1998), 'Immigration et présence ètrangère en France 1997/1998', La documentation Française, Ministère de l'emploi e de la Solidaritè.

Lederer, H. (1998), Illegal Migration: Why Does it Exist and What Do We Know about Numbers and Trends?, Paper presented at the conference 'Managing Migration in the 21st Century: On the Politics and Economics of Illegal Migration', Hamburg, June 21–23.

Lundborg, P. (1991), 'Determinants of Nordic Migration to Sweden', *Scandinavian Journal of Economics*, 3, 363–75.

——(1998), 'The Free Movement of Labour between Sweden and the New EU Members', in *A Bigger and Better Europe?* Final Report from the Committee on the Economic Effects of Enlargement, Stockholm.

Maddison, A. (1995), 'Monitoring the World Economy 1820–1992', OECD, Paris.

Marks, C. (1989), *Farewell—We're Good and Gone: The Great Black Migration*, Bloomington: Indian University Press.

McCormick, B. and Wahba, J. (2000), 'Overseas Employment and Remittances to a Dual Economy', *The Economic Journal*, 110(463), 509–34.

——and Wahba, J. (2001), 'Overseas Work Experience, Savings and Entrepreneurship Amongst Return Migrants to LDCS', *Scottish Journal of Political Economy*, Special Millenium Issue, Royal Economic Society Conference, 48(2), 164–78.

Moulier-Boutang, Y. and Garson, J.-P. (1984), 'Major Obstacles to Control of Irregular Migrations: Prerequisites to Policy', *International Migration Review*, 18(67), 579–92.

OECD (1991), 'Migration: the demographic aspects', OECD, Paris.

——(1999), 'Trends in International Migration', SOPEMI Report, Paris.

——(2000), 'Trends in International Migration', SOPEMI Report, Paris.

Pederson, P. (2000), 'Immigration in a High Unemployment Economy: The Recent Danish Experience', IZA Discussion Paper no. 165.

Pischke, J.S. (1992), 'Assimilation and the Earnings of Guestworkers in Germany', ZEW-Discussion Paper no. 17/92, Mannheim.

——and Velling, J. (1997), 'Labor Market Effects of Foreign Employment in Germany', *Review of Economics and Statistics*, 79(4), 594–604.

Reyneri, E. (2000), 'Integrazione e mercato del lavoro', in G. Zincone (ed.), *Primo Rapporto sull'Integrazione degli Immigrati in Italia, Commissione per le politiche di integrazione degli immigrati*, Il Mulino, Bologna, pp. 206–25.

Richard, J.-L. (2001), 'Une approche de la discrimination sur le marché du travail: les jeunes adultes issus de l'immigration étrangère en France', *Revue Européenne des Migrations Internationales*, Mars 2001.

Riedel, J. and Untiedt, G. (2000), 'Strukturpolitik und Raumplanung in den Regionen der Mitteleuropäischen EU-Aussengrenze zur Vorbereitung der EU Osterweiterung', Draft Final Report, Preparity, WIFO/IFO/ISDEE, Vienna, Dresden, Trieste.

Riphahn, R.T. (1998), 'Immigrant Participation in the German Welfare Program', *Finanzarchiv*, 55, 163–85.

——(2000), 'Dissimilation? Educational Attainment of Second Generation Immigrants', mimeo, University of Munich.

Rosoli, G. (1980), 'Italian Migration to European Countries from Political Unification to World War I', in D. Hoerder (ed.), *Labor Migration in the Atlantic Economies, The European and North American Working Classes During the Period of Industrialization*, London: Greenwood Press, pp. 95–116.

Rotte, R. and Vogler, M. (1998), 'Determinants of International Migration: Empirical Evidence for Migration from Developing Countries to Germany', IZA Discussion Paper no. 12, Bonn.

Roy, A.D. (1951), 'Some Thoughts on the Distribution of Earnings', *Oxford Economic Papers*, 3, 135–46.

Russell, S. (1986), 'Remittances from International Migration: a Review in Perspective', *World Development*, 14, 677–96.

—— and Teitelbaum, M. (1992), 'International Migration and International Trade', World Bank Discussion Paper no. 160, Washington, DC: The World Bank.

Sarris, A. and Zografakis, S. (1999), 'A Computable General Equilibrium Assessment of the Impact of Illegal Immigration on the Greek Economy', *Journal of Population Economics*, 12(1), 155–82.

Schmidt, C. (1992), 'Country of Origin Differences in the Earnings of the German Immigrants', University of Munich Discussion Paper no. 763.

Schmidt, C.M. (1997), 'Immigrant Performance in Germany: Labor Earnings of Ethnic German Migrants and Foreign Guestworkers', *Quarterly Review of Economics and Finance*, 37, 370–97.

Schröder, G. (2000), Rede von Bundeskanzler Gerhard Schröder anlässlich der Regionalkonferenz Oberpfalz 2000 am 18.12.2000 in Weiden, *http://www.bundesregierung.de/frameset/index.jsp.*

Sjaastad, L.A. (1962), 'The Cost and Returns of Human Migration', *Journal of Political Economy*, 70, 80–93.

Sinn, H.-W., Flaig, G., Werding, M., Munz, S., Düll, N., and Hofmann, H. (2001), 'EU-Erweiterung und Arbeitskräftemigration', Wege zu einer schrittweisen Annäherung der Arbeitsmärkte, ifo-Institut für Wirtschaftsforschung, Munich.

SOPEMI (2000), 'Trends in International Migration', OECD, Paris.

Stark, O. (1991), *The Migration of Labour*, Cambridge, MA: Basil Blackwell.

Straubhaar, T. and Zimmermann, K.F. (1993), 'Towards a European Migration Policy', *Population Research and Policy Review*, 12/93, 225–41.

Strozza, S. and Venturini, A. (2001), Italy is no longer a country of emigration. Foreigners in Italy, how many, where they come from and what they do, mimeo.

Swamy, G. (1981), 'International Migrant Workers' Remittances: Issues and Prospects', World Bank Working Paper, no. 481, Washington, DC: The World Bank.

Tapinos, G. (1999), 'Clandestine Immigration: Economic and Political Issues in Trends in International Migration', SOPEMI, OECD Annual Report, Paris.

Trabold, H. and Trübswetter, P. (2001), 'Schätzung der Beschäftigungs- und Lohneffekte der Zuwanderung', in H. Brücker, H. Trabold, P. Trübswetter, C. Weise (eds.), *Migration: Potential und Effekte für den deutschen Arbeitsmarkt*, Draft Final Report for the Hans-Böckler-Foundation, German Institute for Economic Research (DIW), Berlin.

Trefler, D. (1997), 'Immigrants and Natives in General Equilibrium Trade Models', NBER Working Paper 6209, Cambridge, MA.

UN (1999), 'World Population Prospects, 1998 Revision', New York.

UN (2000), 'Replacement Migration: Is it a Solution to Declining and Ageing Populations', UN Secretariat, Geneva.

UNDP (1999), 'Monitoring Human Development'.

United Nations Economic Commission for Europe (1979), 'Labour Supply and Migration in Europe: Demographic dimensions 1950–75 and prospects', Ginevra.

Venables, A.J. (1999a), 'Regional Integration Agreements: A Force for Convergence or Divergence', W.P. World Bank – Country Economic Department.

Venables, A.J. (1999*b*), 'Trade Liberalisation and Factor Mobility: An Overview', in Faini, R., J. de Melo, and K.F. Zimmermann (eds.), *Migration. The Controversies and the Evidence*, Cambridge (UK): Cambridge University Press, pp. 23–47.

Venturini, A. (1999), 'Do Immigrants Working Illegally Reduce the Natives's Legal Employment in Italy', *Journal of Population Economics*, 12(1), 135–54.

—— (2001), 'Le migrazioni dei paesi Sud Europei, Un approccio economico', Utet Libreria, Torino.

—— and Villosio, C. (2000), 'La competizione occupazionale tra lavoratori italiani e stranieri in Italia', Working Paper no. 22, Commissione per le politiche di integrazione degli immigrati Dipartimento per gli Affari Sociali, Presidenza del Consiglio dei Ministri, Roma. Forthcoming AS ILA Discussion Paper 2002. 'Are Immigrants Competing with Natives in the Italian Labour Markets'. The Employment Effect.

Vogler, M. and Rotte, R. (2001), 'The Effects of Development on Migration, Theoretical Issues and New Empirical Evidence', *Journal of Population Economics*, 13, 485–508.

Weil, P. (1994), 'Mouvements de Population. La Politique de la France', *Politique Etrangère*, 59(3), 719–29.

Werner, H. (2001), 'Wirtschaftliche Integration und Arbeitskräftewanderungen in der EU', Aus Politik und Zeitgeschichte, 8/2001, 11–19.

—— (2001), 'Wirtschaftliche Integration und Arbeitskräftewanderungen in der EU', Aus Politik und Zeitgeschichte, 8/2001, 11–19.

Wheatley Price, S. (1998), 'The Employment Adjustment of Male Immigrants in the English Labour Market', University of Leicester Discussion Papers in Public Sector Economics, 98/10, Leicester, *Journal of Population Economics*, 1, April 2001, 193–220.

Winter-Ebmer, R. and Zweimüller, J. (1996*b*), 'Immigration and the Earnings of Young Native Workers', in *Oxford Economic Papers*, 48, 473–91.

—— and Zweimuller, J. (1999), 'Do Immigrants Displace Young Native Workers: the Austrian Experience', *Journal of Population Economics*, 12(2), 327–40.

—— and Zimmermann, K. (1999), 'East–West Trade and Migration: The Austro-German case', in R. Faini, J. De Melo, and K. Zimmermann (eds.), *Migration. The Controversies and the Evidence*, Cambridge University Press, 296–327.

Wihtol de Wenden, C. (2000), 'Illegal Migration. The French Case', mimeo.

—— (2000), 'La politique française de régularisation des sans-papiers', mimeo.

World Bank (1998), 'World Development Report', Oxford University Press, Washington.

—— (1999), 'World Development Indicators', Washington, DC.

—— (2000), 'World Development Indicators', CD-Rom, World Bank, Washington, DC.

Zimmermann, K.F. (1994*a*), 'European Migration, Push and Pull', Proceedings volume of the World Bank Annual Conference on Development Economics, Supplement to the World Bank Economic Review and the World Bank Research Observer.

—— (1994*b*), 'Immigration Policies in Europe, An Overview', in H. Siebert (ed.), *Migration, A Challenge for Europe*, Tübingen, J.C.B. Mohr, 227–58.

Zimmerman, K. (1995), 'Tackling the European Migration Problem', *Journal of Economic Perspectives*, 9: 45–62.

Zincone, G. (ed.), (2000), 'Primo Rapporto sull'Integrazione degli Immigrati in Italia', Commissione per le politiche di integrazione degli immigrati, Il Mulino, Bologna.

Zolberg, A.R., Suhrke, A., and Aguayo, S. (1989), *Escape from Violence, Conflict and Refugee Crisis in the Developing World*, New York: Oxford University Press.

PART II

IMMIGRATION AND THE US ECONOMY: LABOUR-MARKET IMPACTS, ILLEGAL ENTRY, AND POLICY CHOICES

Gordon H. Hanson, Kenneth F. Scheve,
Matthew J. Slaughter, and Antonio Spilimbergo

The authors thank Giuseppe Bertola, Irene Bloemraad, Tito Boeri, George Borjas, Alan Kessler, and participants at the Rodolfo DeBeneditti conference, 'Immigration Policy and the Welfare State,' for helpful comments. The views expressed here are those of the authors and do not necessarily represent those of the IMF or its Board of Directors.

8

Introduction

Since the 1960s, the United States has undergone a surge in immigration. The share of the US population that is foreign born reached 10 per cent in 2000, up from a 150-year low of 5 per cent in 1970 but still below the 1910 high of 15 per cent (see Fig. 8.1). Few other advanced countries have higher foreign-born populations.[1] During the 1990s, an average of one million legal immigrants and 300 000 illegal immigrants entered the United States each year, accounting for 40 per cent of the decade's population growth.[2]

What is surprising about this recent immigration episode is that US immigration policy has *not* become markedly more open. In fact, during this period the United States has liberalized foreign trade and direct investment much more than it has immigration. Cross-border flows of goods, capital, and labour—all help eliminate cross-border differences in factor prices. The United States has reduced barriers to trade and investment on many fronts, such as by helping create the World Trade Organization (WTO) and by enacting the North American Free Trade Agreement (NAFTA). There is no such analogous record on immigration. Instead, in the discussion of how the United States should integrate into the world economy, immigration is the least favoured option.

The lack of liberalization in immigration policy does not, however, indicate a policy consensus. Rather, immigration is a sharply contentious issue with substantial political conflict characterizing every aspect of policy debates. Some groups clearly support expanded immigration. Amidst the tight labour markets of the late 1990s, employers complained that restrictive immigration quotas were helping choke off the long-running US expansion. Interestingly, these sort of concerns came from both high-skill and low-skill industries. In 1998, the US Congress temporarily increased the number of work visas allotted to highly skilled immigrants, thanks largely to intensive lobbying from high-technology companies in Silicon Valley. Claiming that a shortage of manual labour threatens US agriculture, farmers in California, Oregon, Texas, and elsewhere are pushing to reinstate large-scale temporary immigration of field workers, a

[1] Among OECD countries in 1997 (excluding Luxembourg), only Australia (21.1 per cent), Canada (17.4 per cent), and Switzerland (19.0 per cent) had foreign-born population shares higher than the United States.

[2] For the period 1990–2000, growth in the foreign-born population accounted for 33.7 per cent of US population growth. Births to immigrants that arrived in the 1990s accounted for another 6.5 per cent of population growth (Camarota, 2001).

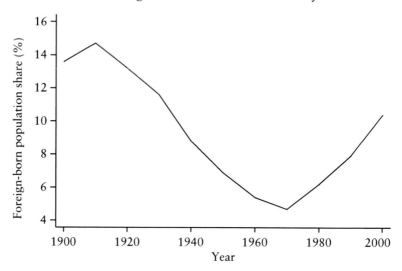

Figure 8.1. *Share of foreign-born in US population*

programme defunct since the 1960s.[3] The Mexican government is also lobbying for expanded temporary immigration, to remedy what it sees as poor treatment of Mexican farm workers in the United States, many of whom are illegal aliens.

A diverse set of groups is lined up against freer immigration. Many in favour of tax reform claim that immigrants receive more in public benefits than they contribute to revenue. Labour activists worry that immigration lowers US wages and labour standards. And nativists, such as perennial presidential candidate Pat Buchanan, fear that ongoing immigration from non-European countries weakens the US social fabric.

Three sets of related policy issues are central to the debate about immigration. One is what should be the level and composition of legal immigration. Despite restrictions on immigration, the labour-market magnitude of US immigration is on par with that of international trade. In 1990, there were 11.7 million foreign-born workers in the United States. This compares with the equivalent net inflow of 8.3 million workers arising from the labour-market services embodied in US exports and imports (Davis and Weinstein, 1998).[4] Immigration on this scale has the potential to alter the structure and growth of US industry. Whether intended or not, current policy appears to favour individuals with relatively low levels of education and other observable skills. Rising immigration of the less skilled may lower wages of less-skilled native workers, shift US comparative advantage, and strain government budgets.

---

[3] Current US policy does allow for the temporary immigration of farm labourers, as discussed in Chapter 11.

[4] The estimated net inflow of foreign workers embodied in US trade is in US productivity-equivalent terms. See Davis and Weinstein (1998) for details.

A second policy issue is what to do about illegal immigration. Currently, illegal aliens account for one-third of new US immigrants. The US government impedes illegal entry by policing the US–Mexico border, where about half of illegal immigrants enter the US, and by monitoring likely employers of undocumented workers. It devotes the vast majority of resources to border enforcement, with, at best, mixed success. Proposals to reinstate temporary immigration from Mexico would have the US government begin to regulate, in effect, the current inflow of illegal labour while proposals to grant an amnesty to some existing illegal immigrants would seek to significantly reduce the stock of these workers living in the country.

A third policy issue is whether immigrants should be eligible for public assistance. Denying eligibility could reduce incentives to emigrate to the United States for the purpose of obtaining government transfers. In recent years, California and other states have passed restrictions on immigrant access to public assistance. While recent US legal decisions have limited the scope of these laws, the possibility of immigrants gaining at taxpayers' expense remains a politically-charged issue.[5]

Despite widespread dissatisfaction with US immigration practices, the delicate political economy of immigration makes changing of policy difficult. Arguable imperfections in the existing system—such as admitting immigrants without consideration of labour-market conditions or forgoing revenue illegal immigrants might pay in return for legal residence—are the outcome of a compromise among the myriad groups favouring and opposing immigration. The relative influence of these groups can change with shocks to the economy or the political system. Rapid economic growth and low unemployment usually strengthen the hand of employers seeking more work visas. Calls for stricter enforcement against illegal immigration are loudest following crashes in the Mexican economy, which lead to more attempts at illegal entry.

In this second part, we examine immigration in the United States over the last several decades in order to gauge the potential for and the consequences of changes in US immigration policy.[6] We aim to elucidate key aspects of the ongoing US debate over immigration policy—with lessons not just for the United States but also for other countries facing rising immigration. Our study has four main chapters.

---

[5] As discussed in Chapter 12, in 1994, California passed proposition 187, which barred children of illegal immigrants from receiving public services (including the right to attend school). It was struck down by a federal court in 1995. In 1996, the US Congress passed legislation to deny eligibility for food stamps, federal disability assistance, and other government benefits to legal immigrants who had not become citizens. These changes did become law, as part of the package of welfare reforms in the Personal Responsibility and Work Opportunity Reconciliation Act (1996).

[6] We focus on a specific set of policy issues and do not attempt a broad coverage of US immigration issues. For recent, more expansive treatments of immigration in the United States, see Smith and Edmonston (1997) and Borjas (1999). For an overview of US immigration from Mexico, in particular, see Mexico–United States Binational Migration Study (1998).

First, to see how immigration affects native workers we consider how regional economies in the United States have adjusted to immigrant inflows. A large body of research finds that the impact of immigration on native wages is very small. We explain how this outcome may occur if regions can adjust to immigration through mechanisms other than wage changes. These include outmigration of native workers, changes in regional imports and exports, or changes in technology. The labour-market impact of immigration depends on which adjustment mechanisms are operative. The recent US experience suggests that wage adjustments need not predominate, but the conditions that have contributed to this outcome may not persist. We identify possible changes in the economic environment, under which the wage impacts of immigration could become more pronounced. The larger the impact of immigration on wages, the stronger the demands for changes in the level or composition of immigration are likely to be.

Second, we examine factors affecting both illegal immigration and attempts to stop it. Economic conditions in Mexico are key determinants of illegal immigration in the United States. Yet, US border enforcement fails to rise in response to what appears to be predictable surges in attempted illegal entry. In addition, the US Immigration and Naturalization Service (INS) fails to monitor aggressively those who employ illegal immigrants. These enforcement practices highlight the conflicting mandate of the INS. The INS is legally obliged to enforce against illegal entry, but severe enforcement brings opposition from industries that rely heavily on immigrant labour. Reinstating the temporary immigration of seasonal labour and granting an amnesty to existing illegal immigrants would convert illegal migrants into legal ones, but, as we explain, will not necessarily give the US government greater control over the inflow of labour from abroad.

Third, we examine the fiscal impact of immigration. Though exact estimation is difficult, it appears that the long-run net fiscal impact of immigration on the aggregate US economy is small. This overall fiscal neutrality hides two important features of immigration and US public finances. One is that the net benefits of immigration may be negative in the short-run as many immigrants are relatively poor and use relatively more public services, such as education. A second is that the fiscal costs of immigration are concentrated in the 'gateway' states that are home to most immigrants, while most fiscal benefits from immigration go to the federal government. The US reform of welfare policies in 1996 has increased this mismatch by devolving the administration of public assistance to state and local governments. The net fiscal contribution of future immigrants will depend crucially on the age and schooling of new arrivals.

Fourth, we consider the factors that influence US immigration policymaking. We identify the preferences of the main actors in the US immigration debate and how successful these actors are in influencing national policymakers. From the opinions of individual citizens about policy to votes on legislation by members of Congress, it is clear that immigration policymaking is affected by the perceived economic consequences of policy alternatives and, in particular, on the distribution of these economic effects. Less-skilled workers are more likely to support restrictionist policies while the employers of these workers generally favour liberalization. The influence of both these groups is observable in the voting behaviour of members of Congress. Beliefs about the impact of immigration on the welfare state also affect policymaking. There is consistent opposition to family-based immigration from political conservatives who favour a smaller welfare state both in the electorate and in Congress.

In Chapter 9, we set the stage for the discussion by giving an overview of trends in US immigration and immigration policy. The overview is followed by the four main chapters of the report. We conclude by considering the potential impact of proposed changes in US immigration policy on the US economy.

9

Immigration and Immigration Policy in the United States

Any policy that restricts immigration must establish a criterion for the admission of foreign nationals. The US policy gives explicit preference to family members of US citizens, with some consideration for an individual's occupational background. Whether desired or not, this policy appears to have contributed to rising immigration of individuals with relatively low levels of discernible skill. Given ample opportunities for illegal immigration, the US government does not exercise full control over which individuals gain entry to the country. By choosing to concentrate enforcement efforts at the border, rather than at the place of employment, the US implicitly gives preference to illegal immigrants who are able and willing to evade border authorities. This may have further contributed to immigration of the less skilled.[1] In this chapter, we briefly review US immigration policy and then discuss recent developments in immigration patterns and the economic performance of immigrants.

9.1. AN OVERVIEW OF US IMMIGRATION POLICY

US immigration policy is based on a quota system, the main elements of which were established by the Hart–Celler Immigration Bill of 1965, an amendment to the Immigration and Nationality Act of 1952 (Smith and Edmonston, 1997).[2] Under the current system, the Immigration and Naturalization Service (INS) assigns applicants for admission to one of seven categories, with each having its own quota level.[3] The law guarantees admission to immediate family

---

[1] Crossing the US–Mexico border illegally imposes costs of time, physical duress, and money, and precludes finding legal employment in the United States. All else being equal, illegal immigration under these circumstances is likely to be more attractive to individuals expecting to be employed as manual labourers.

[2] The first broad numerical limits on immigration (besides bans on Chinese immigration imposed in the nineteenth century) were embodied in the Immigration Act of 1924, which sharply restricted immigration overall and from outside Western and Northern Europe in particular. The 1965 amendments were to the Immigration and Nationality Act of 1952, which had created skill-based categories for immigration (though without changing restrictions on national origin).

[3] The most recent change to immigration levels was the Immigration Act of 1990, which set a flexible cap for overall legal admissions at 675 000 of which 480 000 would be family-based,

members of US citizens. Specific quotas are assigned to other family members of US citizens, immediate family members of legal US residents, individuals in special skill categories, and refugees and asylum seekers facing persecution in their home countries. Of the 660 447 individuals the INS admitted in 1998, 72 per cent gained entry as family members of US citizens or legal residents, 12 per cent gained entry as skilled workers, 8 per cent were refugees or asylum seekers, and 8 per cent were in other categories.[4] Additional admissions to the United States occur through temporary work visas, the two most common classes of which are for highly skilled workers and short-term manual labourers.[5]

Though the United States does not set the level of illegal immigration explicitly, existing policy, in effect, allows substantial numbers of illegal aliens to enter the country. Warren (1999) estimates that in 1997 there were 5.3 million illegal immigrants in the US, which was 20 per cent of the foreign-born US population in that year, up from 2.3 million in 1987.[6] Most such individuals gain entry either by crossing the US–Mexico border illegally or by overstaying temporary visas. The INS, and in particular the US Border Patrol which the INS oversees, enforces against illegal immigration by policing the US–Mexico border and other points of entry and by seeking to prevent the smuggling or employment of illegal aliens.

Current US policy on illegal immigration is based largely on the Immigration Reform and Control Act (IRCA) of 1986, which made it illegal to employ illegal aliens, mandated monitoring of employers, and expanded border enforcement.[7] IRCA also offered amnesty to illegal aliens who could establish that they had resided in the United States continuously since 1982. As a result of IRCA, the INS granted legal residence to 2.7 million individuals, 2 million of whom were Mexican nationals (see Fig. 8.1).[8] In 1998, the Border Patrol

140 000 would be employment-based, and 55 000 would be 'diversity immigrants.' The law also set temporary immigration at 65 000 for the H-1B programme and 66 000 under the H-2B programme, and created new categories for temporary admission of workers (O, P, Q, R). Subsequent legislation created categories for temporary immigration of professional workers from Canada and Mexico as part of the North American Free Trade Agreement (INS, 2000).

[4] The Refugee Act of 1980 created systematic procedures for the admission of refugees 'of humanitarian concern', eliminating refugees and asylum seekers as a category of the existing quota-preference system (INS, 2000).

[5] To obtain a temporary work visa, a worker must be sponsored by a US employer. The H-1B visa applies mainly to workers in high-tech industries. It was created in 1990 to permit foreigners with a college degree to work in the United States for a renewable three-year term for employers who petition on their behalf. In 1998, the US Congress raised the annual number of H-1B visas from 65 000 to 115 000 for a period of three years. The H-2B visa, created by the Immigration Reform and Control Act of 1986, applies to seasonal labourers, most of whom work in agriculture. The bureaucratic steps needed to obtain H-2B visas are onerous, which appears to limit their use.

[6] Estimates for 2000 put the number of illegal immigrants at 8 million (Camarota, 2001).

[7] Prior to this time it had been illegal to 'harbor' illegal aliens but not to employ them (Calavita, 1992).

[8] Subsequent to IRCA, several pieces of legislation modified US treatment of illegal aliens. The Personal Responsibility and Work Opportunity Reconciliation Act of 1996 barred illegal aliens

apprehended 1.5 million illegal aliens at the US–Mexico border and 124 000 illegal aliens through other enforcement efforts (INS, 2000). While the US Border Patrol has enforced the border against illegal immigration since 1924, the modern experience of high levels of illegal immigration dates back to the 1960s and the end of the *Bracero* Programme (1942–64), which allowed seasonal farm labourers from Mexico and the Caribbean to work in US agriculture on a temporary basis.

9.2. RECENT TRENDS IN US IMMIGRATION

The current US immigration wave is the second the country has experienced in the last century and a half. Both are clearly evident in Fig. 9.1, which shows admissions of new legal immigrants by year from 1820 forward. The first wave lasted from the 1880s to the 1920s, bringing in a total of 26 million immigrants. The current one began in the 1960s and has accelerated in each subsequent decade. There are a number of salient features about current US immigration.

Immigrants are concentrated at the extremes of the skill distribution. Table 9.1 shows the educational profile of immigrant and native men and women over the period 1960–98. Immigrants are much more likely to have lower levels of schooling than US native-born individuals. In 1998, 34 per cent of immigrant men had not completed the equivalent of a high-school education, compared to only 9 per cent of US native men. At the same time, immigrants are also more likely to have very high levels of schooling than US natives. In 1998, 13 per cent of immigrant men had at least a master's degree, compared to 10 per cent of US native men. In the 1960s, immigrant men had educational profiles that were more similar to US native men, indicating that the average relative educational attainment of immigrant men has been declining over the past several decades. This reflects in part a shift in the national composition of new immigrants, as shown in Table 9.2, from countries in Europe, where education levels are similar to the United States, to countries in Asia and Latin America, where average education levels are lower than the United States. Women show the opposite pattern from men, as the educational profiles of immigrant and native women have become more similar over time.

from most federal, state, and local government benefits and required the INS to verify an individual's immigration status before he or she could receive most types of federal public benefits. The Illegal Immigration Reform and Personal Responsibility Act of 1996 mandated increases in border enforcement and surveillance; increased penalties for smuggling, illegal entry, and failure to depart; instituted 3- and 10-year bars for legal admissibility in the United States for individuals found to have entered the country unlawfully; and further restricted access of illegal aliens to federal public benefits (INS, 2000).

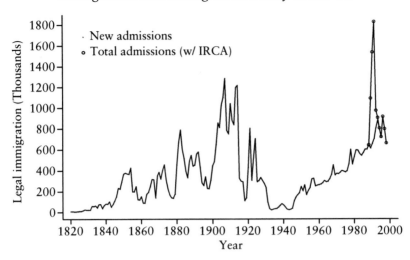

Figure 9.1. *US legal immigration*

Table 9.1. *Changing skills of immigrant and native populations, 1960–98 (in %)*

	1960	1970	1980	1990	1998
Native men					
who are high school dropouts	53.0	39.7	23.3	11.9	9.0
who are college graduates	11.4	15.4	22.8	26.4	29.8
with at least a master's degree	—	—	—	9.2	9.9
Immigrant men					
who are high school dropouts	66.0	49.0	37.5	34.1	33.6
who are college graduates	10.1	18.6	25.3	26.6	28.3
with at least a master's degree	—	—	—	12.9	12.5
Hourly wage differential					
between immigrant and native men	4.2	0.0	− 9.2	− 15.0	− 23.0
Native women					
who are high school dropouts	46.1	35.3	19.7	9.2	6.6
who are college graduates	9.7	11.5	17.9	23.6	28.5
with at least a master's degree	—	—	—	7.7	8.7
Immigrant women					
who are high school dropouts	61.8	47.9	34.6	25.9	24.5
who are college graduates	5.6	9.7	17.5	23.0	28.7
with at least a master's degree	—	—	—	8.0	8.8
Hourly wage differential					
between immigrant and native women	3.4	3.0	− 1.7	− 5.0	− 12.1

Source: Borjas (1999).

Table 9.2. *Sources of legal immigration in the United States*

	Foreign-born pop., 2000		Cohorts by arrival year			
	Level (000s)	Percent distribution	Pre-1970	1970–79	1980–89	1990–99
			(level in 000s)			
All countries	28 379	100.0	4547	4605	8022	11 206
			(percent distribution)			
Mexico	7858	27.7	15.0	30.2	28.4	31.3
Canada	679	2.4	7.0	1.8	1.1	1.7
Central America	1948	6.9	3.8	4.6	9.9	6.9
Caribbean	2815	9.9	13.0	10.7	9.9	8.3
South America	1876	6.6	4.8	6.2	6.7	7.5
Europe	4356	15.3	41.3	11.7	8.2	11.4
East Asia	5085	17.9	9.0	20.2	22.7	17.2
South Asia	1315	4.6	1.4	4.3	4.4	6.2
Middle East	1035	3.6	2.4	6.4	3.8	2.9
Sub-Saharan Africa	511	1.8	0.4	1.5	1.9	2.4
Other/Oceania	904	3.2	2.0	2.3	3.1	4.1

Source: Camarota (2001).

Immigrants earn less than US natives. Table 9.1 shows that in 1998 the average hourly wage for immigrant men was 23 per cent less than that for native men and the average hourly wage for immigrant women was 12 per cent less than that for native women. Such immigrant–native wage disparities have not always existed. In 1960 and 1970, immigrants earned as much or more than native workers. These changing wage patterns reflect the increasing concentration of immigrants at relatively low education levels. We see this more clearly by examining the wages of recent immigrants. In 1960, the average hourly wage of recent immigrant men was 13 per cent less than that for native men; by 1990, this so-called entry wage gap had reached 34 per cent. The rise in the entry wage gap falls somewhat (17 per cent in 1960 vs 29 per cent in 1990) when we control for differences in age and education between immigrants and natives (Borjas, 1999a).

Immigrants tend to concentrate in specific US regions. Table 9.3 shows the immigrant share of the population for the nation as a whole and for selected US states. Upon arriving in the United States, immigrants tend to settle in the 'gateway' states of California, Florida, Illinois, New Jersey, New York, and Texas. In 2000, these states were home to 73 per cent of immigrants but only 36 per cent of natives. Within these states, most immigrants live in a few large cities. In 2000, 53 per cent of immigrants, but only

Table 9.3. *Immigration and population in the United States in 2000*

	State share of national pop.		State share of foreign-born pop.		Share of foreign-born pop.	
	1990	2000	1990	2000	1990	2000
California	12.0	12.4	32.7	30.9	21.7	25.9
New York	7.2	6.8	14.4	12.8	15.9	19.6
Florida	5.2	5.5	8.4	9.8	12.9	18.4
Texas	6.8	7.3	7.7	8.6	9.0	12.2
New Jersey	3.1	3.0	4.9	4.3	12.5	14.9
Illinois	4.6	4.4	4.8	4.1	8.3	9.5
Nation	—	—	—	—	7.6	10.4

Source: Center for Immigration Studies (*http://www.cis.org.*)

23 per cent of natives, lived in just six consolidated metropolitan areas, Los Angeles, New York, San Francisco, Miami, Chicago, and Washington-Baltimore (Camarota, 2001). California stands out as the state of choice for recent immigrants. The share of the state's population that is foreign born rose from 10 per cent in 1970 to 26 per cent in 2000 (compared to the rise in the nation as a whole from 5 to 10 per cent). California has attracted a disproportionately large share of less-educated immigrants. In 1998, the state was home to 32 per cent of all immigrants and 40 per cent of immigrants who had not completed high school, compared to 10 per cent and 9 per cent, respectively, in 1970 (Borjas, 1999). The state is also home to a dispropor-tionate share of illegal immigrants, as shown in Table 9.4. In 1996, an estimated 40 per cent of illegal immigrants in the United States resided in California and another 41 per cent of illegal immigrants resided in one of the other five gateway states.

Immigrants tend to concentrate in specific occupations and industries. Table 9.5 shows the distribution of native and foreign-born workers by occupation for 2000. Relative to native workers, immigrants are much less likely to be managers, professionals, or administrative staff and much more likely to be manual labourers or to work in services, construction, or agriculture. This latter set of low-paying jobs are what we would expect for workers with relatively low levels of education and relatively little US labour-market experience. Table 9.6 shows the share of workers who are foreign born by education level and US industry. In 1990, while immigrants accounted for 19 per cent of all workers with less than a high-school edu-cation, they accounted for more than 30 per cent of workers in agriculture, apparel, food products, and household services. Immigrants with a college

Table 9.4. *Illegal immigrants in the United States, 1996*

Country of origin	Population	State of residence	Population
All countries	5 000 000	All states	5 000 000
Mexico	2 700 000	California	2 000 000
El Salvador	335 000	Texas	700 000
Guatemala	165 000	New York	540 000
Canada	120 000	Florida	350 000
Haiti	105 000	Illinois	290 000
Philippines	95 000	New Jersey	135 000
Honduras	90 000	Arizona	115 000
Poland	70 000	Massachusetts	85 000
Nicaragua	70 000	Virginia	55 000
Bahamas	70 000	Washington	52 000
Colombia	65 000	Colorado	45 000
Ecuador	55 000	Maryland	44 000
Dom. Republic	50 000	Michigan	37 000
Trinidad & Tobago	50 000	Pennsylvania	37 000
Jamaica	50 000	New Mexico	37 000
Pakistan	41 000	Oregon	33 000
India	33 000	Georgia	32 000
Dominica	32 000	Dist. of Columbia	30 000
Peru	30 000	Connecticut	29 000
Korea	30 000	Nevada	24 000
Other	744 000	Other	330 000

Source: US Immigration and naturalization service (*http://www.ins.usdoj.gov.*)

Table 9.5. *Share of employment by occupation, nationality and ethnicity, 2000*

Occupations	% immigrant	Average wages($)	% of workforce	% of immigrants	% of natives
Total Workforce	12.8	33 921	100.0	100.0	100.0
Low-immigrant occupations	10.4	38 616	72.3	58.3	74.3
Managerial and Professional	10.2	49 695	31.2	24.8	32.2
Technical, Sales, Admin. Support	9.0	30 542	27.9	19.6	29.2
Farming Managers, Forestry, Fishing	8.8	12 447	1.1	0.7	1.1
Precision Production, Craft and Repair	14.0	30 949	12.1	13.2	11.9
High-immigrant occupations	19.3	21 674	27.7	41.7	25.7
Operations, Fabricators, Labourers	17.6	24 319	14.8	20.3	14.0
Service Occupations, Non-household	18.1	19 590	11.0	15.5	10.3
Household Service Occupations	39.7	12 195	0.4	1.2	0.3
Farming, Except Managerial	40.3	13 233	1.5	4.7	1.0

Notes: Data are for persons in the labour force, 16 years and over, employed full time for at least part of the year.

Source: Current population survey, March 2000 (*http://www.census.gov/*), Camarota (2001).

Table 9.6. *Foreign-born share (%) of industry employment, 1990*

Industry	Education Level			
	Less than high school	High school graduate	Some college	College graduate
All industry	18.7	5.9	6.3	8.8
Agriculture	31.5	4.2	2.9	2.9
Ag. services	29.5	9.2	6.4	4.1
Mining	5.8	0.7	3.2	8.1
Construction	18.9	4.7	4.6	9.8
Food products	33.6	9.1	8.6	7.8
Textiles	13.3	1.9	2.2	6.4
Apparel	41.9	9.7	18.3	25.1
Lumber	9.8	1.5	1.7	4.0
Furniture	24.4	7.6	5.1	5.1
Paper	16.4	3.3	7.4	5.5
Printing	15.7	5.0	5.6	5.5
Chemicals	22.4	4.1	5.7	8.9
Rubber	28.2	5.2	9.4	6.6
Leather	16.0	13.3	10.6	7.5
Stone, clay, glass	11.0	4.3	5.6	8.5
Primary metals	24.1	3.2	3.0	4.1
Metal products	26.7	7.9	4.9	10.4
Machinery	19.5	4.0	6.3	14.2
Elec. machinery	24.4	8.6	9.7	13.9
Transport equip.	18.2	6.0	4.9	6.9
Misc. manuf.	40.5	9.7	12.9	11.9
Transport., utilities	11.7	4.0	6.2	8.3
Wholesale trade	19.7	7.0	6.0	9.3
Retail trade	15.3	7.0	6.5	11.6
FIRE	15.0	5.7	6.3	8.6
Investment finance	30.2	10.3	12.0	6.9
Lodging services	27.8	12.2	13.5	20.5
Personal services	21.4	9.2	6.1	20.0
Business services	22.5	7.2	6.4	11.0
Auto. services	15.6	7.3	12.8	12.3
Repair services	19.4	1.9	6.9	13.9
Entertainment	12.1	5.6	7.7	5.4
Health services	12.7	6.1	6.1	13.0
Legal services	23.3	4.9	7.0	3.7
Educ. services	10.4	4.7	6.2	6.1
Social services	9.2	5.3	5.5	6.5
Household services	32.3	15.5	14.6	26.8
Government	9.7	2.7	4.4	5.1

Source: Public use Micro. Sample (5%), *US Census of Population and Housing, 1990.*

education were disproportionately concentrated in apparel and lodging, personal, and household services. In these industries, highly educated immigrants may function as entrepreneurs (perhaps hiring workers of the same nationality).

10

How do Economies Adjust to Immigration Inflows?

One important consideration for US immigration policy is the economic impact of arriving immigrants. How does an economy like the United States absorb immigrant inflows? The commonly assumed answer is via wage pressures. This perception has helped make the labour-market impact of immigration a politically charged issue.

> There are advantages [to immigration]. Businesses can hire new immigrants at lower pay; and consumers gain because reduced labour costs produce cheaper goods and services. But, generally speaking, the gains from high immigration go to those who use the services provided by new immigrants. If you are likely to employ a gardener or housekeeper, you may be financially better off. If you work as a gardener or housekeeper, or at a factory job in which unskilled immigrants are rapidly joining the labour force, you lose. The last twenty years of immigration have thus brought about a redistribution of wealth in America, from less-skilled workers and toward employers.
>
> Pat Buchanan, 'To Reunite a Nation', presidential campaign speech delivered in Yorba Linda, CA, 18 January 2000.

But wages are only one possible adjustment mechanism in economies like the United States that are open to flows of goods, capital, and ideas. In this chapter, we delineate these adjustment mechanisms by sketching out some standard models used in both labour and international economics. Immigration-induced changes in labour supplies can be absorbed via changes in relative factor prices, but they can also be absorbed in at least three other ways: changes in industrial specialization, migration of labour and/or capital, and changes in underlying production technology.

Our discussion then turns to the empirical evidence. Most research on immigrant absorption has looked for wage impacts, at the regional and/or national level. There is a large literature on regional wage responses to regional immigrant inflows, and the repeated finding is that immigration has a small negative impact, at best, on local native wages (for surveys, see Borjas, 1994, 1999; Borjas *et al.*, 1997). National wage effects do not seem to be particularly large, either. There is a relatively small literature on whether native migration responds to immigrant inflows, with mixed results. We will discuss evidence that output-mix and/or technology changes have helped accommodate immigrant inflows and thus account for the lack of obvious wage pressures.

After evaluating the past, we look to the future. Although the recent US experience seems to show that wage adjustments have not predominated, the conditions that have contributed to this outcome may not persist. We identify possible changes in the economic environment, both at home and abroad, under which the wage impacts of immigration could become more pronounced. If this happens, the political economy of immigration may shift: the larger is the impact of immigration on wages, the stronger the demands for changes in the level or composition of immigration are likely to be.

10.1. HOW THE US ECONOMY ABSORBS IMMIGRANTS: THEORETICAL FRAMEWORK

To elucidate how economies can absorb immigrant inflows, this section briefly summarizes three models of the labour market: the area-analysis model, the factor-proportions-analysis model, and the Heckscher–Ohlin (HO) trade model. The first two models are commonly used in labour economics (we borrow the terms from Borjas *et al.*, 1996), while the third is the standard model in international trade.

Consistent with the facts about recent US immigration presented in Chapter 9, in all models we treat the US immigrant inflow as an increase in the relative supply of less-skilled workers. To maintain a simple focus on different skill groups in the labour force, in all models we assume just two factors of production, skilled labour and unskilled labour. To maintain focus on equilibrium wage determination, in all models we assume that wages are sufficiently flexible to ensure full employment. Of course, how realistic this assumption is varies in the real world. Our country of interest, the United States, is commonly thought over the medium-to-long run to have flexible labour markets that are reasonably approximated by the full-employment/flexible-wages assumption. In contrast, in recent years many European countries have displayed much higher unemployment rates and more wage rigidity. For these cases, it may be more realistic to consider unemployment as another possible adjustment mechanism.[1]

10.1.1. *The area-analysis model*

This model assumes a single aggregate output sector (the factor demands for which can be proxied by the factor demands for a single representative firm), and also assumes distinct, geographically segmented labour markets within a country. This latter assumption is likely to be untrue in the very long run, but it may be true over shorter time horizons thanks to frictions such as information and transportation costs that people (both natives and immigrants

---

[1] We note that the US–Europe contrast was reversed before the early 1970s: in earlier decades US unemployment rates were generally higher than those in Europe. Davis (1998) models how the labour-market impacts of trade depend on whether or not wages clear at full employment.

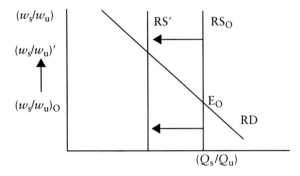

Figure 10.1. *Labour-market equilibrium: the area-analysis model or the factor-proportions-analysis model*

Notes: Skilled labour is subscripted 's' and unskilled labour 'u'. The RS schedule is relative supply and the RD schedule is relative demand. For the factor-proportions-analysis model this picture represents the single national labour market; for the area-analysis model this picture represents each separate local labour market.

upon arrival) must incur to move. Empirically, US 'local' labour markets are usually defined by states or metropolitan areas. Each local market has its own equilibrium wages determined by local supply and demand.

If there is literally no mobility among local labour markets, the effects of immigration on wages are limited entirely to the 'gateway' communities where immigrants arrive. In each community, arriving immigrants must price themselves into employment by accepting lower wages and thereby inducing profit-maximizing firms to demand them. If within each skill category natives are perfect substitutes for immigrants, then wages move for natives as well as immigrants. Thus, immigrant inflows raise the local skill premium, with larger immigrant inflows meaning larger wage changes. At unchanged product prices, real wages move commensurate with relative wages: skilled real wages rise, while unskilled real wages fall.

Figure 10.1 displays the labour market for the area-analysis world. The horizontal axis plots the local supply of skilled labour relative to unskilled labour, while the vertical axis plots the local skill premium. The local relative-labour-demand schedule RD slopes downward everywhere, consistent with most technologies one might assume for the single representative profit-maximizing firm. Initial relative labour supply is given by the schedule RS_O, with initial equilibrium at point E_O and relative wages $(w_s/w_u)_O$. Immigration shifts the supply schedule back to RS', raising the local skill premium to (w_s/w_u). Again, for fixed product prices real wages change, too.[2]

---

[2] Consistent with our full-employment assumption, the relative-supply schedule is vertical: all workers are sufficiently willing to work that they price themselves into employment at any going relative wage.

10.1.2. *The factor-proportions-analysis model*

Like the previous model, the factor-proportions-analysis model also assumes a single output sector employing all workers. The fundamental difference between the two is that this model assumes a national labour market. Thanks to sufficient mobility of natives (and immigrants upon arrival) there are no geographically segmented 'local' labour markets. Natives can leave gateway communities when immigrants arrive; immigrants can move on to other communities; or natives can choose not to enter gateway communities as planned pre-immigration.

The assumption of a national labour market means that the wage pressures created by immigration spread beyond gateway communities. Arriving immigrants must still price themselves into employment as described above, but now wages adjust throughout the entire national labour market.

Graphically, the factor-proportions-analysis model also looks like Fig. 10.1—but with the key difference that now this figure represents national, not local, conditions. Here, immigration shifts relative labour supplies and thus wages economy-wide.

10.1.3. *The Heckscher–Ohlin model*

The key assumption of the HO trade model is that there are more tradeable products (i.e. sectors) than primary factors of production, with products differentiated by their factor intensities. Multiple products are essential for establishing many fundamental trade-theory results, such as comparative advantage.[3] The HO framework usually assumes a single national market for each factor, although many of its key ideas apply to regions within countries as well. We maintain this assumption for now, but revisit it in our empirical discussion of the next section.

With these assumptions, in equilibrium a country chooses (via the decentralized optimization of firms) the 'output mix' that maximizes national income subject to the constraints of world product prices, national factor supplies, and national technology. This output mix consists of both products which actually get produced and the quantities of production. In turn, this output mix helps determine the country's national factor prices. The general intuition is that the technology parameters and world price for each produced sector help determine national wages. In the standard case where the country makes at least as many products as the number of primary factors, equilibrium wages are a function of just the world prices and technology parameters of the produced sectors. These wages do not depend on the prices and technology of the non-produced sectors.

---

[3] Without at least two products, countries (in a static setting) would have no incentive to trade and thereby more optimally allocate scarce national resources. Ethier (1984) generalizes the HO model to settings with many products.

They also do not depend directly on the level of endowments, only indirectly through the endowments' role in selecting the product mix.

The effects of immigration on wages depend on the initial product mix, on the size of the immigration shock, and on whether the country is large or small (i.e. on whether its product mix does or does not have any influence on world product prices). Consider the standard case where the initial output mix is sufficiently diversified for wages to depend on just world prices and technology.

In this case, with 'sufficiently small' shocks the country absorbs immigrants by changing its output mix as predicted by the Rybczynski Theorem (1955): the same products are produced, but output tends to increase (decrease) in the unskill-intensive (skill-intensive) sectors. Whether wages change depends on whether the country is big or small. If the country is small, world prices do not change and thus there are no wage effects. This insensitivity of national wages to changes in national factor supplies Leamer and Levinsohn (1995) call the Factor-Price-Insensitivity (FPI) Theorem. If the country is large, wages do change in the spirit of the Stolper–Samuelson (1941) Theorem: the relative price of unskill-intensive products declines, which tends to lower (raise) wages for unskilled (skilled) workers.

With 'sufficiently large' immigration shocks, national wages do change. Large enough shocks induce the country to make a different set of products, which entails a different set of world prices and technology parameters and thus different wages. This absorption of large shocks via changes in both output mix and wages holds whether the country is big or small: in either case wage inequality rises.

Figure 10.2 displays the national labour market for the case of a small HO country with three products. The distinguishing feature is the shape of relative labour demand. It has two perfectly elastic portions, each of which corresponds to a range of endowments for which FPI holds. The national output mix varies along the demand schedule. A different set of two products is made on each elastic part; accordingly, different relative wages prevail on each elastic part. On the downward-sloping portions the country makes only one product. Along these portions output-mix changes are not possible, so immigrants must price themselves into employment by changing wages. Point E_O designates the initial labour-market equilibrium, with relative labour supply RS_O and relative wages $(w_s/w_u)_O$. Two immigration shocks are shown. The 'sufficiently small' immigration shock shifts RS_O to RS'. Relative wages do not change, as immigrants trigger Rybczynski output-mix effects with no product-price changes. The 'sufficiently large' shock shifts RS_O to RS''. The country now produces a new set of products. As a result the unskilled wage falls relative to the skilled wage (to $(w_s/w_u)''$), and with fixed product prices this relative-wage decline will be a real-wage decline as well.[4]

---

[4] Three additional comments are in order on Fig. 10.2. First, it is important to emphasize that an economy would need to satisfy several crucial HO assumptions for it to manifest portions of

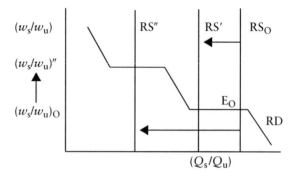

Figure 10.2. *Labour-market equilibrium: the Heckscher–Ohlin model*

Notes: Skilled labour is subscripted 's' and unskilled labour 'u'. The RS schedule is national relative supply and the RD schedule is national relative demand.

10.1.4. *Other adjustment mechanisms for immigrant inflows*

Our discussion thus far has described two possible mechanisms by which economies absorb immigrants. The first is wage changes, a mechanism potentially present in all three frameworks discussed. The second is output-mix changes, as predicted by the HO model.

A third possible mechanism is native labour-supply changes. One version of this mechanism contrasts the area-analysis and factor-proportions frameworks: even if immigrants arrive into gateway communities, they may trigger native labour-supply flows that dissipate any wage effects throughout the entire country. More generally, during the period of immigration inflows there may be changes in native labour supply unrelated to immigrant inflows. For example, it is well known that as the United States has been receiving larger immigrant inflows in recent decades, the educational mix of natives has been rising. But to the extent that natives and immigrants are sufficiently substitutable within each skill category, what may matter for equilibrium wages is not the immigration-related shifts in RS but rather the overall shifts in RS. If

RD that were truly perfectly elastic. Relax these assumptions and the perfectly elastic portions would start to 'tilt'. For example, as discussed in the text, if the country could affect world prices, then output-mix changes would trigger Stolper–Samuelson wage adjustments via world-price changes. Or if some factors were attached ('specific') to certain sectors, this would inhibit output adjustments. Second, underlying the downward-sloping portions of RD is the assumption of flexible production technologies with factor substitutability. With Leontief technology these portions would be vertical. Third, along the national demand schedule the country's output mix progresses according to sector factor intensities. The likely output mixes are as follows. Along the leftmost branch of RD the country makes only the most unskill-intensive product. Along the first flat it makes this product and the 'middle' intensity product, switching to only the middle product along the middle downward-sloping branch. The country picks up the most skill-intensive product as well along the second flat; finally, along the rightmost branch it makes only the skill-intensive product.

immigrant and native labour-supply changes move against each other, then the net supply change depends on the relative magnitudes.

A fourth possible adjustment mechanism is contemporaneous shifts in relative-labour demand. Our HO discussion specified an endogenous shift in labour demand, via output-mix effects. But during periods of immigrant inflows there may be other labour-demand shifters unrelated to immigrant inflows. One is trade-related shifts via the Stolper–Samuelson process. A large number of recent papers have looked for Stolper–Samuelson wage pressures operating on the United States in recent decades (see Slaughter (2000) for a survey).

Another possible labour-demand shifter is technological change. There is a large literature that documents how US technological change in recent decades appears to have shifted firms' relative demand away from less-skilled workers and towards more-skilled workers (Bound and Johnson, 1992; Katz and Murphy, 1992; Berman *et al.*, 1994; Autor *et al.*, 1998; Katz and Autor, 1999). This skill-biased technological change (SBTC) may tend to offset labour-supply shifts from immigrants and/or natives.[5] Economic openness may matter a great deal for SBTC within the United States: regional openness to the flow of ideas may mean innovations discovered in particular locations (e.g. Silicon Valley) diffuse throughout the entire country.

10.1.5. *Summary*

If one assumes economies are closed to flows of factors, goods, and ideas, then immigrant inflows must be absorbed via wage changes. But to the extent that US regions and/or the country overall is open to these flows, other adjustment mechanisms are possible: native factor flows, output-mix changes and resultant trade flows, technological change. As we have discussed, these other adjustment mechanisms may be endogenous responses to immigrant inflows or may be largely unrelated. Either way, if these other mechanisms operate then immigrants need not pressure wages as is commonly assumed. Having set out these possibilities, we now turn to the empirical evidence.[6]

---

[5] See Gandal *et al.* (2000) for a discussion of how skill-biased technical change appears to have helped Israel absorb very large inflows of highly-skilled Russian immigrants.

[6] Even adjustment mechanisms commonly presumed to be unrelated to immigrant inflows may not be. For example, Acemoglu (1999) models how the technologies firms adopt endogenously respond to shifts in labour supplies. Empirically, Saxenian (1999) studies how immigrants have contributed to growth in Silicon Valley in recent years: She reports that in 1990 immigrants accounted for 32 per cent of the region's scientific and engineering workforce, and that in 1998 Chinese and Indian engineers were running 25 per cent of the region's high-technology businesses. Rauch and Trindade (2001) estimate that Chinese immigrants stimulate more bilateral trade between their host countries and China. Gaston and Nelson (2001) also discuss how immigrants can be absorbed into host-country labour markets.

10.2. HOW THE US ECONOMY ABSORBS IMMIGRANTS: EMPIRICAL EVIDENCE

10.2.1. *Wages and labour-supply adjustments*

Wage changes are the obvious first place to look for immigrant absorption. There is by now a very large literature on this issue (for comprehensive surveys, see Borjas, 1994, 1999; Friedberg and Hunt, 1995). Most studies have adopted the area-analysis framework in light of the evidence that recent immigrants concentrate in gateway regions (see Table 9.3). The general approach of these studies is to correlate the fraction of immigrants in a region with native wages (and sometimes other outcomes, like un/employment rates). Different studies take different approaches to measuring regions (cities, metropolitan areas, states); distinguishing skill groups (just distinguish natives from immigrants—which in turn may be separated between new and older arrivals—or separate further, especially by skills measured via educational attainment or occupation); econometric specification (levels, time differences of varying lengths); and treatment of potential endogeneity between immigrant inflows and local labour-market conditions (use OLS, or instrument for immigrant inflows using stocks/flows of immigrants from earlier periods). A representative group of studies includes Altonji and Card (1991), LaLonde and Topel (1991), and Card (2001).

The near uniform finding is that immigration has, at most, a small negative effect on wages. Typical estimates are that a 10 per cent increase in the fraction of immigrants in a region lowers native wages by less than 1 per cent (often an amount not statistically different from zero). This finding has been obtained from a wide range of studies under a wide range of treatments of the relevant measurement, specification, and estimation issues outlined above. It has even been found in event studies such as Card (1990), who documented that although the 1980 Mariel boat lift into the Miami-area labour market unexpectedly increased the local labour supply by 7 per cent in a four-month period, this shock had no discernible effect on native wages or unemployment in the area.

There is ample evidence, then, that regional variation in immigrant inflows generates small pressures, at best, on regional wages. One possible reason for this, suggested by the factor-proportions framework, is that native migration patterns respond to immigrant inflows such that total labour-supply shifts across regions are more uniform than that suggested by natives alone.

It is commonly thought that inter-regional labour mobility is high in the United States relative to most other advanced economies. In Europe, by contrast, inter-regional labour mobility appears to be much lower (Abraham, 1996). It is clear that US labour tends to migrate from low-wage to high-wage regions, at least over medium to long time horizons (Topel, 1986; Blanchard and Katz, 1992). Of particular relevance for immigration, low-skill workers appear to be less mobile across regions than high-skill workers (Borjas *et al.*, 1992; Bound and Holzer, 1996).

But what about labour mobility related specifically to native responses to immigration inflows? There is some evidence that natives respond to immigration inflows by exiting and/or choosing other destinations. Borjas *et al.* (1997) document that before 1970, California's population growth was driven both by immigrants and natives. But since 1970, after the start of large-scale immigration into California and the overall country (see Chapter 9), California's population growth was almost entirely accounted for by immigrants alone. Borjas *et al.* (1997, p. 21) note that, 'This suggests that the increasing number of immigrants who chose California as their destination "displaced" the native net migration that would have occurred and thus diffused the economic effects of the immigration from California to the rest of the country'.

Does the California example of native responses to immigrant inflows generalize to the rest of the country? Different researchers have reached sharply different answers. A representative study answering 'no' is Card (2001). Using a panel of skill-group/city observations, he regresses the city's net outflow rate of natives or earlier immigrants in a skill group on that city's contemporaneous inflow rate of new immigrants in that skill group. A wide range of other control regressors are used, and immigrant inflow rates are also instrumented using earlier immigrant stocks (a sensible instrument given the ongoing tendency of immigrants to concentrate in gateway locations). This analysis finds that mobility flows of natives and earlier immigrants are not very sensitive to new-immigrant inflows—indeed, if anything they are slightly complementary to new-immigrant flows.

The opposite conclusion is reached by Borjas *et al.* (1997). For an initial specification that parallels Card's, they, too, find that native-population growth rates for states (either states' entire population or population by skill groups) are positively correlated with contemporaneous immigrant-population growth rates. But they argue that these specifications, which correlate across states' contemporaneous growth rates of natives and immigrants, implicitly assume that all states would have had the same growth rate of natives absent the immigrants. If this assumption is not warranted—that is, if each state had its own pre-immigration growth path—then contemporaneous correlations without some kind of pre-immigration control are misleading.

Borjas *et al.* estimate a difference-in-differences specification that compares each state's native and immigrant growth rates 'post-immigration' (i.e. 1970–90) with its growth rates 'pre-immigration' (i.e. 1950 or 1960–70). Using the earlier growth rates as their counterfactual control, they now estimate a negative correlation (sometimes significant, sometimes not) between native population growth and immigrant inflows. With this different counterfactual in their analysis, these authors conclude that native population flows do respond to immigrant inflows.[7]

---

[7] One other possible reason that immigrants do not seem to pressure regional wages is that causation also runs from wages to immigrant inflows. Borjas (2001) argues that arriving

As in the factor-proportions framework laid out in Section 10.1.2, with this kind of regional labour mobility immigration inflows should trigger national, not regional, wage adjustments. Accordingly, Borjas *et al.* calculate these national wage impacts as suggested by Fig. 10.1. First, they calculate the labour-supply shifts induced by immigrants across various skill groups. Immigrants post-1970 contributed most to the national supply of high-school dropouts, with smaller contributions for higher skill groups. Second, they translate these labour-supply shifts into wage changes using various assumed values for the elasticity of national labour demand. They conclude that immigrants can account for around half of the post-1980 decline in relative earnings of high-school dropouts, but can account for less than 10 per cent of the rising college/high-school wage premium. Thus, the national wage effects of immigrant inflows are calculated to be sizable only for the very least-skilled workers.

The question of how much native population flows respond to immigrant inflows raises the related question of how large these two sets of flows are. One possible reason immigrant inflows might not substantially pressure wages is that these inflows are small relative to native labour-supply changes. If natives and immigrants are sufficiently substitutable within various skill groups, then small immigrant wage effects might simply result from small immigrant labour-supply changes relative to native changes. This possibility that natives tend to dominate immigrants in overall supply changes is suggested by the just-described wage findings of Borjas *et al.*

Table 10.1 shows the share of US state labour forces accounted for by native and foreign-born workers in four education categories (high-school dropouts, high-school graduates, those with some college education, college graduates) in changes over the period 1980–90. Data are reported for the overall country, the six immigration-gateway states (see Table 9.3), and six other large states. Looking just at immigrants shows that these workers generally increased their share of the labour force in all education categories. This is most true for high-school dropouts in the gateway states (especially California), broadly consistent with the rising immigrant presence documented in Chapter 9.

But the main message of Table 10.1 comes from comparing the relative magnitudes of native vs immigrant changes. In the country overall and in every state shown, except California, the impact of immigrants on the composition of the labour force is overwhelmed by changes in the educational attainment/labour-force participation of natives. Everywhere there is a large decline in the labour-force shares of less-educated native workers and a large increase in the

immigrants tend to choose to locate in US regions that offer them the highest wages for their skills. It is well known that there are sizable cross-state differences in wages paid for observationally equivalent workers in different skill groups. Borjas documents that arriving immigrants by skill group tend to settle in the highest-paying states, and that levels of arriving immigrants are correlated with wage-convergence rates. Thus, the location decisions of immigrants may 'grease' the wheels of the overall US labour market by helping arbitrage differences across regional labour markets within the country.

Table 10.1. *Share of the state labour force by education category for natives and immigrants, change 1980–90*

State	Worker type	HSDO	HSG	SC	CG
United States	Natives	−7.8	−5.1	6.4	3.9
	Immigrants	0.8	0.2	0.8	0.8
New York	Natives	−6.5	−5.2	4.0	4.3
	Immigrants	0.1	0.4	1.4	1.5
New Jersey	Natives	−7.4	−5.4	4.3	5.2
	Immigrants	0.0	0.4	1.1	1.9
Illinois	Natives	−8.6	−5.8	7.2	5.2
	Immigrants	0.4	0.3	0.7	0.6
Florida	Natives	−6.8	−5.1	5.5	2.9
	Immigrants	1.2	0.3	1.2	0.8
Texas	Natives	−9.7	−3.7	6.2	3.1
	Immigrants	2.1	0.4	0.8	0.8
California	Natives	−5.2	−7.6	1.5	2.4
	Immigrants	3.9	0.9	2.1	1.9
Massachusetts	Natives	−6.2	−6.3	3.8	6.8
	Immigrants	−0.3	0.2	0.8	1.2
Ohio	Natives	−7.4	−4.3	8.1	3.7
	Immigrants	−0.3	−0.2	0.1	0.3
Michigan	Natives	−7.2	−6.0	9.9	3.6
	Immigrants	−0.4	−0.4	0.1	0.3
North Carolina	Natives	−12.9	−1.0	9.2	4.1
	Immigrants	0.1	0.0	0.2	0.3
Georgia	Natives	−11.8	−1.0	6.8	4.4
	Immigrants	0.5	0.2	0.3	0.6
Washington	Natives	−5.2	−7.8	7.6	4.1
	Immigrants	0.4	−0.2	0.5	0.5

Notes: Each cell reports the level change in the share of that state's total labour force accounted for by the factor in that cell. 'HSDO' designates high-school dropouts; 'HSG' designates high-school graduates; 'SC' designates those with some college; and 'CG' designates college graduates and beyond.

labour-force shares of more-educated native workers. This relative-supply shift is due to a combination of retirements and other 'exits' from the labour force, rising educational attainment of new labour-force entrants, and further education of continuing labour-force participants. These movements in native educational attainment swamp the comparatively small changes in immigrant labour-force shares. The one exception is California, where less-educated immigrant entrants to the labour force nearly offset exits of less-educated native workers.

Table 10.2 combines the native and immigrant share changes in Table 10.1 to show the net labour-supply shifts in the overall country and in specific states.

Table 10.2. *US state labour supplies, changes over 1980–90*

State	HSDO	HSG	SC	CG
United States	−6.9	−4.8	7.1	4.7
Connecticut	−8.2	−4.6	5.3	7.5
Massachusetts	−6.5	−6.2	4.7	8.0
New Jersey	−7.4	−5.0	5.4	7.0
New York	−6.4	−4.8	5.3	5.8
Illinois	−8.3	−5.5	7.9	5.8
Michigan	−7.6	−6.3	10.0	3.9
Ohio	−7.6	−4.5	8.2	4.0
Pennsylvania	−7.9	−4.3	7.0	5.3
Florida	−5.6	−4.8	6.7	3.8
Georgia	−11.3	−0.8	7.1	5.0
North Carolina	−12.8	−1.0	9.3	4.4
Texas	−7.6	−3.3	7.0	3.9
California	−1.3	−6.6	3.6	4.3
Washington	−4.8	−8.0	8.2	4.6

Notes: Each cell reports the level change from 1980 to 1990 in the share of that state's total labour force (employed plus unemployed) accounted for by the factor in that cell.

Source: Hanson and Slaughter (2001).

The clear message is skill upgrading of the labour force, both for the country overall and for individual states. Again, California is an outlier: relative to the rest of the country, it did not lose the less-than-high-school segment of its labour force—thanks, as Table 10.1 showed, to arriving immigrants offsetting native exits.

Although not shown in Table 10.2, this pattern of skill upgrading of the US labour force has been going on for decades—and it continued over the 1990s as well. This longer-term perspective appears in Table 10.3, which reports for selected years the distribution of the US adult population across four education categories. The skill upgrading for the 1980s shown in Table 10.2 is part of a trend dating back at least 60 years. As we will discuss in Section 10.3, however, this process of strong native skill upgrading is *not* forecast to continue in the coming generation (Smith and Edmonston, 1997). But at least for recent decades, the clear message is that net changes in both national and regional US relative labour supplies have been driven by natives, not immigrants. This may make the apparent absence of wage impacts of immigration seem less puzzling.

10.2.2. *Technology and output-mix adjustments*

So how are these net changes in labour supply absorbed? Beyond wages and factor flows, two other adjustment mechanisms highlighted in Sections 10.1.3 and 10.1.4 were output-mix effects and other labour-demand shifters such as technological change.

Table 10.3. *US labour supplies in recent decades (% of national labour force)*

Year	High-school dropouts	High-school graduates	Some college	College graduates
1940	76	14	5	5
1950	66	21	7	6
1963	52	30	9	9
1970	45	34	10	11
1979	32	37	15	16
1989	23	39	17	21
1999	17	33	25	25

Notes: Each cell reports the per cent share of the total US adult population (aged 25 and over) accounted by that labour group in that year.

Source: Johnson (1997, table 1) for all years but 1999. For 1999, US Bureau of the Census (2000).

Take technology first. Table 10.2 shows an increase in the US supply of more-skilled relative to less-skilled workers—during a period in which the US returns to skill, as discussed earlier, were rising. From the closed-economy area-analysis or factor-proportions perspectives in Fig. 10.1, in the face of rising relative supplies of skill, the skill premium can be rising only if relative labour demand shifts out even more. SBTC is a prime candidate for such a shift.[8] From the HO trade perspective, the supply shifts in Table 10.2 will have either no wage impact (with FPI) or will lower the skill premium. Thus, for the rising skill premium along with these supply shifts to be caused by technological change, this technological change would have to shift 'up' the RD schedule in Fig. 10.2. This upward shift in RD would require technology innovations to be concentrated in the skill-intensive sectors.[9]

What empirical evidence is there on the role of technological change? At the national level, as outlined in this section, there appears to have been

---

[8] More specifically, where the one-sector labour-demand curve is just the demand curve for a representative firm, for commonly assumed production technologies (e.g. CES) the only force that will shift relative labour demand is factor-biased technological change. Hicks-neutral technological change does not alter relative factor demands, and output-mix effects are not possible by construction.

[9] Given the *shape* of RD in Fig. 10.2, it is important to emphasize that its *position* depends on product prices and production technology. Changes in prices or technology shift the position of the relevant parts of RD, and wages change to restore zero profits in all sectors. At initial factor prices, any change in product prices or technology means zero profits no longer hold in one or more sectors. Producers respond by trying to expand output in now-profitable sectors and reduce output in now-unprofitable sectors. Relative labour demand increases for the factors employed relatively intensively in expanding sectors; labour demand decreases for the factors intensive in the contracting sectors. To restore equilibrium, at fixed labour supply, relative wages must respond to the demand shifts until all profit opportunities are arbitraged away. The key empirical implication of this intuition is that the wage effects of changes in product prices and/or technology tend to depend on their *sector* bias, that is, on the distribution across sectors of induced profit changes.

pervasive SBTC within US industries in recent decades. Although the US skill premium has been rising, firms within most US industries have been hiring relatively more, not fewer, more-skilled workers. This employment shift towards skilled workers despite their rising cost strongly suggests SBTC. From the factor-proportions perspective, this raises the US skill premium in the face of rising skill supplies so long as the demand shift predominates.[10] As for the sector bias of this pervasive SBTC, Haskel and Slaughter (2001) estimate that US SBTC was in fact more extensive in skill-intensive sectors over the 1980s. Thus, from the perspective of either the factor-proportions or the trade frameworks, the data suggest SBTC has been an important adjustment mechanism over the 1980s.

The role of SBTC at the regional level is examined by Hanson and Slaughter (2001). For a sample of 14 US states over the 1980s, they decompose changes in state employment by education category into changes in labour demand arising from output-mix changes across industries and changes in production techniques within industries. These changes in production techniques, in turn, further decompose into national changes that mirror shifts in the rest of the country and state-specific changes. The national changes capture the contribution of national SBTC (and other national shocks); state-specific changes capture the contribution of state-specific changes in relative wages. Consistent with the area-analysis empirical results discussed earlier in Section 10.1.1, they find that state-specific changes in production techniques contribute little to factor absorption. Had state-specific wage changes been important, we would have expected to see a much larger contribution from state-specific changes in production techniques, since these production techniques are a function of factor prices. Instead, states absorb changes in employment primarily through changes in production techniques that are common across all states. This is consistent with technology innovations flowing across US states in a manner that happens to offset these states' rising supplies of more-skilled workers.

What about output-mix effects? We know of no study examining these effects at the national level. For US states, Hanson and Slaughter (2001) use a set of accounting decompositions to examine the labour-demand mechanisms through which states absorb changes in labour supplies. One possible mechanism is changes in the mix of outputs of traded goods. To isolate this

---

Any change that initially increases profits in a particular sector tends to raise the economy-wide wage for factor(s) employed relatively intensively in that sector. In terms of Fig. 10.2, segments of RD tend to shift *up* when price growth and/or technological progress is concentrated in skill-intensive sectors. Conversely, segments of RD tend to shift *down* when these changes are concentrated in relatively unskilled-intensive sectors.

[10] As discussed in the text, the US labour force has been skill upgrading for decades. But the skill premium has not been uniformly rising throughout this period; in particular, it declined during the 1970s. From the labour perspectives in Fig. 10.1, a falling and then rising skill premium in the face of ongoing relative-labour-supply shifts requires SBTC to be initially slower and then faster. Thus, much of the empirical literature on SBTC and changing skill premia has examined whether the rising skill premium has been accompanied by an acceleration in SBTC (e.g. Autor *et al.*, 1998).

mechanism, they adjust observed changes in labour supplies both for labour-demand shifts related to national SBTC (because the Rybczynski Theorem is a comparative-static notion with no other shocks) and for labour-demand shifts related to output changes among nontradables (because tradability matters for Rybczynski effects not to pressure wages). They find that these changes in 'effective' labour supplies are accounted for largely by labour-demand changes mandated by output-mix changes among tradables.

To help make their output-mix findings concrete, they examine how the pattern of industrial specialization in California has evolved over time. Table 10.2 shows that relative to the rest of the country, over the 1980s California's labour force became more concentrated at both ends of the skill-distribution: it had far less of a fall in the high-school-dropout share of the labour force, and it had about the same growth in the college-graduate share.[11] From Table 10.1, we see that immigrants accounted for this relative growth in California nearly as much as natives did. Given these labour-supply shifts, the FPI logic of the HO framework would predict California to have shifted towards production in industries intensive in the use either of very low-skilled or very high-skilled labour.

This was precisely what happened. Table 10.4 reports California's six fastest-growing industries relative to the rest of the country over the 1980s (in terms of the California annualized growth rate of real value added less the US annualized growth rate of real value added). Table 10.4 also reports the factor intensity of these six industries, with lower (higher) numbers indicating more skill-intensive (unskill-intensive) industries. Relative to the rest of the country, the six fastest-growing industries in California during this period were either very skill-intensive—machinery (much of which is computers), legal services, finance, insurance, and real estate—or were very unskill-intensive—textiles, apparel, and household services. Industry immigrant intensity is also reported in Table 10.4, with lower (higher) numbers indicating more (less) immigrant-intensive industries. The three unskill-intensive sectors were also among the most immigrant-intensive in California. This is consistent with the FPI logic of arriving less-skilled immigrants tending to gain employment in these unskill-intensive sectors.

To generalize beyond the high-growth industries in Table 10.4 to all sectors, we estimate the following simple regression equation for California:

$$(\text{relative output growth})_i = \alpha + \beta(\text{skill intensity})_i$$

$$+ \gamma(\text{skill intensity})_i^2 + \delta(\text{immigrant intensity})_i + \varepsilon_i, \qquad (10.1)$$

---

[11] Across the four labour groups in Table 10.2, the difference in labour-share changes between California and the overall country were $+5.6$ ($-1.3-(-6.9)$) for high-school dropouts, -1.8 ($-6.6-(-4.8)$) for high-school graduates, -3.5 ($3.6 - 7.1$) for some college, and -0.4 ($4.3 - 4.7$) for college graduates.

Table 10.4. *California high-growth industries, 1980–90*

Industry name	Annualized growth rate	Skill intensity	Immigrant intensity
Machinery	4.3	15	18
Household services	3.9	40	6
Apparel	3.9	37	1
FIRE	2.8	4	36
Textiles	2.5	29	3
Legal services	2.3	1	40

Notes: Each industry's output growth rate is the California annualized growth rate less the US annualized growth rate in terms of real value added. The skill-intensity measure reports each industry's ranking among 40 sectors economy-wide, with lower (higher) numbers indicating more skill-intensive (unskill-intensive) sectors. Skill ranks are constructed from the average across 1980 and 1990 of each industry's nationwide employment of college graduates relative to high-school dropouts. The immigrant-intensity measure reports each industry's ranking among 40 sectors in California, with lower (higher) numbers indicating more (less) immigrant-intensive sectors. Immigrant ranks are constructed from the average across 1980 and 1990 of each industry's immigrant share of total employment.

Table 10.5. *Explaining California industry growth, 1980–90*

Regressor	Estimates
Industry skill intensity	−0.060 (0.024)
Industry skill intensity^2	0.004 (0.002)
Industry immigrant intensity	0.382 (0.314)
Constant	0.119 (0.050)
No. of observations	40
Adjusted *R*-squared	0.08

Notes: Cell entries are parameter estimates (standard errors) for equation (10.1). Output growth is the California growth rate less the US growth rate. Skill (immigrant) intensity is the average employment of high-school dropouts (immigrants) relative to college graduates (all workers) in 1980 and 1990.

where subscript *i* indicates industries and ε_i is an error term. Skill intensity is average employment of high-school dropouts relative to college graduates for 1980 and 1990; immigrant intensity is average employment of immigrants relative to all workers for the same years. Our expectation that California output growth relative to that in the rest of the country be highest in either unskill-intensive or very skill-intensive sectors, and in the immigrant-intensive sectors, suggests that equation (10.1) should reveal that $\beta < 0$, $\gamma > 0$, and $\delta > 0$. Table 10.5 reports estimation results from equation (10.1) using weighted least squares (with California industry output as weights; OLS results are qualitatively the same). The estimated coefficients are just as expected, with the two for skill intensity significantly different from zero at standard levels.

Figure 10.3 visualizes these estimation results. For each industry in California over the 1980s, Figure 10.3(a) plots actual output growth relative to the rest of the country against industry employment of high-school dropouts relative to college graduates; it also plots predicted output growth calculated using the coefficient estimates for skill intensity and the constant from Table 10.5. Figure 10.3(b) is the analogous figure plotting actual and predicted output growth against immigrant intensity (average share of immigrants in total industry employment). The lines of best fit show quite clearly the regression results: output growth tended to be higher in either the very skill-intensive or the unskill-intensive sectors, and in immigrant-intensive sectors.

The case of the California apparel industry, one of the most immigrant-intensive in the state, is particularly compelling. Between 1970 and 2000, the state's share of national apparel employment rose from 6 to 24 per cent. During the 1980s and 1990s it was one of the few states in which apparel employment actually grew. Relative to the rest of the country, California had average annual employment growth in apparel of 5 per cent in the 1970s, 5 per cent in the 1980s, and 7 per cent in the 1990s.[12] About two-thirds of the state's apparel industry is located in Los Angeles, where many less-skilled immigrants live. In 1990, 75 per cent of workers in California apparel were immigrants (up from 41 per cent in 1970), compared with 13 per cent of apparel workers in the rest of the nation (up from 10 per cent in 1970) (McCarthy and Vernez, 1998).

Beyond these cross-industry output-mix effects, one final piece of evidence on the role of immigrants in California comes from looking at employment shifts within industries. Table 10.1 shows large declines in California's supply of natives in the two less-skilled groups, with incoming immigrants helping offset these declines. Independent of any cross-industry shifts, within California industries one would expect to see employers replacing the 'disappearing' less-skilled natives with broadly comparable less-skilled immigrants.

Figure 10.4 shows widespread evidence of this within-industry substitution away from natives and towards immigrants. For each industry in California over the 1980s, Fig. 10.4(a) plots the level change in the immigrant high-school dropout employment share against the level change in the native high-school dropout employment share; Fig. 10.4(b) has native high-school graduates on the vertical axis. In all industries but one (leather goods) the native employment share was falling while the immigrant high-school dropout share was rising.[13] Thus, within all industries the mix of less-skilled workers was shifting away from natives and towards immigrants.

---

[12] In the rest of the country, apparel employment has declined since the 1970s.
[13] The (unweighted) correlation of share changes in Fig. 10.4(a) is −0.68 and in Fig. 10.4(b) is −0.51.

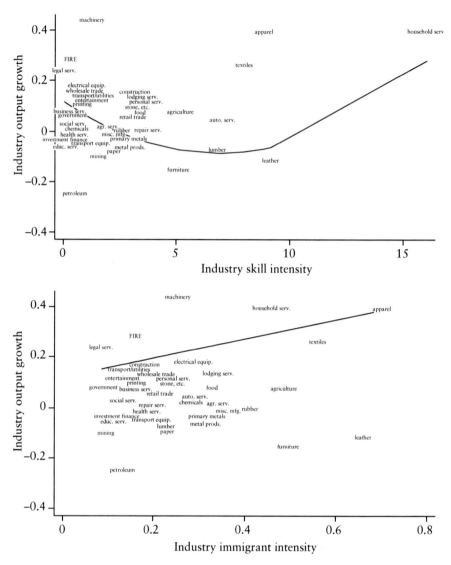

Figure 10.3. *California output growth by industry skill and immigrant intensity, 1980–90*

Notes: Industry relative output growth, skill intensity, and immigrant intensity are defined and constructed as in Table 10.5. The curve in each figure is a line of best fit constructed from coefficient estimates in Table 10.5 (see text for details).

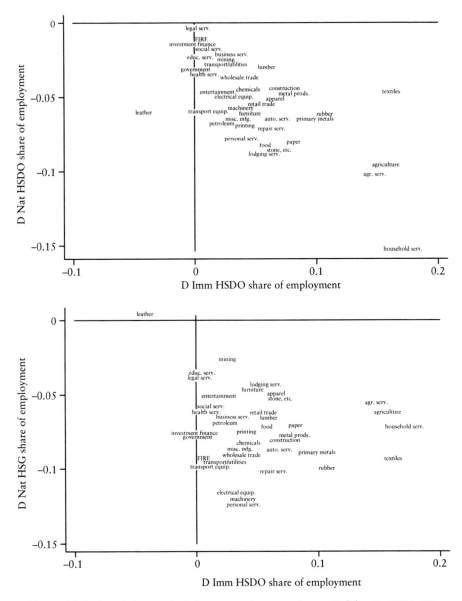

Figure 10.4. *Level changes in industry employment shares: California, 1980–90*

Notes: 'D' indicates level changes; 'Nat' indicates natives; 'Imm' indicates immigrants; 'HSDO' indicates high-school dropouts; 'HSG' indicates high-school graduates.

10.2.3. *Summary of empirical evidence on adjustment mechanisms*

The large immigrant inflows into the United States in recent decades appear not to have triggered large wage adjustments, either at the regional or the national level. The largest estimates for wage pressures appear to be for native high-school dropouts at the national level; outside of this case, a wide range of studies finds no compelling evidence of wage pressures. This is partly because native labour-supply changes have been much larger than immigrant changes, and partly because these net labour-supply changes have been absorbed on the demand side via technology and output-mix changes.

10.3. HOW THE US ECONOMY ABSORBS IMMIGRANTS: FUTURE PROSPECTS

Will the United States maintain its ability to absorb immigrants with very little wage pressures? To answer this question, start with the assumption that arriving immigrants will continue to be less skilled than natives, on average. Barring dramatic changes in US immigration policy, this outcome seems likely (Borjas, 1999).

10.3.1. *Supply-side adjustment mechanisms*

First, consider supply-side adjustment mechanisms. As discussed above, in recent decades shifts in US labour supply from immigrants have been dominated by native labour-supply shifts. But Elwood (2001) forecasts that US labour-force growth in the next 20 years will be very different from that of the previous 20. First, growth in the absolute size of the labour force will be much smaller: From 1980 to 2000 the overall labour force grew by 35 per cent and the so-called prime age workforce—that is, those aged 25–54—grew by a remarkable 54 per cent. Elwood predicts that from 2000 to 2020 these growth rates will fall to only 16 per cent and 3 per cent, respectively. This is mainly because the currently prime-age baby boomers will move into retirement and will be replaced by a much-smaller generation.

Second, the dramatic skill-upgrading of the US labour force will largely stop. From 1980 to 2000 the college-educated share of the labour force rose by over eight percentage points, from 22 to 30 per cent. But from 2000 to 2020, Elwood's baseline prediction is that the college-educated share will rise two percentage points, to 32 per cent. This is because the large, well-educated baby boomers will be replaced by a generation with only marginally higher educational attainment (thanks to declining and then only slowly recovering college enrolment rates in the 1970s and 1980s).

Overall, it appears that the dramatic increase in size and skills of the US labour force in recent decades will not be repeated. Much of this has to do with the ageing of native baby boomers: as this large, educated group exits the labour force into retirement, their replacements will be fewer and not markedly more educated. Because these trends will be driven mainly by natives, immigration will potentially play a larger role in shaping net changes in US labour supplies. With less skill upgrading of natives in coming decades, continued arrivals of less-skilled immigrants will be a more important force reducing the skill mix of the US labour force. This suggests that arriving immigrants will pressure US wages more in the future than they have in the past.

10.3.2. *Demand-side adjustment mechanisms*

We think the possibility of output-mix effects is likely to grow, in so far as the assumptions underlying the HO framework are likely to grow more realistic. The tradability of many goods and services is rising, thanks to ongoing declines in natural and political trade barriers. Inter-industry labour mobility is also rising, thanks to sharp corporate restructuring, continued declines in private-sector unionization rates, and advances in information technology (e.g. job-matching Internet web sites like monster.com) that improve the technology matching workers with vacancies. One piece of country-level evidence is the declining US share of world GDP. At the end of the Second World War, the United States accounted for about half of the world output (and, arguably, an even greater share of output in the economically integrated world excluding largely autarchic countries like those behind the Iron Curtain). By 2000 this share was down to around one-fifth. At the level of individual industries there is at least anecdotal evidence of heightened product-market competition in recent years. For example, many have argued that new information technologies make markets thicker and more transparent.

Graphically, increased potential for output-mix effects means the shape of the US labour-demand schedule will become more like that of Fig. 10.2. What about the position of this demand schedule? One force working against US less-skilled workers may be continued SBTC. Another may be the continued integration of China, India, and other low-income countries into the world economy. Entry into the world economy of these low-income countries is communicated to the US labour market via shifts in the RD curve. Entry of these countries increases the world relative supply of less-skilled labour; in turn, this tends to lower the world relative price of unskill-intensive products, such as textiles and toys. In Fig. 10.2, these price changes shift up the portions of the US RD curve along which the United States would optimally choose to produce these goods—that is, portions corresponding to low skill mixes in the labour force.

Whether the United States will actually be producing these kinds of 'exposed' unskill-intensive goods will depend on the position of the RS curve. As discussed at the outset of this section, in coming decades immigration may very well exert a stronger downward pull on the skill mix of the US labour force.

Immigration and other labour-supply shifts may keep the national RS schedule 'too far' to the left in Fig. 10.2 such that US less-skilled workers are exposed to shifts in RD due to China, India, etc. In contrast, countries with sufficiently skilled labour forces will be insulated from the 'China effect' as they operate farther right on the RD schedule. For these countries, events in low-income countries do not affect relative wages; instead, low-income growth generates real-wage gains for all factors via lower prices for unskill-intensive goods.

10.3.3. *Summary*

The conditions that have prevented US immigrants from pressuring native wages may not persist in coming decades. This is because of both supply-side and demand-side considerations. Instead, a plausible case can be argued that immigration will increasingly work against the skill-upgrading of the US labour force, in a way that exposes US workers to developments in low-income countries.

If this happens, the political economy of immigration may shift. The larger the impact of immigration on wages, the stronger are the demands for changes in the level or composition of immigration likely to be. In Chapter 13, we will turn to consider these political-economy issues.

11

Illegal Immigration

As we have seen, illegal aliens currently account for a large fraction (about one-third) of new immigrants in the United States. This has not always been the case. Illegal immigration arose only after the US government began to restrict legal immigration in the 1920s. Except for a brief episode in the 1950s, it was small in scale until temporary immigration programmes ended in the 1960s (see Figs 11.1 and 11.2). While illegal immigrants come from many nations, Mexico is the single largest source country. From Table 9.4, in 1996 an estimated 54 per cent of US illegal immigrants were Mexican nationals. Over the period 1988–98, above 95 per cent of those apprehended by the Border Patrol attempting to enter the country illegally were individuals from Mexico (INS, 2000). Given large and persistent wage differences between the two countries, restrictive US legal immigration policies, and a long shared land border whose geography complicates enforcement, high levels of illegal immigration from Mexico are hardly surprising.

In this chapter, we examine US policies towards illegal immigration, the factors that contribute to illegal immigration, and the impact of illegal immigration on the US economy. We conclude the chapter with a discussion of recent proposals for changing US policy towards illegal immigration.

11.1. BACKGROUND

Illegal immigration in the United States has its origins in the market for agricultural labour. Historically, the United States has been abundant in land and capital and scarce in labour relative to Mexico, which has helped create large wage differentials between the two countries. Production of perishable crops tends to be very labour intensive and growers of these crops in the US southwest have recruited labourers from Mexico for a century or more. Still, Mexican immigration in the United States was slow to begin. Early last century, a series of positive shocks to US agriculture and negative shocks to Mexican agriculture helped start the south-to-north labour flow.

In the early 1900s, government irrigation projects, beginning with the Newlands Irrigation Act of 1902, expanded the land available for agriculture in the western United States, helping increase agricultural labour demand in the region. Shortly thereafter, the Mexican Revolution (1911–17) pushed many

Mexican peasants off their land, some of whom moved north to escape violence and find work.[1] At the time, there was little enforcement of the Mexico–US border and undocumented immigration was common. The 1917 Immigration Act changed this regime by imposing a literacy test and a head tax on prospective immigrants. This, in effect, made illegal the existing (and continuing) flow of labour across the border (Martin, 1998).[2]

After the First World War, as the United States tightened restrictions on immigration overall, and from non-European countries in particular, pressures for illegal immigration increased. In 1924, the US Border Patrol was created to monitor national boundaries. Initially, the Border Patrol had only 450 officers to enforce both the Canadian and the Mexican borders, making effective enforcement lax. The Great Depression induced a further tightening of restrictions on legal immigration. During this period, illegal immigration from Mexico was relatively low, as high unemployment in the US dissuaded many prospective Mexican workers from migrating north.

In the 1940s, labour shortages caused by the Second World War re-ignited Mexican immigration. To help Mexican workers enter the US labour market, in 1942 the US government established the Bracero Programme, which granted Mexican labourers temporary permits to work in US agriculture. Labourers in Mexico, or braceros, were contracted by US agricultural growers to work in the United States for a single growing season, after which they were obliged to return to Mexico. In an early example of coordination between Mexico and the US on immigration policy, the Mexican government endorsed the programme and negotiated immigration levels with the United States, appealing to the notion that an agreed-upon legal framework would protect Mexican workers from abusive treatment by US employers (Martin, 1998).

Figure 11.1 shows immigration of braceros over the programme's life. At its peak in 1956, 445 200 Mexican workers entered the United States. The number of Mexican workers the Border Patrol admitted each year changed according to US economic conditions. Agency reports from the 1950s indicate that US agricultural labour demand was a major factor in INS decisions of how many braceros to admit. When the Border Patrol launched Operation Wetback in the early 1950s—which raised border enforcement as a means of reducing illegal immigration—growers were allowed to more than double the number of braceros they brought into the country, largely nullifying the impact of increased enforcement on the US supply of manual labour (Calavita, 1992).[3]

---

[1] By some estimates, between 1910 and 1930, 1.5 million Mexicans, or 10 per cent of the country's population, emigrated to the United States (Martin, 1998).

[2] The same year the law was enacted, the US Department of Labor began to allow temporary immigration of Mexican workers, most of whom were farm labourers. They were permitted to work in the country for one year and required to carry a special identification card. Over the period 1917–21, 50 000 to 80 000 Mexican nationals entered the United States under this programme (Martin, 1998).

[3] Operation Wetback was a response, in part, to increasing illegal immigration of individuals attempting to avoid restrictions imposed by the Bracero Programme. In order to obtain jobs as

Figure 11.1. *Temporary immigration under US Bracero Programme, 1942–64*

Not surprisingly, large-scale temporary immigration was controversial in the United States. Labour groups condemned the Bracero Programme, and prevented temporary Mexican workers from joining US unions. Agricultural growers from the United States defended temporary immigration, claiming that the braceros would take jobs that American workers would not. The mechanization of US agriculture gradually reduced the intensity of production in manual labour, helping weaken support for admitting braceros (Martin, 1998). The US Congress abolished the programme in 1964.

Since the end of the Bracero Programme, the formerly legal and temporary labour inflow from Mexico has become illegal and more permanent. Many Mexican illegal aliens in the US return to Mexico one or more times a year (Cornelius, 1992; Reyes, 1997). The number of illegal aliens living in the United States, about half of whom are Mexican, has increased steadily over time, from 2.7 million in 1987 to 5.3 million in 1997 (Warren, 1999). The annual inflow of illegal immigrants is difficult to measure directly.[4] One indirect measure is apprehensions by the INS of individuals attempting to enter the country illegally. While apprehensions overstate illegal immigration, since a given individual

braceros, Mexican workers often had to pay bribes to recruitment officers in Mexico and the United States. By entering the United States illegally workers were able to avoid these bribes. During the early years of the Bracero Programme, enforcement of the border was weak. By increasing both border enforcement and the number of braceros admitted, the United States effectively legalized the flow of labour across the border (Martin, 1998).

[4] A large literature estimates the number of illegal immigrants and their inflow in the United States. See Hans Johnson (1997) for recent estimates for California and a discussion of other estimates. See the Mexico–United States Binational Migration Study (1998) for estimates of illegal aliens from Mexico, in particular.

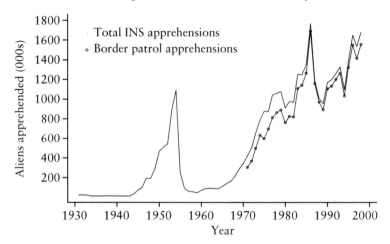

Figure 11.2. *Illegal aliens apprehended by the INS*

may be apprehended multiple times in a given year, its variation over time appears to reflect variation in attempts at illegal entry.[5]

Figure 11.2 shows total apprehensions by the INS and apprehensions by the Border Patrol border for the period 1931–99. Since 1986, when the Immigration Reform and Control Act (IRCA) was passed, apprehensions by the Border Patrol have accounted for 95 per cent of total INS annual apprehensions, with over 95 per cent of Border Patrol apprehensions occurring at or near the Mexico–US border. Apprehensions show a strong upward trend, rising from an average of 133 000 per year in the 1960s to 1.4 million per year in the 1990s. There are spikes in the series during economic crises in Mexico, such as the onset of the Latin American debt crisis in 1982 and the collapse of the Mexican peso in 1994–95, and increases in US border enforcement, as occurred following Operation Wetback in 1953, the passage of IRCA in 1986, and the initiation of special operations by the US Border Patrol in the 1990s.

Being apprehended by the INS does not prevent an individual from attempting to enter the United States again in the near future. Individuals that the INS apprehends who agree to be deported voluntarily are not processed by the US justice system, spend a few days or less in custody before being returned to their home country, and face no restrictions on their ability to enter the United States legally in the future. For Mexican nationals, voluntary deportation often involves little more than a bus ride across the border. During the 1990s, voluntary departures accounted for over 95 per cent of all INS apprehensions.[6]

---

[5] Espenshade (1994) estimates that the correlation between apprehensions and the gross flow of illegal immigrants across the Mexico–US border is 0.9.

[6] Those who do not depart voluntarily are subject to a hearing before a judge. If they are found to have entered the country unlawfully, they may face a ban of up to 20 years before being able to enter the United States legally (INS, 2000).

To help translate apprehensions data into the net inflow of illegal immigrants, Warren (1995) estimates that for 1982–88 the average annual net inflow of illegal immigrants from Mexico was 165 000 individuals and the INS (1998) estimates that for 1988–96 it was 150 000 individuals. Legal Mexican immigration in the United States has risen over time, but remains at lower levels. Discounting the amnesty granted to illegal aliens as part of IRCA (see Fig. 9.2), over the period 1980–98 legal admissions of Mexican nationals by the INS averaged 86 000 individuals per year (INS, 2000).

11.2. US POLICY TOWARDS ILLEGAL IMMIGRATION

Many government policies affect the flow of illegal immigrants into the United States. Some, such as setting quotas for legal immigration or denying immigrants access to public assistance, operate indirectly by affecting the expected rewards from attempted illegal immigration. Others, including the enforcement of US borders and the monitoring of hiring practices by US employers, affect inflows of illegal immigrants more directly. In this section, we focus on these direct policies, which fall under the control of the federal government, and in particular the INS. While immigration quotas and public assistance change slowly over time—typically requiring congressional action—the intensity of border enforcement and employer monitoring are policy instruments that the INS can, in principle, change continuously. Despite federal control over enforcement policy, INS activities often give the appearance of being set on a region-by-region basis, without obvious attempts at national coordination.[7] The variation in enforcement, we shall see, is indicative of both the impact of enforcement on illegal immigration and which factors influence US policies on illegal immigration.

To gauge US efforts to block illegal immigration, Fig. 11.3 shows federal government outlays on enforcement by the INS. INS enforcement spending has increased dramatically over time, more than doubling in real terms in the 1990s. INS enforcement activities include Border Patrol operations, inspections at US points of entry, detaining and deporting apprehended aliens, and investigating those suspected of hiring illegal aliens or smuggling aliens, narcotics, or other contraband.[8] In 2000, of the 23 000 INS employees dedicated to

---

[7] A lack of coordinated enforcement policies is evident not just within the INS but between the INS and other agencies. For instance, the Border Patrol has installed licence-plate readers at about one-third of the 31 border crossing points in the southwestern United States. These readers are connected to a large data bank, which allows the Border Patrol to identify stolen vehicles that are being taken out of the United States (presumably to be resold in Mexico). Approximately 2000 stolen vehicles are identified leaving San Diego each year, alone. Due to the absence of coordination with local police agencies, little, if any, effort is made to stop the illegal export of stolen autos. See 'Customs Officials Spot Stolen Cars but Don't Try to Stop Them,' *New York Times*, February 25, 2001, p. 15.

[8] US immigration law involves the INS in the detention and incarceration of foreign-born criminals. If a foreign-born individual is found guilty of having committed a crime, then the INS

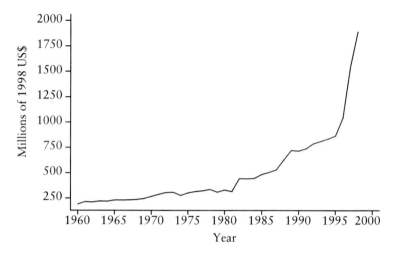

Figure 11.3. *Enforcement budget of the INS*

enforcement, 48 per cent worked for the Border Patrol, 24 per cent worked in inspection, 16 per cent were responsible for detention and deportation, and 12 per cent were responsible for investigations. Relative to its other major activities, the INS devotes few resources to monitoring employers.

Border Enforcement. The level of border enforcement in the United States is the result of several governmental decisions. The US Congress appropriates funds for the US Border Patrol, as part of the overall appropriation to the INS. This appropriation specifies how the funds are to be spent, including what portion of the budget to dedicate to enforcement activities. Given the overall enforcement budget, the INS decides how to divide resources between enforcement of US borders, which consists of policing land borders and ports of entry, or so-called 'linewatch' duty, and internal enforcement, which consists of manning traffic checkpoints, conducting raids on worksites, and investigating employers suspected of hiring illegal aliens.

The Border Patrol concentrates the majority of its enforcement efforts on the Mexico–US border. From 1970 onward, 57 per cent of total Border Patrol

determines whether this individual is deportable. Cause for deportation include having entered the United States unlawfully, having committed an aggravated felony, having engaged in activities deemed contrary to the security of the United States, or having committed certain other crimes. Recent changes in US immigration law have greatly expanded the set of deportable offences. If an individual is deemed deportable, then the INS forcibly 'removes' the person from the country, usually after the individual has finished his or her prison sentence. The number of aliens removed for criminal violations (besides unlawful entry) increased from 2000 in 1986 to 55 000 in 1998 (INS, 2000). Butcher and Piehl (2000) find that criminals subject to deportation by the INS tend to serve longer prison sentences than either native-born prisoners or foreign-born prisoners not subject to deportation. They also find that relative to native-born inmates, foreign-born prison inmates are much more likely to have been convicted of a drug-related offence.

officer hours were devoted to linewatch duty and 91 per cent of linewatch officer hours occurred at the US–Mexico border. With this allocation of enforcement activities, it is not surprising that most apprehensions occur at or near the Mexico–US border. Since 1970, 93 per cent of apprehensions occurred in the US–Mexico border region and 60 per cent occurred as individuals were attempting to cross the border itself.

IRCA and subsequent legislation mandated increases in border enforcement. The INS has implemented these initiatives largely by raising enforcement at specific points along the border where attempts at illegal entry appear to be heaviest.[9] Figures 11.4(a) and 11.5(a) show border apprehensions and total manhours Border Patrol officers spend policing the border by month in Arizona, California, and Texas.[10] Figures 11.4(b) and 11.5(b) show these same data for specific regions inside these states, which have historically accounted for most illegal entry.[11] For the period 1980–93, when the first of the Border Patrol special operations began, California and Texas accounted for 54 and 36 per cent of border apprehensions and 34 and 48 per cent of border enforcement hours, respectively. Within these states, two cities, San Diego and El Paso, were the most active crossing points for illegal aliens, accounting for 50 and 20 per cent of total apprehensions and 27 and 15 per cent of total enforcement hours over the 1980–93 period.

Border Patrol special operations appear to have reduced illegal entry at specific crossing points, without necessarily curtailing illegal immigration overall. The first major initiative, 'Operation Hold the Line', was launched in El Paso, in late 1993 (as indicated by the first solid vertical line in Figures 11.4(b) and 11.5(b)). Within a three-month period, the Border Patrol more than doubled officer patrol hours in and around the city. The effects on attempted illegal immigration are apparent in the apprehensions data for Texas in Figs 11.4(a,b). Within six months of stepping up enforcement, apprehensions in El Paso fell from 15 000 per month to 4000 per month, as many migrants stopped using the city as a US entry point (Bean *et al.*, 1994).

In Figs 11.5(a) and 11.5(b) it is clear that at the moment the Border Patrol raised enforcement in El Paso, it did *not* raise enforcement elsewhere. Not surprisingly, many migrants moved west and began to enter the United States through Arizona (Cornelius, 2000). In the year after Operation Hold the Line began, apprehensions in Tucson, Arizona more than doubled after having been

---

[9] In addition to increasing enforcement office hours, as documented below, the Border Patrol has also installed walls, fences, and underground sensors along the border, and acquired high-tech surveillance equipment.

[10] Apprehension figures are seasonally adjusted (by subtracting off the monthly mean and adding in the sample mean).

[11] The Border Patrol organizes its enforcement activities in the United States according to geographic sector. From West to East, the nine sectors along the Mexico–US border are San Diego and El Centro in California; Yuma and Tucson in Arizona; and El Paso, Marfa, Del Rio, Laredo, and McAllen in Texas.

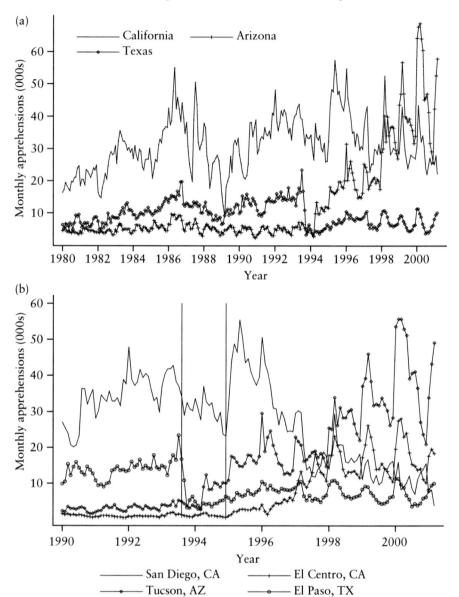

Figure 11.4. *(a) Border apprehensions by the US Border Patrol and (b) Border apprehensions at major crossing points*

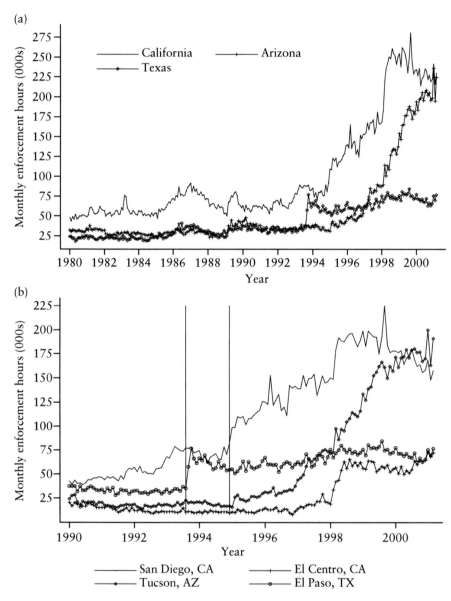

Figure 11.5. *(a) Border enforcement by the US Border Patrol and (b) Border enforcement at major crossing points*

stable for over a decade.[12] While apprehensions declined in El Paso, they did not decline for the border overall, resulting in a fall in the city's share of total apprehensions from 22 per cent in 1992 to 7 per cent in 1994. Had the Border Patrol been intent on reducing illegal immigration along the border as a whole, one might have expected the agency to have complemented its efforts in El Paso by stepping up enforcement at other major crossing points. But it was not until the late 1990s that Border Patrol responded to the changing crossing patterns of illegal migrants by increasing enforcement in Arizona.[13]

The next major border enforcement initiative, Operation Gatekeeper, began in San Diego in 1995 (as indicated by the second vertical line in Figs 11.4(b) and 11.5(b)). Between the middle of 1994 and the end of 1995, the Border Patrol more than doubled officer patrol hours in San Diego and built steel barriers along the border where the city adjoins Tijuana. Between 1995 and 1998, the Border Patrol increased enforcement hours in the region by another 50 per cent.[14] In 1995, apprehensions in San Diego first rose and then fell sharply, as illegal migrants began to stop using the city as a crossing point. At the same time, apprehensions jumped dramatically in El Centro (in eastern California) and in Arizona.[15] Again, overall border apprehensions did not decline. San Diego's share of all border apprehensions simply fell from 53 per cent in 1994 to 20 per cent in 1998. As with Operation Hold the Line, migrants reacted to Operation Gatekeeper by changing the points at which they crossed the border. In the late 1990s, the Border Patrol responded to these changing crossing patterns by increasing enforcement in eastern California and Arizona, but this came several years after it had raised enforcement in San Diego.

The practice of raising enforcement at one location but not others affects *where* illegal immigrants cross the border but not necessarily *how many* cross. Figure 11.2 shows that total border apprehensions, as an indication of attempted illegal immigration, increased in the 1990s. Warren (1995, 1999) estimates that from the late 1980s to the mid 1990s the average annual inflow of illegal aliens from Mexico was steady at 150 000–165 000 individuals per year.[16] Between 1988 and 1997, on net 1.3 million new illegal immigrants from Mexico entered the United States.

---

[12] This has led, not surprisingly, to an increase in illegal immigrants residing in Arizona. The INS estimates that the Mexican illegal alien population in Arizona increased from 115 000 in 1995 to 400 000 in 2000. See Michael Jonafsky, 'Phoenix Counts its Many Challenges: Illegal Immigration, Unrelenting, Has Put a Strain on Services,' *New York Times*, April 11, 2001, p. A12.

[13] In the late 1990s, the Border Patrol launched two new special enforcement initiatives, Operation Safeguard in Arizona, and Operation Rio Grande in south Texas.

[14] This increase occurred as the Border Patrol expanded Operation Gatekeeper into Eastern California and Arizona.

[15] The disadvantage to crossing in Arizona is that the natural environment is harsh. The Sonoran desert, which extends from Mexico into southern Arizona, has freezing temperatures in winter and scorching temperatures in summer. In the last decade, over 600 individuals have died attempting to cross the border (Cornelius, 2000).

[16] Initial estimates for 1997–2000 suggest that the inflow of illegal immigrants from Mexico has continued apace.

The Border Patrol strategy of targeting enforcement in specific regions may serve to appease groups opposed to illegal immigration, such as residents of large border cities like El Paso and San Diego,[17] without disrupting industries intensive in manual labour (by shutting down illegal immigration entirely). As one San Diego resident characterized Operation Gatekeeper, 'It's great for San Diego—people don't have illegal aliens traipsing through their yards and littering, but of course they are all being pushed elsewhere.'[18] The INS is, directly or indirectly, subject to political pressure from groups that favour lax enforcement, including agricultural growers in the western US states that specialize in labour-intensive, perishable crops. Growers frequently declare that without low-wage foreign labour they would be forced to cut back production or shutdown altogether. In defence of hiring illegal aliens, one California grower declared, 'The reality is that if the government was able to stop everybody at the border, there would be no agriculture. You wouldn't be eating asparagus.'[19]

In the current, highly politicized environment, it is difficult to document overt attempts by interest groups to undermine border enforcement. Historical evidence of anti-enforcement efforts, however, is abundant.[20] Calavita (1992) finds that in the 1940s and 1950s the district commissioner of the US Border Patrol in El Paso would routinely issue orders to stop apprehending illegal immigrants during the agricultural harvest season. During the few occasions when the Border Patrol actually did increase apprehensions, Texas farmers complained formally to their congressional representatives, who then pressured the INS publicly to cut back enforcement.

One is left with the impression that, whether intended or not, border enforcement in the United States is designed to work, just not very well. That said, the INS has raised total border enforcement substantially in the last 15 years. Though it appears not to have coordinated the timing of its operations at different points along the border, by 2001 it had raised enforcement at most major crossing points. It remains to be seen whether these increased enforcement efforts will reduce illegal immigration.

Interior Enforcement. As already noted, relative to border enforcement the INS devotes few resources to investigating or monitoring employers that hire or appear likely to hire illegal immigrants. In 1990, less than 8 per cent of INS

[17] See Marcus Stern, 'La Raza Blasts Move in State to Crack Down on Illegal Immigration', *The San Diego Union-Tribune*, July 20, 1994, p. A8; Daniel B. Wood, 'Can Crackdown Halt Border Crossings?' *The Los Angeles Times*, May 8, 1996, p. 4; and statement of Raul Yzaguirre, National Council of La Raza, Subcommittee on Immigration, US House of Representatives, June 29, 1995.

[18] See Joe Cantlupe, 'Arrests up since 1994 Crackdown at Border; Costly Effort Fails to Deter Illegal Flow', San Diego Union-Tribune, February 20, 2001.

[19] Denny Walsh, 'Valley Grower Guilty: Admits Farm Used Illegal Workers', *The Sacramento Bee*, April 30, 1999.

[20] This influence has infuriated politicians sympathetic to organized labour. In 1952, Senator Hubert Humphrey of Minnesota lamented, 'Because of the economic interests that are involved in the wetback problem, no real, sincere effort has been made to solve it. As long as it is possible to hire the wetbacks at 10 cents an hour, they will be coming across the border until kingdom come' (Calavita, 1992: 37).

Table **11.1.** *Illegal aliens apprehended by activity*

Year	Mexican nationals apprehended by US border patrol	Of which		
		Working in agriculture	Working elsewhere	Seeking employment
1992	1 168 946	5488	7165	1 065 159
1993	1 230 124	5393	7403	1 117 414
1994	999 980	5162	8068	901 826
1995	1 293 508	4487	12 552	1 185 761
1996	1 523 141	2684	9413	1 405 314
1997	1 387 650	3521	10 146	1 279 923
1998	1 522 918	3270	6616	1 398 892

Source: INS (2000).

enforcement manpower was devoted to worksite inspections (Juffras, 1991). Table 11.1 shows Border Patrol apprehensions of Mexican nationals by the type of activity illegal aliens were engaged in at the time of apprehension. Of the 1.5 million apprehensions the Border Patrol made in 1998, fewer than 10 000 occurred at US farms or other worksites.[21] As we have seen, most apprehensions occurred at or near the border. The low level of worksite apprehensions is surprising, perhaps, given that in 1996 more than two-thirds of the 2 million Mexican illegal aliens resided in US states bordering Mexico (INS, 1998), with a large fraction of these individuals living and working near the actual border.

Viewed in terms of efficiency, the strategy of favouring border enforcement over interior enforcement may seem puzzling. It is difficult to detain illegal immigrants as they cross somewhere along the 2000 mile US–Mexico border, but it is relatively easy to do so at many places of work, especially during peak production periods, such as agricultural fields at harvest time or apparel factories prior to the annual pre-Christmas production boom. One interpretation of this enforcement strategy is that the INS is pressured by one means or another to avoid enforcement activities that directly injure specific US parties, such as agricultural growers or factory owners.

Periodic attempts by the INS to increase interior enforcement are often met with stern political opposition. Following INS raids of onion fields in the state of Georgia during the 1998 harvest, the US Attorney General, both Georgia senators, and three Georgia congressional representatives publicly criticized the INS for injuring Georgia farmers.[22] The raids ceased shortly thereafter.

[21] Low worksite apprehensions do not reflect any legal mandate of the Border Patrol to focus enforcement on the actual border. The agency's jurisdiction includes interior regions proximate to US borders.

[22] See Mark Krikorian, 'Lured by Jobs, Illegal Immigrants Risk Death at Border Crossings', *Santa Barbara News-Press*, April 25, 1999.

Large-scale raids of farms in California, Florida, or Texas, which are home to the largest concentrations of undocumented workers are very rare. This may be due to the political strength of agricultural interests in these states. Similarly, the INS recently investigated the meat-packing industry in Nebraska and Iowa, which is reputed to use illegal labour intensively, but made no large-scale raids on any plants. Most plant visits by INS agents were announced in advance.[23] In defense of the inaction an INS official stated, 'We don't want to have a negative impact on the production capabilities of these companies.'[24]

A further constraint on interior enforcement efforts by the INS has been that until recently employers faced few penalties for hiring illegal immigrants. Prior to IRCA in 1986 it was not explicitly illegal to hire undocumented workers. Though it was illegal to 'harbour' illegal immigrants, under the so-called Texas Proviso of 1951 employment was not interpreted legally as harbouring. Agricultural political interests appear to have been instrumental in getting the Texas Proviso adopted (Calavita, 1992).

While IRCA did institute penalties for employers that hire undocumented workers, sanctions are infrequent and appear to have little bite. Table 11.2 shows INS investigations of employers suspected of hiring illegal aliens and the number of cases in which it issued warnings or notices of intent to fine, or imposed actual sanctions. During the period 1992–98, the INS investigated 5000 to 8000 employers per year. The agency fined relatively few employers, ranging from a low of 235 in 1998 to a high of 799 in 1993. In no year were more than 20 employers fined in excess of $20 000 and only one fine collected over the entire period exceeded $185 000 (*http://www.cis.org*).

Temporary Immigration. One alternative to illegal immigration is temporary immigration of low-skilled workers, as occurred under the Bracero Programme. Current US law allows for such temporary immigration, but only on a small scale. In 1998, the INS granted temporary work visas to 27 000 agricultural workers and 25 000 low-skilled, non-agricultural workers (INS, 2000).[25] Nearly all agricultural and most non-agricultural workers are from either Mexico or the Caribbean.[26] To obtain a temporary work visa on behalf

---

[23] The INS strategy was to announce plant visits, ask employers for permission to review employee records, and then to interview workers whose records looked suspicious. The many workers who failed to report for their INS interviews lost their jobs. The result of the INS investigation, then, was not monetary sanctions on employers but (indirectly) forced quits by workers. See 'Immigration: In the Vanguard', *The Economist*, October 16, 1999, pp. 31–2.

[24] Barbara Hagenbaugh, 'US, Meatpackers Make Deal on Immigration Crackdown', Reuters, May 7, 1999.

[25] The H-2 visa applies to temporary immigrants working in low-skill occupations. Agricultural workers enter under H-2A visas and non-agricultural workers enter under H-2B visas. Temporary work visas are also granted to individuals in high-skill occupations or who have demonstrated extraordinary abilities.

[26] In 1998, of the 27 308 H-2A visas granted, 21 594 went to individuals from Mexico and 4277 went to individuals from Jamaica; and of the 24 895 H-2B visas granted, 10 727 went to individuals from Mexico, 4293 went to individuals from Canada, 2583 went to individuals from Jamaica, 1678 went to individuals from Europe (largest source country being the United Kingdom),

Table 11.2. *INS investigations of employers*

Year	Investigations of employers	Warnings issued	Notices of intent to fine	Sanctions imposed	Fines above $20 000
1992	7053	840	1461	777	10
1993	6237	758	1302	799	14
1994	6169	683	1063	737	13
1995	5283	550	1055	792	16
1996	5149	668	1019	689	20
1997	7537	733	862	451	9
1998	7795	642	1023	235	9

Source: INS (2000), Employer Sanctions Database (*http://www.cis.org/*).

of an employee, employers have to demonstrate that no US workers would be displaced by admitting the foreign worker. This restriction appears to account for why the programme is little used in practice.

Current provisions for the temporary immigration of farm workers were a result of IRCA. IRCA permitted undocumented agricultural workers in the United States to qualify as special agricultural workers (SAWs), which gave them legal resident status. It also allowed farmers to bring in temporary, undocumented labourers as replenishment agricultural workers (RAWs), subject to government approval. Provisions for SAWs and RAWs appeared to be necessary to convince agricultural interests to support passage of IRCA. They initially opposed the legislation due to its provisions for sanctioning employers that hired illegal aliens (Martin, 1990).

Recently, there have been attempts by the Administration of President George W. Bush and by US congressional representatives from agricultural states to pass legislation that would expand the guest-worker programme and grant an amnesty to illegal immigrants who had been residing in the country for an extended period of time. Current proposals would increase temporary immigration to 250 000 workers a year. The Mexican government has publicly supported this initiative. Allowing temporary emigration generates export earnings for Mexico and potentially allows the country to retain workers with US job experience. A widespread amnesty would acknowledge the obvious fact that millions of illegal aliens live and work in the country and also remove from these individuals the legal uncertainty that clouds their participation in the economy and in their communities. Until now, passage of a new large-scale temporary immigration programme has been unable to surmount political opposition from diverse quarters.[27]

2460 went to individuals from Asia (largest source country being China), and 1799 went to individuals from Central and South America (largest source country being Guatemala) (INS, 2000).

[27] There have been several recent, unsuccessful attempts to re-instate temporary immigration. The most recent failed initiative was in 1996 (Martin, 1998).

11.2.1. *Summary*

US policies to control illegal immigration focus on enforcing the US–Mexico border against illegal entry. During the 1990s, the US government dramatically increased resources devoted to border enforcement, though in an uneven manner across border regions. These efforts do not appear to have eliminated or even reduced significantly illegal immigration from Mexico. Relatively few resources are devoted to monitoring and inspecting employers likely to hire illegal immigrants. Political pressure from special interests, including employers in labour-intensive industries, may help explain these choices of how intensively to combat illegal immigration.

11.3. FACTORS THAT CONTRIBUTE TO ILLEGAL IMMIGRATION

As we have discussed, current US policy on illegal immigration is based largely on border enforcement, though the US government is contemplating proposals to augment this policy with large-scale temporary immigration of low-skilled guest workers. To consider how these policies might influence US immigration and the US economy, we turn to recent academic research on the determinants of illegal immigration and the impact of illegal immigration on the US economy. Research on these subjects is complicated by the absence of direct data on illegal immigrants. In the literature, researchers compensate through one of three strategies: by using data on apprehensions and enforcement at the Mexico–US border, by using US census data on recent Mexican immigrants (a majority of whom appear to be in the country illegally), or by performing case studies of communities that send or receive large numbers of illegal immigrants.[28] We organize the discussion around the main findings in the literature.

Over time, the population of illegal immigrants has shifted away from itinerant agricultural workers towards more permanently settled urban workers. The characteristics of the illegal immigrant population in the United States are difficult to estimate precisely, since these individuals naturally tend to hide their immigration status. The available evidence is drawn from surveys in US or Mexican communities and data from the US population census on individuals recently arrived from Mexico.

In the 1950s and 1960s, most illegal immigrants appeared to have had a profile similar to workers admitted under the Bracero Programme: they were primarily young males from rural Western Mexico coming to the United States to work in the agricultural sector for a single growing season, after which they would return home (perhaps to migrate again the following year) (Cornelius, 1992; Reyes, 1997). Since then, the population of recently arrived Mexican

---

[28] For surveys on recent literature on illegal immigration, see Durand and Massey (1992) and Espenshade (1995).

immigrants in the United States has become more heterogeneous, in particular, becoming more female, more educated, less-oriented towards agriculture, more likely to be from urban areas in Mexico and to reside in urban areas in the United States, and more likely to be living with family members (Cornelius, 1992; Massey *et al.*, 1994; Borjas, 1996; Bustamente *et al.*, 1998; Cornelius and Marselli, 2001; Durand *et al.*, 2001). Living with family members in the United States is notable, as it reflects long-term settlement.

These changes in immigrant characteristics in part reflect changes in Mexico's population. Since the 1960s, Mexico has become a more urban, less agricultural economy with higher rates of female labour-force participation. They also reflect changes in US labour demand. Western US states, where most illegal immigrants settle, have grown substantially in the last four decades, increasing demand for low-wage manual labour in a wide array of service and manufacturing activities. Urban workers tend not to face the seasonal lulls in labour demand that are characteristic of agriculture, allowing them to establish a more permanent residence.

There appear to be sharp differences among individuals in Mexico in terms of who migrates and who does not. Comparing Mexican adults who have returned from the United States to Mexican adults who have never migrated (in a sample of rural Mexican communities), migrants are on average much younger (indicating more recent cohorts are more likely to migrate), more likely to have started or finished primary school but less likely to have finished secondary school (indicating migrants are more likely to have moderate but not high levels of education), and much more likely to have relatives who have also migrated to the United States (Orrenius and Zavodny, 2001). The importance of relatives suggests that family networks influence migration decisions. Families provide a US support base, which may help immigrants assimilate. This may lower the uncertainty associated with immigration, especially for illegal aliens who are likely to be wary of using formal channels to search for jobs or housing.

Illegal immigration appears to be highly sensitive to changes in Mexican wages and moderately sensitive to changes in US wages. Hanson and Spilimbergo (1999), building on earlier work by Bean *et al.* (1990) and Borjas *et al.* (1991), use apprehensions at the Mexico–US border as a proxy for attempted illegal immigration from Mexico and examine how border apprehensions respond to changes in Mexican wages, US wages, border enforcement, and other factors. Changes in Mexican wages have a dramatic effect on border apprehensions. A 10 per cent decline in Mexican wages leads to a 6–8 per cent increase in attempted illegal immigration from Mexico. Over the past three decades, Mexico has experienced wide variation in real wages, as periodic devaluations of the peso have led to bursts of inflation, which have caused real wages to fall sharply. These real wage declines have been followed by surges in attempted illegal entry. Figure 11.6 plots log border apprehensions against log average hourly real wages for production workers in Mexican manufacturing.

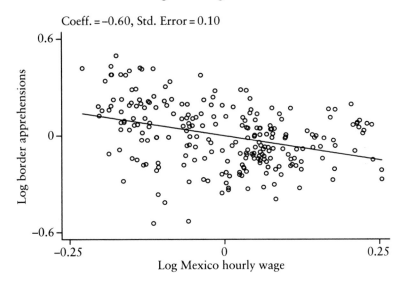

Figure 11.6. *Border apprehensions and Mexican wages*

Apprehensions rise as Mexican wages fall, indicating that volatility in Mexican wages contributes to illegal immigration. Much research on inter-regional migration in the United States and elsewhere finds that it is labour earnings in the receiving region, and not the sending region, that matter for migration flows (e.g. Shaw, 1986). This does not appear to be the case in Mexico, where low and volatile wages are a strong push factor for illegal migration.

Border apprehensions are positively correlated with US wages. This is true for US wages expressed both in peso terms and in dollar terms. That border apprehensions rise when the purchasing power of US wages in Mexico rises is consistent with the fact that Mexican immigrants in the United States remit a substantial portion of their labour earnings to family members and others in Mexico.[29] In deciding to migrate illegally to the United States, immigrants appear to count on supporting family members in Mexico or returning to Mexico eventually. Other factors one might expect would be associated with illegal immigration, such as unemployment in the United States (or in US border states) or minimum wages in Mexico and the United States, are only weakly correlated with border apprehensions. While some of these factors may matter in the long run, they do not matter for changes in illegal immigration at monthly frequencies.

There is mixed evidence about whether border enforcement reduces illegal immigration. Border enforcement does not eliminate illegal border crossings.

---

[29] In the early 1990s remittances (income migrants earned abroad and sent home) totalled 10 per cent of Mexico's export earnings (Durand, 1996). They rose from $2.5 billion in 1990 to $5.6 billion in 1998 (Woodruff and Zenteno, 2001).

It does, in many cases, force migrants to make multiple attempts at crossing the border before they succeed in evading the Border Patrol (Espenshade, 1994). Each time a migrant is caught, he or she is detained and sent back across the border, usually within a few days. This allows the migrant to make two or more attempts at illegal entry within a period as short as a week. Of migrants who had illegally entered the United States one or more times and then returned to Mexico, Kossoudji (1992) finds that on a given trip to the United States in the late 1970s 25–40 per cent were apprehended. Also using data on repeat migrants gathered in Mexico, Massey and Singer (1995) estimate the probability of apprehension for any given trip in the 1970s and 1980s to be 35 per cent.[30] To improve the likelihood of successful entry, a migrant may choose to cross the border at remote locations, such as in the Arizona desert. This brings with it greater risks of physical injury or even death (Cornelius, 2000). Another option is to hire the services of a smuggler, known as a coyote, for help in crossing the border.[31]

There is considerable debate about the effectiveness of border enforcement, due in part to the fact that its total effect on illegal immigration is difficult to observe. Border enforcement affects illegal immigration directly, in that more enforcement means fewer attempts to cross the border illegally on a given day are successful. This direct effect is abundantly clear in the data. Hanson and Spilimbergo (1999) find that the elasticity of apprehensions with respect to enforcement is approximately 0.8–1.0, which means that a 10 per cent increase in border enforcement produces an 8–10 per cent increase in border apprehensions.[32] More apprehensions do not necessarily mean less illegal immigration, as migrants may respond to greater enforcement by increasing the number of attempts they make to enter the United States illegally.

The indirect effects of border enforcement are harder to observe. Enforcement may have a deterrent effect, in that higher enforcement—by raising the

---

[30] Using the same data as Massey and Singer, but focusing on a three-year period following implementation of IRCA, Donato *et al.* (1992) estimate the apprehension probability to be 40–60 per cent.

[31] Coyotes offer a variety of services, ranging from transport immediately across the border to transport to a city in the US interior and the provision of fake US documents (Donato *et al.*, 1992). Crane *et al.* (1990) report that among individuals apprehended by the INS in 1993 8 per cent had used a coyote, compared to 5 per cent in 1988 and 15 per cent in 1976. For individuals in Mexico, the price of coyote services appears to vary from a few hundred dollars to a few thousand dollars, depending on the type of service the coyote provides and on the current state of border enforcement. Prior to Operation Gatekeeper in San Diego, coyotes charged about $300 for assistance in crossing the border and transportation to Los Angeles. By the late 1990s, these fees had risen from $800 to $1500. Similarly, as the INS increased border enforcement in Arizona, coyote fees for transportation from Agua Prieta (across the border from Douglas, AZ) to Phoenix rose from $150 in 1999 to $800 to $1300 in 2000 (Cornelius, 2000).

[32] These elasticities are based on instrumental-variables estimates of the impact of enforcement on apprehensions. An elasticity that is less than one implies there are diminishing returns to border enforcement. These diminishing returns are evident in the data. As the INS has increased border enforcement, the number of apprehensions the Border Patrol yields per hour spent policing the border has declined from 0.29 in the 1980s to 0.24 in the 1990s.

costs of entering the United States—may reduce the number of individuals that attempt to cross the border. The INS cites the success of its special operations as evidence of such a deterrent effect. While apprehensions do fall at locations where the Border Patrol has stepped up enforcement (indicating fewer attempts to cross the border), they later rise at other locations, casting doubt on the presence of border-wide deterrence. Further, as we have seen there is no clear evidence that the net inflow of Mexican illegal immigrants has fallen much following the recent large increases in border enforcement.

Greater enforcement may change the border-crossing behaviour of illegal immigrants, without having much of an effect on the number of illegal aliens that enter the country on balance. When the INS increases enforcement, migrants who prefer to return to Mexico one or more times a year may simply reduce the number of these trips. Consistent with this idea, Kossoudji (1992) finds that after being apprehended illegal Mexican migrants who move back and forth between Mexico and the United States tend to stay in the United States longer on each trip and to make fewer return trips to Mexico. If migrants respond to a higher risk of apprehension by reducing their return trips to Mexico, greater enforcement may have the perverse effect of making the illegal immigrant population in the United States more permanent.

There is some evidence that greater enforcement changes the composition of individuals who cross the border. Orrenius and Zavodny (2001) find that for a sample of young males in rural Mexican communities greater border enforcement reduces the likelihood of migrating to the United States among those with very low education levels (zero to five years of schooling) but not among those with higher education levels. Higher enforcement raises the costs of crossing the border—which an individual may incur directly by paying higher fees to coyotes or indirectly by having to spend more time and energy crossing the border—and individuals with low education levels may be unable to incur these extra costs. These results suggest it is conceivable that higher enforcement raises the skill profile of illegal immigrants in the United States.

Changes in enforcement of US borders against illegal immigration do not affect wage outcomes for workers in US border regions. One important question is whether border enforcement—by changing the level or location of illegal entry—affects the US regional economies in which immigrants settle. Hanson *et al.* (2001) examine the impact of border enforcement on wages in border regions of the United States and Mexico. As most illegal immigrants embark from a Mexican border city and choose a US border state as their final destination, they consider the border regions of California, Texas, and Mexico. If enforcement impedes illegal immigration and if illegal immigrants depress wages in the regions in which they settle, then wages in border regions will tend to rise after an increase in enforcement.

For high-immigrant industries (apparel, textiles, food products, furniture) in California and Texas, there is zero correlation between wages and enforcement of the Mexico–US border in that state. There is also no evidence of a positive effect of border enforcement on the wages of workers with low-education levels (high-school dropouts, high-school graduates) in border regions of California or Texas.[33] For Mexico, the impact of US border enforcement is larger. There is a moderate negative impact of border enforcement on wages for low-education workers (six years of education or less) in Tijuana, which is the most active crossing point for illegal immigrants during the sample period. This is consistent with higher US border enforcement increasing the supply of low-wage workers looking for jobs in Tijuana.

That border enforcement has small US wage effects suggests that illegal immigration may not depress wages in US border labour markets. This interpretation is consistent with the absence of regional wage effects for immigration overall, as discussed in Chapter 10, and with the existence of labour-market institutions that help illegal immigrants rapidly find work in the United States.[34]

Border enforcement appears to be sensitive to political pressure from industry. Lax employer monitoring by the INS is indirect evidence that political factors influence the intensity with which the US government enforces against illegal immigration. Hanson and Spilimbergo (2001) search for more systematic evidence of such effects. They examine whether sectoral shocks influence US border enforcement in order to see whether border enforcement is correlated with the fortunes of industries that use illegal immigrants most intensively. Political lobbying is one mechanism that could create such a correlation. As open lobbying *in favour* of illegal immigration is unlikely, they look for factors that affect the economic return to lobbying on border enforcement and see whether these factors are correlated with changes in enforcement activities.

To motivate this analysis, consider the apparel industry, which is a major employer of illegal immigrants. To guarantee a supply of undocumented workers, apparel firms may lobby the government to maintain weak border enforcement. Opposing these efforts, labour unions and other groups may pressure the government to keep illegal immigrants out. Out of this situation emerges an equilibrium level of enforcement. Now, suppose there is a positive shock to apparel demand. This shock raises the apparel industry's demand for illegal labour, as well as the return to lobbying for lower enforcement, resulting in a lower equilibrium level of border enforcement.

Hanson and Spilimbergo (2001) estimate the sensitivity of border enforcement to relative price changes in industries that use undocumented workers intensively (apparel, perishable fruits and vegetables, slaughtered livestock,

---

[33] Both sets of results remain true even after instrumenting for border enforcement (since the INS may set enforcement in response to economic conditions in the US or Mexican border areas) using data on US political cycles and activity at other US international boundaries (ports and Canadian border crossings).

[34] For evidence on labour-market integration between the United States and Mexico, see Robertson (2000).

construction). Controlling for general economic conditions in the United States and Mexico, they find that increases in the relative product price (or capacity utilization rate) for an immigrant-intensive industry today is associated with a *decrease* in border enforcement 6–10 months in the future. This suggests that authorities relax enforcement when the demand for undocumented workers increases. Border enforcement also rises when overall labour-market conditions in the United States tighten, which suggests that the US government raises enforcement when attempted illegal immigration is expected to be high. It appears, then, that enforcement softens when specific sectors that use illegal aliens intensively expand but not when the overall demand for labour is high. This is consistent with free-rider problems in special interest group activity, in which sectors that benefit greatly from lower border enforcement, such as apparel and agriculture, lobby heavily on the issue while remaining sectors that benefit modestly are politically inactive.

11.3.1. *Summary*

Over time, the population of illegal immigrants in the United States has shifted from being primarily male itinerant farm labourers to being a more heterogeneous group, including long-term residents who live and work in cities. Illegal immigration from Mexico tends to rise quickly following declines in Mexican wages (which in recent decades have been associated with macroeconomic instability in the country). Border enforcement does not appear to have strong deterrent effects against illegal immigration or to have affected labour-market outcomes in US border regions. Border enforcement appears to respond to economic fluctuations in immigrant-intensive industries, suggesting that political pressures influence immigration policy choices.

11.4. POLICY ISSUES AND FUTURE PROSPECTS

Since the end of large-scale temporary immigration programmes in the 1960s, illegal immigration in the United States has increased dramatically. About half of US illegal aliens are from Mexico and enter the country by crossing the Southwest US border illegally. Illegal immigration surges during economic downturns in Mexico, which have occurred with an unfortunately high frequency over the last two decades. The US government attempts to impede illegal immigration mainly by policing borders and public spaces in border regions, where illegal immigrants tend to congregate, and by monitoring US employers. These enforcement efforts have been inconsistent across time and space and appear not to have reduced noticeably the annual inflow of illegal aliens. The US government devotes relatively little energy to employer monitoring and often seems reluctant to apply laws banning the employment of illegal aliens.

If the United States intends to reduce illegal immigration sharply in the future, it has four broad policy options: intensify border enforcement, increase employer monitoring and sanctions against those found to hire illegal aliens, attempt to replace illegal immigration with the large-scale temporary immigration of low-skilled guest workers (coupled with current enforcement policies), and/or grant an amnesty to illegal immigrants currently living in the country.

The get-tough border enforcement policies of the 1990s succeeded in reducing illegal entry at certain active crossing points but have yet to produce a noticeable reduction in net inflows of illegal aliens. Perhaps the clearest evidence of this lack of success is that apprehensions continue to rise with enforcement. Were the new high levels of border enforcement a sufficient deterrent, attempts at illegal immigration would fall, but they have not. To curtail illegal immigration from Mexico may require a much larger enforcement effort, through an expanded Border Patrol or other security presence. If past events are any guide, a large security presence on the border would face strong political opposition from residents of border regions, agriculturalists and other employers in industries that depend on manual labour, and the Mexican government.

The apparent failure of border enforcement to eliminate illegal immigration is not to say that the policy is completely ineffective. For many prospective migrants, the fact that the Border Patrol actively polices US borders surely makes the risk of apprehension too great to warrant attempting illegal entry. It does appear, however, that those individuals who are on the margin between migrating and not migrating are relatively insensitive to changes in border enforcement. They appear to be much more responsive to fluctuations in Mexican and US wages.

There is currently little discussion of increasing interior enforcement against illegal immigration. Attempts by the INS to mount extensive campaigns to locate and penalize employers of illegal aliens have been condemned by the employers themselves and often by their congressional representatives or other political actors. Few of these campaigns have produced onerous sanctions against employers.

The revealed US preference for border over interior enforcement may reflect the relative political power of employer groups. While enforcement of any kind reduces the likelihood that a US employer is able to hire an illegal alien, border and interior enforcement operate quite differently. For employers, the costs of border enforcement have low variance. More border enforcement simply means a lower probability of finding an illegal worker at a given wage. The costs of interior enforcement, on the other hand, have high variance, as with some probability an employer may face a very negative outcome involving fines, legal fees, and perhaps other legal repercussions. Given the option of two policies that yield the same level of illegal labour supply, we would expect employers to prefer border over interior enforcement and to advocate against interior enforcement on this basis. Current US policy choices support this reasoning.

The third US policy option is resuming large-scale temporary immigration. This option is usually mentioned in concert with an amnesty for illegal aliens who have resided in the United States for several years or more. In the past, the United States has only been willing to admit large numbers of temporary immigrants during and following major wars (1917–21, 1942–64), which tend to be times of labour shortage. In the current environment, labour shortages have come not from war but from two apparently unrelated events: the declining labour-force participation of less-skilled native workers and a boom in high-tech industries that are intensive in engineers, computer programmers, and other high-skilled workers. Current proposals to increase temporary immigration both of college graduates in technical occupations (through H-1B visas) and of low-skilled manual labourers (through H-2A and H-2B visas) would increase US labour supplies at the extremes of the skill distribution.

How would increased temporary immigration of manual labourers affect illegal immigration? Let us assume that current levels of border and interior enforcement are maintained. Let us assume also that the US chooses to admit 200 000 temporary workers from Mexico per year (the current proposal is for 250 000, but we will assume that some of these quota slots get allocated to other countries), a number roughly equal to the net annual inflow of illegal aliens from Mexico (Warren, 1999). Should not we expect that attempted illegal immigration would cease or at least drop off substantially?

There are at least two reasons why we may not. First, as a practical matter, though net illegal immigration from Mexico is 150 000–200 000 individuals per year, gross illegal immigration is much higher. As we have seen, many Mexican illegal immigrants in the United States return home one or more times a year, to spend the Christmas holidays with their families, to tend to business interests, etc. There is no reason to believe that illegal border crossings by existing illegal migrants would cease just because some fraction of new migrants received temporary work visas.

Second, and more importantly, temporary immigration and illegal immigration confer different bundles of citizenship rights. For manual labourers, a temporary work visa gives an individual the right to work in the United States for a given US employer for some time period, typically up to a year in length. The worker receives no other citizenship rights and is usually not permitted to bring along other family members. Illegal immigration, obviously, confers no immediate citizenship rights. But in expectation illegal immigrants who succeed in staying in the United States would be eligible for any future amnesty for illegal aliens.[35] For illegal immigrants, then, squatter's rights may apply—if

---

[35] Short of an all-out amnesty, illegal aliens occasionally have other options for obtaining legal residence. For instance the Legal Immigration and Family Equity Act of 2000 temporarily gave illegal immigrants the option to apply for US legal residence, despite the fact that their presence in the country violates US law. After paying a $1000 fine, an illegal alien, under certain restrictions, could file an application for legal residence without having to return to his or her country of origin.

they can remain in the United States long enough they stand a reasonable chance of gaining legal residence.

It is conceivable that for some prospective immigrants the uncertain but potentially expansive citizenship rights conferred by illegal immigration are superior to the certain but highly restricted citizenship rights conferred by temporary immigration. It is also conceivable that some prospective immigrants who are deterred by existing US enforcement practices (e.g. those who view being apprehended and deported as an excessively harsh outcome) would find temporary immigration attractive. If these two groups are sufficiently large, then expanded temporary immigration could potentially have only a small impact on current levels of illegal immigration.

Similar to the situation in the 1980s, when the United States was debating passage of the Immigration Reform and Control Act, a substantial illegal-immigrant population appears to be cause for policy action of some kind. An amnesty would formalize what is an obvious circumstance to many: a large fraction of illegal aliens in the United States are long-term residents of the country and, whether or not they ultimately become legal residents, are unlikely to return home soon. Legalizing the status of these individuals would allow the country to enact a new set of immigration policies with a clean slate. While an amnesty would not *directly* affect the size of the immigrant population in the United States, it would affect the existing immigrant population in two important ways. First, an amnesty would accelerate the granting of legal status to individuals awaiting the outcome of applications for US permanent residence. Second, for illegal aliens with no prospect of gaining legal admission, an amnesty would remove legal uncertainty surrounding their presence in the country. By becoming legal residents, these individuals might have improved job prospects and might be able to command higher wages and better working conditions.

But there is little reason to expect that the direct effects of an amnesty on US labour markets or public finances would be large. Employment of illegal aliens is widespread and has been for some time. Indeed, given the proliferation of fake immigration and social security documents following the Immigration Reform and Control Act, many employers hire illegal aliens as though they were legal residents. Also, since welfare reform in 1996 excluded immigrants from access to many forms of public assistance, an amnesty would be unlikely to produce large new welfare claims by the legalized population. Children of illegal immigrants already have access to public education, which accounts for nearly half of the public benefits immigrants receive.

There are, however, possible *indirect* effects of an amnesty on the size of the immigrant population in the United States. An amnesty would allow newly legalized immigrants to help their relatives gain legal residence in the United States through the family reunification provisions of US immigration policy.

Legalization today would thus beget more applications for legal immigration in the future. An amnesty might also reinforce the belief on the part of prospective migrants that one way or another most illegal immigrants in the United States are eventually able to become legal residents. This would perhaps raise the incentive for illegal immigration. Legalization today could then induce more attempts at illegal entry in the future.

12

Fiscal Impacts of Immigration

The fiscal impact of immigration figures prominently in recent debates over US immigration policy. The issue has attracted attention only recently, as the 1980s and 1990s were the first decades in which there were both large immigrant inflows and a relatively generous welfare state. During the massive immigration of the early twentieth century, the social state was largely non-existent, with the noticeable exception of public education. And in the 1960s, when the modern US welfare state was created, the US foreign-born population was at a historically low level and falling as a share of the total population (see Fig. 9.1). The current immigration wave has occurred during a period in which the role of the welfare state *per se* is heavily debated. This combination of rising immigration and political conflict over welfare policy has moved the fiscal impact of immigration to the centre of academic and political discussions.

The surge in immigration over the last thirty years, as described in Chapter 9, is due in large part to recent changes in US immigration policy. Before the 1960s US immigration was regulated by the Immigration and Naturalization Act of 1924, which had imposed numerical limits on immigration and established a quota system based on national origin.[1] This system was biased in favour of Northern Europeans, implicitly limiting the number of immigrants and selecting relatively educated workers. The Immigration and Nationality Act Amendments of 1965 repealed national-origin quotas, established a seven-category preference system based on family unification and skills, and imposed a ceiling on immigration from the western hemisphere. The Refugee Act of 1980 set up systematic procedures for admitting refugees, removing them as a category from the preference system. These legislative changes helped increase the number of immigrants from developing countries, opening the doors to relatively poor workers and, in the case of refugees, poor families. The composition of immigrants has changed dramatically since 1970. As Chapter 9 shows, the average educational gap between natives and immigrants has increased and convergence between native and immigrant wages has slowed.

In the 1990s, the US welfare state became the subject of intense political debate, culminating in 1996 with the passage of the Personal Responsibility and Work Opportunity Reconciliation Act (PRWORA). This was the first major

---

[1] The first instance of migration policy selecting immigrants on the basis of education was the 1917 Immigration Act, which introduced a literacy test and a head tax on prospective immigrants.

reform of the US welfare system since the 1960s. The main goals of the 1996 reform included reducing the use of public assistance and increasing the employment and earnings of the poor (Blank, 1997). To achieve these goals the 1996 reform mandated work requirements as a precondition to receive benefits, limited the life-time use of certain benefits, and gave states more discretion over programme design. In particular, state entitlements to open-ended federal funds were substituted with block grants, leaving states with autonomy over individual eligibility criteria. The 1996 reform was expected to save about $23 billion, almost half of which was to come from restricting the access of immigrants to public benefits, in particular Supplemental Security Income. Partly as a result of the 1996 reform, the fiscal impact of immigration has become an important issue at both the federal and local level.

The main issues in the debate on the fiscal impact of immigration are: the relative use of public resources by immigrants, the sensitivity of location choice by immigrants to state welfare benefits (welfare magnet effects), cost sharing between federal and state and local authorities, the overall impact of immigration on public finances (especially social security), and the design of fiscal policy. We consider each issue in turn.

12.1. USE OF PUBLIC RESOURCES BY IMMIGRANTS

Though the topic is controversial, most academic studies agree that immigrants have higher welfare participation rates than natives.[2] The main points of disagreement are on how to measure this 'excessive' use of public resources and on its causes. In particular, the methodological issues include the definition of welfare benefits, the reliability of data sources, and how to select the unit of analysis (Fix *et al.*, 1996).[3]

Immigrant welfare participation has increased in the last thirty years. Before 1980, immigrants had a lower probability of receiving public assistance than US natives (Blau, 1984). In 1970, 5.9 per cent of immigrant households received cash benefits, compared to 6.9 per cent of native households; in 1990, 9.1 per cent of immigrant households received cash benefits, compared to

---

[2] For a review of the literature before the 1996 welfare reform see OECD (1996).

[3] The major methodological difference across empirical studies is the definition of welfare programmes. Before 1996, means-tested welfare programmes comprised three cash programmes (Aid to Families with Dependent Children, Supplemental Security Income, and General Assistance) as well as several non-cash programmes (Medicaid, Food Stamps, Special Supplemental Food Programme for Women, Infants, and Children, Low Income Energy Assistance, and School Lunch Programmes), with the cash programmes accounting for about one quarter of all expenditure in means-tested programmes. The Current Population Sample (CPS) reports only if an individual uses cash subsidies while the Survey of Income and Programme Participation (SIPP) reports all kinds of participation in welfare programmes but has less coverage over time. The sample size of CPS is much larger than SIPP, allowing more precise estimates and a larger set of control variables. Borjas and Hilton (1996) and Borjas (1996) use a broader definition of welfare benefits (which includes non-cash benefits) than other researchers and find that in the early 1990s 20.7 per cent of immigrant households received means-tested public benefits as opposed to 14.1 per cent of native households.

Table 12.1. *Use of means-tested programmes by head of household's nativity,
by year of entry (%)*[a]

Welfare Programme	Native households	Immigrant households	Pre-1970 immigrants	1970–79 immigrants	1980–89 immigrants	1990–2000 immigrants
Public assistance[b]	2.1	3.2	1.8	2.9	4.1	3.9
Supplemental security	3.9	5.3	4.9	7.1	5.5	4.1
Income food stamps	5.3	6.7	4.1	6.1	7.5	8.4
Medicaid	12.1	18.6	11.7	17.9	23.5	19.7
Households using any of the above	13.3	19.7	21.1	24.3	18.8	12.5
Earned income tax credit	13.1	25.5	10.7	22.9	31.5	32.7

[a]Immigrants and native households defined by nativity of household head. Year of entry based on household head.
[b]Includes TANF and General Assistance Programme.

Source: Camarota (2001), Center for Immigration Studies (*http://www.cis.org.*)

7.4 per cent of native households (Borjas, 1996). When considering also non-cash benefits, the difference is even larger (see Table 12.1).[4] The reasons behind these differences are still debated but appear to include changes in national origin of immigrants, quicker assimilation of the immigrants to the welfare system, and increases in the number of refugees.

First, the national and education composition of immigration has changed and the new immigrants have demographic characteristics that make them more likely to participate in welfare programmes than in previous years. Given that welfare transfers are negatively correlated with income, the simple change in composition of immigrations resulted in an increase in welfare benefits for immigrants. Table 12.2 illustrates large differences in use of means-tested programmes across households from different countries of origin. For instance in 2000, 54 per cent of the head of households from Dominican Republic used at least one means-tested welfare programme while only 2.9 per cent of households from United Kingdom did.

Second, as immigrants have become accustomed to the welfare system the welfare participation of each cohort has increased over time, holding constant observable characteristics (Borjas and Trejo, 1991; Borjas and Hilton, 1996). There is also evidence that ethnic networks play an important role in spreading information on the availability of welfare programmes. For instance, Mexican immigrants are 50 per cent more likely to receive energy assistance than Cuban immigrants but the latter are more likely to receive housing subsidies (Borjas, 1999). Confirming this anecdotal evidence, Borjas and Hilton (1996) show

---

[4] The extent of the public assistance is even larger if we consider the Earned Income Tax Credit (EITC), which is the largest means-tested cash programme with a cost of about $25 billion (Camarota, 2001). Individuals qualifying for EITC pay negative federal taxes, that is, they receive cash assistance from the federal government. In 2000, 25.5 per cent of immigrant households received the EITC compared with 13.1 per cent of native households.

Table 12.2. *Use of means-tested programmes by head of household's country of origin, 2000 (%)*

Country	Public assistance	Supplemental security income	Food stamps	Medicaid	Using any of these	EITC
Mexico	5.5	4.1	10.2	27.2	28.9	49.2
China/Taiwan/HK	0.5	6.5	1.9	12.1	12.6	13.3
Philippines	2.6	8.0	2.2	16.2	16.2	13.2
India	0.5	1.4	0.9	6.6	7.3	10.7
Vietnam	1.1	19.6	15.2	26.6	31.1	21.9
El Salvador	6.1	3.1	8.0	25.6	26.0	48.5
Korea	0.0	4.7	1.6	7.9	7.9	15.0
Dominican Rep.	15.7	16.0	27.5	53.0	54.0	41.8
Cuba	1.5	8.0	14.3	23.3	24.8	17.0
Colombia	0.5	10.4	7.7	25.1	25.1	25.1
Russia	2.5	18.3	15.3	23.8	24.8	7.9
Canada	0.6	1.2	1.2	2.7	3.6	6.0
Jamaica	1.8	5.4	7.1	26.3	26.3	25.4
Haiti	3.0	1.2	5.5	15.9	17.1	38.4
United Kingdom	0.6	0.6	1.2	2.6	2.9	4.3
Guatemala	1.9	3.7	5.6	26.2	26.2	32.7
Peru	2.5	2.5	2.5	20.3	20.3	32.8
Poland	0.0	0.9	0.0	5.1	5.1	9.8
Iran	0.0	8.3	0.0	15.2	15.2	4.5
Ecuador	1.8	7.2	3.6	30.6	32.7	36.9
All Others	2.7	4.3	4.6	13.4	14.4	16.5
All immigrants	3.2	5.3	6.7	18.6	19.7	25.5
All natives	2.1	3.9	5.3	12.1	13.3	13.1
Immigrant avg. payment amt.[a]	$4673	$6369	—	—	—	$1692
Native avg. payment amt.[b]	$3038	$4926	—	—	—	$1456

[a]Average is only for those who receive payments.
[b]Average is only for those who receive payments.
Source: Camarota (2001), Center for Immigration Studies (*http://www.cis.org.*)

that use of welfare services by earlier immigrants of a particular ethnic group is a good predictor of future use of the same services by new immigrants of the same group.

Third, use of welfare benefits by refugees, which was relatively high thirty years ago, has increased further, as the share of refugees among all immigrants has risen from 12 per cent in the 1970s to 17 per cent in the 1980s. Borjas (1995a) finds that the welfare participation rate was 7.8 per cent among non-refugee households in 1990 compared to 7.4 per cent among native households but it was 16.1 per cent among refugee households. Moreover, the use of cash welfare benefits has increased considerably among refugee households, from 7.1 per cent in 1970 to 11.6 per cent in 1980, and to 16.1 per cent in

1990.[5] There appear to be three reasons why refugees use more welfare benefits than other immigrants. First, refugee households are relatively poor, have more problems in being integrated in the labour force, and demand more special assistance. Second, refugees are also older than the other immigrants, accounting for 27 per cent of the immigrants over 65 who receive public benefits (Fix *et al.*, 1996). Third, for humanitarian reasons the US Congress has exempted refugees from the public charge provision of immigration law, making them eligible for benefits upon arrival.

In addition to the aforementioned reasons, the increasing use of welfare by immigrants is due in part to the specific situation of California, which has relatively generous welfare programmes and a large share of poor immigrants. Because of these factors, California has become a national laboratory of many issues regarding immigration, the welfare state, and cost sharing between federal and local governments.

12.2. WELFARE MAGNETS

... it was enacted by the 43d of Elisabeth, c. 2 that every parish should be bound to provide for its own poor ... By this statute the necessity of providing for their own poor was indispensably imposed upon every parish. Who were to be considered as the poor of each parish, became, therefore, a question of some importance. This question, after some variation, was at last determined by the 13th and 14th of Charles II. When it was enacted, that forty days undisturbed residence should gain any person a settlement in any parish... Some frauds, it is said, were committed in consequence of this statute; parish officers sometimes bribing their own poor to go clandestinely to another parish... (Chapter X. Wealth of Nations. 1776. Adam Smith).

The lines above, which were written more than 200 years ago, highlight many relevant issues of the present debate on immigrants, the perverse effects of welfare magnets, and the different and sometimes conflicting interests of national and local authorities. The names of the actors have changed but the plot is similar. First, the central authority (the Queen then, the US Congress and federal courts now) gives a mandate to local authorities to care for poor immigrants. Second, some local authorities (parishes then, states now) become welfare magnets and try to restrict the access to welfare benefits for immigrants. Third, central authorities (the King then, the Federal Courts now) mandate criteria for eligibility. The issue of welfare magnets is crucial in a decentralized welfare system.

California, which has relatively generous welfare transfers, is host to more than 30 per cent of the US foreign-born population (see Table 9.3). These facts have brought up the question whether poor immigrants choose their location

---

[5] The US census does not contain information on the type of entry visa used by households but provides information on the country of origin. For these reasons, Borjas (1995*a*) uses nationality as a proxy for being a refugee.

according to the generosity of welfare benefits at the local level. Borjas (1999*c*) documents that welfare-recipient immigrants are more likely to cluster than immigrants who do not receive welfare. In the 1980s California was home to 29 per cent of new immigrants who did not receive welfare benefits but 45 per cent of new immigrants who did.[6]

Welfare magnets could have a second undesirable effect by inducing a sub-optimal provision of public goods in reaction to a presumed abuse of welfare benefits. Providing evidence on this point, Brueckner (2000) suggests that benefit levels in nearby states affect a given state's level of benefits. The size of the distortion is unclear given that welfare levels are the result of a strategic interaction among states, the federal government, and voters. Moreover, it is difficult to quantify a benchmark for the optimal level of welfare benefits.

Overall, it seems that there is some evidence on the existence of welfare magnets. As the quotation from Adam Smith suggests, this may be an inevitable feature of a decentralized welfare system, which gives more control at the local level but can induce opportunistic behaviour. One important issue is to quantify welfare costs and to weigh them against benefits derived from local control. The US welfare reform of 1996 is still too recent for a full evaluation of its impact.

12.3. SHARING THE COSTS BETWEEN CENTRAL GOVERNMENT AND LOCAL AUTHORITIES

Before 1996, the United States had a limited set of federal policies explicitly aimed at immigrants. In practice, legal immigrants had access to the same welfare programmes as natives. This situation had been sanctioned by several rulings of federal courts that established that local authorities could not discriminate against legal immigrants in public welfare programmes. Moreover, before 1996 the federal government was ultimately funding and regulating the use of welfare programmes by immigrants. In addition, some states, such as Massachusetts, had supplemented federal aid with additional programmes targeted at immigrants, such as teaching English as a second language (Fix and Tumlin, 1997).

The 1996 Personal Responsibility and Work Opportunity Reconciliation Act and the 1997 Balanced Budget Act changed this situation and affected both eligibility criteria and the funding structure. In the short run, the change of eligibility criteria was the most important innovation; in the long run, however, the change in financing scheme was more relevant as it has moved the immigration debate to the local level. The 1996 Act restricted immigrant access to

---

[6] This has happened because California attracts a disproportionate number of less-skilled and poor immigrants, who are more likely to receive welfare benefits. This evidence is consistent with the existence of welfare magnets but is also compatible with other explanations such as immigrant network effects.

welfare benefits, marking a clear break with the previous policy of equality between legal immigrants and natives. The 1997 Act restored some benefits such as Medicaid to all elderly and disabled immigrants but did not change the principle that natives and legal immigrants have different access to welfare benefits.[7] There is still concern over the effects of welfare reform on poor immigrant groups, and in particular on children. Moreover, many critics have raised concerns about the cost effectiveness of excluding immigrant children from Medicaid. Currie (2000) observes that curtailing Medicaid eligibility for immigrant children may not save money if children remain eligible for costly emergency care. In addition, even entitled immigrants appear to have received fewer welfare benefits after 1996, perhaps because of uncertainty about their immigration status and eligibility for assistance.[8]

The biggest changes of the 1996–97 reforms were for immigrants arriving after August 1996, who are barred from using Medicaid, Temporary Assistance to Needy Families, and other federal means-tested benefits for the first five years after they enter the United States. After the five-year period, their eligibility will depend on the state in which they reside.[9] Table 12.3 summarizes the eligibility criteria for non-citizens before and after the recent welfare reforms.

The decentralization of the welfare system will likely be the most important long-run legacy of the 1996 reform. Since 1997, state entitlements to open-ended federal funds for welfare programmes were substituted with block grants, which were fixed at the nominal level of the transfers at the beginning of the 1990s. This new legislation makes poor natives and immigrants compete for the same resources at the local level, especially in states with high immigration and relatively generous social benefits. In this respect, the debate has been particularly strong in California because public benefits have been perceived as 'too generous' towards immigrants, with the undesired results of attracting the 'wrong' immigrants.

After the 1996 welfare reform, there have been three major developments in the provision of welfare benefits to immigrants: a partial reversal of the benefits cuts in 1996 at the federal level; increasing state involvement in providing welfare benefits to immigrants, especially in states with a large proportion of immigrants; and an increase in legal challenges to the provisions of welfare reform regarding immigrants at both the state and federal levels. We briefly address each of these developments in turn.

First, many provisions of the 1996 reform—especially those regarding assistance to the elderly—were considered politically untenable and have never

---

[7] The effectiveness of this measure is somewhat limited given that many immigrants have been excluded from the extension. For instance, only 1.4 million non-citizens lost food stamps after 1996 (Fix and Tumlin, 1997).

[8] By far, the largest 'chilling' effect has been in California after the approval of Proposition 187.

[9] Asylum seekers, refugees, Cubans, Haitians, and a few other groups are eligible for means-tested programmes in their first five to seven years after entering the United States.

Table 12.3. *Overview of non-citizens' benefits eligibility*

	SSI	Food stamps	Medicaid	TANF	Other federal means-tested benefits	State/local public benefits
Qualified immigrants arriving before August 23, 1996						
Legal permanent residents	Yes	No	State option	State option	State option	State option
Asylum seekers, refugees[a]	Eligible for first 7 years	Eligible for first 5 years	Eligible for first 7 years	Eligible for first 5 years	Eligible for first 5 years	Eligible for first 5 years
Qualified immigrants arriving after August 23, 1996						
Legal permanent residents	No	No	Barred for first 5 years; state option afterward	Barred for first 5 years; state option afterward	Barred for first 5 years; state option afterward	State option
Asylum seekers, refugees	Eligible for first 7 years	Eligible for first 5 years	Eligible for first 7 years	Eligible for first 5 years	Eligible for first 5 years	Eligible for first 5 years
Unqualified immigrants						
Illegal immigrants	No	No	Emergency services only	No	No[b]	No[c]
PRUCOL immigrants	No[d]	No	Emergency services only	No	No	No[c]

[a]Cuban and Haitian entrants, Amerasians, and aliens granted withholding of deportation are also included in this group.
[b]States have the option to provide WIC to unqualified immigrants.
[c]Selected programmes are exempted, including short-term non-cash relief, immunizations, testing and treatment for communicable diseases, and selected assistance from community programmes.
[d]Those immigrants receiving SSI as of August 22, 1996, will continue to be eligible until September 30, 1998.
PRUCOL = Persons Residing under Cover of Law.

Source: Urban Institute (1997).

been enforced. Almost immediately after the 1996 reforms, Congress quietly started repealing the tougher provisions. In 1997, the Balanced Budget Act brought back SSI for the disabled and Medicaid benefits to 420 000 legal immigrants who were in the country before August 1996. The 1998 Agriculture Research Act provided food stamps for 225 000 legal immigrant children, senior citizens, and individuals with disabilities who were in the country before August 1996. In 1999, the administration proposed $1.3 billion to close remaining gaps in medical and food stamp benefits for legal immigrants who lost these benefits with the 1996 welfare reform. Together with this roll back, came a change in the political attitude in the 1998 Congressional elections, as, in contrast with previous years, immigration became a muted issue.

Second, above and beyond benefits being rolled back at the federal level, an even larger reversal has occurred at the state level. In several cases, states have simply taken over the expenditures that were previously financed by the federal government. For instance, California has committed to providing food stamps to many poor legal immigrants barred from receiving federal assistance at the estimated cost of around $60 million annually (Urban Institute, 2001). Similarly, several states, including New Jersey, Massachusetts, Pennsylvania, and Connecticut, have subsidized Medicaid for legal immigrants. While the 1996 reform shifted to the states the responsibility for the administration of some welfare programmes, it explicitly barred the states from providing other benefits. For instance, states could not provide benefits to immigrant children who came into the country after August 1996. This prohibition was repealed in 1999, sanctioning a trend towards states providing higher levels of welfare benefits to immigrants.

This state-level reversal of federal benefit cuts has been most pronounced in high-immigration states. The pattern seems in direct contradiction to arguments that high-immigration states are inclined to spur a 'race to the bottom' via benefit cuts. It may be related to the rising influence of immigrants as a coherent political group (see Chapter 13). This is particularly evident in California, where Hispanics accounted for about 4 per cent of the electorate in the 1990 gubernatorial election but 14 per cent in the 1998 election.[10]

Finally, while in the past immigration policy was mostly in the hands of executive and legislative powers, since 1995 the judiciary has become increasingly involved. Judicial intervention has occurred at two levels. First, local authorities in regions with a high proportion of immigrants—such as the city of New York, the city of Chicago, the state of Florida, and Dade county in Florida—have challenged in court the constitutionality of federal welfare laws that cut off benefits for legal immigrants. In general, the courts have confirmed the constitutionality of the 1996 reform on the ground that the reform, while indeed penalizing immigrants' welfare, did not violate the immigrants' right to equal

---

[10] While part of this increase was due to changing demographics, another part was due to increased political mobilization in response to Proposition 187.

Table 12.4. *Immigration's contribution to the school-age population (2000)*[a]

	School-age (5–17) pop.		Young children (0–4)	
	Percent with immigrant mothers	Number with immigrant mothers (thousands)	Percent with immigrant mothers	Number with immigrant mothers (thousands)
California	43.3	2939	45.0	1184
New York	27.1	954	27.6	350
Florida	28.1	740	22.1	198
Texas	22.0	857	23.1	386
New Jersey	22.1	323	21.4	113
Illinois	15.2	365	18.0	169
Massachusetts	17.1	195	12.7	51
Arizona	23.1	232	29.9	118
Entire Country	16.3	8612	17.6	3456

[a]Values have been rounded to the nearest thousand.

Source: Camarota (2001), Center for Immigration Studies (*http://www.cis.org.*)

protection.[11] Second, state judiciaries have intervened to rule illegal local provisions against immigrants. For instance, the New York appellate court has ruled that the state has violated the state and federal constitutions in denying Medicaid benefits to the immigrants who arrived in the United States after August 1996.[12] Local judicial rulings have not always enlarged welfare benefits for immigrants. For instance, the Texas attorney general has declared in a written opinion that federal law prohibits hospitals from using public funds to provide non-emergency services such as prenatal care. This opinion is non-binding but does open hospitals to legal challenges.

There is one important set of public benefits that immigrants receive that have been unaffected by welfare reform. Apart from standard welfare programmes, immigrants also use educational services, which, as we discuss below, may represent the largest source of fiscal transfers from native taxpayers to immigrant families. Table 12.4 illustrates the estimated contribution of immigrants to the school-age population. McCarthy and Vernez (1998) document that enrolment in primary and secondary schools in California increased substantially after 1980 thanks largely to immigrant children. In 2000, 43.3 per cent of the school-age population in California had foreign-born

---

[11] Significantly, the courts have also confirmed the constitutionality of the welfare reform provision barring illegal immigrants from prenatal care, overturning a 1987 ruling by a lower court judge who ordered the federal government to provide prenatal care for illegal immigrants.

[12] Note that, given that the New York appellate court cannot compel the federal government to pay for the benefits, the state of New York will pay the additional cost.

mothers. Moreover, given higher fertility rates among immigrants, children of immigrants will represent an increasing share of the school-age population in the future. This fact and a high concentration of refugees largely explain why California transfers more on net to immigrants than do other states.[13] For this reason, it is not surprising that the political debate in California has focused on immigration. Voters in the state have passed anti-immigrant initiatives, such as Proposition 187, which have received much attention at the national level (see Box 12.1).

Box 12.1. *Proposition 187 in California*

After a heated debate in 1995, Californian voters approved Proposition 187, which denied education, health, and social services to illegal immigrants. While Proposition 187 concerned only the provision of public benefits to illegal immigrants in one state, its passage had huge political significance and influenced the reform of federal welfare in 1996.

Even though the public debate focused on education and health issues, fiscal considerations seemed to play an important role in the passage of Proposition 187. Over the past two decades, California has been struggling to contain state public expenditure, given self-imposed taxation limits passed in 1978. Public expenditure in education takes a large share of the state budget (for instance, Proposition 99 earmarks 40 per cent of California's general state public revenues for K to 12 education) and a large proportion of students are children of legal and illegal immigrants. Proposition 187 thus would have likely lowered substantially transfers in the form of public education to immigrants. Passage of the measure may have been helped by the fact that it cut benefits for immigrants who are ineligible to vote and that immigrants in general have historically had lower voter participation rates in local and national elections. One consequence of Proposition 187 appears to have been to increase the political participation of immigrants at local and national levels.

Proposition 187 did not become law because it was successfully challenged by a federal lawsuit on the grounds that it would have unconstitutionally usurped federal authority by enacting immigration laws in conflict with federal authorities, violated due process and equal protection guarantees, and conflicted with the 1982 Supreme Court decision in Plyler vs Doe, which affirmed the right of immigrant children to a public education.

Even though Proposition 187 has been rejected in court, the 1996 Personal Responsibility and Work Opportunity Reconciliation Act implicitly implemented many of its provisions with the exception of those regarding primary and secondary education.

---

[13] Smith and Edmonston (1997) have calculated that the net fiscal deficit for providing services to immigrants was $1178 per native family in 1996 in California, while it was $232 per native household in New Jersey.

12.4. OVERALL ANNUAL FISCAL IMPACT OF IMMIGRATION

Though the debate has mainly focused on immigrant use of public programmes, a very important economic issue is the overall net fiscal impact of immigrants. Does immigration increase or decrease fiscal costs for native taxpayers?[14]

In order to address this question the US Congress appointed a Commission on Immigration Reform, which requested the National Academy of Science to examine the overall fiscal impact of immigration. The results are contained in two reports by Smith and Edmonston (1997, 1998). These reports and especially the case studies of New Jersey and California laid down a framework to study the problem. Notwithstanding myriad conceptual and data problems, these studies give a broad idea of the magnitude of transfers between native and immigrant households. In 1996, the net annual fiscal burden of immigration considering all transfers at local and national levels is estimated to be between $166 and $226 per native household. The main reasons for transfers from natives to immigrants appear to be differences in family structures and income levels: immigrant families have more dependent children who use publicly funded schools and immigrant households are poor and so receive more transfers and pay fewer taxes.[15]

One major finding of Smith and Edmonston (1997, 1998) is that there are large differences in transfers across states. Tables 12.5 and 12.6 summarize their results. In the absence of immigration, the average native household would have taxes reduced by $1174 in California and by $229 in New Jersey. The average immigrant household receives transfers of $3463 in California and $1484 in New Jersey. The reasons for these cross-state differences are differences in demographic structures and welfare schemes across states. In particular, the foreign-born population in California is younger and poorer, and has more dependent children. It is important to note that the largest transfer between natives and the foreign-born is related to public education.[16]

---

[14] The overall economic impact of immigration, which is the sum of fiscal, product, and labour market effects, appears to be small. Borjas (1999) calculates that through its impact on factor markets immigration increases native GDP by about 0.1 per cent. This section discusses results that suggest that the fiscal impact is also negligible. Therefore, the total economic impact of immigration in the United States appears to be limited, at least under present policies.

[15] These studies must address difficult conceptual and data problems. One problem is the classification of public goods, for which by definition there is no additional cost due to immigration. For instance, defence expenditure does not in principle depend on the number of immigrants. This is one reason why the study finds that immigrants are net contributors to the federal government, which is the main provider of public goods. Another problem is to establish who ends up paying for a given tax, which could be a different entity from the one on which the tax is levied. Given the many assumptions required and the complex nature of the issue, most estimates are at best indicative.

[16] There is evidence that there is also an implicit education subsidy beyond K to 12 education. Data from the General Accounting Office suggest that foreign-born students are more likely to receive grants in Californian universities (see 'Distorted Incentives: The United States Pays the

Table 12.5. *Local, state, and federal expenditures, revenues, and average fiscal balance by foreign-born and native households in New Jersey and California (1996, US$)*

	New Jersey		California	
	Foreign-born	Native	Foreign-born	Native
Expenditures				
Local	4236	2969	6208	5290
Of which K12 education	2985	2162	1581	768
State	3146	2647	4973	2510
Of which K12 education	1878	1585	2496	1212
Federal	—	—	13 326	13 625
Revenues				
Local	3314	3113	5377	5573
State	2584	2735	2341	3405
Federal	—	—	10 644	16 347
Fiscal Balance				
Local	−922	144	−831	283
State	−562	88	−2632	895
Federal	—	—	−2682	2722

Note: Figures for New Jersey are for FY 1990, figures for California are for FY 1995. Both are adjusted upward to reflect December 1996 prices. Average fiscal balance equals revenues minus expenditures. If the average fiscal balance is greater than zero, then the average household in this category makes a net contribution.
*The net effect of immigrants on the federal level is available only for California.
Source: Smith and Edmonston (1997).

Table 12.6. *Net annual fiscal impact imposed by current immigrant-headed households on native residents in New Jersey and California (1996, US$)*

	New Jersey	California
Local	−144	−283
State	−88	−895
Federal	3	4
Total	−299	−1174

Source: Smith and Edmonston (1997).

Apart from these specific estimates, the studies contained in Smith and Edmonston (1997, 1998) highlight the key determinants of immigrants' fiscal contribution and show how the impact differs across states. For instance, the

University of California Twice as Much to Educate Foreign Graduate Students as American Ones', CIS Backgrounder, February 2000, *http://www.cis.org*.)

age structure and the ethnic composition of the immigrants have large effects on the fiscal effect of immigration. An average immigrant household in California receives net benefits for $4977 if the members are from Latin America, but contributes $1308 if the members are from Europe or Canada.

12.5. LONG-TERM IMPACT OF IMMIGRATION ON PUBLIC FINANCES

While estimating the annual effect of immigration is indicative of its short-run fiscal implications, looking at the dynamic impact is conceptually more appropriate for several reasons. First, an immigrant's net fiscal contributions may vary over his or her life cycle. Being relatively young, immigrants may be net beneficiaries shortly after arriving but net contributors later on. Second, the composition of new immigrants may change over time with important fiscal effects. Third, fiscal policy may also change over time. Given these factors, a simple extrapolation from the annual estimates may be misleading.

Smith and Edmonston (1997) evaluate the long-run net fiscal impact of immigration under different assumptions. Under a baseline scenario, fiscal policy is set so that the debt/GDP ratio is kept constant, newly arriving immigrants have the average characteristics of the current foreign-born population, and the speed of assimilation to natives' wages and family structure is the same as in the past. In this case, Smith and Edmonston (1997) find that the overall present discounted value of the effect of immigration is positive, with significant variations over time. Immigrants' annual net contributions in the first two decades are negative but afterwards become positive. The estimated long-run fiscal impact of 100 000 more immigrants (with average characteristics) per year would be a decrease in taxes by less than 1 per cent (Lee and Miller, 2000). This result *is* influenced by small variations in the aforementioned assumptions.

As with static exercises, one contribution of this study is to highlight the important factors in determining the long-run fiscal effects. Table 12.7 reports the present discounted value of the estimated fiscal contribution of immigrants with different education levels. Again, the most important variables are age and education. The net present value of the fiscal impact is at the maximum for an individual with an arrival age between 10 and 25 years, right after most educational expenditure has been incurred, and declines afterwards. More educated immigrants are positive net contributors, while immigrants with an education of less than high school are negative net contributors. A second important insight of the study is that the mismatch between net federal fiscal gain and net local fiscal loss will increase over time. This is largely due to the fact that the goods provided at federal level are mostly public goods whose cost does not increase with immigration, while many public services used by immigrants, such as education, are funded at the local level.

Table 12.7. *Average fiscal impact of an immigrant and descendants by education level (1996, US$)*

Educational level	Original immigrant only	Immigrant plus descendants over the next 300 years*
< High School	−89 000	−13 000
High School	−31 000	51 000
> High School	105 000	198 000
Overall	−3000	80 000

*Based on estimated educational transition probabilities.

Source: Camarota (2001), Center for Immigration Studies (*http://www.cis.org.*)

The study in Smith and Edmonston (1997) has limitations. First, it assumes that future taxes and/or cuts in benefits will stabilize the national debt, while public debt has already been reduced since the late 1990s. Second, it does not consider the observed trend of a decline in the relative earnings ability of immigrants. Third, it does not consider political economy mechanisms, which could change fiscal policy.

Addressing the first two issues, Auerbach and Oreopoulos (1999) argue that the fiscal impact will be more positive (or less negative) if the burden of taxation is shifted to the future when immigrants will be net contributors. Hence, the present reduction of federal budget deficits reduces immigrants' net fiscal contribution. Moreover, Auerbach and Oreopoulos (1999) find that the educational composition of immigration is key and the present trend towards relatively less educated immigrants could decrease net fiscal benefits in the long-run. It is worth reiterating that the evaluation of the overall fiscal impact depends on how broad is the definition of public goods. In sum, these studies indicate that the fiscal impact of immigration is likely to be small, such that immigrants are neither a solution to fiscal problems nor the cause of sizeable imbalances.[17]

The third issue to be considered is how immigration changes the political economy of fiscal policy. While the aforementioned studies have considered how immigration affects fiscal policy under the present rules (Smith and Edmonston, 1997) or with exogenous changes (Auerbach and Oreopoulos, 1999), endogenous changes to the fiscal stance are relatively unexplored. Spilimbergo (1999) points out that free mobility of workers between a rich (North) and a poor country (South) often leads to fiscal transfers from North

---

[17] After the studies by Smith and Edmonston (1997, 1998) and Auerbach and Oreopoulos (1999), other studies have confirmed the basic results that immigration has a negligible effect on fiscal position over the long run. For instance, by calibrating an overlapping generation model Storesletten (2000) finds little fiscal impact of current immigration. However, he shows that a selective immigration policy favouring high-skilled working age immigrants has sizeable fiscal benefits.

to South (e.g. between United States and Puerto Rico, Western and Eastern Germany, Northern and Southern Italy). This could be rationalized in the context of a political equilibrium in which workers in the North are willing to be taxed and pay a subsidy to avoid excessive migration. In this case, migration (or threat of migration) results in higher taxation.

The previous reasoning presupposes that immigrants are not yet present in the country. If, however, there are relatively poor immigrants already in the country, then the incentives can be turned around. Razin *et al.* (1998) argue and show evidence that low skill immigration may lead to a lower tax burden and less redistribution than would be the case with no immigration. Using a similar argument, Wildasin (1994) shows that migration can lead to a Pareto-inferior outcome in the destination region if immigrants are beneficiaries of redistributive transfers.

12.6. IMMIGRATION AND SOCIAL SECURITY

If the overall long-term fiscal impact of immigration is small and ambiguous, its impact on Social Security is easy to determine using the present contribution and benefit rules. Gustman and Steinmeier (2000) argue that immigrants arriving after 1980 receive more benefits than taxes and so are net beneficiaries of the social security system. The reason is that the social security benefit formula transfers benefits toward those with low lifetime covered earnings, and all years an immigrant spends outside the United States are treated as years of zero earnings. Moreover, immigrants with high income who have worked in the United States for only a decade benefit even more, so the present social security system appears to favour relatively rich foreign-born individuals.

Though the previous study carefully computes the effects of immigration within the present rules, it does not account for dramatic increase in 'illegal contributions' to social security. Since the Immigration Reform and Control Act (IRCA) was passed in 1986, employers have required social security cards from their employees. Many illegal aliens have met this requirement by obtaining fake social security cards, which can be purchased in many cities for as little as a few hundred US dollars. The contributions made using these fake Social Security numbers, which cannot be matched to names legally recorded in the Social Security System, are collected in a 'suspense file' with other contributions to the Social Security System that will not generate corresponding benefits. A relatively small amount of money in this 'suspense file' is normal given that people make mistakes in assigning their contributions. However, the increase in funds in this category has been dramatic in the years following the passage of IRCA. The taxes collected from suspended W2 forms rose from $1.2 billion in 1990 to nearly $4 billion in 1998. During the 1990–98 period, these contributions amounted to more than $20 billion (Sheridan,

2001).[18] Consistent with the idea that illegal immigrants are responsible for this surge, most of these contributions come from areas and industries that typically employ many illegal workers, such as agriculture, restaurants and bars, etc.

12.7. SUMMARY

The net fiscal impact of immigration appears to be small at the aggregate level in the long run. The key variables in determining the size and the sign of the net fiscal contribution are the age and education level of immigrants at the time of entry in the United States. Present policies, which allow for admissions of refugees and family reunification, may heighten (directly and indirectly) the fiscal cost of immigration.

Even if the aggregate fiscal impact is negligible, the fiscal costs and benefits of immigration are not distributed equally between local and federal governments or across time. In general, the federal government is a net gainer, while many states lose because redistributive programmes are often locally funded and because the federal government provides more public goods whose cost does not rise with immigration. Moreover, the burden is distributed unequally across states because relatively poor immigrants cluster in a few gateway states. The welfare reform in 1996, which has devolved the administration and financing of many welfare programmes to the states, appears likely to worsen this financing mismatch. It is notable, however, that these gateway states have been at the forefront of choosing policies to reverse at the state level aspects of the 1996 federal welfare reform. In the short run, immigrants appear to make a negative net contribution to fiscal accounts because they are relatively young and poor. In the long run, however, immigrants are estimated to make a positive net contribution to fiscal accounts.

We should stress the uncertainty of the assumptions under which these conclusions are drawn. In the short run, we do not know very well how the 1996 welfare reform will affect fiscal accounts during a recession. In the long run, there is uncertainty about demographic and economic variables. Even a small variation in the average education and age at entry could change significantly the fiscal impact. It is also difficult to predict the speed of convergence

---

[18] The IRS and the Social Security System are bound by law to keep personal information confidential and so do not share this information with other governmental agencies such as the Immigration and Naturalization Service. Another way in which 'illegal taxpayers' contribute to fiscal accounts is through automatic deduction from wages. Illegal immigrants who pay taxes through automatic deduction cannot claim a rebate at the end of the year because their Taxpayer Identification Number is illegal. Finally, it seems that many illegal immigrants who are paid in cash pay taxes in order to build a record to prove their presence in the country in case of a future amnesty (Sheridan, 2001).

between immigrant and native wages. In addition, past experience suggests that immigration policies react quickly to changes in the economic environment (Hanson and Spilimbergo, 2001) so that we expect that corrective measures will be taken promptly if the fiscal impact becomes large, especially in specific states.

13

The Political Economy of Immigration Policy

As the previous sections have made clear, immigration has important—if contested—effects on the US economy and so on this basis alone is an important political issue. Immigration is also, however, about deciding membership in a political community and, as such, is one of the most fundamental and controversial political choices facing national policymakers. Given the critical economic and political issues at stake, what are the factors that have shaped US immigration policy over recent decades?

Like all areas of policymaking in democracies, US immigration policy is determined by the preferences of voters, firms, and interest groups and by how the political system aggregates these preferences. The aggregation of preferences is particularly sensitive to how successful different groups are in solving their respective collective action problems and organizing themselves effectively to influence policy decisions. US political institutions also influence the costs and benefits of various political actions and thus advantage some groups over others in the policymaking process. In this section, we identify the preferences of the main actors in the US immigration debate and how successful those actors are in getting their views implemented into policy. We focus on explaining the patterns of political conflict about immigration rather than accounting for why particular pieces of legislation have succeeded or failed in becoming law over recent decades. This approach allows us to learn as much as possible about the systematic factors that are likely to influence future US policy choices about immigration and avoids excessive attention on the idiosyncratic events that have determined the fate of various legislative proposals.

Our analysis shows that political conflict over immigration policy has a number of important dimensions. From the opinions of individual citizens about policy to votes on legislation by members of Congress, it is clear that the politics of immigration policymaking is influenced by the perceived economic consequences of policy alternatives and, in particular, on the distribution of these economic effects. The evidence also demonstrates, however, that other considerations play an important role in the course of policymaking, such as beliefs about the impact of immigration on the welfare state.

In addition to this description of the sources of political conflict about immigration, we also argue that the common characterization of immigration policymaking in the US as a process dominated by organized interests and uninfluenced by diffuse interests in the electorate is incorrect. While it is clear that organized interests play an important role in the making of immigration policy, there are substantial theoretical reasons why diffuse interests may also get represented, and we present empirical evidence consistent with this argument.

The remainder of this section examines the preferences of the American public and other important groups involved in the immigration debate and how those preferences are aggregated in the making of national immigration policy.

13.1. PREFERENCES

Our analysis begins with the identification of the preferences of US citizens and employers about immigration policy. For individuals, our approach is to use survey data to determine what, if anything, US citizens think about immigration policy and why they hold the opinions that they do. Our discussion will highlight the key patterns of public opinion in the US based on our review of a large dataset of survey results over the last several decades.[1]

The most striking characteristic of US public opinion about immigration is that there is substantial support for more restrictive immigration policies. For example, the following questions suggest that, at best, Americans are divided between decreasing the number of immigrants and maintaining the status quo. More often than not, a plurality to majority of Americans prefer increased restrictions to the status quo, while fewer than 10 per cent of respondents favour increasing the number of immigrants.

Question 'Do you think the number of immigrants from foreign countries who are permitted to come to the United States to live should be increased a little, increased a lot, decreased a little, decreased a lot, or left the same as it is now?'

Answers, 2000	Increased a lot	3.8%
	Increased a little	5.5%
	Left the same	43.4%
	Decreased a little	14.4%
	Decreased a lot	28.8%
	Don't Know/No Answer	4.1%
Answers, 1998	Increased a lot	2.7%
	Increased a little	7.9%
	Left the same	38.7%
	Decreased a little	28.2%

[1] This review builds on previous research on public opinion in the US about immigration policy. See, for example, Simon and Alexander (1993); Espenshade and Hempstead (1996); Citrin *et al.* (1997); Gimpel and Edwards (1999); Fetzer (2000); Andreas and Snyder (2000); and Scheve and Slaughter (2001*a,b*).

	Decreased a lot	19.8%
	Don't Know/No Answer	2.8%
Answers, 1996	Increased a lot	1.6%
	Increased a little	3.1%
	Left the same	32.9%
	Decreased a little	26.5%
	Decreased a lot	24.5%
	Don't Know/No Answer	11.5%
Answers, 1994	Increased a lot	1.7%
	Increased a little	3.5%
	Left the same	28.2%
	Decreased a little	21.9%
	Decreased a lot	41.0%
	Don't Know/No Answer	3.7%
Answers, 1992	Increased a lot	2.6%
	Increased a little	5.1%
	Left the same	41.6%
	Decreased a little	24.5%
	Decreased a lot	22.4%
	Don't Know/No Answer	3.9%

(*Source*: National Election Studies Survey, 1992, 1994, 1996, 1998, 2000)

Underlying these policy preferences is recognition by the majority of Americans that immigration has some clear economic and cultural benefits. When asked a simple question about whether immigrants bring benefits to the country, nearly 70 per cent of respondents agree that they do.[2]

Question 'Do immigrants help improve our country with their different cultures and talents?'

Answers	Yes	69%
	No	28%
	Don't Know	3%

(*Source*: Gallup/*Newsweek*, August 1990)

On the other hand, surveys also suggest that Americans are clearly concerned about the possible labour-market costs of immigration. In particular there is

---

[2] Although this question is asked at a very general level, other surveys indicate that the US public attributes to immigrants many of the benefits we would expect. For example, when asked in 1986 'What do you think is the most important thing immigrants have done for this country?', the most frequent answers include 'built US', 'variety of cultures', and 'work hard/help the economy' (*Source*: CBS News, *New York Times*). Moreover, the view that immigrants work hard and contribute to economic productivity is not confined to immigrants of previous eras. In the same survey, respondents were asked 'Generally, do today's immigrants work harder than people born here, not as hard, or isn't there much difference?' A full 45 per cent of respondents chose the 'harder' response with only 8 per cent indicating 'not as hard' (*Source*: CBS News, *New York Times*).

a perception that immigrants may take jobs from American natives. The following question asks respondents whether immigrants 'take jobs away' from people already in the United States, and indicates that the large majority thinks immigrants do take jobs—with a plurality responding this outcome is either extremely or very likely.

Question 'The growing number of Hispanic immigrants [in the US economy]: How likely is it to take jobs away from people already here?'

Answers Extremely likely   17.7%
       Very likely   25.6%
       Somewhat likely   33.2%
       Not at all likely   11.9%
       Don't Know/No Answer   11.6%

(*Source*: National Election Studies Survey, 1992)

Question 'The growing number of Asian immigrants [in the US economy]: How likely is it to take jobs away from people already here?'

Answers Extremely likely   16.7%
       Very likely   26.8%
       Somewhat likely   32.8%
       Not at all likely   11.9%
       Don't Know/No Answer   11.8%

(*Source*: National Election Studies Survey, 1992)

It is worth pointing out that these questions do not specify whether the respondent is expected to consider the short-run or long-run effects of immigration. As indicated in Chapter 10's discussion of the labour market effects of immigration, economists think immigration has little influence on national unemployment rates—particularly in economies with flexible labour markets. Nevertheless, the answers to this question indicate that individuals are sensitive to the effects of immigration on labour-market competition generally, and that they think about competition in terms of jobs. Below, we will consider whether the effects of immigration on the labour market outcomes that economists emphasize—specifically wage pressures—help to explain cleavages in public opinion about immigration.

Another consideration that seems to underlie public concern about immigration is its impact on the welfare state. The economic effects of immigration are not limited to its impact on outcomes in the labour market or its possible small but positive effects on economic growth. Immigration clearly affects the welfare state as well. A key concern of the American public is whether or not immigrants pay their way. In the following questions, nearly 55 per cent of respondents think that it is extremely or very likely that the growing number of Hispanic immigrants will cause higher taxes due to increased demand for public services. When the reference group is Asian immigrants, a lower but still substantial 38 per cent give the 'extremely' or 'very likely' response.

Question 'The growing number of Hispanic immigrants [in the US economy]: How likely is it to cause higher taxes due to more demands for public services?'

Answers Extremely likely   18.8%
           Very likely   36.1%
           Somewhat likely   34.5%
           Not at all likely   7.1%
           Don't Know/No Answer   3.4%

(*Source*: National Election Studies Survey, 1992)

Question 'The growing number of Asian immigrants [in the US economy]: How likely is it to cause higher taxes due to more demands for public services?'

Answers Extremely likely   11.1%
           Very likely   26.6%
           Somewhat likely   41.6%
           Not at all likely   16.9%
           Don't Know/No Answer   3.8%

(*Source*: National Election Studies Survey, 1992)

It is clear from these questions as well as other survey evidence that concerns about the fiscal effects of immigration contribute substantially to public scepticism about liberal immigration policies.[3]

Our discussion thus far has focused on how the US public assesses the aggregate economic costs and benefits of immigration and on how the public prefers generally more restrictive policies compared to the status quo. It remains unclear from this description, however, whether there are important cleavages in public opinion about immigration.

As discussed in the previous sections, the evidence suggests that some of the biggest effects of immigration on the US economy may be distributive. For example, under current immigration laws, there are theoretical reasons—albeit supported by mixed empirical evidence—to think that the flow of relatively less-skilled workers into the US harms the labour market outcomes of similarly skilled native workers while more-skilled natives are left better off. To the extent that different immigration policy alternatives have clear distributive consequences, this is likely to generate conflict in the policy debate with winners and losers from liberalization advocating policies consistent with their interests. The importance of distributive issues is likely to be particularly

---

[3] Many of the fiscal costs associated with immigrants like public education are financed at the state and local level and so are likely to be especially salient to voters. When asked to make an overall economic assessment of the total costs and benefits of immigration, a majority appear to believe that the costs outweigh the benefits. In 1985, Americans were asked 'Generally speaking, do you think that refugee immigrants to the United States take more from the US economy through social services and unemployment than they contribute to the US economy through taxes and productivity—or haven't you heard enough about that yet to say?' Respondents chose the 'take more' response 46 per cent of the time and the 'contribute more' response 19 per cent of the time.

significant in a policy area like immigration for which the net balance of the aggregate costs and benefits to the US economy seems to be small (and the direction contested).

If the distributive consequences of immigration influence individual policy preferences, then public opinion about policy will be characterized by distinct economic cleavages. The key question is whether the types of individuals who are most likely to be hurt economically from current immigration are most supportive of further restrictions. Evaluating this question requires assessing the determinants of individual opinions about immigration. Why do some individuals support more-restrictionist policies while others are opposed? Individual opinions surely depend on a host of considerations, including political ideology, ethnic and racial identity, expectations about the economic impact on the nation as a whole as well as on how policy alternatives affect individuals' own personal economic welfare. Among distributive concerns, the anticipated effect of immigration on wages is likely to play a key role, as labour income is a major determinant of individual economic welfare. Because labour income depends primarily on individual skill levels, there may be a significant link from skills to wages to immigration-policy preferences. Our distributive question then becomes, do individuals with different labour market skills have different preferences about immigration policy?

Recall from Chapter 10 that different economic models make contrasting predictions about the nature of the link from immigration to labour income. Here we consider the simple prediction that immigration increases relative wage inequality and lowers the real wages of less-skilled workers. This prediction accords with the current US law increasing the pool of less-skilled workers, and is consistent with both the Heckscher–Ohlin and factor-proportions models (assuming fixed product prices) reviewed in Chapter 10.[4] To the extent that individuals expect such a relationship between immigration, skills, and wages, we anticipate a link between the skills of workers and the policy preferences that they hold: increasing skills should be associated with less restrictive immigration opinions.

We examined individual responses to the following question asked in the 1992, 1994, and 1996 National Election Studies (NES) surveys: 'Do you think the number of immigrants from foreign countries who are permitted to come to the United States to live should be increased a little, increased a lot, decreased a little, decreased a lot, or left the same as it is now?' We estimated how skill levels, measured by years of education and average wages for an individual's occupation, and other individual characteristics affected the probability of supporting immigration restrictions (see Section 13.4 for a more detailed description of our methodology).

---

[4] Recall though that Chapter 10 emphasized that economies can adjust to immigration through changes in industrial specialization, migration of labour and/or capital, and changes in underlying production technology in addition to changes in wages.

Table 13.1. *Estimated effect of increasing skill levels on the probability of supporting immigration restrictions*

Increase skill measure by two standard deviations	Year	Change in probability of supporting immigration restrictions
Occupation wage	1992	−0.049 (0.021)
		[−0.083, −0.013]
Education years		−0.102 (0.020)
		[−0.133, −0.069]
Occupation wage	1994	−0.135 (0.022)
		[−0.171, −0.100]
Education years		−0.141 (0.022)
		[−0.175, −0.105]
Occupation wage	1996	−0.095 (0.023)
		[−0.133, −0.057]
Education years		−0.121 (0.025)
		[−0.162, −0.082]

Notes: Using the ordered probit estimates reported and discussed in the Appendix, we simulated the consequences of changing each skill measure from one standard deviation below its mean to one standard deviation above on the probability of supporting immigration restrictions. The mean effect is reported first, with the standard error of this estimate in parentheses followed by a 90 per cent confidence interval.

Our main empirical finding is clear evidence that individuals with greater skill levels were significantly less likely to support further immigration restrictions, controlling for a wide number of other characteristics such as age, gender, race, ethnicity, and political ideology.[5] Table 13.1 reports the key results assessing the impact of increasing our two skill measures from typical low values—one standard deviation below their sample means—to typical high values—one standard deviation above their sample means—on the probability of supporting further immigration restrictions. For the skill measure *Education Years*, increasing the variable by two standard deviations (from a typically low level of about 11 years of education to a high level of about 16 years) reduces the probability of supporting immigration restrictions by 10–14 per cent over the three survey years. What this means is that if you could put a respondent who was a high school dropout but with otherwise average characteristics through both high school and college, then the probability that this hypothetical individual supports immigration restrictions would fall by about 12 per cent. Preferences about immigration divide strongly across labour-market skills, consistent with immigration's potential distributional consequences in the national labour market, and individuals explicitly make the connection between immigration and labour-market pressures.

[5] The correlation between skills and immigration policy preferences is robust to changing or eliminating the conditioning information. Details about the data, estimation procedures, and results are available in Scheve and Slaughter (2001*a,b*).

These findings may seem puzzling in light of the evidence presented in Chapter 10 that immigration has made, at best, a small contribution to the wage pressures faced by less-skilled native workers. It is important not to see these perceptions and the actual impact of immigration on wages as necessarily inconsistent. First, even if the effect of immigration on wages has been small, it makes sense for less-skilled workers to oppose policies that have a marginal negative impact on their welfare. Second, some of the alternative adjustment mechanisms discussed in Chapter 10, such as immigration changing the migration patterns of natives, are also indicators of labour market pressure on natives from immigration. Third, and perhaps most importantly, individuals may be forward-looking in forming their policy opinions. Chapter 10 discusses reasons why the conditions that have mitigated the wage adjustment mechanism may not persist in the future. Consequently, it is certainly reasonable for individuals to be concerned about the impact of immigration on wages in the future.

Our analysis establishing a correlation between skill levels and immigration policy preferences pools all regions in the United States. An obvious question raised by the finding is whether the concentration of immigrants in some regions of the country affects policy opinions. The area-analysis model discussed in Chapter 10 predicts that wage pressures on less-skilled workers should be strongest in the gateway communities where immigrants are concentrated. This suggests that the link between skill levels and preferences may be stronger among workers in these areas. We tested this prediction using the survey data from the NES along with information about the concentration of immigrants in the region in which the respondent was located. Our analysis suggests that the correlation between skill levels and immigration policy preferences is not higher among people in high-immigration areas than among people elsewhere.[6] The differences between less- and more-skilled workers in opinions about immigration policy are similar throughout the country.[7] Moreover, we find no evidence that, controlling for individual characteristics, opinions are generally more or less restrictionist in regions with higher concentrations of immigrants.

The skill cleavage that we do observe raises a number of questions regarding public opinion about immigration policy. Note that the question that we analyse does not ask what skill mix immigrants would have relative to natives. We assume that respondents think that immigrant inflows would increase the relative supply of less-skilled workers. This assumption is reasonable as it clearly reflects the facts about US immigration in recent decades. However, the

---

[6] See Scheve and Slaughter (2001a,b) for details about the estimation procedures and results on this point.

[7] The finding of a skill correlation that does not vary across regions according to the concentration of immigrants is consistent with the factor-proportions and Heckscher–Ohlin models that assume a single national labour market but is inconsistent with the area-analysis model.

options that policymakers face include changing not only levels of immigration but also the characteristics of those entrants. Although there is clear evidence of a skill cleavage in current public opinion about immigration, this should be understood in the context of current US policy and immigration experience. It is perfectly possible for this cleavage to disappear or even reverse itself if the skill mix of immigrants was altered. In fact, theoretically we would expect such a change.

It is, of course, difficult to assess what preferences would look like in a different policy regime in which immigrants were relatively more skilled. Nevertheless, although we do not have much evidence on what would happen to the skill correlation, indirect evidence suggests that restrictive opinions about immigration policy might be significantly reduced as the skills of immigrants increase.

The first piece of evidence on this point takes advantage of the fact that different communities have different skill mixes of immigrants. Do individuals have more or less restrictive policy preferences in geographic regions with more-skilled immigrants? To answer this question, we obtained data on the educational attainment of the immigrant population in the local communities represented in the NES surveys discussed above. We found evidence that individuals living in communities with more-skilled immigrants were somewhat less likely to support further immigration restrictions. This finding is only suggestive as the immigration question queries respondents about national policy and it is not clear how heavily individuals weigh local immigrants in evaluating policy. Moreover, it is important to recognize that increasing the skill level of immigrants is just as likely to affect individuals' assessment of the fiscal effects of immigration as it is to impact their evaluation of its consequences for the labour market. Respondents may have less restrictive opinions in areas with more-skilled immigrants because they expect skilled entrants to contribute more in taxes than they take away in government services and transfers.[8]

The second piece of indirect evidence on how the skills of immigrants might affect public preferences about immigration policy is that opinion varies substantially with the geographic origin of immigrants. Although immigrants from different parts of the world may differ in many characteristics, one difference that is well documented is their skill levels (Borjas, 1994, 1999a). Consider the following question posed to the US public in 1965.

---

[8] Note that in 1984, Americans were asked 'Let's imagine that you were a US government official and that your job was to make decisions about who should and should not be admitted into this country. For each of the persons I describe, please tell me if you think that person should or should not be admitted into the US . . .'. Sixty-four per cent responded that a person 'with job skills very much in demand in the US' should be admitted. This question does not explicitly state that the skills in demand are high skills but it is clear from the question that the hypothetical immigrants will likely pay their way.

Question 'Here is a list of countries and parts of the world. If we are going to allow more people into this country as immigrants, which places on this list would you most prefer they come from...Canada, England or Scotland, Scandinavia, Germany, Ireland, France, Italy, Poland, Mexico, Latin America, Eastern Europe, Middle East, Asia, or Russia?

Selected Answers	Canada	28%
	England or Scotland	28%
	Germany	17%
	Italy	7%
	Mexico	5%

(*Source*: Harris, 1965)

Similarly, more recent surveys have asked whether the US accepts too many, too few, or about the right number of immigrants from various parts of the world. The proportion responding 'too many' ranges from over 50 per cent for 'Latin America' to about 30 per cent for 'Europe'.[9] There are obvious limitations to each of these types of questions.[10] Nevertheless, the evidence suggests that the US public is more receptive to immigration from countries whose immigrants have been relatively more skilled. Consider the five countries for which answers are reported in the Harris question above. The average years of education of immigrant men in the US for 1990 are 13.8 for Canada, 14.6 for the United Kingdom, 13.9 for Germany, 10.9 for Italy, and 7.6 for Mexico (Borjas, 1994).[11]

The evidence that we have reviewed so far has focused on the economic considerations that determine the overall direction of US public opinion about immigration policy and the variation in opinions among different types of individuals. Immigration policy, however, is also a political decision and, as such, preferences are likely to be influenced by considerations beyond its labour market effects. For example, opinion may be influenced by preferences about

---

[9] See, for example, 1990 Gallup/*Newsweek* results.

[10] The wording for the question asking respondents 'Are the numbers of immigrants now entering the United States from each of the following areas too many, too few or about the right amount?' is particularly problematic as the differences in percentages may just reflect that more immigrants arrive from some regions than others, and so an individual wanting less immigrants overall would be more likely to focus on the regions sending the most immigrants. Consequently, differences in responses across regions may or may not reflect the differences in the skill of immigrants in these regions. Nonetheless, the pattern is not inconsistent with the argument that the skills of immigrants matter for patterns of public preferences about policy.

[11] As discussed above, the increasing support for immigrants by skill level may also indicate assessments about the fiscal effects of immigration. For example, Chapter 12 notes evidence that immigrants from Canada make a positive contribution to fiscal balances while immigrants from Latin America do not. Moreover, the countries that have high-skilled immigrants tend to be European so these survey results raise the further question of the role of attitudes about race and culture on immigration policy opinions, a question we address below. The point made here is simply that differences in attitudes about immigration by country of origin are not inconsistent with the skills of immigrants being a key determinant of public opinion about policy.

the welfare state and beliefs about how immigration affects the welfare state. Alternatively, opinion may be affected by beliefs about whether immigration affects American culture and whether any perceived changes are desirable or not. One strategy for determining whether these types of considerations influence public opinion is to again look for cleavages in policy opinions about immigration. Do identifiable demographic groups have systematically different policy views? Do individuals with certain political ideologies or attitudes tend to think differently about immigration policy?

We examined these questions in our evaluation of responses to the 1992, 1994, and 1996 NES survey question discussed above. We found there to be systematic differences in the opinions of African Americans and in the views of immigrants and their children. For example, we estimate that African Americans were nearly 10 per cent less likely to support further restrictions on immigration policy than the rest of the population, controlling for other determinants of opinion like skill levels. We found about the same difference to exist for the category of immigrants and children of immigrants. Importantly, political ideology also plays a role in opinion formation. Our analysis suggests that individuals who identify themselves as very conservative are about 10 per cent more likely to support immigration restrictions than individuals who place themselves in the middle of a liberal-conservative ideological scale. The interpretation of this correlation is hardly unambiguous because liberalism and conservatism mean different things to different voters. Nonetheless, it is likely that this correlation is related to preferences about the size of government and, more specifically, the size of the welfare state. Individuals who identify themselves as political conservatives are, all else equal, more likely to prefer small government. Given the trends in use of the welfare state by immigrants reported in Chapter 12, conservatives may object to immigration in part because of the demands it puts on public services and the tax and transfer system.[12]

In addition to these ideological and demographic cleavages, individual immigration opinions may vary due to different levels of tolerance. The political conflict surrounding immigration often seems to be closely intertwined with more general civil rights debates in US politics. Moreover, the public opinion

---

[12] The interpretation of the ideology/immigration policy preferences correlation requires some caution. In one view, individuals have political ideologies that affect and guide their opinions about all sorts of political issues. In this sense, ideology causes immigration opinions. An alternative perspective is that individuals develop policy opinions consistent with their interests and values and ideology is largely a summary statistic for individuals' collective set of policy opinions. In this sense, ideology is a consequence rather than a cause of policy opinions. Even if ideology is to some extent exogenous and a meaningful explanatory variable, it should be interpreted cautiously as although different preferences about the size of government is a salient feature of liberal/conservative political debate in the US so are other issues that may be related to immigration policy. It is worth noting that to the extent that there are ideological differences in opinion about immigration due to its impact on the welfare state, this source of opinion does not fit into a simple economic/non-economic dichotomy. Debate about the size of government reflects distributive conflict as well as differences in tastes.

literature has shown that general attitudes toward racial, ethnic, and religious groups can affect opinions about a wide array of public policies. We investigated this possibility by examining the extent to which immigration policy opinions were correlated with general measures of tolerance. We measured tolerance by respondents' answers to three different tolerance statements or questions (e.g. 'We should be more tolerant of people who choose to live according to their own moral standards, even if they are very different from our own'). We found a robust correlation between the tolerance measures and immigration opinions with those with more tolerant attitudes having less restrictionist policy opinions. Further, this relationship held even after controlling for the skill measures, demographic identifiers, and political ideology variables discussed above.[13]

Although it is surely the case that both economic and non-economic considerations influence public opinion about immigration, determining the relative weight of these factors is a much more difficult, if not impossible, task. For example, how to identify the relative role of labour market competition and individual tolerance in explaining opinions about immigration policy is not clear. Intolerance is, of course, in part a symptom and consequence of economic competition. Thus, inferring the relative role of intolerant attitudes and economic threat requires a theoretical model for the relationship between the two that is much more precise than we have available. Adding to the challenge is that tolerance is actually a very difficult attitude to study through the use of public opinion surveys for a number of reasons including the fact it is one of the areas for which it is most difficult to elicit truthful responses. Our view is that while it is clear that both economic and non-economic factors influence public opinion about immigration, the importance of economic factors has generally not been weighted as heavily as it should.

In addition to individual citizens, another large and diverse group that plays a critical role in immigration policymaking is US employers. Firms in a wide variety of industries have expressed preferences for significant changes in US immigration policy. As discussed in Chapter 11, employers requiring relatively less-skilled and often seasonal workers in industries such as agriculture and apparel manufacturing have been among the principal advocates of policy liberalization. More recently, firms employing highly skilled workers such as software programmers have joined the chorus for immigration liberalization. Employers have not only lobbied for higher immigration quotas within the existing policy regime but also have advocated sweeping changes in immigration law. Many firms, particularly in the context of the tight labour markets of the 1990s, have urged that admission based on family membership criteria be

---

[13] It is important to note that the skill-preferences correlation is robust to controlling for these other factors including tolerance. Critically, this indicates that skill measures are not proxies for tolerance. See Scheve and Slaughter (2001*a*,*b*) for more discussion on this point. The ideology correlation is also robust to including the tolerance measures which suggests that ideology is not simply a proxy for tolerance.

substantially curtailed in favour of skill-based and other criteria that reflect the needs of employers and arguably the national economy. Skill-based immigration policies are especially favoured among high-technology companies but in principal may be designed to garner the support of employers of workers with varying skill levels. Thus, the immigration policy opinions of US employers generally favour increasing levels of immigration and other reforms designed to make the levels of immigration allowed as beneficial as possible to their respective industries.

There are, however, important differences among employers in emphasis and in the intensity of preferences. For example, the reintroduction of large-scale temporary immigration favoured by many agricultural employers would not meet the needs of many other types of firms. Also, some industries do not employ many workers with the skills of the immigrants admitted under current laws and have not experienced acute shortages for the workers that they do employ. Many of the firms in these industries have fairly indifferent preferences about changes in immigration policy.

13.2. AGGREGATING PREFERENCES IN THE POLITICAL PROCESS

The previous discussion has suggested that there is substantial variation among and between citizens and firms in immigration-policy preferences. Given this variation, how does the political system aggregate these preferences and ultimately set US immigration policy?

To start, consider the breadth of variation in preferred policies. Firms, particularly those employing relatively less- and more-skilled workers, have a strong interest in policy liberalization. Among individual citizens, policy opinions seem to be clearly related to the perceived effects of immigration on labour market outcomes. This link is most evident in the differences in preferences between more- and less-skilled workers. Less-skilled workers who have the most to lose from immigration under current laws and patterns of immigration are more likely to favour restrictive policies. The public opinion evidence suggests, however, that there are other groups in society that seem to have systematically different preferences about immigration that are not necessarily related to its labour market effects. For example, the surveys suggest that beliefs about the impact of immigration on the welfare state may distinguish different groups of voters. The public is generally concerned about whether immigrants burden public services and the tax and transfer system, but political conservatives are especially sensitive to this issue. There is also variation among demographic groups with, for example, blacks, immigrants, and children of immigrants being more likely to oppose further immigration restrictions. Each of these groups regardless of the source of its policy preferences represents a potential interest group that either directly or in coalition with others seeks to influence US immigration policies.

We, of course, do not actually observe active interest groups for every category of individuals or firms that has a clear preference about the direction of US immigration policy. The formation of an interest group with the resources to influence policy requires that those like-minded individuals and firms solve their respective collective action problems. The challenge is simply that individuals or firms that may be better off if they all contribute to a common effort such as lobbying for their preferred immigration policy may not have an incentive to do so because their own contribution is not decisive in the success of the common effort. Consequently, many potential groups with similar preferences are never organized into active interest groups engaged in the policy-making process.

The literature on collective action problems generally, and interest groups in particular, suggests that small groups for which the benefits of organization are concentrated and for which the costs of monitoring each member's efforts are low will be more successful in lobbying for their preferred policies than large groups with diffuse interests.[14] This literature also suggests that many groups will rely on selective benefits not necessarily directly related to the collective good to create incentives for participation. The provision of the collective good is then in some sense a by-product rather than the main output of the interest group.

The recognition that not all interests are equally likely to solve their collective action problems is important for understanding immigration policy-making. Most studies of the determinants of US immigration policy contend that interest groups dominate the policymaking process and that the interest groups that are successfully organized to exert influence reflect the preferences of only some of the relevant groups in society.[15] In particular, this research suggests that diffuse interests like the ordinary citizens polled in the public opinion surveys presented above are unorganized and largely unrepresented in the policy process. To understand the asymmetries in organization for immigration policy lobbying, it is instructive to consider what types of interest groups have been active in the US immigration debate. There are, of course, lots of different interest groups that have taken explicit positions on immigration policy. However, three categories of groups are widely recognized to have been important forces in influencing policy debates.

Employers of immigrants are the most obvious and their success in organizing the least surprising. These firms are typically organized in industry groups. Within each industry, the number of firms is small compared to the number of individuals in most of the other groups with clear preferences about immigration policy, and the firms have substantial economic interests at stake in changes in immigration policy. Moreover, they often have common interests

---

[14] See, for example, Schattschneider (1935); Olson (1965); Milner (1988); Alt and Gilligan (1994); Grier *et al.* (1994); and Gilligan (1997).   [15] See Gimpel and Edwards (1999).

in a variety of policy areas such as trade and regulation in addition to immigration. Once organized, they can lobby across a number of policy areas.

Immigrant groups have also been successful in organizing. These groups face a more difficult collective action problem. Although, as noted above, immigrants are more likely to support liberal immigration policies, they are a large, diverse group for which the benefits of liberalization for any single individual are small. The success of immigrant groups in organizing seems to be due to the fact that many of these groups are organized for entirely different purposes— often for social and/or professional reasons—and then develop a capacity for lobbying. In this sense, their organization for purposes of lobbying for particular immigration policies is a by-product of other activities.

The same can be said of African-American and other civil rights groups that have been successful in organizing lobbying efforts about immigration policy. These groups are organized for completely different purposes, but nonetheless have played an important role in the national policy debate about immigration.

This list is not exhaustive but it is indicative of the general point that the interest groups lobbying about immigration policy are likely to represent concentrated interests or to represent the views of groups organized for reasons other than influencing national immigration policy. Moreover, it is not at all evident that the concerns of the electorate observed in the public opinion surveys are represented by well-organized and well-funded interest groups.[16] This leads, then, to a standard interest group explanation for why US immigration policy has remained relatively liberal in the face of often restrictive preferences among the American public. The argument is simply that a coalition of employers, immigrant groups, and civil rights groups have lobbied effectively to prevent a significant restrictionist turn in policy. Put differently, the concerns of diffuse groups such as less-skilled workers and fiscal conservatives are not effectively organized on this issue, and immigration has not become salient enough in electoral politics to seriously constrain national policymakers.

This account of immigration policymaking is no doubt accurate in its main insight that there is asymmetry in the organization of interests reflecting alternative policy views. To this insight, however, must be added consideration of the strategic situation that faces national policymakers—particularly members of the House of Representatives in the US Congress—and how it may affect the representation of diffuse interests. A number of congressional scholars (Kingdon, 1973; Denzau and Munger, 1986; Arnold, 1990; Bailey, 2001) have argued that representatives are sensitive to the concerns of even uninformed voters because they anticipate efforts to mobilize these groups. So, although taxpayers and low-skilled workers may not be particularly well-organized compared to other groups with distinct preferences in the immigration debate,

---

[16] See Gimpel and Edwards (1999) and Kessler (1999) for a detailed description of interest groups active in immigration lobbying.

members of Congress are likely to consider their preferences when making policy decisions in order to insure themselves against mobilization of these groups by political opponents. The argument is simply that the electoral concerns of members of Congress are such that diffuse, unorganized interests may be represented in the policy process even if we observe limited interest group activity.[17] This insight does not imply that interest-group formation and activity is not important for understanding patterns of support for alternative immigration policies, but rather that these influences will be checked by the electoral calculations of policymakers.[18]

So, given the expected role of organized interests and the electoral constraints faced by politicians, what are the key determinants of the policymaking behaviour of members of Congress? In the discussion of immigration policy preferences, we observed differences among individuals in opinions about immigration based on skill type, political ideology, immigration status, and ethnicity. We also noted the generally more favourable view toward immigration of US employers. We expect the relative strength of these groups in each member's congressional district to account for variation in voting behaviour in the House of Representatives. This includes both those groups that have been widely recognized as well organized and influential in the immigration debate such as employers, immigrants, and civil rights groups and relatively more diffuse groups such as less-skilled workers and fiscal-conservatives.

Although a comprehensive analysis of congressional voting on immigration is beyond the scope of this review, we examine a number of key votes in the 1990s to illustrate how these factors can explain political conflict among national policymakers over immigration policy.[19] The objective of this analysis is to explain votes on immigration legislation in the House of Representatives. Although a given position on each vote can be characterized as more or less restrictive, the interests and preferences of various groups in society (and in each representative's district) depend critically on exactly what aspect of immigration policy is under consideration and what its expected consequences are.

To start with, we analyse votes on the Chrysler amendment during key immigration debates during the 104th Congress. This amendment proposed

---

[17] See Bailey (1999, 2001) for a full development of this idea within a formal probabilistic voting model with applications to trade policy. He argues that skilled workers are a diffuse group that favours free-trade and finds that members of Congress from districts with relatively more skilled workers are more likely to cast votes consistent with free trade positions.

[18] Note that it is not necessary that we observe individual citizens actually voting on the basis of the immigration issue for this constraint to hold. It is as much the threat of the mobilization of interests as actual voting behaviour that induces the constraint.

[19] Explaining variation in congressional behaviour provides relatively more insight about the political conflict associated with immigration policymaking than a guide to actual changes in policy. Major immigration legislation is rare and notoriously difficult to anticipate. Moreover, the analysis here is limited to the House of Representatives while the passage and implementation of legislation is the result of complex interactions between the House, the Senate, the president, the courts, and even state and local governments.

that immigration reform legislation separate issues that were primarily associated with restriction and reform of legal immigration from those associated with restriction and reform of illegal immigration. It was arguably the critical vote determining whether new restrictions on legal immigration would be made, with passage of the amendment damaging any prospects for new restrictions.[20] Consequently, a 'yes' was a vote in favour of relatively liberal immigration policy under the current policy regime dominated by family-based immigration. Given this content, the following factors are hypothesized to account for variation in Congressional voting behaviour.

1. *Immigrant Population.* Representatives in districts with greater immigration population are more likely to support relatively liberal policy, particularly for family-based immigration.[21]
2. *Black Population.* Representatives in districts with more African Americans should, all else equal, be more supportive of liberal policies, again particularly for family-based immigration.
3. *Economic Activity.* Representatives in districts with industries that employ less-skilled workers intensively should also be more supportive of liberal immigration policies. The employers in these districts may prefer reforms that allow for more employment-based immigration but the current regime characterized by family-based immigration does predictably supply the less-skilled workers these industries demand. However, representatives in districts with lots of activities in high-technology sectors are likely to be more supportive of liberalization only when it includes reforms that actually increase the flow of the skilled workers they require.
4. *Organized Labour.* Representatives in districts with higher rates of unionization are likely to be more responsive to the views of organized labour on immigration policy. Although labour has traditionally opposed immigration because of its potential to put downward pressure on wages, it developed a more strategic view in the 1990s. Organized labour remains generally opposed to employment-based immigration liberalization. However, some important labour organizations have become more supportive of family-based immigration. At the very least unions cannot be counted on as consistent restrictionist voices in the immigration debate.[22] The reasons for this distinction lie in the success of unions in recruiting recent immigrant workers. Many unions believe that their long-term interests are served in alliance with rather than in opposition to immigrants and the groups that

---

[20] The amendment was passed.

[21] Note that in addition to immigration's distributive consequences for natives and immigrants in the receiving country, it has an impact on the welfare of sending states. Consequently, changes in immigration policy can be influenced by international relations considerations. One mechanism for sending states to influence policy is through their immigrant communities.

[22] The AFL-CIO has recently even endorsed an amnesty for illegal immigrants. Although the AFL-CIO officially called for labour and business to work on new mechanisms to meet legitimate demands for new workers, they remain opposed to the expansion of temporary worker programmes.

represent them.[23] The implications for congressional voting then are that representatives in districts with high unionization are more likely to take a negative view toward liberalizing employment-based immigration but more likely to be supportive of the current family-based policy regime.

5. *Less-skilled Workers.* Not all less-skilled workers are union members and even among those that are members, some may not share the long-term strategic partnership views of union leaders. Moreover, the public opinion evidence suggests that these individuals have distinctly more restrictive preferences about immigration. Consequently, this is a diffuse group whose preferences may affect the calculations of members of Congress. We expect that, all else equal, representatives in districts with higher concentrations of less-skilled workers are more likely to take restrictionist positions on legislation.

6. *Political Conservatism.* The public opinion evidence suggests that voters are generally concerned about the fiscal effects of immigration. Moreover, political conservatives who typically favour a smaller welfare state have significantly more restrictive policy opinions about immigration. This suggests that congressional representatives in conservative districts are likely to be more supportive of restrictive legislation. This will be especially true of legislation dealing with family-based immigration and the access of immigrants more generally to public services and the welfare state. We have emphasized the connections between ideological conservatism and views about the welfare state and immigration policy. This is consistent with considerable empirical evidence that the main dimension of ideological political competition in the US over the last several decades is about the size of government and the extent of redistribution.[24] Nonetheless, fiscal conservatism and nativist sentiments are correlated to some degree and the measures of ideology available may also indicate differences in views about the cultural impact of immigrants in addition to the distributive conflicts we have emphasized.[25]

We analysed the impact of various measures of these factors on congressional votes on the Chrysler amendment. We found evidence that representatives from districts with more immigrants, blacks, and union members were more likely to vote for the Chrysler amendment and thus prevent restrictive reforms of current legal immigration laws. Districts with more less-skilled workers and more-conservative House members were less likely to vote for the amendment.

---

[23] There are no doubt tensions in this calculation as the distinction between employment and family-based immigration for the potential labour market impacts on low-skilled workers is minimal. Family-based immigration means more low-skilled workers.

[24] See, for example, Poole and Rosenthal (1991, 1997).

[25] See Kessler (1999) for further discussion of the content of ideological and partisan differences in policy preferences about immigration policy.

Table 13.2. *Estimated effect of explanatory variables on the probability that a member of Congress votes against the Chrysler amendment*

Increase variable by two standard deviations	Change in probability of voting against Chrysler amendment
Per cent immigrant	−0.089 (0.047)
	[−0.181, −0.024]
Per cent black	−0.142 (0.076)
	[−0.262, −0.011]
Manufacturing employment	0.022 (0.061)
	[−0.076, 0.117]
Unionization	−0.142 (0.082)
	[−0.291, −0.029]
Per cent less than H.S.	0.139 (0.062)
	[0.036, 0.240]
Ideological conservatism	0.320 (0.048)
	[0.243, 0.399]

Notes: Using the logit estimates reported and discussed in the Appendix, we simulated the consequences of changing each explanatory variable from one standard deviation below its mean to one standard deviation above on the probability of voting against the Chrysler amendment and thus expressing a restrictionist policy preference. The mean effect is reported first, with the standard error of this estimate in parentheses followed by a 90 per cent confidence interval.

Table 13.2 reports the key results assessing the impact of increasing the variable measuring each factor from typical low values—one standard deviation below their sample means—to typical high values—one standard deviation above their sample means—on the probability of voting *against* the Chrysler amendment.[26] Immigration population is measured by the percent of the total population in the Congressional district that is foreign born. Increasing this measure from a low value to a typical high value—two standard deviations—decreases the probability that the representative of that district takes a restrictive position and votes against the amendment by 9 per cent. A similar effect is estimated for the percentage of the total population that is African American. These results are broadly consistent with the observation that these groups are more supportive of the current family-based immigration regime and oppose restrictive reforms. These groups are relatively well organized and it is not surprising that, all else equal, representatives appear to be influenced by their concerns.

---

[26] The dependent variable was coded as votes against the amendment so it is consistent with the public opinion and other results discussed in this section—more restrictionist opinions and votes are assigned higher values.

Economic activity or the interests of employers is measured in this analysis by the percentage of total district employment in manufacturing. In results not reported, we included alternative measures such as the percentage of employment in agriculture and the percentage of total campaign receipts received by the representative from corporations. For none of these measures is the effect significantly negative as hypothesized. This null result may be because of limitations with these measures. It is clear from immigration debates that employer interests are weighted heavily in US policymaking whether or not they account for differences in voting patterns across legislators not explained by the other variables in all Congressional votes. We will discuss below Congressional voting evidence for which these measures of district employer interests do have the hypothesized negative effect.

The estimates in Table 13.2 are consistent with our expectation that for some types of policy votes organized labour and less-skilled workers may exert opposing pressures on national policymakers. Consistent with the observation that national union leaders have become more supportive of family-based immigration, increasing unionization from relatively low to relatively high levels decreased by 14 per cent the probability that the representative took the restrictionist position on this vote. In contrast, members of Congress in districts with more less-skilled workers—as measured by the percentage of the population above the age of twenty-five with less than a high-school education—were, all else equal, more likely to cast restrictionist votes and the magnitude of the effect was comparable in absolute value to that of unionization. Part of the answer to the question of who resisted the efforts of immigrant, civil rights, and other groups to prevent restrictionist reform of legal immigration is members of Congress who anticipated potential negative electoral consequences from less-skilled workers.

Our analysis suggests that opposition was also ideological. The measure of ideology used is the Poole–Rosenthal NOMINATE score (Poole and Rosenthal, 1991, 1997). This variable is based on the voting behaviour of members of the House of Representatives throughout each Congress. Strictly speaking, the variable measures the ideology of each representative. Under most theories of representation, including a median voter model, each member's ideology should be at least sensitive to that of his or her district. Like any multi-dimensional scaling technique, the actual content of NOMINATE scores is open to interpretation. Poole and Rosenthal argue that the single dimension measure used in this analysis reflects primarily economic conflict between liberals and conservatives over, among other things, the size of government and the extent of redistribution.[27] Consequently, we employ this measure to

[27] Although this makes the variable a suitable measure for fiscal conservatism, alternative interpretations are that it is primarily measuring partisan effects (to the extent this is an exogenous explanatory variable) or that it is primarily measuring nativist sentiment. Partisan interpretation is consistent with the main point made here because empirically the primary differences between the US political parties in legislative behaviour have been about the size of government and the extent

account for differences among districts and representatives in views about the welfare state. The variable is increasing in conservatism. The estimate reported in Table 13.2 indicates that increasing this ideological measure from a typically liberal value—one standard deviation below the mean—to a typically conservative value—one standard deviation above the mean—increases the probability of taking a restrictionist position and voting against the amendment by 32 per cent. This finding is consistent with the ideological differences that we observed among individuals in opinions about immigration policy.

One strategy for checking these results is to examine the determinants of votes for which a particular aspect of immigration policy making is clearly salient. For example, do the coalition patterns observed over the Chrysler amendment hold up when the legislation in question is explicitly about immigrant access to public services? To some extent we would expect the answer to be 'yes' because we have argued that the coalitions for and against family-based immigration are, in part, determined by the perceived effects of immigration on the welfare state.

We analysed votes in the 104th Congress on passage of a bill to permit states to bar illegal immigrants from public education.[28] The results of the statistical analysis are reported in the Appendix. We again find that representatives in districts with high concentrations of immigrants are significantly less likely to cast restrictionist votes. Further, representatives in districts with relatively more less-skilled workers are again more likely to take restrictionist positions as are members of Congress in ideologically conservative districts. Not surprisingly, in this analysis, the magnitude of the effect of ideological conservatism is even larger than for the Chrysler amendment. When public services is the issue in immigration debates, the positions taken are substantially determined by the preferences that voters and legislators have about the welfare state generally.[29]

Although the expected coalitions for votes about restrictionist reforms to the current family-based policy regime and for votes explicitly about immigration and public services are similar, this is not the case when liberalization of employment-based immigration is the issue in question. First, organized labour is still generally opposed to these forms of liberal immigration policy. Consequently, the tension between organized labour and less-skilled workers

---

of redistribution. Gimpel and Edwards (1999) and Kessler (1999) both emphasize the importance of partisan conflict over immigration policy and their evidence is consistent with fiscal conservatism constituting the substance of those partisan differences.

[28] The bill was passed. This vote took place in the House on 25 September 1996 after the schooling provisions had been stripped from the main immigration legislation during negotiations with the White House. The schooling provisions in the latter bill had no chance of becoming law due to both Senate and White House opposition. Our analysis of the original Gallegly amendment to bar illegal immigrants from public education revealed substantively similar results to those discussed here.

[29] The importance of the interactions between immigration and the welfare state are also evident in the politics of welfare reform. Chapter 12 discussed the extent to which immigrants were targeted for cuts in recent welfare reforms.

should disappear with both groups in opposition to liberalization. Second, ideological differences may shift substantially especially if the legislation is about temporary workers. In particular, ideological liberals can be expected to protect their base labour constituency. Third, we might expect the influence of employer interests to be more apparent when the legislation is specifically about employment-based immigration.

To test how the salience of employment issues affects political conflict over immigration policy, we analysed votes on a motion in the 104th Congress to recommit legislation to the House Judiciary Committee to require certain limitations on replacing US workers with temporary foreign workers.[30] The results of the statistical analysis are reported in the Appendix. Representatives in districts with higher concentrations of immigrants remain less likely to support any restrictive policies including measures making it more difficult to employ temporary foreign workers. The expected reversal of the impact of unionization is apparent in the results with members of Congress from more unionized districts more likely to support restrictions on temporary foreign workers. Similarly, ideological conservatism is now associated with less support for the restrictionist position. Interestingly, the concentration of less-skilled workers no longer has a systematic impact on votes, controlling for the other factors. While this variable has the expected positive correlation when regressed on this Congressional vote absent control variables, once organized labour and liberals in Congress—less-skilled workers' natural ideological representatives— take positions consistent with the economic interests of less-skilled workers, the concentration of these workers no longer has a marginal effect on the votes of representatives. Finally, the influence of employers is evident in this analysis with members of Congress in districts with greater manufacturing employment (and greater campaign contributions from corporations) being less likely to cast votes for further restrictions on hiring foreign temporary workers.

The foregoing discussion illustrates the plausibility of the argument that the relative strength of both organized and diffused groups in each member's Congressional district account for variation in voting behaviour in the House of Representatives. The arguments resonate with many of the findings in recent comprehensive studies of Congressional immigration policymaking by Gimpel and Edwards (1999) and Kessler (1999). Nevertheless, the results reported here reflect the analysis of a small number of votes in a single Congress and so must be taken with some caution.

13.3. SUMMARY

In this section, we have identified the preferences of the main actors in the US immigration debate and how successful those actors are in influencing national policymakers. Our analysis shows that political conflict over immigration

---

[30] The motion was rejected.

policy has a number of important dimensions and that both organized and diffuse interests influence policymaking. From the opinions of individual citizens about policy to votes on legislation by members of Congress, it is clear that the politics of immigration policymaking is affected by the perceived economic consequences of policy alternatives and, in particular, on the distribution of these economic effects. Less-skilled workers are more likely to support restrictionist policies while employers of these workers generally favour liberalization. The influence of both these groups is observable in the voting behaviour of members of Congress. Our evidence also demonstrates that other considerations such as beliefs about the impact of immigration on the welfare state play an important role in the course of policymaking. We observe, for example, consistent opposition to family-based immigration from political conservatives both in the electorate and in Congress. We also find clear preferences among identifiable groups such as immigrants and their children that probably impact on the electoral strategies of national politicians. As the previous sections have suggested, immigration has the potential to have substantial effects on a number of key aspects of the nation's political economy including outcomes in the labour market and the size of the welfare state. The politics of immigration policymaking reflects conflict among groups with very different interests and preferences about these issues.

13.4. APPENDIX

Determinants of immigration-policy preferences

The simulations reported in Table 13.1 examining the impact of individual skill levels on the probability of supporting further immigration restrictions are based on our statistical analysis of the determinants of immigration preferences. The dependent variable for this analysis is from the NES question about immigration-policy preferences: 'Do you think the number of immigrants from foreign countries who are permitted to come to the United States to live should be increased a little, increased a lot, decreased a little, decreased a lot, or left the same as it is now?' We construct the variable *Immigration Opinion* by coding responses 5 for those individuals responding 'decreased a lot' down to 1 for those responding 'increased a lot'. Thus, higher levels of *Immigration Opinion* indicate preferences for more-restrictive policy. To test whether skill levels are a key determinant of policy preferences, for each individual-year observation we constructed two variables measuring skills. One was *Education Years*, recorded in the NES survey as years of education completed. The other was *Occupation Wage*, which was that year's average weekly wage nationwide for the three-digit Census Occupation Code occupation reported for the individual. Educational attainment is a common skills measure; *Occupation Wage* assumes that average national earnings for a given occupation are determined primarily by the skills required for that occupation. We also constructed several measures of possible non-economic determinants of preferences. These measures include variables such as gender, age, race, ethnicity, personal immigrant status, party identification, and political ideology.

The empirical work aims to test how skills affect the probability that an individual supports a certain level of legal immigration. The level of immigration preferred by a respondent could theoretically take on any value, but the NES data only report which of five ordered categories the respondent chose. Because there is no strong reason to think *ex ante* that these five ordered categories are separated by equal intervals, a linear regression model might produce biased estimates. The more appropriate model for this situation is an ordered probit, which estimates not only a set of effect parameters but also additional parameters representing unobserved category thresholds.

Given these considerations, we estimate ordered probit models where the expected mean of the unobserved preferred immigration level is hypothesized to

Table 13.3. *Determinants of immigration-policy preferences*

Regressor	1992		1994		1996	
	Model 1	Model 2	Model 1	Model 2	Model 1	Model 2
Occupation wage	−0.349		−0.811		−0.541	
	(0.130)		(0.135)		(0.133)	
Education years		−0.044		−0.074		−0.059
		(0.010)		(0.011)		(0.012)
Gender	−0.022	−0.008	0.022	0.083	−0.020	0.024
	(0.048)	(0.046)	(0.056)	(0.054)	(0.060)	(0.057)
Age	−0.000	−0.002	0.000	−0.002	0.004	0.002
	(0.001)	(0.001)	(0.002)	(0.002)	(0.002)	(0.002)
Race	−0.207	−0.225	−0.222	−0.211	−0.238	−0.241
	(0.080)	(0.080)	(0.091)	(0.092)	(0.096)	(0.097)
Hispanic	−0.064	−0.122	−0.306	−0.360	−0.124	−0.172
	(0.111)	(0.110)	(0.136)	(0.137)	(0.120)	(0.121)
Immigrant	−0.158	−0.150	−0.213	−0.193	−0.220	−0.207
	(0.066)	(0.066)	(0.076)	(0.076)	(0.087)	(0.087)
Party ID	0.003	0.008	−0.006	−0.002	−0.023	−0.016
	(0.013)	(0.013)	(0.016)	(0.016)	(0.016)	(0.016)
Ideology	0.057	0.050	0.054	0.041	0.080	0.072
	(0.020)	(0.020)	(0.028)	(0.029)	(0.025)	(0.025)
Observations	2485	2485	1795	1795	1714	1714

Notes: These results are multiple-imputation estimates of ordered-probit coefficients based on the 10 imputed data sets for each year. Each cell reports the coefficient estimate and (in parenthesis) its standard error. In both models the dependent variable is individual opinions about whether US policy should increase, decrease, or keep the same the annual number of legal immigrants. This variable is defined such that higher (lower) values indicate more-restrictive (less-restrictive) policy preferences. For brevity, estimated cut points are not reported.

be a linear function of the respondent's skills, a vector of demographic identifiers, and political orientation. Each year of data is analysed separately to allow for any differences across years and further details about data definitions, estimation procedures including the methods used to deal with missing data problems, and results can be found in Scheve and Slaughter (2001a,b). Table 13.3 reports the main ordered probit results on which the simulations in Table 13.1 are based.

Determinants of Congressional votes on immigration policy

The simulations reported in Table 13.2 examining the impact of various congressional district characteristics on the probability of voting against the Chrysler amendment are based on our statistical analysis of the determinants of voting on this amendment. The dependent variable is equal to 1 if the representative voted against the amendment and 0 if they voted for it. Thus, a 1 or a success indicates favouring restrictive reforms. The independent variables constructed to explain the votes are described in the text, and the statistical model estimated was a logit regression with heteroskedastic consistent standard errors. Table 13.4 reports the logit results on which the simulations in Table 13.2 are based. Table 13.4 also reports the logit regression estimates for two other congressional votes for which the results are discussed in the main

Table 13.4. *Determinants of Congressional immigration votes*

Regressor	Chrysler amendment	Educational restriction	Employment restriction
Per cent immigrant	−3.775	−7.848	−5.366
	(1.424)	(1.674)	(3.387)
Per cent black	−1.989	0.114	3.137
	(1.163)	(1.156)	(2.413)
Manufacturing employment	1.443	−0.043	−14.846
	(3.867)	(5.313)	(8.714)
Unionization	−8.280	2.005	15.255
	(2.571)	(3.333)	(5.275)
Per cent less than H.S.	5.766	6.745	0.113
	(2.743)	(3.642)	(5.164)
Ideological conservatism	4.014	6.978	−10.022
	(0.477)	(0.629)	(1.368)
Constant	−1.440	−0.245	1.880
	(0.541)	(0.711)	(0.912)
Observations	420	428	418

Notes: These results are logit regression coefficients. Each cell reports the coefficient estimate and (in parenthesis) its standard error. The dependent variable is the votes of members of Congress on immigration policy. The variable for each vote is defined such that 1 indicates more restrictive policy preferences and 0 less restrictive.

text. The dependent variable for the first is equal to 1 if the representative voted for passage of the bill to permit states to bar illegal immigrants from public education and 0 if they voted against. The dependent variable for the second of these analyses is equal to 1 if the representative voted for motion to recommit legislation to the House Judiciary Committee to require certain limitations on replacing US workers with temporary foreign workers and 0 if they voted against.

14

Conclusion

Setting immigration policy in any country raises a dizzying array of interrelated questions. Immigration may have substantial implications for the economic welfare of both those countries that send immigrants and those that receive them. Aggregate impacts are just a starting point, however, as many of immigration's biggest effects are distributive. The interests of native citizens can conflict with those of immigrants; in addition, interests can conflict among different groups of natives. These distributive battles have always been a feature of the politics and economics of immigration. However, the rise of the modern welfare state has introduced new sources of economic conflict and cooperation that substantially alter how individuals perceive immigration affecting their interests.

To this mix of economic issues is added the political issues of citizenship, national identity, and international relations. Choosing immigration policy requires countries to answer difficult questions about the definition of and requirements for membership in a political community. In answering these questions, racial and ethnic conflict often arises because immigrants are, by definition, from different communities. An immigrant's decision to leave his or her country of birth is one with substantial costs and risks. More often than not, it is a decision born of economic and political instability in the home country. Consequently, immigration policy helps define a nation's strategy both for responding to political repression around the world and also for addressing the acute poverty that often accompanies such instability.

With all this at stake, there is every reason to expect substantial variation across countries and over time both in immigration policy and also in what aspects of the immigration political debate are most salient. Some of this variation is likely to be systematic and predictable. For example, countries have very different national histories of settlement and colonialism. Those countries with long histories of immigration may or may not be more welcoming to new immigrants, but they are unlikely to spend much time debating whether immigration is in principle consistent with their understanding of citizenship. Differences in political institutions are also likely to account for some systematic variation in the policies and politics of immigration. These institutions can affect the costs and benefits of alternative political strategies for various groups in society (e.g. interest-group vs electoral politics).

To explain all these variations in immigration policymaking in receiving states, a sensible first step is a detailed account of each country's immigration experience. In this Part, we have attempted to produce such an account for the United States. We have evaluated recent patterns in the flows of immigrants, the policies governing those flows, and the effects of those flows on the US economy. Our analysis focuses particular attention on how US regional economies adjust to immigrant inflows, the factors that influence illegal immigration, what the fiscal impact of immigration has been, and what are the key factors that have shaped US policymaking over recent decades. We briefly summarize key findings for each of these issues.

First, we find that the large immigrant inflows into the United States in recent decades appear not to have triggered large wage adjustments, either at the regional or the national level. The largest estimates for wage pressures appear to be for native high-school dropouts at the national level; outside of this case, a wide range of studies finds little compelling evidence of wage pressures. Regions have adjusted to immigrant inflows through other mechanisms, including outmigration of native workers, shifts in output mix towards immigrant-intensive industries, and skill upgrading of the native labour force. This last mechanism may be less important in coming decades, as the educational composition of the US labour force is projected to stabilize. Should this happen, future immigration may be more harmful to the economic well-being of less-skilled US natives.

Second, we document important patterns in the flow of illegal immigrants into the United States over the last two decades. Most illegal immigrants enter the country either by crossing the Mexico–US border or by overstaying entry visas. Mexico is the largest source country for illegal immigration and illegal entry tends to surge following economic downturns in the country. The US government has dramatically increased expenditure on enforcement against illegal entry at the Mexico–US border, raised penalties for hiring illegal aliens, and broadened monitoring of employers deemed likely to hire illegal aliens. These reforms have increased border enforcement at specific points where illegal crossing has been particularly heavy in the past. But enforcement has been slow to increase at other points along the border, which perhaps accounts for why the net inflow of illegal aliens does not appear to have diminished. Illegal migrants change their border-crossing behaviour very quickly in response to changes in enforcement. This renders operations in specific border regions relatively ineffective at curtailing overall illegal immigration.

Despite widely publicized legislation in the 1980s that increased sanctions against hiring undocumented workers, the US government seems reluctant to monitor intensively US employers. Many illegal aliens responded to new sanctions simply by obtaining fake documents, which employers often accept at face value. The hiring of illegal aliens—though not technically of 'undocumented' workers—remains widespread in many labour-intensive industries, particularly in the western United States. The US government focuses the vast majority of its efforts against illegal immigration on the border, where illegal migrants, and not US employers, bear the direct costs of enforcement. These enforcement practices appear to be at least partly a response to pressure from farmers and employers in other labour-intensive sectors, who strongly oppose policing of their hiring practices.

Third, we examine the fiscal impact of immigration. Prior to US welfare reform in 1996, immigrants were more likely than natives to receive public assistance. New laws restrict immigrant access to many benefits, one important exception being costly public education. For some types of public assistance, individual US states have the discretion to offer benefits after an individual has been in the country for at least five years. Excluding immigrants from public assistance has been subject to numerous judicial challenges. Despite immigrant use of public assistance, the net fiscal transfer from natives to immigrants appears to be very small at the national level, though it is higher in a few specific states that have both generous welfare benefits and large immigrant populations. In general, the older and the less educated the adult immigrant population is, the larger are native-to-immigrant net fiscal transfers.

One important feature of recent US welfare reform is devolution: states were granted more discretion over the level of welfare benefits, in general, and whether immigrants have access to specific programmes, in particular. Devolution has reduced the federal government's ability to coordinate a national policy over the attractiveness of the United States as an immigrant destination. This moves the United States closer to the situation of the EU, within which countries differ considerably in the generosity of their welfare systems. Some US states, such as Massachusetts, have committed to replace lost federal benefits for immigrants. Others, such as California, offer more generous welfare programmes of one kind or another. Cross-state variation in immigrant access to public assistance may contribute to the continued geographic concentration of immigrant populations in specific US regions.

Finally, we reviewed the politics of US immigration policymaking. We find that individual opinions about immigration policy are influenced by expectations about its impact on outcomes in the labour market and on public services and the welfare state. In particular, less-skilled workers and political conservatives are among those most opposed to freer immigration. Congressional representatives seem to respond to these concerns in their districts when voting on legislation.

A common theme underpinning political debate over immigration has been distributive conflict. The economic interests of employers, workers, and taxpayers have helped shape the policy preferences and political strategies for immigration policymaking in the United States. Immigration debates have, of course, been marked by other concerns; in particular, those that mobilize nativist sentiments for cultural homogeneity. It is not clear, however, whether non-economic forces have had substantial influence in national policymaking. In contrast, the role of economic interests and the building of strategic coalitions to protect those interests is evident at all levels of US debate and political activity.

To summarize, the US experience in recent decades is one of sharply rising levels of immigration; a shift in the composition of immigrants towards individuals from Asia and Latin America, who tend to have less schooling than US natives; an increase (at least until the welfare reforms of 1996) in the use of means-tested welfare benefits by immigrants; and a substantial rise in illegal immigration. Against this background, immigration debates have quite naturally focused on the level and composition of immigration, whether immigrants should have access to public assistance, and how to control illegal immigration. We turn to these three issues in Section 14.1 which explores the policy implications of our findings.

14.1. US IMMIGRATION POLICY CHOICES

In the current environment, the United States faces several important choices with regards to immigration policy. Key decisions include whether to replace family-based immigration with skills-based immigration, whether to continue to exclude immigrants from access to public assistance, whether to expand temporary immigration, how to balance border and interior policing in enforcing against illegal immigration, and whether to grant an amnesty to illegal immigrants already in the country. In evaluating these policy choices, it is important to be explicit about one's objectives for setting immigration policy. Actual policymaking involves the aggregation of diverse interests, including concerns about how immigration affects the economic livelihood of workers, the fiscal burden of taxpayers, the availability of public services to US citizens, and the short-run or long-run profitability of firms in different industries. Beyond these narrow economic interests, policymakers may also consider how immigration influences the political power of different interest groups and the cultural identity of specific communities or the nation as a whole. Moreover, the impact of policy alternatives on the welfare of other countries and the United States' relationship with those countries may also be a factor. It is well beyond the scope of this study to propose how policymakers should balance these divergent interests.

Our aim in this concluding section is considerably more modest. We evaluate immigration-policy choices with an eye to minimizing three outcomes: the adverse consequences for low-skilled US workers, net fiscal transfers from native taxpayers to immigrants, and overall levels of illegal immigration. We identify these objectives because they represent concerns that have been at the centre of the US debate about immigration policy; we recognize that they may not necessarily be justifiable in terms of maximizing US national welfare, global welfare, or some other commonly accepted welfare criterion. By identifying policies that recent academic research suggests will address (or fail to address) common complaints about current US immigration policy, we hope to contribute to the debate about what are appropriate sets of immigration policies for the United States and other countries. Along the way, we also try to highlight how possible future events (e.g. a slowdown in skill upgrading by US workers) or indirect effects of policy changes (e.g. changes in the behaviour of illegal immigrants) may influence the impacts of specific policies.

14.1.1. *Family reunification vs skills-based immigration*

US immigration policies based on family reunification are associated with rising immigration of the less skilled. An alternative policy would be to admit individuals based on consideration of their level of human capital. One commonly-cited possibility would be to establish a point system, in which individual applicants for admission to the United States would be evaluated more favourably the higher their level of education or job-specific work experience, the more in demand their specific occupational abilities, or the more desirable their overall skill profile (see, e.g. Borjas, 1999). Such a system would resemble the framework that Canada has adopted in admitting immigrants (Smith and Edmonston, 1997).

In theory, a shift in immigration policy to favour the admission of young workers with high skill levels would reduce any negative impacts of immigration on low-skilled native workers, enhance the US comparative advantage in knowledge-intensive industries, and generate positive net fiscal transfers from immigrants to natives. The first two of these effects operate through changes in labour supply. Increasing the relative supply of more skilled workers would be expected to increase the relative wage of less-skilled workers, and their absolute wage as well if high-skilled labour complements low-skilled labour in production by firms. The selection for admission of foreign scientists, engineers, and computer programmers, for instance, may increase the level of innovative activity in the United States, and so, following the successful application of these innovations, the demand for and wages of US production labour.

A larger supply of more skilled labour would tend to shift the pattern of specialization towards industries that use this factor intensively, including high-technology sectors, finance, and business services. By shifting the US comparative advantage towards industries that are intensive in the use of skilled labour, less-skilled workers would be more likely to work in these sectors and less likely to work in apparel, food processing, and other labour-intensive activities where they would be effectively competing against workers from low-wage countries.

The third effect of replacing family-based immigration with skills-based immigration—the reversal of net fiscal transfers from natives to immigrants—reflects the fact that young, highly-educated immigrants have had their schooling financed by taxpayers abroad and stand to make tax contributions to the US government over most of their working life. That is, these individuals require few if any public resources to become productive members of the labour force and they start paying US taxes virtually upon arrival in the country. Given their high earnings ability, these individuals are also unlikely to use much in the way of public assistance.

To the extent US objectives in setting immigration policy are to soften the economic impact on low-skilled native workers, strengthen the country's position in knowledge-intensive industries, and avoid fiscal transfers from natives to immigrants, replacing family-based immigration with skills-based immigration is sensible. But this switch may face some important limitations.

One is that favouring the immigration of the young and highly educated promotes fiscal transfers from other countries to the United States, a policy that may anger foreign friends and undermine development prospects in poor regions. Many in the United States may prefer to replace low-skilled immigrants with engineers from China and India, but the governments of China and India might be highly opposed to such a policy change, for obvious reasons. Apart from harming the economic well-being of poor countries, promoting brain drain at their expense may also undermine US security interests abroad by making immigrant-sending countries less stable economically or politically.

A second limitation of skills-based immigration is that in the long run the distinction between skills and family-based immigration policies may not be so sharp. Given political pressures from immigrant and civil rights groups and the long-standing US tradition of family-based immigration, the US public may find it difficult to admit skilled individuals and not their family members. If this ends up being the case, the admission of one highly-skilled individual may ultimately lead to the admission of four or five individuals in total, via spouses, children, and possibly other dependents. Given the shortage of skilled labour that exists in most countries, we would expect these family members to be less skilled, on average, than the highly skilled individual who seeks admission to the United States. In this case, though skills-based immigration may still raise the skill composition of new immigrants relative to family-based immigration, it may not do so by as much as some might expect.

It is also worth recognizing that a change from skills to family-based immigration would probably encounter intense political opposition. Family-based immigration, though perhaps not intended in its original design, is currently the primary source of new low-skilled workers in the United States. If, as expected, the education attainment of US residents stabilizes in future years, a continuation of family-based immigration could actually increase, for the first time in many decades, the relative supply of less-skilled labour force in the US economy. Employers in labour-intensive sectors would likely object strenuously to the elimination of family reunification as an objective in US immigration policies, as this could undermine their future economic viability.

Another source of opposition would come, quite obviously, from immigrants themselves. An end to family-based immigration would probably leave some family members of US residents stranded abroad. It would also slow the growth (and size of the future potential vote bloc) of specific immigrant groups, perhaps undermining their political power. In the last few years, some politicians have begun actively tailoring their campaigns to target the interests of immigrants, in part because they are among the fastest growing groups of actual or potential voters. Slowing the growth of specific immigrant communities could dent their political appeal. In the light of these potential effects, we might expect political allies of immigrant voters, such as civil-rights groups, to also oppose an end to family-based immigration.

14.1.2. *Immigrant access to public benefits*

To limit fiscal transfers from natives to immigrants, an obvious policy would be to expand immigrant exclusions from access to public assistance. In practice, however, such direct policies may be ineffective.

One issue is that the largest transfer most immigrants receive is in the form of publicly funded education. As we saw in Chapter 12, it is both legally and politically quite difficult to restrict the access of immigrants, even those who are in the country illegally, to public education. More broadly, excluding immigrant access to public assistance may be difficult to sustain in the long run. For one, it may violate the equal-protection clause of the US Constitution. Recent experience shows that such exclusions are often challenged and overturned in court. Though fiscal conservatives succeeded in attaching tough immigrant-exclusion provisions to US welfare reform in 1996, these provisions are slowly being chipped away over time thanks to judicial challenges, US states choosing to restore benefits taken away by the federal government, and the US Congress reversing some aspects of welfare reform deemed too harsh on immigrant families (or too costly politically). Immigrant exclusions remain a political battlefield. In the near term, at least, it seems likely that they will be eroded further.

An alternative means to limit native-to-immigrant fiscal transfers, if this indeed is the desired policy objective, is the indirect policy of selecting immigrants who are likely to make positive net fiscal contributions, as would conceivably be accomplished by a switch from family-based immigration to skills-based immigration. Adopting skills-based immigration sidesteps the politically and legally complex issue of which individuals can have access to public benefits. If immigration standards select individuals who make relatively little use of public assistance and who make relatively large tax contributions, then fiscal transfers from natives to immigrants are likely to be negative (or at least small, if positive) under any set of rules governing which individuals may receive public benefits. Along with a switch to skills-based immigration, however, would come the potential pitfalls we have just discussed.

14.1.3. *Controlling illegal immigration*

A change from family- to skills-based immigration may alter the behaviour of illegal immigrants. Individuals who find themselves cut off from opportunities for legal immigration—such as those with family members in the United States but who do not meet the skill requirements of a new policy—may choose to immigrate illegally. Indeed, many individuals who have applied for US legal residence under family-based immigration provisions are already in the United States, having chosen to wait out the often-lengthy application period as illegal aliens (with apparently little prospect of facing US legal repercussions). Many current legal immigrants thus have been willing to become illegal immigrants, at least for a period of a few years. All else equal, a switch from skills- to family-based immigration could increase attempted illegal immigration, possibly by a substantial amount. If the US objective is to reduce illegal immigration, or at least maintain it at somewhere near current levels, complementary policies would be needed.

The current US policy mix of heavy border enforcement, light interior enforcement, and low levels of temporary immigration of manual labourers appears to be ineffective at stemming the tide of illegal immigrants. One alternative is to reduce the supply of illegal immigrants indirectly by increasing temporary immigration of manual labourers, coupled with an amnesty of existing illegal immigrants; another is to reduce the demand for illegal immigrants by increasing employer monitoring.

Current proposals by the administration of President Bush would increase temporary immigration of manual labourers to a level roughly equal to the current level of illegal immigration and grant an amnesty to some fraction of the illegal immigrants currently living in the United States. Such a policy would in effect seek to replace an unregulated, long-run supply of illegal workers with a regulated, short-run supply of legal workers. By granting an amnesty to illegal immigrants, perhaps similar to that enacted by the Immigration Reform and Control Act of 1986, the United States would begin with a clean slate, so to speak, in the sense of having legalized both the stock and flow of immigrants in the country. In theory, large-scale temporary immigration would be effective at curtailing illegal immigration if US firms viewed illegal workers and temporary legal workers as close substitutes and if potential migrants viewed temporary migration as reasonably comparable to illegal migration.

There are reasons to doubt that the latter condition holds. An increasing fraction of illegal immigrants live and work in cities. They have long-term relationships with employers and an established presence in their communities. They also may expect to become legal US residents some day, either because they have pending applications for legal residence with the Immigration and Naturalization Service or because they expect to be eligible for some future amnesty offered to illegal immigrants. Temporary immigration precludes such permanence, precarious as it may be, as well as eligibility for an amnesty. For some migrants, then, temporary immigration may be an inferior option to illegal immigration. This suggests that for expanded temporary immigration to be effective, it would need to be coupled with effective enforcement against illegal entry.

Even if temporary immigration were to succeed in reducing illegal immigration, the question remains of what objective would have been achieved. The impact on labour markets and industrial specialization of equivalent inflows of temporary and illegal workers may be very much the same. And the impact of the two inflows on fiscal balances may also be similar. Temporary immigrants would probably have access to certain restricted public benefits while in the United States, but could be taxed to pay for these benefits, leaving a neutral impact on government budgets. Illegal immigrants are barred from receiving public assistance, but are entitled to receive emergency medical care and to send their children to public schools. At the same time, they appear to make contributions to social insurance coffers, on which they do not collect. On balance, it is unclear whether their fiscal contribution is positive or negative. Even if it were negative, there are other factors favouring illegal immigration. Having a long-term presence in the country may induce illegal migrants to make productive investments in human or physical capital that temporary migrants, given their short-run employment contracts, are unwilling to make. Illegal immigrants, then, may be more likely than temporary immigrants to acquire labour-market experience and skills that are matched to the specific needs of US employers. In sum, expanded temporary immigration may change illegal immigration in name only, without much changing its impact on US labour markets, public finances, or industrial competitiveness.

An amnesty for illegal immigrants would carry symbolic importance, and might modestly improve the living conditions of these individuals, but it would be unlikely to have large impacts on national labour-market outcomes or public finances. Employment of illegal aliens is widespread in the country. A large fraction of these individuals have fake documents testifying to their permanent legal residence and to their membership in the social security system. From the perspective of some employers, these individuals are legal immigrants. Given that native-to-immigrant fiscal transfers are small, that recent immigrants, whether legal or illegal, have lost access to many forms of public assistance, and that children of illegal immigrants already have access to public education, an amnesty would be unlikely to lead to large new claims on public benefits by legalized immigrant households. An amnesty may, however, lead to an increase in applications for legal admission, as the relatives of newly legalized residents become eligible for family-sponsored immigration, and an increase in illegal immigration, as the belief that by holding out long enough illegal aliens can attain legal status is reinforced.

An alternative policy on illegal immigration is expanded monitoring of employers. Though US law forbids hiring illegal aliens, enforcement of the law appears to be quite lax. Fines are small and infrequently applied, and many plant visits by the Immigration and Naturalization Service are announced in advance. By establishing large fines for hiring illegal immigrants and by conducting random, unannounced inspections of worksites the US government could curtail the demand for illegal labour. In a given year, a single INS agent can inspect dozens of firms employing thousands or tens of thousands of workers but can apprehend relatively few illegal immigrants at the border (and even fewer illegal aliens in the country as a result of overstaying temporary entry visas). A reduction in demand for illegal labour would in theory lead to a reduction in illegal entry, as the reduction in wages and/or loss in jobs would potentially dissuade many prospective migrants from attempting to cross the border. The main obstacle to greater employer monitoring appears to be intense and highly organized political opposition by employers.

Switching from an emphasis on border enforcement to one on worksite enforcement would also probably shift the incidence of some enforcement costs from illegal immigrants to employers, which perhaps accounts for employer opposition to interior policing (a further reason they may oppose interior policing is that they may expect it to be a more effective policy). Either border or interior enforcement may lower the level of illegal immigration, raising the expected wage employers must pay (due to a lower supply of illegal labour) and lowering the expected wage illegal immigrants receive (due to higher expected costs of crossing the border and/or finding a job). But the relative variance in outcomes for employers and illegal immigrants differs sharply under the two policies. With border enforcement, the variance in outcomes for employers is low (lower labour supply and higher wages) but for illegal immigrants it is high (given uncertainty regarding evading the Border Patrol, being treated fairly by smugglers, or crossing through harsh environments safely). With a comparable level of interior enforcement (in terms of the supply of illegal labour), the situation is reversed as the variance in outcomes for employers is high (small probability of large fines and other legal repercussions) but for illegal immigrants is low (lower labour demand and wages). Given a desire to lower illegal immigration, switching from attempting to manage the supply of illegal labour to attempting to manage the demand for illegal labour targets agents who are relatively easy to identify (hiding agricultural fields, construction sites, or hotels or restaurants is difficult) and prosecute (treating a few guilty subjects harshly sends a strong signal). It may also be a more humane policy in that it may tend to replace physical risk taking (illegal immigrants crossing deserts) with legal risk taking (employers facing large fines).

The key to changing current and future economic impacts of immigration appears to be changing the skill composition of new immigrants. This could be accomplished by replacing family reunification with a skill criterion as the basis for legal immigration. It would also require as a complementary policy stronger enforcement against illegal immigration, including more active worksite monitoring. At the present time, political conflict over immigration policy has produced an impasse, making wide-ranging reform unlikely in the near future. But, as the process of welfare reform in the 1990s makes clear, pressure for large-scale policy changes can build very quickly.

Comments

GIUSEPPE BERTOLA

Since my lifecycle trajectory includes some intra- and inter-continental migration, even before reading this wide-ranging and very enjoyable report I knew only too well some details of US immigration rules and procedures for members of the 1990s immigration wave's highly qualified segment. From the report, I learned about many interesting features of immigration into the US by the vastly more controversial and numerous low-skill component of the US immigration phenomenon: the Statue of Liberty's wretched, poor, and huddled masses.

Economics and Migration

The report offers much more than facts, in the form of a lucid review of economic interactions and policy issues. When studying immigration, economists cannot invoke the competitive market paradigm. Immigration is a most heavily regulated economic phenomenon. Perhaps only the supply and demand of pharmaceuticals and other drugs are as heavily interfered with as those of labour across country borders. Emotions and the distribution, rather than efficient production, of economic welfare motivate much of immigration regulation.

Economics remains relevant, however, in a variety of respects. Economically motivated illegal immigration flourishes alongside heavily regulated flows, and immigration interacts with local provision of costly fiscal support for the poor. Together with the obvious conflict of interest between employers and workers, these phenomena shape a complex political debate, where economic considerations play a much more important role than more or less avoidable ethnic and cultural tensions. The report builds a careful conceptual structure along these lines, and uses it to support a blow-by-blow account of facts and figures (not only from the US experience, but also from the English parish-based social assistance scheme of Elizabethan times!)

Europe and North America

I did come back to Europe, and I gave up my hard-earned US permanent residency permit a while ago. I still follow US developments with a measure of personal interest, both as regards the desperate, thirsty, and sometimes dead Mexican workers crossing the desert, and the possible supply-side role of immigration in shaping US labour market outcomes in the light of changing demographic and educational trends. When I read the report, however, I was naturally inclined to draw European lessons from American facts. And it was especially nice to perform that exercise in Trieste, where—at least in my experience—taxi drivers are quite unlike their US colleagues in that they are native and well dressed, and are spontaneously inclined to offer their customers a long speech about the differences between Slovenian and Chinese immigration in the area.

Lessons come in two forms. Europe can learn a lot from America in the light of increasing similarity of economic and policy conditions on the two sides of the Atlantic. After all, Europe is in some respects similar to a sideways version of North America: the East–West relationship between the EU and its CEEC neighbours is much like the North–South relationship between the US and Mexico. This was of course not the case 20 or even 10 years ago, when the EU was not as tightly integrated, and the Iron Curtain fenced poor neighbours out much more efficiently than the Rio Grande. Portugal, however, is not Alaska, and Germany is very different from Texas. So, lessons from America need to be qualified and filtered in the light of important differences.

Lessons and Qualifications

The scale and character of actual and potential interactions of migration with national fiscal and social institutions is quite likely different across the two sides of the Atlantic. In Europe, and everywhere, immigrants are poorer and more attracted to welfare benefits than natives. But in Europe immigrants do not need to draw benefits themselves to put fiscal pressure on unemployment and social benefit systems: they can price segments of the native labour force out of employment and into subsidies. The textbook example of this as an actual rather than only theoretical phenomenon is the early-1990s experience, which saw almost all construction work on East German soil performed by non-German workers while German construction workers enjoyed unemployment benefits higher than foreigners' reservation wages. In the US, low-wage natives may or may not see their wages lowered further by immigration: the report documents quite clearly both the theoretical reasons why this should be the case, and the elusive empirical character of these and other effects. In an unreformed Continental European labour market, immigration is more likely to increase the fiscal and unemployment costs of existing institutional constraints than to reduce market wages of any native worker.

Another relevant difference is the degree of labour mobility, and its interaction with differently generous welfare systems. The US has a fairly mobile native population, and it is not unheard of for American single mothers to cross State lines in search of more generous welfare benefits. Such mobility, like that motivated by wage differentials, is much less hindered in America by language, cultural, ethnic, and extended-family considerations than it is in Europe. Even in the US, however, migrants from outside are more likely to be sensitive to benefits differentials. Starting from an essentially frozen within-EU mobility landscape, substantial external immigration in the EU can dramatically increase the (direct, or indirect as mentioned above) fiscal implications of institutional differences. If immigrants are drawn to local constituencies that offer high wages and generous subsidies to low-skills workers, that status quo situation can quickly become fiscally unsustainable, and may foster more or less subterranean ethnic barriers to mobility and economic integration.

Problems and Policies

An important lesson of the US immigration-regulation experience, and of the comparison to the EU current situation, is that more stringent official limits to immigration are associated with larger illegal migration flows. Across the two continents, legal migration is 25 per cent higher in the US than in the EU on a per-resident basis... and, on the same basis, illegal migration is 25 per cent higher in the EU than in the US. Within the US experience, tighter quotas have also spilled over into more intense illegal migration flows, and even variation in enforcement effort appears to have much stronger effects on the localization and composition of illegal migration than on the total size of resilient aggregate migration flows.

This is, of course, quite familiar from the experience of other strictly regulated economic phenomena. Not only drugs, but also workers and jobs are traded in illegal or informal segments on the side of official regulated markets. And, of course, the size of informal or 'submerged' labour markets is much more importantly affected by the stringency of official regulation than by enforcement effort.

The report documents that US border enforcement is quite expensive: almost 2 billion dollars per year (without counting the cost of other Immigration and Naturalization Service duties). Or about $1000 per apprehension—a quite crude measure of the enforcement effort's output, which presumably includes some discouraged attempts and should be assessed on the basis of apprehension hazards, but quite an impressive figure in comparison to the apprehended workers' marginal productivity. At minimum wage, the captured worker should work several hundred hours to pay the cost of his apprehension. This is food for thought for Europeans who used to let the Soviet army and Berlin Wall guards patrol some borders.

Setting Rules and Enforcing Them

Europeans should also be alerted by the report's evidence that this costly effort is essentially and perhaps intentionally ineffective. The rich statistical, political opinion, and enforcement information provided by the report could in fact support a perhaps simplistic, but quite intriguing view of the US immigration policy problem. Voters pretend to be worried about immigration flows in spite of almost completely lacking evidence of significant labour market or any other effects. And, to appease those fears, politicians pretend to address the problem funding highly visible, expensive, and almost completely ineffective immigration regulation.

Among the policy options considered and carefully discussed in the report, the most prominent speaks in favour of

(1) biasing immigration quotas in favour of highly-skilled labour, and
(2) avoiding illegal immigration of low-skill workers not by border patrols, but by workplace inspections.

These are indeed excellent policy recommendations not only for the US, but for all advanced countries, at least if internal efficiency and distributional considerations are the objective of immigration regulation by domestic policy-makers. Of course, the interests of less developed countries may be better served by different policies. The current Mexican administration, not unlike English parish officials who bribed 'their' poor to move to other parishes, does support its poor citizens' desert-crossing efforts. Policies meant to keep out the wretched and tax the more useful component of immigrant flows make a lot of sense from the economic point of view. In practice, however, political inter-actions in the immigration field are influenced by economic considerations but quite forcefully shaped by more emotional considerations: one only needs to imagine replacing the Statue of Liberty's motto with a simpler 'Huddled Masses Keep Out' sign to realize that such policies are hard to sell politically.

Enforcement of immigration constraints by inland inspection, however, is clearly the most effective mean of enforcing any regulation. As mentioned above, such enforcement is almost comically non-existent in the US. Public figures subject to confirmation procedures and characters of movies such as 'Wag the Dog' are worried about being caught violating Federal immigration rules, but on the basis of the figures reported here I guess everybody else can quite safely employ illegal aliens in the US. In Europe, regulation is much heavier than in the US for many other aspects of employment relationships, and enforcement effort would be welcome, as part of a careful re-thinking of all labour market regulation, in many other areas. Simplification and possible harmonization of labour market regulation and welfare provision in EU countries are both urgent. As noted above, informal labour markets and immigration flows interact importantly with all institutional features of European labour markets, and efficient workplace enforcement of clear and rational regulation is, in this wider context, clearly a primary policy objective.

GEORGE BORJAS

In the 1950s, only around 250 thousand immigrants entered the United States annually. By the 1990s, almost 1 million legal and 300 thousand illegal aliens entered the United States annually. This resurgence of immigration has motivated many economists and other social scientists to examine how immigration affects economic opportunities in the United States. Hanson, Scheve, Slaughter, and Spilimbergo (henceforth HSSS) have written an ambitious survey of this voluminous literature.

In their survey, HSSS focus on four related issues.

(1) What is the impact of immigration on the job market opportunities of native workers? It is often claimed that immigrants 'take jobs away' from natives. What is the nature of the empirical evidence that supports or contradicts this assertion?

(2) What factors determine illegal immigration to the United States? There are at least 6 million illegal aliens currently residing in the country. What role do economic conditions and border enforcement play in determining the size of the illegal flow?

(3) What is the fiscal impact of immigration? It is well known that immigrant households have higher welfare participation rates than native households. What is the magnitude of the tax burden that immigrants impose on native taxpayers?

(4) What is the political economy of immigration policy? For decades, most surveys of the US population have shown that natives consistently prefer lower levels of migration. At the same time, however, policymakers have consistently opted to admit more immigrants. Why is there such a striking discrepancy between popular preferences and policy choices?

The HSSS survey is comprehensive and touches on most of the key points that are relevant in the immigration debate. Instead of providing a point-by-point discussion of the many issues and concerns raised by HSSS, I have chosen to present a more detailed appraisal of some selected questions in the literature. In particular, I have selected to focus on two or three issues that I feel should be at the frontier of the immigration research agenda. I believe that these issues not only lie at the core of the immigration debate in the United States and in many other source countries, but also that a resolution of these issues would help us get a much better understanding of how the immigration debate will evolve in the next decade.

The labour market impact of immigration

Do immigrants have an adverse impact on the earnings and employment opportunities of native workers? If so, how large is the loss in the economic welfare of natives? And are all native groups equally affected by the entry of immigrants into the labour market? A large literature now purports to document the impact of immigrants on the native labour market in a number of host countries. As HSSS implicitly note, this literature has evolved through three different (and not entirely successful) phases in attempting to answer these important questions.

In the first phase, many economists exploited the fact that immigrants typically tend to cluster in a relatively small number of geographic areas in the host country. Each geographic area was then treated as a closed labour market. The intuition guiding the empirical analysis was that if we could observe a number of closed labour markets which immigrants penetrate randomly, we could relate the change in the wage of native workers to the proportion of immigrants in the population, and the estimated parameters would summarize the impact of immigration on native employment opportunities.

Almost all of the early empirical studies in the literature conducted this exercise in estimating 'spatial correlations' by defining a city or metropolitan area in the United States as the empirical counterpart of the closed labour market in the conceptual framework. The typical study then regressed a measure of the native wage in the locality on the relative quantity of immigrants in that locality (or the change in the wage in the locality over a specified time period on the change in the number of immigrants in the locality). As HSSS note, the spatial correlations estimated in this literature tend to be small and vary erratically over time.

The next phase of the literature pointed out the (now) obvious fact that the comparison of economic conditions across different metropolitan areas, as well as the pre- and post-immigration comparison in a particular metropolitan area, presumes that the labour markets are closed (once immigration takes place). However, metropolitan areas in the United States and abroad are not closed economies; labour, capital, and goods flow freely across localities and tend to equalize factor prices in the process. As long as native workers and firms respond to the entry of immigrants by moving to areas offering better opportunities, there is no reason to expect a correlation between the wage of natives in a local labour market and the presence of immigrants. As a result, the comparison of local labour markets may be masking the 'macro' effect of immigration.

Because of these responses, Borjas *et al.* (1992) proposed shifting the analysis to the national labour market, which was presumed to be relatively more closed than the local labour market. This shift in the unit of observation led to the factor proportions approach, which effectively simulated how the (national) wage differential between skilled and unskilled workers responded to changes in the factor proportion of skilled and unskilled workers in the national labour force. This methodology has typically suggested that there may be sizeable effects of immigration on relative wages in the United States, particularly at the bottom end of the skill distribution.

The third (and current) phase of the literature attempts to synthesize the results from the spatial correlation methodology with the factor proportion approach by documenting the existence of equilibrating flows that tend to equalize opportunities across labour markets. If these flows were sufficiently important it would then be possible for immigration to have an impact at the national level, but there would be little difference in economic outcomes across local labour markets. The equilibrating flows that have been investigated include the internal migration of native workers or the internal migration of jobs and capital (which HSSS call the 'output-mix' approach). This literature is not yet fully developed and has not yet generated a widely accepted set of 'stylized facts'. Nevertheless, there are strong empirical suggestions, discussed in HSSS, that equilibrating flows of both workers and jobs exist across regions of the United States, so that the spatial correlation approach may be masking much of the presumed impact of immigration.

Although I have contributed to all three phases of this literature—and changed my mind about the relative attractiveness of the various methodologies a number of times in the process—there remains a fundamental question in my mind, a question that HSSS do not pose. As I first noted in my *Journal of Economic Literature* survey (Borjas, 1994, p. 1700), there is an unresolved puzzle facing those who wish to interpret the weak spatial correlation between immigration and native wages in terms of an economy-wide equilibrium process: *Why should it be that many other regional variations persist over time, but that the local impact of immigration on native workers is arbitraged away immediately?* Put differently, many economists have made a career of documenting how regional differences across labour markets can be explained in terms of differences in unemployment rates, or unionization rates, or the industrial structure, or many other variables. Why should all of these spatial correlations be so readily observed and so easy to measure, yet the spatial correlation between immigration and wages be so difficult to find? Why should flows of native workers and capital help to equilibrate the regional wage differentials that can be attributed to immigration, but not the regional wage differentials that are due to other factors?

I suspect that part of the answer to this puzzle lies in an issue that has not yet received sufficient attention in the empirical literature: immigrants are not randomly distributed across the labour markets in the host country. Immigrants typically choose to settle in some labour markets and avoid others. It is easy to demonstrate that the spatial correlation approach would fail to yield any evidence of adverse wage effects if immigrants were income-maximizers with respect to their location decision in the host country—even if there were no equilibrating flows across labour markets.

In particular, suppose there exist sizeable wage differences across regions or states in the host country (for concreteness, the United States), even for workers of particular skills looking for similar jobs. Persons born in the United States and living in a particular state often find it expensive to move across states. Suppose that migration costs are, for the most part, fixed costs—and that these fixed costs are relatively high. The existing wage differentials across states may then fail to motivate large numbers of native workers to move because the migration costs swamp the interstate differences in income opportunities. As a result, native internal migration will not arbitrage interstate wage differentials away.

In contrast, newly arrived immigrants in the United States are a self-selected sample of persons who have chosen to bear the fixed cost of the geographic move. Suppose that once this fixed cost is incurred, it costs little to choose one particular state of destination over another. Income-maximizing immigrants will obviously choose the destination that offers the best income opportunities. Newly arrived immigrants will then tend to live in the 'right' state, in the sense that they are clustered in the state that offers them the highest wages.

The income-maximization hypothesis thus leads to two important insights. First, immigrants will choose to live in high wage areas. More specifically, low-skill immigrants will tend to cluster in the states that pay relatively high wages to low-skill workers, while high-skill immigrants will tend to cluster in those states that pay relatively high wages to high-skill workers. Second, immigrants may play a crucial—and neglected—role in a host country's labour market: they are 'marginal' workers whose location decisions arbitrage wage differences across sectors. The immigrant population may then play a disproportionately large role in helping the national labour market attain an efficient allocation of resources.

Is there any evidence that new immigrants do, in fact, tend to locate themselves in high-wage areas? The hypothesis that immigrants tend to cluster in high-wage states would seem to contradict a well known 'stylized fact': immigrants have clustered and continue to cluster in a relatively few number of areas in the United States. In 1990, 74 per cent of newly arrived immigrants, the immigrants who had been in the country for fewer than five years, lived in one of the six main immigrant-receiving states: California, New York, Texas, Florida, Illinois, and New Jersey. In contrast, only 36 per cent of natives lived in those states.

Although this clustering might raise serious doubts about the validity of the income-maximization hypothesis, it is simply not true that all immigrants cluster in the same states. It turns out that different types of immigrants tend to live in different states. Table 14.1 describes the geographic distribution of newly arrived immigrants in 1990. Half of the immigrants with fewer than 9 years of schooling lived in California, as compared to only a quarter of the immigrants with a college education. In contrast, 9.2 per cent of the immigrants with fewer than 9 years of schooling and 14.9 per cent of college graduates lived in New York. Overall, the data reveal that although fewer than 20 per cent of the immigrants who were high school dropouts lived *outside* the six main immigrant-receiving states, almost 40 per cent of the immigrants with a college degree lived outside those states.

Let $M_{jk}(t)$ be the number of immigrants who arrived between 1980 and 1984, reside in state j, and belong to skill group k, and let $M_k(t)$ be the total number of the new immigrants who belong to that skill group. The variables $N_{jk}(t)$ and $N_k(t)$ give the respective number of native workers in the state-education cells at that particular time. One can define the index of relative

Table **14.1**. *Geographic distribution of the immigrant population in the*
United States in 1990

Per cent of immigrants living in	Educational attainment				
	Less than 9 years	9–11 years	12 years	13–15 years	At least 16 years
California	50.1	41.9	32.7	33.2	26.5
New York	9.2	14.8	18.6	14.1	14.9
Florida	5.6	8.1	8.1	7.8	5.0
Texas	10.1	7.2	5.1	5.4	5.2
New Jersey	2.9	4.1	5.8	4.7	6.3
Illinois	4.4	3.9	5.0	4.3	4.7

Source: Borjas (2001*a*).

supply for the state-education cell (j, k) as:

$$R_{jk}(t) = \frac{M_{jk}(t)/M_k(t)}{N_{jk}(t)/N_k(t)}. \tag{1}$$

The variable $R_{jk}(t)$ measures the relative supply of newly arrived immigrants in education group k to state j. The denominator in (1) effectively 'deflates' the supply of immigrant workers in a particular skill group to a particular state by the relative importance of that state in the employment of similarly skilled native workers. The relative supply index equals one when immigrant and native workers belonging to the same education group have the same geographic distribution, and would be greater than one if immigrants in education group k were over-represented in state j.

It is well known that there are significant interstate differences in real wages in the United States, and that the structure of these differences probably differs across skill levels. In other words, different states tend to offer relatively different wages to different skill groups. I used an earnings function to calculate the regional wage structure as of 1980. In particular, I calculated the average wage paid by each state (after adjusting for the age and gender of workers) to workers in each education group.

Table 14.2 summarizes the cross-section relationship between interstate wage differentials and the location of newly arrived immigrants. For each education group, the table differentiates between the 'highest-paying' states and the 'lowest-paying' states. The highest-paying states are those where the adjusted wage ranks among the top five for that skill group, while the lowest-paying states are those where the adjusted wage ranks in the bottom five. For each of these sets of states, I then calculated the average index of relative supply. The data strongly suggest a behavioural clustering effect for new

Table 14.2. *Cross-section relation between relative supply of new
immigrants and wages in 1980*

Education group (in years)	Measure of relative supply			
	New immigrants relative to natives		New immigrants relative to earlier immigrants	
	5 high-wage states	5 low-wage states	5 high-wage states	5 low-wage states
Less than 9	4.964	0.045	1.210	0.691
9–11	2.709	0.082	1.196	0.513
12	2.360	0.143	1.217	0.523
13–15	1.880	0.192	1.134	0.721
At least 16	1.920	0.312	1.143	0.850

Source: Borjas (2001a). The 5 high-wage states pool data from the states with the five highest values for the adjusted log wage in 1980 for a particular skill group. The 5 low-wage states pool data from the states with the five lowest values for the adjusted log wage. The 'new' immigrants entered the United States between 1980 and 1984; the 'earlier' immigrants entered the country before 1975.

immigrants. Consider, for example, the geographic distribution of workers who are high school graduates. In 1980, the relative supply index giving the number of new immigrants relative to natives in the five 'best' states for high school graduates is 2.4. In contrast, new immigrants are relatively absent from the five states that offer the lowest wages for high school graduates; the relative supply index in the 'worst' states is 0.14. Generally, new immigrants tend to be over-represented in the states that offer the highest wages, and under-represented in the states that offer the lowest wages.

It turns out that the newest immigrant arrivals are over-represented in high-wage states not only relative to natives, but also relative to immigrants who arrived in earlier waves. To show this, the last two columns of the table use a slightly different definition of the relative supply index. Let $I_{jk}(t)$ be the number of immigrants in earlier waves who reside in state j and belong to skill group k at time t, and $I_k(t)$ be the total number of these earlier immigrants belonging to that skill group. The 'earlier' immigrants have been in the United States for at least five years prior to the measurement of the log wage index. One can then define an alternative relative supply index:

$$R'_{jk}(t) = \frac{M_{jk}(t)/M_k(t)}{I_{jk}(t)/I_k(t)}. \tag{2}$$

The data reported in Table 14.1 suggest that the two cohorts of immigrants locate themselves in somewhat different states, with the new immigrants tending to be over-represented in the states that offer the best economic opportunities for their skills. Consider, for example, workers who have between 9 and 11 years of schooling. In 1980, the relative supply index defined in equation (2) was 1.2 in the five states offering the highest wages, but was only 0.5 in the five states offering the lowest wages.

The possibility that immigrants cluster in high-wage states has implications for a number of the important issues and concerns that HSSS raise about the current status of the 'economics of immigration' literature. First, the income-maximization hypothesis could help resolve the empirical puzzle noted earlier. Because immigrants deliberately choose to enter those labour markets that offer the highest wages, it will be very difficult to document that increased immigration lowers the native wage in the penetrated geographic areas. The literature has sometimes attempted to control for this endogeneity problem by using instrumental variables, where the instrument for the measure of immigrant penetration in the local labour market is typically a variable indicating the number of immigrants who resided in that labour market at some point in the past. The clustering of immigrants in high-wage areas suggests that this is not a valid instrument. Immigrants cluster in those labour markets that offer them the best opportunities for the skills that they bring to the country, and hence the size of the pre-existing stock of immigrants will not, in general, be uncorrelated with the wages offered by a particular locality.

More important, the clustering of immigrants in high-wage states raises a number of questions about the macroeconomic impact of immigration. The endogenous clustering of immigrants in high-wage regions suggests that the spatial distribution of new immigrants in the United States should help reduce regional wage differentials. This finding has significant macroeconomic implications for it suggests that regional wage convergence will occur at a faster rate among those skill groups and in those periods that experience high levels of immigration.

A large literature examines the rate of wage convergence across states in the United States (Barro and Sala-i-Martin, 1991; Blanchard and Katz, 1992). These studies typically find that the half-life of interstate wage differentials is roughly 35 years. The income-maximization hypothesis developed above suggests that there is a structural relationship linking the rate of regional wage convergence and the size of the immigrant flow into that market.

In Borjas (2001a), I used data drawn from the 1950–90 Censuses to estimate a particular specification of the generic convergence regression model. Consider the following regression model:

$$\log w_{jk,t+1} - \log w_{jkt} = \alpha + \beta_{kt} \log w_{jkt} + \varepsilon_{jkt}, \qquad (3)$$

where $w_{jkk}(t)$ is the adjusted log wage of workers in state j and skill group k in Census year t; and the parameter β_{kt} is the convergence coefficient describing the evolution of the regional wage structure for that skill group in the $(t, t+1)$ time period. The time periods are 1950–60, 1960–70, 1970–80, and 1980–90. I annualized the dependent variable by dividing by 10, so that β gives the annual rate of regional wage convergence. I estimated the regression model in equation (3) separately for each skill group in each time period. The empirical analysis, therefore, yields a total of 20 estimated convergence coefficients (or 4 periods × 5 education groups).

The income-maximization hypothesis suggests that there should be greater wage convergence in those labour markets (defined for a particular skill group over a particular time period) that experience larger immigrant flows. Let the index of immigrant penetration in a particular labour market be given by:

$$m_{kt} = \log \frac{M_k(t, t+1)}{N_{kt}}, \tag{3}$$

where $M_k(t, t+1)$ gives the total number of immigrants in skill group k who entered the United States between periods t and $t+1$, and N_{kt} gives the size of the native-born population in skill group k at the beginning of the period.

Figure 14.1 presents the scatter diagram illustrating the basic data. There is a clear downward sloping (and statistically significant) relationship between the convergence coefficient in any particular market (defined by time period and skill group) and the relative number of immigrants entering that labour market. It seems, therefore, that immigration 'injects' the host country's labour market with workers who are very responsive to regional wage differentials. As a result, immigrants speed up the process of wage convergence and improve labour market efficiency.

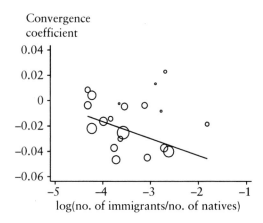

Figure 14.1. *The relation between the convergence coefficient and immigration*

Source: Borjas (2001a). Each observation represents a convergence coefficient estimated in a particular decade for a particular skill group. The measure of immigrant penetration gives the log of the number of immigrants in a particular skill group who arrived during a particular decade relative to the number of natives in that skill group at the beginning of the decade. The points on the scatter diagram are weighted by the inverse of the square of the standard error of the convergence coefficient.

It is worth stressing that the clustering of immigrants in high-wage areas implies that immigration generates a new type of gain for the host country's economy. The HSSS survey, like most of the studies in the immigration literature, emphasizes various aspects of the cost that immigrants impose on various sectors of the host country's economy—whether they be the wage losses suffered by native workers or the increase in taxes borne by native taxpayers. Remarkably, very little attention is paid to the possibility that immigrants impart benefits to the host country's economy.

In the traditional one-sector model, immigration increases the net income accruing to native workers because immigrants enter the labour market, lower wages, and thereby raise the return to a fixed capital stock (which is typically assumed to be owned by natives). In the US context, this 'immigration surplus' has typically been found to be relatively small, less than 0.1 per cent of GDP.

The clustering of immigrants in high-wage states implies that there are additional gains from immigration. In particular, native migration flows, perhaps because of relatively high fixed migration costs, cannot fully arbitrage the regional wage differences. The immigrant flow, in contrast, is self-targeted to those regions of the country where their productivity is highest. This clustering effect 'greases the wheels of the labour market' by speeding up the process of wage convergence, and improves economic efficiency. It is important to emphasize that these gains from immigration differ conceptually from the productivity gains captured by the immigration surplus.

As indicated by the topical content of the HSSS survey, the immigration literature has paid remarkably little attention to the source and magnitude of the economic gains from immigration. This is one area of study that clearly requires much additional research.

The political economy of welfare reform

HSSS present an excellent discussion of the political economy of immigration policy. Their description of the polling data shows that most Americans consistently prefer lower levels of immigration. This description raises a fundamental question in the political economy of immigration: why has the US government consistently ignored voter preferences regarding immigration and increased the size of the legal immigrant flow each time that it has reformed immigration policy in the past few decades?

Although HSSS do not link their discussion of the political economy of immigration policy with another topic that they survey at length—immigrant use of welfare—recent changes in welfare policy in the United States suggest that much can be learned by considering the link between these two topics. It is well known that due to increasing concerns over the link between immigration and welfare, Congress included a number of immigrant-related provisions in the 1996 Personal Responsibility and Work Opportunity Reconciliation Act (PRWORA). In fact, it has been estimated that almost half of the $54 billion savings attributed to the welfare reform bill can be traced directly to the restrictions on immigrant use of welfare (Primus, 1996–97, p. 14). In general terms, the legislation, as signed by President Clinton, contained three key provisions:

(1) Most non-citizens who arrived in the country *before* August 22, 1996, the 'pre-enactment' immigrants, were to be kicked off from the SSI and food stamp rolls within a year. (This provision of the legislation, however, was never fully enforced).
(2) Immigrants who entered the United States *after* August 22, 1996, the 'post-enactment' immigrants, are prohibited from receiving most types of public assistance. The ban is lifted when the immigrant becomes an American citizen.
(3) Post-enactment immigrants are subject to stricter deeming regulations. The eligible income and assets of the immigrant's sponsor will be deemed to be part of the immigrant's application for most types of public assistance, and the deeming period can last up to ten years.

The restrictions on immigrant use of welfare brought together a number of powerful interest groups after the 1996 presidential election—all of which lobbied hard for their repeal. And, in fact, many of the immigrant-related provisions of the legislation were never enforced. The balanced budget agreement reached in 1997 between President Clinton and the Republican-controlled Congress effectively repealed some of the most draconian aspects of the legislation. The partial restoration of federal aid, combined with actions taken by individual states (discussed below), implies that relatively few of the pre-enactment immigrants ended up being kicked out of the SSI and Food Stamp Programs. The mandated waiting period for post-enactment immigrants, however, remained on the books.

A superficial glance at the *national* trends suggests that welfare reform was a success—at least in terms of reducing the number of immigrants on the rolls. Table 3 reports the per cent of immigrant and native households that received some type of assistance (defined as cash benefits, Medicaid, or food stamps) in each year between 1994 and 1998. The probability that either immigrant or native households received some type of assistance was roughly constant prior to 1996. About 24 per cent of immigrant households received some type of assistance both in 1994 and 1995, as compared to about 16 per cent of native households. The participation rate of both groups fell immediately after the enactment of PRWORA, but the post-1996 decline was much steeper in the immigrant population. In particular, the participation rate dropped by about 2 percentage points among native households, but by about 4 percentage points in immigrant households.

These national trends seem to suggest that the welfare reform legislation had a particularly strong impact on the likelihood that immigrant households receive assistance, helping to create the perception that PRWORA had a

Table 14.3. *Trends in welfare participation rates (1994–98) (per cent of households receiving some type of assistance)*

Calendar year	Entire Country		California		Outside California	
	Natives	Immigrants	Natives	Immigrants	Natives	Immigrants
1994	15.6	23.4	15.2	31.2	15.6	20.0
1995	15.0	23.8	14.5	31.1	15.1	20.6
1996	15.3	21.9	13.6	26.3	15.5	20.1
1997	14.0	20.2	13.5	23.7	14.1	18.8
1998	13.4	20.0	13.6	23.2	13.4	18.7

Source: Borjas (2001*b*).

'chilling effect' on immigrant participation in welfare programmes. However, the national trends are quite misleading, for they do not reflect what went on in much of the country during the 1994–98 period.

The demographic importance of California, a state that is home to about a third of the immigrants, suggests that it might be of interest to examine the trends separately for California and for other states. As Table 14.3 also shows, it turns out that almost all of the relative decline in immigrant welfare participation at the national level can be attributed to what happened to immigrant welfare use in California. The fraction of native households in California that received some type of assistance dropped slightly by 1.6 percentage points, from 15.2 per cent before PRWORA to 13.6 per cent afterwards. In contrast, the fraction of immigrant households in California that received assistance fell precipitously, from 31.2 to 23.2 per cent. Outside California, the welfare participation rate of native-born households declined by about 2.2 percentage points, while the participation rate of immigrant households declined by less than 2 percentage points, from about 20 per cent before PRWORA to 18.7 per cent by 1998. It is also interesting to note that the *timing* of the decline in immigrant welfare use differs between California and the rest of the country. The decline in California began before PRWORA, but occurred later (after PRWORA) in the rest of the country.

Why are the trends in California so distinctive? One obvious candidate is the enactment of Proposition 187 in November 1994. This proposition, supported by 59 per cent of California's voters, denied almost all types of assistance (including schooling) to *illegal* aliens. Although most of the provisions in the proposition were never enforced, its impact on the political and social climate in California is undeniable. Soon after the enactment of Proposition 187, there were numerous newspaper accounts of the chilling effect that the proposition had on aliens applying for particular types of publicly provided benefits.

Although the trends in welfare participation outside California suggest that PRWORA had relatively little impact on immigrant welfare use, this conclusion is premature for it ignores the fact that the states responded to the legislation. A closer look at the trends suggests that much of the potential chilling effect of PRWORA on immigrant welfare use was undone by the political reactions of state governments. Some states—*and particularly those states where immigrants live*—offered state-funded benefits to their immigrant populations.

An important, though little publicized, provision in PRWORA grants states the option to offer state-funded welfare programmes to immigrants. The Urban Institute has calculated an index of 'welfare generosity' that measures the extent to which particular states offered their state-funded safety nets to the immigrant population after 1996 (Zimmermann and Tumlin, 1999, table 18). The Urban Institute's index classifies states into four categories according to the availability of the state safety net. The states where such aid was 'most available' included California and Illinois; the states where the aid was 'somewhat available' included New York and Florida; the states where the aid was 'less available' included Arizona and Michigan; and the states where the aid was 'least available' included Ohio and Texas. It is worth noting that five of the six states with the largest immigrant populations (the exception being Texas) tended to provide above-average levels of state-funded assistance to immigrants.

Table 14.4 uses the Urban Institute index to classify states into 'more generous' (where aid was 'most available' or 'somewhat available') and 'less generous'. The table shows how the chilling effect of welfare reform depends on these state programmes. The fraction of non-citizens receiving assistance in the less generous states—the states that offered minimal levels of state-funded assistance to immigrants—dropped by 10 percentage points (from 29.4 to 19.4 per cent). In contrast, the fraction of non-citizens receiving assistance in the more generous states dropped by about 5 percentage points (from 29.7 to 24.4 per cent).

Table 14.4. *Impact of state-funded programmes on welfare participation rates (per cent of households receiving some type of assistance)*

Sample and period	Households in					
	Less generous states			More generous states		
	Native	Citizen	Non-citizen	Native	Citizen	Non-citizen
All households						
Pre-1996	16.3	15.5	29.4	14.3	14.9	29.7
Post-1996	14.3	14.4	19.4	13.1	17.0	24.4
Non-California households						
Pre-1996	16.3	15.5	28.4	14.2	13.1	23.9
Post-1996	14.3	14.4	19.4	13.0	16.4	22.6

Source: Borjas (2001*b*). The household is defined as a native, citizen, or non-citizen household depending on the birthplace and naturalization status of the household head.

Moreover, much of the presumed chilling effect observed in the more generous states disappears if we look at the immigrants who live outside California. The participation rate of non-citizens living outside California dropped by about 9 percentage points if they lived in less generous states, and dropped by only 1.3 percentage points if they lived in the more generous states.

In sum, the fact that some states chose to offer a state-funded safety net to their immigrant populations helped cushion the impact of federal welfare reform on immigrant welfare use. Put differently, PRWORA could indeed have caused a chilling effect outside California, but the political reactions of individual states, and particularly the states where most immigrants live, prevented much of that chilling effect from occurring.

The political economy of welfare reform, therefore, provides an important lesson about the politics of immigration reform. In 1996, Congress granted individual states the option to supplement the federal benefits available to immigrants. Most of the states with large immigrant populations accepted this invitation and offered state-funded safety nets to immigrant households. From an economic perspective, the responses made by the states with large immigrant populations seem puzzling. One could have easily argued that once states were free to pursue their own welfare policies, many of the states most affected by immigration would have chosen to discourage welfare use—rather than adopt policies that further encouraged it.

Why did the race to the bottom not occur? Was it perhaps because the immigrant population in these states is now sufficiently large that elected officials found it politically essential to cater to the needs of this large minority?

HSSS note that there is a great deal of evidence that large immigrant populations tend to alter the nature of how elected representatives act on immigration issues. It seems, in fact, that the clustering of immigrants in a relatively small number of places can substantially alter the intended political outcomes of federal legislation in the United States. The trends in welfare use after 1996, therefore, could well provide an excellent case study of the political constraints that are likely to frame any future reform of immigration policy.

References

Abraham, F. (1996), 'Regional Adjustment and Wage Flexibility in the European Union', *Regional Science and Urban Economics*, 26(1), February: 51–75.

Acemoglu, D. (1999), 'Patterns of Skill Premia', NBER Working Paper no. 7018.

Alt, J.E. and Gilligan, M. (1994), 'The Political Economy of Trading States', *Journal of Political Philosophy*, 2, 165–92.

Altonji, J. and Card, D. (1991), 'The Effects of Immigration on the Labor Market Outcomes of Less-Skilled Natives', in J. Abowd and R. Freeman (eds.), *Immigration, Trade, and the Labor Market*, Chicago, IL: University of Chicago Press, 201–34.

Andreas, P. and Snyder, T. (eds.) (2000), *The Wall Around the West: State Borders and Immigration Control in North America and Europe*, Lanham, MD: Rowman and Littlefield.

Arnold, R.D. (1990), *The Logic of Congressional Action*, New Haven, CT: Yale University Press.

Auerbach, A.J. and Oreopoulos, P. (1999), 'Analysing the Fiscal Impact of U.S. Immigration', *American Economic Review. Papers and Proceedings*, 89(2), 176–80.

Autor, D.H., Katz, L.F., and Krueger, A.B. (1998), 'Computing Inequality: Have Computers Changed the Labor Market?' *Quarterly Journal of Economics*, 1169–214.

Bailey, M. (1999), 'The Other Side of the Coin: The Hidden Benefits of Campaign Finance', Georgetown University Manuscript.

——(2001), 'Quiet Influence: The Representation of Diffuse Interests on Trade Policy, 1983–94', *Legislative Studies Quarterly* Vol. XXVI (1), 45–80.

Barro, R.J. and Sala-i-Martin, X. (1991), 'Convergence across States and Regions'. *Brookings Papers on Economic Activity*, 1, 107–58.

Bean, F.D., Lowell, B.L., and Taylor, L.J. (1988), 'Undocumented Mexican Immigrants and the Earnings of Other Workers in the United States', *Demography*, 25, 35–52.

——Chanove, R., Cushing, R.G., de la Garza, R., Freeman, G.P., Haynes, C.W., and Spencer, D. (1994), 'Illegal Mexican Migration and the United States/Mexico Border: The Effects of Operation Hold the Line on El Paso/Juarez', U.S. Commission on Immigration Reform Research Paper (July).

Berman, E., Bound, J., and Griliches, Z. (1994), 'Changes in Demand for Skilled Labor Within U.S. Manufacturing Industries', *Quarterly Journal of Economics*, 109, 367–98.

Bernstein, J.R. and Weinstein, D.E. (1998), 'Do Endowments Predict the Location of Production? Evidence from National and International Data', NBER Working Paper no. 6815.

Blanchard, O.J. and Katz, L.F. (1992), 'Regional Evolutions', *Brookings Papers on Economic Activity*, pp. 1–75.

Blank, R.M. (1997), 'The 1996 Welfare Reform', *Journal of Economic Perspectives*, 11(1).

Blau, F.D. (1984), 'The Use of Transfer Payments by Immigrants', *Industrial and Labor Relations Review*, 37, 222–39.

Borjas, G.J. (1994), 'The Economics of Immigration', *Journal of Economic Literature*, 32, 1667–717.

Borjas, G.J. (1995*a*), 'Immigration and Welfare', *Research in Labor Economics*, 14, 253–82.

—— (1995*b*), 'Know the Flow', *National Review*, April 17.

—— (1996), 'The Earnings of Mexican Immigrants in the United States', *Journal of Development Economics*, 51, 69–98.

—— (1999*a*), *Heaven's Door: Immigration Policy and the American Economy*, Princeton, N.J.: Princeton University Press.

—— (1999*b*), 'The Economic Analysis of Immigration', in O.C. Ashenfelter and D. Card (eds.), *Handbook of Labor Economics*, Amsterdam: North Holland, pp. 1697–760.

—— (1999*c*), 'Immigration and Welfare Magnets', *Journal of Labor Economics*, 17(4), 607–37.

—— (ed.), (2000), *Issues in the Economics of Immigration*, Chicago: The University of Chicago Press.

—— (2001*a*), 'Does Immigration Grease the Wheels of the Labor Market?', *Brookings Papers on Economic Activity*, 1.

—— (2001*b*) 'Welfare Reform and Immigration', in Blank R. and Haskins, R. (eds.), *The New World of Welfare: An Agenda for Reauthorization and Beyond*, Brookings Press.

—— and Hilton, L. (1996), 'Immigration and the Welfare State: Immigrant Participation in Means-Tested Entitlement Programs', *Quarterly Journal of Economics*, 111(2), 575–604.

—— and Trejo, S.J. (1991), 'Immigrant Participation in the Welfare System', *Industrial and Labor Relations Review*, 44, 195–211.

—— Bronars, S.G., and Trejo, S.J. (1992), 'Self-Selection and Internal Migration in the United States', *Journal of Urban Economics*, 159–85.

—— Freeman, R.B., and Kevin, L. (1991), 'Undocumented Mexican-Born Workers in the United States: How Many, How Permanent?' in J.M. Abowd and R.B. Freeman (eds.), *Immigration, Trade, and the Labor Market*, Chicago, IL: University of Chicago Press, pp. 77–100.

—— Freeman, R.B. and Katz, L.F. (1992), 'On the Labour Market Effects of Immigration and Trade', in Borjas, G.J. and Freeman, R.B. (eds.), *Immigration and the Work Force: Economic Consequences for the United States and Source Areas*, Chicago, IL: University of Chicago Press, pp. 213–44

—— —— and —— (1996), 'Searching for the Effect of Immigration on the Labor Market', *American Economic Review*, 86(2), 247–51.

—— —— and —— (1997), 'How Much Do Immigration and Trade Affect Labor Market Outcomes?', *Brookings Papers on Economic Activity*, 1, 1–90.

Bound, J. and Holzer, H. (1996), 'Demand Shifts, Population Adjustments, and Labor Market Outcomes during the 1980s', NBER Working Paper no. 5685, July.

—— and Johnson, G. (1992), 'Changes in the Structure of Wages in the 1980s: An Evaluation of Alternative Explanations', *American Economic Review*, 371–92.

Brueckner, J.K. (2000), 'Welfare Reform and the Race to the Bottom: Theory and Evidence', *Southern Economic Journal*, 66(3), 505–25.

Bustamente, J.A., Jasso, G., Taylor, J.E., and Legarreta, P.T. (1998), 'Characteristics of Migrants: Mexican in the United States', in Mexico–United States Binational Migration Study, pp. 91–162.

Butcher, K.F. and Piehl, A.M. (2000), 'The Role of Deportation in the Incarceration of Immigrants', in G.J. Borjas (ed.), *Issues in the Economics of Immigration*, Chicago, IL: University of Chicago Press, pp. 351–86.

Calavita, K. (1992), *Inside The State: The Bracero Program, Immigration, and The I.N.S.* New York, NY: Routledge.

Camarota, S.A. (2001), 'Immigrants in the United States—2000'. Mimeo, Center for Immigration Studies (http://www.cis.org/).

Card, D. (1990), 'The Impact of the Mariel Boatlift on the Miami Labor Market', *Industrial and Labor Relations Review*, 43(2), 245–57.

—— (2001), 'Immigrant Inflows, Native Outflows, and the Local Labor Market Impacts of Higher Immigration', *Journal of Labor Economics*, 19(1), 22–64.

Chiswick, B.R. (1984), 'Illegal Aliens in the United States Labor Market: Analysis of Occupational Attainment and Earnings', *International Migration Review*, 28(3), 714–32.

Citrin, J., Green, D., Muste, C., and Wong, C. (1997), 'Public Opinion Toward Immigration Reform: The Role of Economic Motivation', *Journal of Politics*, 59(3), 858–81.

Cornelius, W.A. (1992), 'From Sojourners to Settlers: The Changing Profile of Mexican Immigration to the United States', in J.A. Bustamante, C.W. Reynolds, and R.A. Hinojosa (eds.), *U.S.-Mexico Relations: Labor-Market Interdependence*, Stanford, CA: Stanford University Press, pp. 155–95.

—— (2000), 'Death at the Border: The Efficacy and "Unintended" Consequences of U.S. Immigration Control Policy, 1993–2000', Center for Comparative Immigration Studies, Working Paper no. 27.

—— and Marselli, E.A. (2001), 'The Changing Profile of Mexican Migrants to the United States: New Evidence from California and Mexico', *Latin American Research Review*, (forthcoming).

Crane, K.W., Asch, B.J., Heilbrunn, J.Z., and Cullinane, D.C. (1990), 'The Effect of Employer Sanctions on the Flow of Undocumented Immigrants to the United States'. Washington, DC: Urban Institute Report 90–8.

Currie, J. (2000), 'Do Children of Immigrants make Differential Use of Public Health Insurance?' in G.J. Borjas, (ed.), *Issues in the Economics of Immigration*, Chicago, IL: The University of Chicago Press.

Davis, D.R. (1998), 'Does European Unemployment Prop Up American Wages? National Labor Markets and Global Trade', *American Economic Review*, 88(3), 478–94.

—— and Weinstein, D.E. (1998), 'An Account of Global Factor Trade', NBER Working Paper no. 6785.

Denzau, A. and Munger, M. (1986), 'Legislators and Interest Groups: How Unorganized Interests Get Represented', *American Political Science Review*, 80, 89–102.

Donato, K.M., Durand, J., and Massey, D.S. (1992), 'Stemming the Tide? Assessing the Deterrent Effects of the Immigration Reform and Control Act', *Demography*, 29(2), 139–57.

Durand, J. (1996), 'Migradollars and Development: A Reconsideration of the Mexican Case', *International Migration Review*, 30(2), 423–45.

—— and Massey, D.S. (1992), 'Mexican Migration to the United States: A Critical Review', *Latin American Research Review*.

—— —— and Zenteno, R.M. (2001), 'Mexican Immigration in the United States', *Latin American Research Review*, 36(1), 107–27.

Elwood, D.T. (2001), 'The Sputtering Labor Force of the 21st Century: Can Social Policy Help?', mimeo.

Espenshade, T.J. (1994), 'Does the Threat of Border Apprehension Deter Undocumented U.S. Immigration?', *Population and Development Review*, 20(4), 871–91.

—— (1995), 'Unauthorized Immigration to the United States', *Annual Review of Sociology*, 21, 195–216.

—— and Hempstead, K. (1996), 'Contemporary American Attitudes Toward U.S. Immigration', *International Migration Review*, 26(4), 1144–67.

—— Baraka, J.L., and Huber, G.A. (1997), 'Implications of the 1996 Welfare and Immigration Reform Acts for US Immigration', *Population and Development Review*, 23(4), 769–801.

Ethier, W.J. (1984), 'Higher Dimensional Issues in Trade Theory', in R.W. Jones and P.B. Kenen (eds.), *Handbook of International Economics Volume 1*, Amsterdam: North Holland Press, 131–84.

Fetzer, J.S. (2000), *Public Attitudes toward Immigration in the United States, France, and Germany*, Cambridge, UK: Cambridge University Press.

Fix, M.E. and Tumlin, K. (1997), 'Welfare Reform and the Devolution of Immigration Policy', The Urban Institute.

—— and Passel, J.S. (1994), 'Immigrations and Immigrants. Setting the Record Straight', The Urban Institute.

—— and —— (1999), 'Trends in Noncitizens' and Citizens' Use of Public Benefits Following Welfare Reform: 1994–97', The Urban Institute.

—— —— and Zimmermann, W. (1996), 'Facts about Immigrants' Use of Welfare', The Urban Institute.

Flier, R.K. (1992), 'The Impact of Immigrant Arrivals on Migratory Patterns of Natives', in G.J. Borjas and R.B. Freeman (eds.), *Immigration and the Work Force: Economic Consequences for the United States and Source Areas*, Chicago, IL: University of Chicago Press.

Friedberg, R. and Hunt, J. (1995), 'The Impact of Immigrants on Host Country Wages, Employment, and Growth', *Journal of Economic Perspectives*, 9(2), 23–44.

Gandal, N., Hanson, G.H., and Slaughter, M.J. (2000), 'Technology, Trade, and Adjustment to Immigration in Israel', NBER Working Paper no. 7962.

Gaston, N. and Nelson, D. (2001), 'Immigration and Labor-Market Outcomes in the United States: A Political-Economy Puzzle', *Oxford Review of Economic Policy*, 16.

Gilligan, M. (1997), *Empowering Exporters: Reciprocity, Delegation, and Collective Action in American Trade Policy*, Ann Arbor, MI: University of Michigan Press.

Gimpel, J.G. and Edwards, J.R. (1999), *The Congressional Politics of Immigration Reform*, Boston, MA: Allyn and Bacon.

Grier, K., Munger, M., and Roberts, B.E. (1994), 'The Determinants of Industry Political Activity, 1978–1986', *American Political Science Review*, 88, 911–26.

Gustman, A.J. and Steinmeier, T.L. (2000), 'Social Security Benefits of Immigrants and U.S. Born' in G.J. Borjas (ed.), *Issues in the Economics of Immigration*, Chicago, IL: The University of Chicago Press.

Hanson, G.H., Robertson, R., and Spilimbergo, A. (2002), 'Does Border Enforcement Protect U.S. Workers from Illegal Immigration?', *The Review of Economics and Statistics* (forthcoming).

—— and Slaughter, M.J. (2002), 'Labor-Market Adjustment in Open Economies: Evidence from U.S. States', *Journal of International Economics* (forthcoming).

—— and Spilimbergo, A. (1998), 'Mexican Migration and U.S. Policy Options', in P. Hakim and N. Lustig (eds.), *Immigration in U.S.–Mexican Relations*, Washington, DC: Brookings Institution and Inter-American Dialogue.

—— and —— (1999), 'Illegal Immigration, Border Enforcement and Relative Wages: Evidence from Apprehensions at the U.S.–Mexico Border', *American Economic Review*, 89, 1337–57.

—— and —— (2001), 'Political Economy, Sectoral Shocks, and Border Enforcement', *Canadian Journal of Economics*, 34(3), August: 612–38.

Haskel, J.E. and Slaughter, M.J. (2002), 'Does the Sector Bias of Skill-Biased Techno-logical Change Explain Changing Skill Premia?', *European Economic Review*, (forthcoming).

Johnson, G. (1983), 'Intermetropolitan Wage Differentials in the United States', in J. Triplett (ed.), *The Measurement of Labor Costs*, Chicago: University of Chicago Press, pp. 309–30.

—— (1997), 'Changes in Earnings Inequality: The Role of Demand Shifts', *Journal of Economic Perspectives*, 11, 41–54.

Johnson, H.P. (1997), *Undocumented Immigration to California: 1980–1993*, San Francisco: Public Policy Institute of California.

Juffras, J. (1991), 'Impact of Immigration Reform and Control Act on the Immigration and Naturalization Service', The RAND Corporation Report JR-09.

Juhn, C., Murphy, K.M., Chin, K.M., and Pierce, B. (1993), 'Wage Inequality and the Rise in Returns to Skill', *Journal of Political Economy*, 101, 410–42.

Katz, L.F. and Murphy, K.M. (1992), 'Changes in Relative Wages, 1963–1987: Supply and Demand Factors', *Quarterly Journal of Economics*, 107(1), 35–78.

—— and David Autor. (1999), 'Changes in the Wage Structure and Earnings Inequality', in Orley Ashenfelter and David Card (eds.), *Handbook of Labor Economics*, Vol. 3A, Amsterdam: Elsevier, 1463–1555.

Kessler, A.E. (1999), 'Globalization, Domestic Politics, and the "Curious Coalitions" of Postwar American Immigration Reform', paper presented at the 1999 Annual Conference of the American Political Science Association.

Kingdon, J. (1973), *Congressman's Voting Decisions*, New York: Harper and Row.

Kossoudji, S.A. (1992), 'Playing Cat and Mouse at the U.S.–Mexico Border', *Demography*, 29(2), 159–80.

LaLonde, R. and Topel, R. (1991), 'Labor Market Adjustments to Increased Immi-gration', in J. Abowd and R. Freeman (eds.), *Immigration, Trade, and the Labor Market*, Chicago, IL: University of Chicago Press, 167–200.

Leamer, E.E. and Levinsohn, J. (1995), 'International Trade Theory: The Evidence', in G.M. Grossman and K. Rogoff (eds.), *Handbook on International Economics Volume 3*, Amsterdam: North Holland Press, 1339–94.

Lee, R. and Miller, T. (2000), 'Immigration, Social Security, and Broader Fiscal Impact', *American Economic Review. Papers and Proceedings*, 90(2), 350–4.

McCarthy, K.F. and Vernez, G. (1998), *Immigration in a Changing Economy. California's Experience—Questions and Answers*, Santa Monica, CA: The RAND Corporation.

Martin, P.L. (1990), 'Harvest of Confusion: Immigration Reform and California Agriculture', *International Migration Review*, 24(1), 69–95.

Martin, P. (1998), 'Guest Workers: Past and Present', in Mexico–United States Binational Migration Study, *Migration Between Mexico and the United States*,

Volume 3, Washington, D.C.: U.S. Commission on Immigration Reform and Mexican Ministry of Foreign Affairs, pp. 877–96.

Massey, D.S., Goldring, L., and Durand, J. (1994), 'Continuities in Transnational Migration: An Analysis of Nineteen Mexican Communities', *American Journal of Sociology*, 99(6), 1492–533.

—— and Singer, A. (1995), 'New Estimates of Undocumented Mexican Migration and the Probability of Apprehension', *Demography*, 32(2), 203–13.

Mexico–United States Binational Migration Study (1998), *Migration Between Mexico and the United States, Volumes 1, 2, and 3*, Washington, DC: U.S. Commission on Immigration Reform and Mexican Ministry of Foreign Affairs.

Milner, H. (1988), *Resisting Protectionism*. Princeton, NJ: Princeton University Press.

Montgomery, E. (1991), 'Evidence on Metropolitan Wage Differences across Industries and over Time', *Journal of Urban Economics*, 31, 69–83.

OECD, Various Years, 'Trends in International Migration'. Annual Report. Paris. Various issues.

Olson, M. (1965), *The Logic of Collective Action*, Cambridge, MA: Harvard University Press.

Orrenius, P.M. and Zavodny, M. (2001), 'Self-Selection among Undocumented Immigrants from Mexico', mimeo, Federal Reserve Bank of Dallas.

Poole, K. and Rosenthal, H. (1991), 'Patterns of Congressional Voting', *American Journal of Political Science*, 35(1), 228–78.

—— and —— (1997), *Congress: A Political-Economic History of Roll Call Voting*, Oxford, UK: Oxford University Press.

Primus, W. (1997), 'Immigration Provisions in the New Welfare Law', *Focus*, 18, 14–18.

Rauch, J.E. (1993), 'Productivity Gains from Geographic Concentration of Human Capital: Evidence from the Cities', *Journal of Urban Economics*, 34, 380–400.

Rauch, J. and Trindade, V. (2002), 'Ethnic Chinese Networks in International Trade', *Review of Economics and Statistics*, (forthcoming).

Razin, A., Sadka, E., and Swagel, P. (1998), 'Tax Burden and Migration: A Political Economy Theory and Evidence', NBER Working Paper 6734.

Reyes, B.I. (1997), *Dynamics of Immigration: Return Migration to Western Mexico*, San Francisco: Public Policy Institute of California.

Robertson, R. (2000), 'Wage Shocks and North American Labor-Market Integration', *American Economic Review*, 90(4), 742–64.

Rybczynski, T.M. (1955), 'Factor Endowments and Relative Commodity Prices', *Economica*, 22, 336–41.

Saxenian, A.L. (1999), 'Silicon Valley's New Immigrant Entrepreneurs', Public Policy Institute of California Working Paper.

Schattschneider, E.E. (1935), *Politics, Pressure and the Tariff: A Study of Free Private Enterprise in Pressure Politics, as Shown in the 1929–1930 Revision of the Tariff*, Hamden, CT: Archon Books.

Scheve, K.F. and Slaughter, M.J. (2001a), 'Labor Market Competition and Individual Preferences Over Immigration Policy', *The Review of Economics and Statistics*, 83(1), 133–46.

—— and —— (2001b), *Globalization and the Perceptions of American Workers*, Washington D.C.: Institute for International Economics.

Shaw, Paul, R. (1986), 'Fiscal versus Traditional Market Variables in Canadian Migration', *Journal of Political Economy*, 94(3), June: 648–66.

Sheridan, M.B. (2001), 'Illegals paying Millions in Taxes', in *Washington Post*, April 15.

Simon, R.J. and Alexander, S.H. (1993), *The Ambivalent Welcome: Print Media, Public Opinion and Immigration*, Westport: Praeger.

Slaughter, M.J. (2000), 'What Are the Results of Product-Price Studies and What Can We Learn From Their Differences?' in R.C. Feenstra (ed.), *International Trade and Wages, The Impact of International Trade on Wages*, Chicago: University of Chicago Press, 121–70.

Smith, J.P. and Edmonston, B. (eds.) (1997), *The New Americans: Economic, Demographic, and Fiscal Effects of Immigration*, National Academy Press: Washington, D.C.

——and——(eds.) (1998) *The Immigration Debate*, National Academy Press: Washington, D.C.

Spilimbergo, A. (1999), 'Labor Market Integration, Unemployment, and Transfers', *Review of International Economics*, 7(4), 641–50.

Stolper, W. and Samuelson, P.A. (1941), 'Protection and Real Wages', *Review of Economics and Statistics*, 9(1), 58–73.

Storesletten, K. (2000), 'Sustaining Fiscal Policy Through Immigration', *Journal of Political Economy*, 108(2).

Topel, R.H. (1986), 'Local Labor Markets', *Journal of Political Economy*, 94, S111–143.

——(1994), 'Regional Labor Markets and the Determinants of Wage Inequality', *American Economic Review*, 84(2), May, 17–22.

U.S. Bureau of the Census (2000), *Educational Attainment in the United States*, March 1999. Washington, D.C.: U.S. Government Printing Office.

U.S. Immigration and Naturalization Service, Department of Justice (1998), 'Illegal Alien Resident Population'. http:/www.ins.usdoj.gov/.

U.S. Immigration and Naturalization Service, Department of Justice (2000), *1998 Statistical Yearbook of the Immigration and Naturalization Service*. Washington, D.C.: U.S. Government Printing Office.

Warren, R. (1995), 'Estimates of the Undocumented Immigrant Population Residing in the United States, by Country of Origin and State of Residence: October 1992', Mimeo, U.S. Immigration and Naturalization Service.

—— (1999), 'Unauthorized Immigrants Residing in the United States: Estimating the Population, Components of Change, and Trends, by Broad Area of Origin, 1987 to 1997', mimeo, U.S. Immigration and Naturalization Service.

Weintraub, S. (1998), 'IRCA and the Facilitation of the U.S.–Mexico Migration Dialogue', in Bean *et al.*, *Binational Study*.

Wildasin, D.E. (1994), 'Income redistribution and migration', *Canadian Journal of Economics*, 27(3), 637–56.

Woodruff, C. and Zenteno, R.M. (2001), 'Remittances and Microenterprises in Mexico', mimeo, UC San Diego.

Zimmermann, W. and Tumlin, K.C. (1999), 'Patchwork Policies: State Assistance for Immigrants under Welfare Reform', Washington, DC: The Urban Institute, Occasional Paper no. 24, May.

Final Remarks

OLIVIER BLANCHARD

Let me start by sketching a toy model of immigration. Think of all the capital as being in the West (Western Europe). Think of all the labour as being in the East (Eastern Europe). Now remove the barriers to factor mobility. Some capital is likely to move East, in order to work with the abundant labour there. Some labour is likely to move West, to work with the abundant capital here. Make the extreme assumption that, so long as the rate of return is higher in the East, capital moves East, and that, so long as the wage is higher in the West, labour moves West.

How much capital will move East, how much labour will move West is not obvious from this description. There is, it would appear, an infinity of equilibria, one with all the capital and labour in the West, one with all the capital and labour in the East, and all the equilibria in between. What will actually happen? This depends on frictions, or more formally, on relative adjustment costs for capital and labour. If adjustment costs are higher for labour than for capital, most of the capital will end up in the East, and immigration to the West will be limited. If instead, adjustment costs are higher for capital than for labour, immigration to the West will be much larger. Small differences in relative adjustment costs can end up making a large difference to the final outcome. If, for example, capital is a bit slow to respond, immigration will start, decreasing the incentives for capital to move East.

Are there reasons for either Eastern or Western states to intervene in this adjustment process? The answer is a very conventional one: If there are no externalities, that is, if private and social adjustment costs coincide, then the outcome will be efficient. There is no reason to intervene on efficiency grounds. This does not imply however that, with limited transfers across countries or across groups, both countries gain, or all groups within a country gain. Thus intervention may still be justified, but this time on equity grounds.

This toy model is just that, a toy model. The distribution of capital and labour between East and West is much less extreme than I have assumed. The long-run supply of both capital and labour is not fully elastic: Many workers will not want to move, even in the long run. But it has all the basic mechanisms and so is a useful conceptual framework. It raises a number of issues, among them.

1. How can we be sure that some of the countries of Eastern Europe will not simply empty of labour and capital?
2. What are the externalities or distributional issues we should be worried about, and do they lead us to want to slowdown immigration from the East?
3. Should not we be thinking of immigration and foreign direct investment together, and how much can one help reduce the other?

Let me take each of these three issues, and make a few remarks based on what I have learned both from the papers and from the discussion at the conference.

The potential size of immigration flows.

The basic numbers are as follows: The EU has a population of 375 million, including 19 million foreigners, of which about one million comes from the CEECs (Central and Eastern and European Countries) candidate to EU accession—Current flows from the CEECs to the EU are around 0.3 to 0.4 million, mostly to Germany.

Population in the CEEC is about 100 million. The estimate given in the first part of this volume—based on the effect of time variation in barriers to immigration from various countries to Germany between 1967 and 1998—is that, in due time, we can expect about 3 per cent of the CEEC population to move, so approximately 3 million people, at a flow rate of 0.2–0.3 million a year.

The empirical work from which this estimate is derived represents genuine progress. But I suspect the estimate is too low. The reason: the countries in the sample used by Brücker *et al.* fall roughly into two groups. Those that are quite similar to Germany in both their income per capita and their culture (for example, France); and those which are quite different from Germany in both dimensions: their income per capita is much lower, and their culture is quite different (for example, Turkey). For either group, a decrease in barriers to immigration is likely to have a modest effect. In the first case, differences in income per capita are too small to trigger a large immigration; in the second, income differences are large, but cultural differences stand in the way. CEECs present a new combination: income per capita is much lower than in Germany, but the culture is quite similar to that of Germany. It is plausible that, as barriers to labour mobility are reduced, this combination will lead to much higher migration than estimated by Brücker *et al.*

In that context (i.e. similar culture, differences in income per capita), the US evidence on mobility across states may be relevant. Here, the raw evidence is quite striking. For example, from 1950 to 1990, the population of Pennsylvania decreased by 60 per cent relative to that of the United States over the last 40 years, that of Illinois by 50 per cent, that of West Virginia by 75 per cent: There is indeed such a thing as states or regions emptying of capital and labour ... The econometric evidence is equally striking: the estimates by Barro and Sala i Martin (1991) imply for example that a 10 per cent differential in income per capita leads to a net migration of roughly 0.25 per cent of the population per year. If we take income per capita in the CEECs to be about half that of Germany, and use the Barro–Sala i Martin coefficient, this implies a net migration rate of $(\ln(2) - \ln(1)) \times 0.025$ per cent, so roughly 1.75 per cent, or 1.75 million. CEECs and the EU are not like the states in the US and this is obviously a generous upward bound. But it still serves as a warning, and to my first conclusion, the estimate of 0.3–0.4 million a year may be very conservative.

Which Externalities?

The argument is often made that immigration into the EU can help tilt the age composition from retirees towards workers, and thus help balance the retirement system in EU countries. The argument is correct as far as it goes. And if our focus was only on improving welfare in the EU (in its current composition), it would indeed be right. If we think, as I believe we should, of the joint welfare of the EU and the CEEC, the argument is much less obvious: What helps in the West hurts in the East. The argument must then be that retirement systems are in worse shape in the West than in the East. (Even then, the argument is not straightforward. It requires that the transfer of workers from East to West allows a decline in marginal tax rates in the West, the positive effects of which more than offset the increase in marginal tax rates in the East). But this does not seem to be true: The coming change in demographic structure seems, if anything, more adverse in the East than in the West.

A related argument is that the EU should allow for the immigration of skilled workers. The argument is made on various grounds. Distributional: if a group of workers is going to be hurt, it had better not be the unskilled workers in the West. Externalities: skilled immigrants are less likely to trigger racism. They are less likely to use the welfare system. They may well contribute to growth beyond their direct effect on production: they contribute to the quality of civil society. They may contribute to total factor productivity growth. Again, if our focus was just on the EU, all these arguments might be right. But, again, what helps in the West is likely to hurt in the East. In particular, skilled workers are likely to have larger externalities in transition economies than they do in the EU. I remember how, as transition started in Poland, the quality of the staff at the finance ministry steadily decreased over time: Whoever exhibited talent and knowledge was hired away within weeks by a Western consulting or financial firm. Not to denigrate the usefulness of consulting or financial firms, it was painfully clear that the effect on the quality of decisions at the Ministry, and the cost to Poland, was substantial. For this reason alone, it may well be best if skilled workers stay in the CEECs, rather than move to the EU.

If, however, skilled workers return home, and do so having acquired new and better skills, the initial loss to the East may be more than offset by the gain later on, and migration may prove useful to both the EU and the CEECs. The few pieces of evidence we have suggest that this effect may be quite relevant (McCormick and Wahba, 2001, for example). Thus, my second conclusion: I find the idea of temporary contracts for immigrants discussed in Chapter 6 of the Brücker *et al.* report to be a very attractive one.

How Much Difference can FDI Make?

Can capital flows to the East (as well as domestic capital accumulation) really stem the flow of immigration to the EU? To get a sense of the answer, consider the evolution of the capital labour ratio in the East (the capital–labour ratio, and by implication, the output–labour ratio is at the centre of the adjustment process described earlier). By definition, the rate of growth of the ratio is equal to the rate of growth of capital minus the rate of growth of labour. We saw earlier that immigration may contribute—0.3 per cent (the Brücker *et al.* best guess) to—1.75 per cent (the generous upper bound based on extrapolation of Barro and Sala i Martin's results for the United States to the CEECs) to the rate of growth of labour. How much could FDI contribute to the rate of growth of capital? The answer is: Easily as much. Take for example a ratio of FDI to the CEEC's GDP of 5 per cent. Take a ratio of capital to output of 2. This implies a contribution of FDI to the growth rate of capital of 2.5 per cent, a number above the upper bound on the (negative) contribution of immigration to the growth rate of labour. In other words, FDI can easily contribute as much as immigration to the process of convergence.

Is a ratio of FDI to GDP of 5 per cent totally unrealistic? Looking around the world, one concludes it is not. Some of the poorer countries of the EU (Portugal, Greece) are now running current account deficits of close to 10 per cent of GDP (although admittedly, FDI accounts only for part of the capital flows). But the current ratio of FDI to GDP for the CEECs is indeed considerably lower, around 1 per cent of GDP. And much of it represents privatization revenues, acquisitions of existing firms rather than additions to the capital stock.

This leads me to my third conclusion. It may be a good idea, not only conceptually but also politically, to link immigration issues with FDI in discussing transitional arrangements for the entry of the CEECs into the EU. Restrictions on immigration may be easier to sell, and eventually more successful, if coupled with incentives for investment of Western firms in the East.

DANI RODRIK

Here is a question for policymakers at the WTO, IMF, World Bank, the OECD, and finance and trade ministries around the world: which remaining impediments to international economic exchange would probably produce upon their removal the greatest bang in terms of improved efficiency in the global allocation of resources? (a) agricultural protection? (b) differential tax treatment of investment? (c) weak protection of intellectual capital? (d) inadequate prudential regulation in financial markets? Or (e) immigration restrictions? Without any doubt, the answer is (e).

As every economist knows, the efficiency cost of any policy-imposed ('artificial') price wedge is proportional to the square of the wedge. Where international markets for commodities and financial assets are concerned, these price wedges rarely exceed a ratio of 2 : 1. Where labour services are concerned, however, wages of similarly qualified individuals in the advanced and low-income countries differ by a factor of 10 or more. So the gains from liberalizing labour movements across countries are enormous, and much larger than the likely benefits from further liberalization in the traditional areas of goods and capital. If international policy makers were really interested in maximizing worldwide efficiency, they would spend little of their energies on a new trade round or on the international financial architecture. They would all be busy at work liberalizing immigration restrictions.

Except, of course, for politics. The liberalization of trade and capital flows has benefited greatly from the push of political forces. The same forces have been conspicuous by their absence in the case of international labour movements. Why is it that the politics of immigration restrictions plays out differently than in the case of trade and capital flows? The answer is not immediately obvious.

Look for example at Table 14.5, where I have summarized some cross-national evidence on popular attitudes towards trade and immigration in the advanced economies. Given the wildly different policy outcomes in these two areas, it is surprising to learn that popular opinion is as a rule equally hostile to immigration *and* trade. In fact, the only country in Table 14.5 where anti-immigration sentiment greatly exceeds anti-trade sentiment is the Netherlands. By contrast, popular opinion in the US, Canada, New Zealand, and Ireland is significantly friendlier to immigration than it is to trade. It is hard then to explain the difference by appealing to the preferences of the median voter.

A more promising avenue is to focus on the manner in which beneficiaries of liberalization organize and become politically effective. In trade, export-oriented firms have been instrumental in pushing for multilateral trade negotiations, as they have been quick to see the link between enhanced market access abroad and increased profits. With respect to capital flows, multinational enterprises and financial interests have been similarly influential. In both areas, liberalization has had a well-defined constituency in the advanced countries.

Table 14.5. *Attitudes towards trade and immigration*
(per cent of respondents who think imports/immigration
is good for the economy)

	Imports are good	Immigration is good
Germany	38	34
UK	14	15
Italy	23	21
Netherlands	39	15
Sweden	25	22
USA	13	28
Japan	36	36
Ireland	23	55
New Zealand	24	44
Canada	26	57

'Imports are good': respondents who disagree or disagree strongly that imports should be restricted to protect the national economy.
'Immigration is good': respondents who agree or agree strongly that immigrants are good for the economy.
Respondents whose parents are not citizens are excluded.

Source: International Social Survey Programme (1995).

Not so with immigration. When an additional Turkish worker enters the EU (or a Mexican worker enters the US), the ultimate beneficiaries *within* Europe (or the US) cannot identify themselves ex ante, and therefore have no incentive to ensure that the worker is allowed to come in in the first place. It is only after the worker has a specific job that the firm in which he is employed develops a direct stake in keeping him in the country. An interesting implication of this, documented nicely in the second part of this volume is that the US federal government spends a lot of resources on border controls (preventing *hypothetical* immigrants from coming in), but is virtually incapable of deporting employed illegals or fining their employers once they become actual immigrants. Once the border is crossed, gains accrue to specific, identifiable groups in the host economy. Otherwise, there is no readymade constituency for immigration in the way there is for trade or capital flows.

In recent years, an exception of sorts has developed with regard to skilled immigration. High-tech firms have begun to organize themselves to lobby for an enlarged quota of skilled immigrants. This has borne some fruit in the United States (in terms of expanded temporary H-1 visas for IT professionals) and has led to a wider debate on the reform of immigration policy in the EU. This shows that greater labour mobility becomes politically feasible once a clear set of beneficiaries—high-tech employers—can be identified ex ante in the host country.

Expanding the scope of skilled migration is better than nothing, but it does create some problems, particularly for home countries. Note first that wage gaps (between North and South) are much larger at the low-skill end of the labour market than at the high end. Therefore, from an efficiency standpoint—as well as a global distributive justice standpoint—the gains are mostly in low-skill migration. In addition, the emigration of skilled workers deprives poor countries of the human capital they need to develop their industries, acquire new technologies, and build high quality public institutions (on the latter point, see Desai *et al.*, 2001). Such brain drain is bad news for the sending countries, and is unlikely to be sufficiently offset by remittances and 'network' benefits.

One potentially Pareto-efficient solution is to institute a system of *temporary* contract employment in the host countries, with various penalties on the migrant and/or his employer to ensure that there is repatriation after a set number of years. In principle, the return migrants would then be in an even better position to contribute to the development of their home economies. This policy option is usefully presented and discussed in the first part of this volume. I am sufficiently convinced by the argument developed therein to think that this would be something worth trying on some scale, even if a very high degree of compliance is likely to prove elusive. A system of temporary contract employment for skilled migrant workers can be useful even if a (small) minority of workers manage to stay on forever.

But there is a broader issue that neither paper touches on. As long as we are thinking of sensible reforms of existing immigration restrictions, why do we keep on thinking in unilateral (or at best bilateral) terms? In trade and capital flows, we are used as economists to emphasize the superiority of multilateral arrangements. Non-discrimination and the most-favoured nation principle are taken to be the norm, with a price to be paid if and when countries depart from it. Even regional trade arrangements are sanctioned multilaterally (by requiring that they comply with WTO rules on such arrangements). Multilateralism ensures that what A and B negotiate does not create adverse effects on C. It guarantees that rules, rather than power, dominates—at least once the rules have been negotiated. Once the rules are in place, it enables a dispute settlement process.

I think it is high time we thought of multilateralizing immigration rules as well. We need to embed existing unilateral/bilateral schemes in a multilateral framework. This does not imply that preferential schemes cannot exist. The US may work out a separate deal for Mexicans, and the EU may want to have special arrangements for workers from candidate member countries. But such schemes need to be governed by multilateral disciplines to ensure that immigration rules minimize adverse spillovers to third countries.

Is a relaxation of restrictions on temporary labour mobility (both at the low- and high-skill end) realistic or even desirable, given the distributional and other adjustment costs that are involved in the host countries?

Note that the advanced countries expect developing countries to make a large number of costly adjustments at home in order to integrate to the world economy. Poor countries have to abide by a long list of WTO agreements, put in place a demanding set of financial codes and standards, and institute in short order 'governance' reforms that took today's advanced countries centuries to accomplish. The asymmetry of expectations imposed on the North and South is simply staggering. So the short answer to the question posed above is that developed countries cannot have it both ways. Either they put their money where their mouth is, and include labour flows in the agenda of liberalization; or they recognize the need for national autonomy and space, in which case they must extend to the developing countries the same privileges in the areas of trade and capital flows.

One final word about the role of economists. I think economists need to be considerably more outspoken on the sins that politicians commit in this area. I am struck by how tolerant we are of the political realities that support an excessively restrictive regime of international labour mobility, while we continually decry the 'protectionist' forces that block further liberalization of an already very open trading system. It is time to redress the balance.

GIOVANNI SARTORI

I shall be brief because I am very peripheral to this volume. Most contributors are by and large economists, whereas I am a political scientist. Thus, my focus on the issues discussed in this volume will appear out of focus.

The economic stance basically is that immigrants are needed and are a useful work force. This is often the case. Yet, is usefulness an overriding criterion for the evaluation of immigration policies? To begin with, if immigrants are needed for times of boom, of economic expansion, what if the economic cycle enter a slump, a phase of depression?

The hitherto needed imported worker eventually becomes unneeded and unemployed. What is useful today may become damaging tomorrow. Benefits should be weighted *vis-à-vis* their foreseeable costs.

Furthermore, the notion of 'useful worker' is an excessively broad blanket. Clearly, there are immigrants who cannot be employed usefully. So, who is useful? The second part of this volume offers a good discussion about skills. Obviously, some places require high skill imports (e.g. Silicon Valley), while other countries need unskilled workers (as most Africans). Across generations, however, the illiterate, unskilled immigration turns out to be undesirable, for it tends to be severed from, and incapable of, upward socio-economic mobility. Latinos in California live poorly in segregated slums, their kids go to degraded schools, and this brings about a somewhat permanent underclass brought up in neighbourhoods of juvenile gangs, drugs and violence, that develops into a nasty social problem.

Be that as it may, the issue that is generally neglected by economists is the issue of integration, of cultural and socio-political integration. What kind of society is a 'good society'? A homogeneous, a pluralistic, or a multicultural society? Western civilization has come to believe in pluralism and thus in the pluralistically integrated society. But this view is currently challenged by the ideology of multiculturalism. The multicultural programme does not seek integration but 'recognition' of separateness, of the separate identities of each and all cultures. Whatever the theoretical merits of this vision, its practical implication is the disintegration of the pluralistic community and a fragmentation of the polity into closed and eventually hostile sub-communities. Now, how does the immigrant fit into these separate ways?

Clearly, the more the host country embraces the multicultural programme, the lesser the integrative pressures (and the greater, I believe, the socio-cultural conflict). Assume, however, that integration (pluralist integration, to be sure) is still perceived by most people as a good thing. Even so, some immigrants are more easily integrated than others. The report in the second part of this volume basically envisaged the surge of Mexican and Latin American entries in the United States. Needless to say, massive flows of illegal, uncontrolled immigration create problems everywhere. Yet, the European ones are of unprecedented difficulty. But let me immediately qualify this statement. Europe has two borders: east–west and south–north. Along the first border the pressure is not worrisome. Eastern immigrants hardly pose problems (just like Latino immigration in the United States). Furthermore, many Eastern Europeans do not plan to leave their homeland for good. They leave because they are attracted by Western salaries. But they are not interested in changing nationality. When they have made money they tend to return to their native country.

The south–north immigration instead is of a very different kind. Most African and Arab immigrants are no-return immigrants. They escape starvation. On the other hand, they are largely Moslems. This entails that they belong to a non-western and indeed anti-western vision of the world. The Islamic culture is theocratic, it does not abide by the state–church separation, and is currently experiencing a fundamentalist heating, a return to invasive and harsh Islamic fundamentals. This is then a most difficult and potentially destructive kind of immigration. Yet, at this meeting nobody has confronted the question of how and whether Islamic communities will coexist and/or conflict with the western-type community. Our society must 'adapt' says Prodi in his message to the Trieste Conference that this book draws upon. Clever guy. In what terms? This should be spelled out. It seldom is.

Let me now pick on some specific points. Here we have discussed the rejoining of the immigrant's families. Fine. But what about Islamic families? Tunisia and Turkey happen to be the only Islamic countries that forbid polygamy. Small exceptions. The estimate is that in Paris there are about 200 000 Islamic polygamic families. How do we deal with this issue? Quite aside from a most serious matter of principles, in practice the French government plays dumb and recognizes only the first wife and thus enrols in the welfare benefits only her children. But there are no records. Thus, all the children of a multi-wife father become, in France, children of the first wife. Is this the way of adapting?

Another point touched at the meeting is the one of racism. The issue exists; but the word must be handled with care and with a proper understanding of the issue. For 'racism' is a boo word, a scare word, an insult word. I was thus flabbergasted to read (in the report in the first part of this volume) the question (in Chapter 5, Section 5.2, page 108) of the 1996 Eurobarometer about racism. In this report about 33 per cent of the respondents described themselves as 'quite racist'. Considering that most people do not like to be considered racist, and that they do not perceive themselves as being racists, the Eurobarometer finding is horrifying. Fortunately, the explanation of the finding is in the horrendous way in which the questions are formulated!

My point is, then, that economists should not neglect the non-economic aspects and implications of immigrations.

Index